TEN SENDING CHURCHES

TEN SENDING CHURCHES

Edited by

Michael Griffiths

MARC EUROPE

STL BOOKS

EVANGELICAL MISSIONARY ALLIANCE

STL Books are published by Send The Light (Operation Mobilisation), PO Box 48, Bromley, Kent, England.

The Evangelical Missionary Alliance is a fellowship of evangelical missionary societies, agencies and training colleges that are committed to world mission. Its aims are to encourage cooperation and provide coordination between member societies and colleges, and to assist local churches to fulfil their role in world mission. The EMA offices are at Whitefield House, 186 Kennington Park Road, London SE11 4BT.

MARC Europe is an integral part of World Vision, an international Christian humanitarian organisation. MARC's object is to assist Christian leaders with factual information, surveys, management skills, strategic planning and other tools for evangelism. We also publish and distribute related books on mission, church growth, management, spiritual maturity and other topics.

Ten sending churches: ten ministers share how they and their churches have caught the vision for mission.
1. Missions
I. Griffiths, Michael, *1928 -*
266   BV2061

ISBN 0-9508396-7-1 (MARC)
ISBN 0-9502968-3-X (EMA)
ISBN 0-903843-92-7 (STL)

Contents

Ten Sending Churches

1. St Philip & St Jacob
   Bristol

2. Baptist Tabernacle
   Stockton on Tees,
   County Cleveland

3. Gold Hill Baptist Church
   Gerrards Cross, Bucks

4. Charlotte Chapel
   Edinburgh

5. St George's
   Leeds

6. Selly Oak Methodist
   Birmingham

7. St John & St Germain
   Harborne, Birmingham

8. Alton Evangelical Free Church
   Alton, Hants

9. Cranleigh Chapel
   Bournemouth, Dorset

10. Elim Church
    Portsmouth

Introduction

Appetizer: An Overview of the Ten Sending Churches

Michael Griffiths

Dr. Michael Griffiths is Principal of London Bible College, and Consulting Director of the Overseas Missionary Fellowship. Prior to his present appointment he served as General Director of the OMF, and he and his wife have spent many years as missionaries in Japan and Singapore. He is author of a number of books including Take My Life *and* Cinderella with Amnesia.

When I was first asked to write an introductory chapter to this book, owing to the illness of the original editor, our beloved Harry Sutton, I had my own personal doubts about the validity of the idea. How would ten different authors work together?

Would not ten accounts of missionary involvement in ten churches all be rather the same? Would we not be bored to tears with repetitive, overlapping accounts of missionary weekends (ghastly inadequate approach), missionary prayer groups and the detailed organisation of missionary committees? So I was delighted to discover how different these ten churches are from one another – yet each one is making its own special contribution to our thinking.

While these churches belong to differing traditions, and each is in that sense 'typical', yet on the other hand each has been chosen as 'successful' within its own denominational tradition: would this not seem rather daunting to those of us in more ordinary congregations, who might therefore be discouraged rather than helped? Again I was interested to discover that the honesty of the writers means that no one church could necessarily be regarded as the one ideal model for the rest of us all to imitate. For example, there is the admission from Dr. Copley of Moorlands that the teaching programme at Cranleigh Chapel was weak as far as world mission was concerned. Even the strongest of these churches shows some glaring weakness, though I will leave you, the reader, to decide exactly which these are!

So probably all of us will find plenty of new insights and innovations which can be adopted or adapted to our own particular situations. We will glean something from one church and something else from another – for example, many churches seemed content with a ritual mention of missionary names in ministerial praying, while (to some people perhaps surprising in an Anglican context) St. John's, Harborne, provided opportunities week by week for congregational participation in extempore prayer for specific missionaries.

I have written previously on this subject and thought about it a great deal from the missionary receiving end, but have found it beneficial to see it now from the opposite sending-church viewpoint. Let me then attempt to whet your appetite for studying this book and sucking it dry of ideas, by commenting on aspects which seem to me both interesting and significant. This will help to keep you on your toes in deriving the greatest possible benefit from reading the book as a whole.

Centrality

Jim Graham of Gold Hill draws out 'seven very clear principles' that the Lord gave them; the first reads:

   Mission needed to be removed from the periphery of the church's life and put at the heart of our life together. Involvement and responsibility had to be moved from the "enthusiast" to the "ordinary" church member. This was achieved by teaching . . .

This is indeed basic and primary: one must reject the idea of missions as the peripheral passion of a few enthusiasts on the fanatic fringe. Somehow New Testament priorities have to be re-established in present-day churches. It is clear from these ten accounts, that few even of these churches have yet done this completely successfully. Some churches still seem satisfied that the annual missionary weekend is adequate involvement (as though the annual ceremonial paddling of the toe in the sea on the annual church outing could be confused with serious swimming!), and the polite weekly mention of missionaries by name in the ministerial prayer seems not too great an improvement on Christopher Robin's 'God bless Daddy – I quite forgot!' Missionary society prayer groups have always been the property of the extra-keen and already committed – so how can we help the non-committed, for whom world mission still signifies anthropological bric-a-brac and free dog-eared pamphlets at the annual missionary exhibition?

To some of us the Methodist contribution from Selly Oak could seem astonishingly 'dutiful, traditional and denominational' (Jim Graham) in its preoccupations, yet in spite of this the description of the Methodist ideal must surely start all of us thinking:

> Ever since its foundation the basis of the Methodist Missionary Society . . . is that every member of the Methodist Church is automatically a member of the society. Mission and all that it means is not just for the enthusiasts – it is not an optional extra tacked on for those who choose it – it is for everybody.

Wow! That is certainly telling it the way it ought to be. Few of our churches share that same identity between church and mission, and we all wish that we did. St. John's, Harborne, tried to simplify the chaos of missions from Andes to Zambesi by deciding that their 'primary call was to back Anglican evangelical societies' and there must be at least five of those left still. 'John Wesley declared "The world is my parish" and from their origins Methodists have been brought up to have a world vision . . .' (Donald Knighton).

This, then, is the essential problem to be solved with all church members anywhere in the world: how do we help them to grow out of childish parochialism and denominationalism to a true sense of world concern for the

universal church of Christ and for the vast legions of the
unreached (see Jim Graham's powerful statistics) who are
therefore the lost, through our inaction and indifference?

Motivation

'People need targets, goals, aims – visions. Otherwise they
become lackadaisical, lazy, complacent, parochial and
ineffective. Christians are no exceptions.' So writes Malcolm
Widdecombe, whose opening contribution interests me
because it shows how his own motivation and commitment to
missions started – by reading a book by Oswald Smith. Unless
the minister sees the need to make mission central, unless the
leaders are well motivated, it is hard to make any progress. I
remember some years ago preaching my heart out in a famous
Scottish church, and realising that my efforts were almost
certainly in vain unless its famous preacher-minister was
really listening and accepting what I was trying to get across.
That church is now much more involved because the minister
who followed was invited overseas to speak at conferences of
missionaries (crafty move by the society concerned!) and
having seen the need with his own eyes, came home all fired
up to get more missionaries sent out from that congregation.
Again and again you will notice how the personal experience
of the minister is often a significant step to motivating a whole
church. St. John's sent Tom Walker to Latin America, while
Jim Graham went to Asia. I found Barrie Taylor's honest
account very moving: 'The problem right then was my own
heart, a heart cold towards mission, lacking in biblical
perception, vision and zeal in this vital area' and he goes on to
describe his visit to Africa, and those hot tears which some of
us experience when we share in the need we find in many
places.

   Stockton Baptist Tabernacle speaks of elders and church
members making visits to the overseas areas where their
missionaries are working, and the story is repeated in report
after report. This would have been virtually impossible in the
old leisurely days of steamship travel (it still took us five
weeks to get home from Japan by the cheapest available route
in the early sixties) but is so easy (albeit expensive) today
when most missionaries are within twenty-four hours'

journey of home. The remarkable example is that of the Portsmouth Pentecostal church whose whole account concentrates upon the involvement of the congregation in visiting just one country – travelling across Europe to Poland to meet social needs in days of crisis, in more direct evangelism and as a witnessing choir. It is so much easier to pray for people that you have met in person. Their report helps to underline the fact that many parts of Europe are needy mission fields, perhaps none more so than our immediate neighbour France which has fewer Christians proportionately than Japan or India. There is no doubt that field visits by young people through Operation Mobilisation and many other missions have done a great deal to increase motivation.

The account from St. John's, Harborne, pinpoints the remarkable contribution made by the personal influence of utterly committed individuals (in that instance a former missionary candidate prevented from service himself because of bad health). That story could be repeated over and over again and the infectious enthusiasm of such Christians is significant in motivating others. I still remember a walk taken as a student with the late Prof. Rendle Short of Bristol: I was fascinated that such a busy surgeon was so interested in missions and talked of little else but Africa and Asia throughout a three- or four-hour birdwatching walk together.

Selly Oak Methodists again show the considerable influence of overseas visitors, who help to make the world-wide church real to us, especially when they help to lead worship as they are invited to do there, and participate also in the class meetings. It is this personalisation of mission in warm human beings which arouses many of us to greater concern and involvement. I think of one Korean student at what was then Clifton Theological College, who stirred up several of his British contemporaries to form a Korean Prayer Fellowship – one of whom was John Wallis, mentioned several times in the account from St. George's, Leeds. Possibly many of us can remember significant individuals we once met or entertained in our homes, whom we (and often our children as well) will never forget. This personal impact of people upon other people, whether overseas visitors or missionaries on furlough, is probably the one single factor used most of all by the Lord in a kind of infectious motivation of one another. It was the missionary Paul's total lifestyle and ministry that inspired and involved young Timothy in Lystra all those years ago (2 Tim.3:10–11). I myself was led to work in Japan through meeting in succession three Japanese studying in this country – the first two got me really interested and reading everything on Japan I could lay my hands on, so that when the third asked me to pray seriously about coming to serve in Japan, I was all ready to move.

Notice in passing that both Selly Oak and Cranleigh Chapel were considerably influenced by nearby Christian training colleges. We should pray for and expect an aura of influence around all such teaching centres and mission offices upon neighbouring churches.

Motivation, then, is crucial. It is not achieved by the teaching of missions once a year by a visiting missionary enthusiast. I have been cast in that role too often to overvalue its effectiveness. The annual missionary weekend is a very powerful form of non-verbal communication. It speaks volumes. Apparently the usual full-time teacher does not think mission important enough to teach on it himself – he often takes the opportunity of accepting an invitation to preach somewhere else! It says loud and clear that missions are peripheral – an extra bit of razzmatazz like the Boy Scout parade or Remembrance Sunday that happens now and again. Please do not follow those models who seem to have accepted this level of motivation only. We may not all feel able to go as far a Pip 'n' Jay in devoting three successive Sundays every May and November each year – that certainly shows great seriousness – but we must all agree with the folk at Alton who feel that for teaching on mission to be effective it should be seen as part of the regular teaching ministry of the church (see their section called 'Sharing with the church'.) The motivating power of good Bible teaching is plain.

> The very first such sermon God winged to the ears and hearts of a young couple in the congregation. It was to be a link in the chain that led them to dedicate and offer their lives in missionary service. Beware if you start preaching mission. God does not hang about – you may well lose your best members to the mission field!

But then what an irresponsible thing it would be to send anyone other than 'your best members' to overseas service. Crossing cultural barriers, ministering in a foreign language and engaging in spiritual warfare will test the commitment of our best workers.

The annual weekend is better than nothing: that way every mission could get an innings each every hundred years or so; but as a way of teaching and motivating it is too brief and sporadic, and has proved to be woefully inadequate. Some churches are predictable in their programmes, and have held a mid-week Bible Study and Prayer Meeting since anyone can remember. However, there are today some courageous congregations who get away from programme orientation, and ask basic questions about what they are aiming to achieve and whether they are succeeding in achieving it; and so every autumn they rethink their winter's programme so as to meet the current needs of the church according to defined biblical goals. Thus they may decide to devote a series lasting a few weeks for 'magazine style meetings on mission' (i.e. an interesting mix of teaching sessions, quizzes, interviews, book reviews, audio visuals) which help concentration and retention of information, a useful teaching approach.

Involvement

'Missionary support means, of course, much more than money' (Tom Walker). We are told a good deal about the raising of money for missions, but I believe they are right who see this as a necessary by-product of realistic involvement, and not just as a worthy thing in itself. It is a tangible expression of Christian love. Nowadays we are so used to transferring money by impersonal cheques and bank drafts, that we fail to notice that in the New Testament, after money had been raised, it had to be literally carried by some individuals in the church to the individual or group for whom it was intended. That meant a considerable journey on foot 'in peril of robbers', often lasting three or four weeks each way. The Berean Christians who escorted Paul to Athens must have walked a thousand kilometres, if they went overland.

We are sometimes critical of societies for being impersonal, but it is worth now recalling the origin of most of these societies in personal involvement of committed individuals.

Even 'church' societies like the Church Missionary Society
and the Church's Mission to the Jews were first started by
small independent groups of concerned individuals who gave
their money and time on a voluntary basis to get something
started – Charles Simeon was involved in starting both. Such
missionary societies depended for their support not on
official church funds, but on occasional cheques from
wealthy or generous individuals: much as George Müller sent
again and again to help Hudson Taylor. Most interdenominational 'faith' missions were supported for many
years on the basis of individual donations rather than regular
church giving. What we see, in the frozen instant of time
represented by these reports, is the healthy realisation that
this is not good enough, and that as our understanding of the
significance of the local church grows, the assumption of
corporate responsibility grows with it. The American scene is
somewhat different from ours because through the influence
of people like Oswald Smith (see Malcolm Widdecombe's
account) and Harold Ockenga, church support for individuals
through societies became general (partly because of
legislation that prevented personal gifts to individuals being
tax-deductible). Moreover the vastness of North America
meant that often only one or two missionaries were known
from any one society, so that it became regarded as normal
and proper for such giving to be earmarked for the support of
known individuals. This did not happen at first in Britain
because the enthusiastic donor in Britain may well know
twenty missionaries in Wycliffe, or WEC or OMF, and will not
bother to divide a £20 gift up between them all by earmarking
it, rather trusting that the society will divide it equitably
according to need. Thus the 'keen fringe' used to support the
missions almost entirely (and still do a tremendous amount).
Even in these reports you can see the difference in realism
between Stockton Baptist Tabernacle's recognition that for a
family £6,600 is about right (as of 1983) and another church
that was splitting up some £4,500 between nine individuals.
You can contrast Harborne helping to support their
candidates delayed from going abroad, with another church
that wanted to train people, but hoped they would find a part-
time job to support themselves. The same discrepancies can
be found in the realism with which different churches support

their candidates in Bible college training.

Increased giving, then, may show an increased concern and love for missionaries as human beings. There is some stirring stuff from Malcolm Widdecombe:

> I came back good and hopping mad. I saw there with my own eyes what others had told me, that British missionaries are not well supported by the British Church. I contacted a friend who had been a missionary in Zaire to ask his experience. 'Yes, brother' he said, 'it's true generally. In the international missionary community of Africa we British missionaries were often made to feel like second-class citizens.'

Certainly in the past there were many churches that would cheerfully go on sending two or three hundred pounds a year to 'our missionaires' without asking the obvious question: For how many weeks could a family in Britain survive on that? Answer: less than a month. It's partly the old-fashioned image that sees missionaries living in areas where food is cheap, whereas countries like Japan, Nigeria and Hong Kong are much more expensive than this country. Thankfully all this lack of realism is changing fast.

But what cheered me most were those contributors who majored on areas other than money as an index of their achievement in supporting missionaries (while money can also be a useful index of genuine concern, it is an impersonal form of non-involvement sometimes, if it is seen as an easy substitute for love and caring).

It is a tremendous encouragement to the missionary to know that he has a home church full of friends, who are committed to him or to her; that every fresh item of news is treasured and prayed over (like the mother who carries around photos of her children in her handbag and will read you snippets from their latest letters given only the slightest encouragement!). The various contributions contain excellent illustrations of this: Stockton renting a home for the missionary family on furlough, paying for those air tickets, helping with the education of teenage children of missionaries; Harborne letter writing, caring for children, establishing prayer support cells for individual missionaries, as well as linking people in with Fellowship groups.

Merely formal 'fellowship' is not enough: it is committed, caring friendship that heartens missionaries most when they are far away from home. I shall never forget the occasion when our three older children joined us in Singapore for several weeks of the summer; as the last day came the unspoken question was whether we would be able to afford to fly three of them out again the following year, for such expenditures are often a private personal responsibility not undertaken by a society. That very morning a letter came from our home church in Guildford to say that they already had sufficient in hand to bring out at least one of our children the following summer. Knowing that, a whole year in advance, was a wonderful encouragement to us all. Somebody cared and was thinking about us: praise the Lord for his goodness in giving us a church like that.

Furlough

I became quite excited at the increasing recognition that the missionary needed a time of real refreshment and renewed involvement with the church that sent him out. The old deputation syndrome (criticised by Stockton, who insist that it should be primarily a time for 'rest and re-establishment of home church links') sprang at least partly from a need to raise more funds (inappropriate, to say the least, from so-called 'faith' missions) largely because at that time churches were unrealistic in their support. Once support becomes realistic, deputation can become properly a wider sharing of information with the larger church constituency, who want to hear about the Lord's work in parts of the world not represented among their own missionaries. Having heard hardly anyone but himself preach (and in a foreign language at that!) for some three or four years, the missionary is often spiritually dry and needs refreshment in his soul and not just in mind and body. But there is more to it than this. Often the returned worker has become, deliberately, redundant in handing over his job to a national Christian – that is the aim of the operation after all. Not until he returns will he have another clear job description for initiating some fresh work. The furlough missionary is in a strange kind of limbo and often suffers an identity crisis. To send this rootless, insecure person straight off on a several-week tour, repeating endlessly the same two or three talks on one-night stands in different towns, every night in a different bed, is cruel. I noted with amusement the church which liked its missionaries to stay for a whole week, and seemed astonished when one stayed a whole month! And approved that Charlotte Chapel expected at least 'a part of furlough' to be spent with them, while others felt this should be several months. The missionary 'rolling stones' need time to become 'living stones' properly bonded back into their home church again. However, this will not help if they are not given any status, any definable role or identity. Unemployment will deepen their alienation and frustration. Interviewing them on arrival, arranging a reception when they get home and commissioning them when they depart (full marks to Stockton), and giving them an opportunity to show their slides at a mid-week meeting is still not sufficient help. Wise churches bring them in as elders or assistant ministers to fulfil a clearly defined role on the pastoral team. It is not that they want status so much as work to do. Then they belong and cease to be oddities smelling like their long disused winter clothes – of mothballs. Deputation has often been a psychological necessity because their home church cannot think of anything better to do with them.

It lies then in the hands of the sending church to give to 'the returned empty' – tired and jaded, jetlagged and reverse-culture-shocked, as he may be – a clear identity as a church worker, valued, loved and cared for. That caring will have begun much earlier in the first building of the relationship with the home church. Several reports stress the need for the individual to test his call by opening it up for consideration by church leaders 'from the outset'. Many of them, you will notice, want the candidate to serve as a full-time worker with them for a probationary period before going out. This practical, pastoral training is invaluable.

The local church and missionary societies

One of the most interesting aspects of these contributions is the repeated reference to the respective roles of local church and missionary society. This seems worth mentioning because of the question that naturally arises about whether the society is needed any longer once the local church is aroused to its responsibilities, with its own Mission Board.

It must be asserted in the strongest terms that it is the local church which is the sending body – that is entirely biblical. Moreover, it is the local church which can best evaluate the usefulness and gifts of the candidate evidenced thus far, and which provides the spiritual and emotional support needed by the missionary. But exactly the same biblical principles which establish the significance of the corporate emphasis at home, decree likewise that the missionary overseas should relate to other missionaries in a responsible way and not be an individualist, a freelance, answerable to nobody within sight, doing only that which is right in his own eyes. The very high incidence of mental breakdown among 'Third World Missionaries', sent out without any pastoral care or oversight, as solitary individuals to new fields on behalf of new missions, bears clear witness to this.

I recently prepared a list of the advantages of belonging to a society rather than trying to go it alone in an individualistic way. I came up with the following list (admittedly incomplete).

What the Missionary Society offers the Missionary

1. Knowledge and experience of the field
2. Language teaching
3. Orientation (culture, society, religions)
4. Medical officer (prophylaxis and treatment)
5. Pastoral care as a person
6. Oversight of his work
7. Support services (visas, money)
8. Communications (with others and home)
9. Fellowship and prayer
10. Policy discussion and strategy
11. Children's schooling
12. Middleman with local church

Neville Atkinson of the Stockton Baptist Tabernacle writes as follows:

We do not send out our missionaries to a missionary society feeling that it is now the society's responsibility to look after them and support them. The society is regarded as a necessary channel working in partnership with the home church. We see the accumulated expertise of the society as being at the service of the sending church and the national church overseas. It is also a channel of contact from home church to missionary and vice versa.

Ian Finlayson of Charlotte Chapel too says some sensible things under the same head.

Churches in this country are not sufficiently aware of all the implications of the local parameters affecting the missionary on the field to presume to determine mission priorities. If several missionaries from different church backgrounds are working together on any project, it is surely the responsibility of the mission under whose umbrella the team is working to dictate policy and to define principles and to determine objectives. For the sending churches to do this would result in chaos!

This is certainly true in pioneer areas, but once the emerging national church is directing policies, there should be order and discipline. Even then, though, the national church is often glad to have a society act as a go-between and middleman in ensuring that the missionary is doing what the national church requires. This is especially so when the missionaries come from different home countries and differing church traditions. Barrie Taylor of Alton also has some good things to say about the local churches not abdicating responsibility to the missionary society and as always Gold Hill provides a goldmine of good sense and experience.

Well now, has that whetted your appetite and stirred you up to recognise some of the issues which these varied contributions raise in our minds? I hope so, and that this book will fulfil its purpose in helping other local churches to find the way forward in achieving an effective worldwide mission outreach.

I finished reading with a question from Jim Graham ringing in my ears:

How can we, as a church, release more and more resources into the harvest fields of the world?

That is more than a question in our minds: it must become a prayer from our hearts.

Michael Griffiths
London Bible College, July 1984

Chapter 1

St. Philip and St. Jacob, Bristol

Malcolm Widdecombe

St. Philip and St. Jacob, popularly known as 'Pip'n'Jay', is an Anglican inner-city church in Bristol. The congregation, however, is eclectic, some travelling over thirty miles on a Sunday. The total attendance on the average Sunday is around 350.

'Pip'n'Jay, supports about twelve full-time missionaries and a good number of short-term personnel, many working with Operation Mobilisation. The church has strong links with WEC International, Regions Beyond Missionary Union, the Mission Aviation Fellowship, the Diocese of the Arctic, the Red Sea Mission Team, the Belgian Evangelical Mission, and Operation Mobilisation. The church has personnel with all these societies, and also has strong bonds, though no staff at present, with the Bible Churchmen's Missionary Society, the South American Missionary Society, and the Church Missionary Society (Ruanda).

The Rev. Malcolm Widdecombe has been responsible for the ministry at St. Philip and St. Jacob since 1965, and became Vicar in 1974. In 1979 he was appointed Rural Dean of Bristol City Deanery. Born in Gibraltar in 1937, he was converted at Capernwray Hall in 1955, left school the following year to work on a chicken farm ('10,000 birds – my largest congregation' he comments), and following training at Tyndale Hall Theological College was ordained in 1962.

He is married to Meryl, and they have two sons and one daughter. He lists his interests as gardening, jogging, reading crime novels and watching Westerns.

The missionary call

No one likes catching flu. An overflowing waste-paper basket of used Kleenex, pyjamas drenched with perspiration, and the growing conviction that one's case was probably terminal, hardly provided the context for a meeting with God. But that is what happened. No visions or audible voices, but God spoke to me clearly from a book. I was in my last year at Monkton Combe School. It was February and I was in the sick bay. Tony Bush, a school friend, had been to visit me and left me a book he had found in the school library.

'You'll like it,' he said. 'This man really has something to say.' So I started into *The Challenge of Missions* by Dr. Oswald J. Smith, pastor of The People's Church, Toronto.

During the previous Christmas vacation I had been with Tony to Capernwray Hall for a New Year houseparty led by Major Ian Thomas. There I had made a personal commitment of my life to the Lord Jesus. I had believed in God ever since I could remember, and had worshipped him and had been involved in Christian activities for some years. My name was already given by the school Chaplain to the Bishop of Chelmsford, that I might be considered for ordination. I had thought for some time that this was what I wanted to do with my life. The message that got through to me at Capernwray was the direct question, 'Do you *know* you are a Christian?' I worshipped God with Christians, I tried to serve him with other Christians, and I thought I was one. But I didn't know. So my individual prayer of personal commitment had taken place. And now I knew. I had the testimony of God's Word, which I had known for some time. But I also had the testimony of God's Spirit in my heart. The Spirit did indeed bear witness with my spirit that I was God's child. This posed a question. I had thought I was a Christian. That was not good enough, because I needed to know. Hence my conversion. I thought God wanted me in the ministry. This was no longer good enough. I needed to know. Did God want me in the ministry or not?

There was a second question. Under Ian Thomas's dynamic leadership the Capernwray Missionary Fellowship of

Torchbearers was formed. Its emphasis was on personal soul-winning and evangelism. I thought God wanted me in full-time service. I also thought evangelism would play a large part in that service. Was God calling me to evangelise?

Someone once asked a rabbi 'Why is it you Jews always answer a question by asking another one?' The rabbi replied 'Why shouldn't we?' I knew the feeling as I began Oswald Smith's book. The Lord was asking me a third question. (Well, Jesus was a Jew after all.) What place was missionary work going to have in my ministry?

In the second chapter of his book, Oswald Smith pointed his readers to the book of the prophet Ezekiel. He drew special attention to God's call to Ezekiel in chapter 3 verses 17–19, and in particular to the words 'but his blood will I require at thine hand.' Read the verses for yourself in any version of the Bible you care to choose. The message comes across loud and clear. Allow me to paraphrase it for you. 'Christian, I have put you on guard duty. The enemy is approaching. I am the enemy coming in dreadful judgement on the human race that has despised and rebelled against me. So sound the alarm. If wicked people hear and do something about it by turning to me, I will forgive them and save them. If they ignore your warning, on their own heads be it. However, if you neglect to sound the alarm, they will still experience my dire judgement, and further I will hold you personally responsible for every soul that is lost.' I believe God used those verses in Ezekiel to seal my call to the ministry. I was suddenly aware of the Christian's individual responsibility for those who are outside the church of Jesus Christ. Paul's words in Romans 1:14 about his being a debtor to all nations took on a new meaning for me. I had salvation, but that salvation had not been provided for me alone but for everyone. Therefore I was in debt to anyone who did not know the Lord. The only way to repay the debt was to tell them about Jesus and what he had provided for them by dying on the cross.

It was not just the other fellows in school who did not know the Lord, but the folk over Combe Down living in Bath. And the people of Somerset. And all the residents of the United Kingdom. The thousands who lived in Europe. The millions of the whole world. Bishop Stephen Neil was yet to make his famous statement 'Every Christian is either a missionary or a mistake.' But I understood then, in spite of a streaming nose, the enormity of the call of God.

Dr. Smith had not finished with me yet. He now went on to discuss the financial implications of the missionary task given to the church. He recounted his early days at the People's Church, Toronto. When he went there the church was in decline and in debt. The pews were as empty as the treasury. For his first eight days with them he preached his heart out on missions and the Christian's individual responsibility for the world. On the eighth day, his second Sunday, he held three services. At each he took up a missionary offering. Everyone thought the new pastor had taken leave of his senses. Did he not know that the church was in debt? How could he possibly ask the congregation to give to foreign missions?

Oswald Smith gave them Matthew 6:33 'Seek ye first the kingdom of God and his righteousness, and all these things will be added unto you.' Put missions first and God will take care of your own needs. Dr. Smith went to the People's Church at the beginning of the 1930s, the years of the Great Depression. That is a very significant fact for us who live in days of inflation and massive unemployment. I was reading his book, in between mouthwash and gargles, in 1956. The book reported that all debts were paid and all seats filled, and in addition the People's Church was supporting over 300 missionaries. They were giving much more to missions than they were spending on themselves. That pattern has continued to the present time. Today the People's Church is still solvent, still full, and supports over 500 missionaries.

I finished *The Challenge of Missions* duly challenged, blew my nose, and listed my three questions.

Did God want me in the ordained ministry? Was it to be evangelistic? Was it to have a clear missionary emphasis?

I had the sneaky feeling inside that the answer was 'Yes' on all three counts. I wanted to know. Thinking and believing were not sufficient. I asked God for a sign. 'Putting out a fleece' is the correct jargon, I believe. Gideon only asked for this particular sign once in his life. Some Christians get hung up on the sign thing. They need signs from heaven before they do anything – even like deciding what time they are to rise in the morning. I have always found an alarm clock to be guidance enough in such matters. But there may be just one or two occasions in life, when it is permissible to come humbly before God and ask a sign. The rest of the time guidance is God's business which he does in his way in direct proportion to our trusting with all our hearts, consulting him about everything, and confessing our own inadequacy. (Proverbs 3: 5,6.) So I asked for a sign, something I have only done on one occasion since.

In Eddystone House we did our own thing on Friday nights. At Monkton morning and evening worship were held in the school Chapel every day. On Fridays we at Eddystone did our own thing with our housemaster, Tom Watson. Usually the senior boys took it in turns to lead the sessions – just fifteen minutes or so containing a hymn, a Bible reading, a short talk, and a closing prayer. We all crammed into the largest dormitory, sang lustily, and sat on the beds for the talk and prayers.

Having recovered and left the sick bay, I found my name was down for the next Friday's prayers. Shortly before it was time to go to the dormitory I slipped into the school chapel, got on my knees and asked for my sign. My prayer went something like this: 'Lord Jesus, I think you do want me in the ministry. I think you do want me to be concerned for evangelism. I think you do want me to concern myself with the missionary task of the church. If that is really so, please give me one soul tonight when I take house prayers. Amen.'

And off to house prayers I went. Instead of the statutory fifteen minutes we went well over twenty, and I've been preaching long sermons ever since. I simply explained my conversion the previous vacation. Many of the boys had known me for some time. They had seen me in the chapel, at the Christian Union meetings, attending the voluntary Bible Studies, leading house prayers and so on. They thought I was a Christian, and so did I. But now I knew I was a Christian. Was there anyone else like me, who thought they were Christians but didn't know and wanted to? I think the hymn I chose was 'O Happy Day that fixed my choice'. I closed with prayer, and we all prepared for bed. A few minutes later just one fellow came up to me. 'Widdecombe,' he said (we were terribly formal at Public School in those days). 'I want to know Jesus too.' God had given me the confirmation I needed. It was Yes

to the ministry. Yes to evangelism. And it was Yes to missions
It was simply a matter of getting ordained . . .

The missionary base

Ordination is no simple matter. Dr. Faulkner Allison, then
Bishop of Chelmsford, met me and nominated me to the
selectors. Meanwhile there was a year to fill in before I went
to theological college. Dr. Allison wanted me to work in the
East End in a boys' club for three or four months. First I spent
some nine months or so working on a chicken farm in Surrey.

I often say that I believe in purgatory because I have been
there. Five years in an Anglican Theological College was the
stretch given me.

In fact I was most fortunate to get a place at Tyndale Hall in
Bristol. At that time it was the college of the Bible
Churchmen's Missionary Society. There were missionaries in
training, there were missionaries returning for refresher
courses, and endless missionary speakers in college chapel.
Bishop Donald of the Arctic and two of his missionaries
Canon Tom Dalby and Peter Emerson, came on separate
occasions with their illustrated talks on the frozen North
West Territories of Canada. I established a link with the
Diocese of the Arctic which has been maintained to this day.
Canon Alan Neech, on furlough from India, was one of the
most enthusiastic missionary speakers I have ever heard. And
these are to mention but a few. In addition every Tuesday
there were missionary prayer groups. There was no way the
missionary vision imparted by Oswald Smith was going to
dim; indeed, it was enhanced, enlarged and brightened.

The purgatorial side was the academic work. I have never
seen the point of treating the Bible as a piece of literary work
to be dissected and criticised like any other piece of history,
drama or fiction. For me it is a collection of writings of men
who had an experience of God. They wrote what they wrote
to feed readers who had a hunger and a longing to experience
God for themselves. It is the word of God, written by men
inspired by the Holy Spirit. At Tyndale Hall we were privileged
to be lectured by men like Dr. Jim Packer, John Wenham, and
Canon Stafford Wright, all believers in the reliability and truth
of the scriptures.

Somehow I scraped through the necessary minimum of examinations and in June 1962 was ordained in Bristol Cathedral by Bishop Oliver Tomkins. My first curacy was to be at Holy Trinity in East Bristol. My vicar was also the Priest-in-Charge of the adjoining parish of St. Philip and St. Jacob, which was in the process of being declared redundant. Probably, we were told, it would be officially closed by the end of 1964. Apparently the necessary alternative use for the building was that it should become a potato warehouse, doubtless signifying that the parish had had its chips.

St. Philip and St. Jacob with Emmanuel or the Unity, to give the parish its full title, is really a mouthful. We called it Pip'n'Jay for short. And the name has stuck. Once the Mother Church of East Bristol, Pip'n'Jay had gradually experienced the fate of other inner-city churches. Industry and commerce had moved in, and the resident population had largely moved out.

In 1962 the population was around 800. When there were parishes (especially in the north) of many thousands without priests, clearly there was no case for Pip'n'Jay to have a full-time minister. The congregation (about eight at 8 a.m., twenty-five at 11 a.m., and sometimes as many as forty at 6.30 p.m.) were mainly elderly, though nowhere near as old as the building they worshipped in. As the second oldest church in Bristol, the first historical mention being in 1174, Pip'n'Jay had an expensive fabric problem. The maintenance of this building was an unfair burden on a congregation made up largely of pensioners. It all added up to a clear case for redundancy. The Churchwardens and congregations were sad, but there were no plans for appeals to Her Majesty in Privy Council. The inevitable had to be accepted.

However, God had other plans. The promise was that if you put God's kingdom first, he will take care of your needs. Pip'n'Jay had always been concerned for the Kingdom. In 1714 the church gave £29.7s.0d. to the Society for the Propagation of the Gospel. In 1739, when George Whitefield preached there, an offering of £18 was taken up for his orphanage in Georgia. Both gifts were considerable sums in those days. As well as Whitefield, John Wesley had preached from the pulpit, so obviously there had been a concern for souls. Perhaps God was about to reward that faithfulness of the past.

Briefly, what happened was this: a small group of young people began attending the church evening service in December 1963. Along with their Youth Club leader they were all committed Christians. Looking for club premises, they discovered that Pip' n'Jay had a church hall. It was not in very good shape. It was used only once a year by the Pigeon Fanciers Association, and it smelt like it – and of damp, too. But they asked permission, got it and the Pip' n'Jay Youth Club was formed. Since this church had provided the premises, the logical step was to worship there. The regular congregation had settled in their seats, behind pillars, and as far away from me and one another as possible, when in trooped twenty or so young people aged between sixteen and twenty-three.

They filled in from the front and would have done Cranmer's heart good with the manner in which they took part in the old 1662 service of evening prayer. Having recovered from the culture shock, the rest of the congregation took heart at seeing signs of new life. The Pip'n'Jay Youth Club members were normal young people enjoying sports and pop music. But they also enjoyed Youth for Christ Rallies, Bible Studies and Prayer Meetings. They willingly invited friends to special Youth Services, or went on to the street with tracts and invitations. Slowly the congregation began to grow. The average evening attendance had gone comfortably over the sixty mark and was still increasing. Then in June 1964 came the bishop's letter officially announcing the closure of the church at the end of the year.

The Churchwardens wrote immediately to the bishop. They pointed out that the congregation was now growing. They asked him to make me the vicar. They assured him the church had a future. Bishop Oliver was very gracious. His pastoral committee would review the situation, he promised. He added that he certainly didn't want to kill new life. The usual round of meetings took place. In the late autumn of 1964 I was summoned to Bishop's House, and the bishop told me what had been decided. First, there was no way I could be made vicar. I had only been in the ministry for two years, so my apprenticeship was only just beginning. Secondly, he would act on one of our suggestions that had come up in the discussions. He would give us a trial period of three years,

beginning in June 1965, with two targets to aim at. By the end
of the three years the average congregation must be 120 at the
evening service. 'If over 100 people are gathering for worship'
the bishop said, 'I think they need a full-time minister to look
after them.' The other target was a financial one. £500 would
have to be raised in each of the three years, over and above all
running expenses, to prove we could do something about the
fabric of the church. It was something we would have to do
ourselves. There were to be no public appeals. Thirdly, the
bishop informed me that I would serve a second curacy at St.
Luke's on Barton Hill in Bristol. Roy Henderson, the vicar of
St. Luke's, would be Priest-in-Charge of Pip'n'Jay and take the
chair at the Annual General Meetings to prove it. But for the
trial period I would be the minister responsible for Pip'n'Jay.
Fourthly, the bishop made it quite clear he was raising no false
hopes or making empty promises. 'Even, Malcolm, if you do
achieve the targets, I cannot possibly guarantee that the
church will stay open.'

We called a night of prayer to seek the Lord's guidance for
what our strategy should be. We certainly didn't spend the
whole night praying. We had many coffee breaks to stay
awake. In between prayer times we talked and discussed
together. As far as the young people were concerned, the first
target presented no problem. They were already inviting and
bringing friends. They intended to go on doing so. The tracts
and invitations would still be given out. Special Youth
Services with an old-fashioned altar call would continue. The
big problem was the money.

Now £500 may not seem a large sum even for the 1960s.
However, our income as a church was only around £1,000 a
year and our expenditure tended to be in excess of that. If we
were going to get a surplus of £500 in each year of the trial
period, our income had to go up by at least fifty per cent.
Taking a quick look at the giving potential of the congregation
did not provide grounds for encouragement. Only about ten of
us were salaried. The rest were pensioners, school children
on pocket money, and a few students on grants. How were we
going to get the cash? Someone proposed a jumble sale. Well,
we were open to any suggestions. But having examined the
proceeds from previous jumble sales, we learned that if we
were going to achieve the bishop's target that way, we would

need to hold two jumble sales every week through the entire three-year programme!

I am encouraged by the Lord's patience with me. It always takes a long time to get through to me. As we prayed on through the night, the blueprint became clear. Oswald Smith had provided it. And so we at Pip'n'Jay took Matthew 6:33 as our motto. We interpreted 'Seeking first the kingdom' to mean putting missions first on the programme. We believed that if we gave more to missions, then God would take care of the bishop's targets.

We had no particular policy of giving a tenth of our church's income or anything like that. I did have my own secret longing that the time would come when like the People's Church of Toronto we would be giving more away than we spent on ourselves. As we started our trial period our aim was simply to give more to missions.

What did we mean by mission? Basically we understood that a mission was an organisation or an individual that was concerned with the salvation of souls. We included relief organisations that cared for the body in the name of Christ and other specifically Christian charitable institutions. We also included home missions as long as they were operating outside our parish. Internal gifts to our own staff or members would not be included. Our Lord's marching orders to his church were that they were to have a world concern. This comes across in all four gospels and the Acts. 'Teach all nations.' 'The Gospel to every creature.' 'Ye are witnesses of these things.' 'As my father hath sent me, even so send I you.' 'Ye shall be witnesses unto me both in Jerusalem, and in all Judaea, and in Samaria, and unto the uttermost part of the earth.' Pip'n'Jay, Bristol was to be our Jerusalem, our missionary base. By our prayers and by our gifts others would become our representatives to take the gospel elsewhere.

Various tables have been drawn up to show the increase in giving over the years. The table below is only approximate but is based on the definition of what we understood as missionary giving. I have not included charitable giving to members of our own fellowship which is quite a sizeable sum. Nor have I included our contribution to the central funds of the diocese, which now more than covers my salary and house. In 1965 we nearly doubled what we gave away in 1964.

We more than doubled the amount again in 1966.

The bishop's three-year trial period began in June 1965. So at the close of 1966 we were at the half-way mark. We had sought first the kingdom to the best of our ability. God had kept his word. In only eighteen months we had an average 120 attending our evening services, and we had a surplus of £1500 for the building. Of course we jubilantly informed the bishop. He continued to encourage us but told us we would have to wait for a final decision on the future of Pip'n'Jay. I did in fact become the Priest-in-Charge in the summer of 1967, which meant I was the temporary vicar. It was not until May 1974 that the bishop and his pastoral committee were finally convinced that we were a going concern, and I was then instituted as vicar. My own personal target, that we should give more away than we spent on ourselves was achieved in 1969. (Home expenditure £1,681 – Give Away £1,840).

INCREASE IN MISSIONARY SUPPORT

1964	£79	1971	£4215
1965	£137	1973	£8054
1966	£291	1974	£12,496
1967	£705	1977	£28,990
1968	£1247	1980	£53,023
1969	£1840	1983	£67,976

To my knowledge we have no millionaires in the congregation. Nor are we a large company. 1964 saw an average of 60 attending the evening service. In 1983 it was roughly 250. Whereas the congregation has increased by 416% the giving has increased by thousands per cent. As Oswald J. Smith says 'You can't beat God giving.' He always adds the other things.

The missionary support we give

To maintain missionary giving on what can only be described as a miraculous level means that the congregation needs supporting as much as the missionaries. Proverbs 29:18 says 'Where there is no vision the people perish.' Again we owe a debt of gratitude to Oswald Smith for pointing out the

importance of this verse. People need targets, goals, aims -
visions. Otherwise they become lackadaisical, lazy
complacent, parochial, and ineffective. Christians are no
exception.

In our drive to increase missionary support we never
resorted to money-raising efforts. It was all direct giving. But
people need to know where their money is going. They need
to get a vision. In the same way Dr. Martin Luther King cried
'I have a dream!' So the Christian missionary supporter needs
to be able to say 'I have a vision!' We therefore embarked on
a missionary education programme. It was a fairly easy matter
to make 'Seek First' our church motto as well as the title of
our new-look church magazine. We always try to include
missionary items in every edition. It was in the area of
missionary speakers that we had to have a shake-up. It was
the custom then, as it still is for many today, to have a special
Sunday – Leprosy Hospital Sunday, Tear Fund Sunday, etc. In
fact there were so many special Sundays around, that there
were never any Sundays left to do your own thing. Being a
small church we tended to be the Cinderella when it came to
missionary speakers. The big churches got the star, the rest
did a pulpit exchange. At best we got a missionary who was
tired and depressed, at worst a local vicar who was equally
tired and depressed. We needed communicators, salesmen.

We scrapped all special Sundays and instead arranged two
missionary conventions a year (three Sundays in May and
three in November). We appealed to the Missionary Societies
to send us their best speakers. In spite of our meagre
donations in those early days, they responded wonderfully.
Canon Harry Sutton was one who came, won our hearts, and
gave us the sort of vision we were after. Alan Neech came for
BCMS, Dr. Norman Green came for Ruanda, Ernest Oliver for
RBMU, and a host of others whose enthusiasm was infectious,
and I'm heartily glad we all went down with it.

We believed as a church council that we had a
responsibility to our members to encourage and direct wise
spending of their resources. Our missionary giving has gone
through three stages.

First we gave to societies. This was because we had no real
deep personal links with individual missionaries. Our only
link at the beginning of the trial period in 1965 was with Dr.

Arthur Wright of the RBMU. He happened to be a brother of one of our former Sunday school superintendents. The other link we had then was with the Leprosy Mission. This was because Dr. Ian Cochrane's name had been given to me when I had requested a personal missionary for whom I could pray. I believe every Christian should have their own personal missionary. The question for us at Pip'n'Jay was which societies should we support. There are many about. We went for what we called the Big Seven. These were societies we felt in complete sympathy with. From them we drew information and speakers, and to their conferences we tried to send representatives. On three occasions we have ceased official support when we felt a mission was out of line or had lost its way.

The second stage came when although giving to societies, we were giving for the full support of our own missionary personnel. There is nothing like having a member of your congregation leave for the mission field to stir people up.

Today we are in the third stage. Now that we have more personnel than ever, we have to give for the proportionate support of our missionaries, otherwise there would be no latitude to engage in one-off projects or to respond to particular and urgent needs. Taking part in a particular project can stir a church. We sent a team of men to help with building a clinic in the Middle East two or so years ago. It was estimated that in two months they had brought forward the Mission's building programme by eighteen months. As a direct result of that project, one of the men we sent has now gone to work full time with the mission concerned. Another project was to send one of our missionaries in the Arctic the wherewithal to buy himself a new skidoo. On another occasion we sent the finances for another missionary in the Arctic to build an extension so that he could have a study attached to his house. These sort of projects gave us a more personal link with the mission and missionaries concerned.

At every Communion Service now, thanks to the revised liturgy, we declare 'We are the body of Christ.' Pip'n'Jay believes in corporate giving. Take missionary boxes. In 1965 we asked for people to give them up! Instead we issued our own missionary boxes labelled 'Pip'n'Jay Missions'. This meant the Church Council could divide the contents (we open them twice a year) among the Big Seven, or our own missionary personnel according to the present need. We realised some people would have their own pet societies that were not supported by the rest of us. Providing they were bona fide Christian missions we encouraged members to earmark their gifts and give through the Church. It meant more work for the church treasurer, but it meant each year when the accounts were published all could see where the money was going. Individual missionary concern became shared concern. As a result the vision grew.

Of course, if something good is going on you can be sure that the devil will try and spoil it. Earmarking of gifts can be a way of making a protest or causing financial embarrassment to a church. For example if a church member does not approve of the way the money is being spent in a church, he can earmark all his giving for a particular person or organisation, thus making no provison for the general running of the church. Such a person sponges on the generosity of other members who, although they may not always agree with the leadership, nevertheless are prepared to give loyally to the general running of the church.

My own view is that one should give a tenth of one's income (covenanted if possible) to the church of which one is a member with no stipulations or strings attached. By all means earmark gifts over and above one's tenth. The giving of a tenth may seem a high and impossible standard. I believe it is biblical. I believe it is the standard that every Christian should aim for. Further I believe that up to that standard the church to which you belong has first call. If you cannot give your church that commitment, then perhaps you should find another church.

Of course, the other person who needs educating is the minister. Allowing your minister freedom to travel is bound to keep his vision bright. At least give him the opportunity, but don't force him if he doesn't want to go! After all, there are plenty of books that he can read to keep himself informed of what is going on on the mission field. Bishop Oliver once said 'An ounce of imagination can be worth pounds of experience.' In any case the airways are jammed these days with globe-trotting clergy. However, Pip'n'Jay has been very good in allowing me to travel to other churches and indeed to other

lands. I do not like travelling particularly. I prefer terra firma
– the more firmer the less terror. And I am certainly no tourist
or sightseer. That sort of thing bores me stiff. I go only where
the work the Lord has given me takes me. In 1976, for
example, I was invited by Japanese Christians to tour their
country and preach on missions. I hope they got something
from it. I certainly did. I came back good and hopping mad. I
saw there with my own eyes, what others had told me. British
missionaries are not well supported by the British church. I
contacted a friend who had been a missionary in Zaïre to ask
his experience. 'Yes, brother,' he said, 'it's true generally. In
the international missionary community of Africa we British
missionaries were often made to feel like second-class
citizens.' I made a rededication of my life to the Lord shortly
after that, vowing that as long as he gives me strength I will do
all in my power to promote the missionary task of the church
in general, and the support of British missionaries in
particular.

How do we go about choosing which missionaries to
support, now that we are mainly concerned with the support
of individuals? Bible colleges and missionary societies have
their own selection procedures, and some are more
bureaucratic than others.

At Pip'n'Jay we operate a system of elders. If someone
expresses a feeling that they are called of God to serve in
some mission full-time then I or the elders will see them. Our
aim is simply to advise on possible training and societies to
approach. If the person is obviously unsuitable we can say so
then, but this rarely happens. Interviews of this kind are fairly
low key. We reckon that if people are prepared to go to Bible
school or to theological college they deserve our support.
Once they are accepted by a missionary society it is then up to
the elders to make a recommendation concerning financial
support to the Church Council. When a person is a candidate
or a full-blown missionary he or she is adopted by one of our
prayer groups. The prayer group writes to the missionary,
even telephones him or her from time to time, and makes sure
that the rest of the church is kept well informed about news
and prayer requests. In addition we have a missionary support
group. Their task is to maintain a close personal link with the
missionaries and make sure that at all times the Church

Council is fully aware of their financial needs. It has always been our policy, when we are able to do so, to spoil our missionaries thoroughly when they come home.

I am often invited to other churches to share the Pip'n'Jay story. In some I am particularly invited by the minister who wants his people stirred up. The only blockage I have found is the one of fear. People are afraid that they cannot afford to invest in missions. I always try and point out that God's perfect love does away with all fear. If we allow his love to be poured out into our hearts by the Holy Spirit, then we cannot help but have a concern for the lost in our world. In obedience to the dictates of that love we then begin to give to missions. Any church, chapel, assembly, or fellowship of believers can prove for themselves that what Oswald Smith says is true. It is absolutely impossible to out-give God.

The missionary task of the church is not only the church's first priority, it is also any church's secret of personal blessing.

Chapter 2

Baptist Tabernacle, Stockton on Tees

Neville Atkinson

The Baptist Tabernacle at Stockton on Tees, Co. Cleveland, is situated in the centre of the town. In an industrial area, which suffers from high (twenty per cent) unemployment, the 'Tab' has a morning congregation of 500-600, and an evening congregation of 350-450.

The Baptist Tabernacle supports nine missionaries, and has particular links with the Baptist Missionary Society, Regions Beyond Missionary Union, and the European Christian Mission.

The Rev. Neville Atkinson comes from a village working-class background, and left grammar school at fifteen – 'as soon as the law would let me'. The following year he was converted at a Cliff College Mission. After a spell in market gardening he spent two years at Bible college, and became a Baptist minister in 1958, spending ten years at Torquay and fifteen at Stockton. He is married to Cynthia, and they have three grown-up children. His particular interests are gardening, hiking and watching football.

The situation

Stockton on Tees is a typically northern industrial town, with few salient features or points of interest for anyone who does not live there. Its main claim to fame seems to lie in the fact that John Walker, the inventor of the friction match, lived here; as also did Thomas Sheraton the furniture designer. The world's first passenger railway, the Stockton to Darlington line, ended here (or began here, depending on whether you were coming or going). A wide High Street plays host, on a twice-weekly basis, to one of the largest open-air markets in England.

The people depend heavily on the steel and petro-chemical industries for a living. In common with the rest of the population of the north-east, they have suffered badly through long periods of industrial recession and consequent unemployment. At the present time twenty per cent of the working population are jobless, and the prospects for young people are bleak indeed.

Stockton Tabernacle

At the centre of the town and just off the main High Street is Stockton Baptist Tabernacle. A population of 85,000 people live within 2½ miles of its doors. Considerably less than ten per cent of those people attend church with any degree of regularity.

Every bus into town terminates within five minutes' walk of the church, and across the road from the Church Fellowship Centre is a large municipal car park. Obviously a strategic position in a large mission field.

The Tabernacle was built at the beginning of this century. It was the third home of a Christian Fellowship which began about 1775 and which had outgrown its accommodation on two previous occasions. The spacious building at that time seated 900 people. It was built to last. The bricks are like armour plating. When the church was remodelled in 1972, it was rather like trying to remodel a battleship. An interesting point for the economist is that the whole structure cost only £9,000 in 1908.

In 1972 the remodelling process produced a church with 600 seats. At that time this was more than adequate for a church of 285 members.

Through continuing evangelistic work the membership was more than 480 in 1984. Most of this growth has been conversion growth, and a large proportion of these converts have been adults. On numerous special occasions through the year the church is now more than full.

A large Fellowship Centre next door was purchased from the North Eastern Co-operative Society in 1976. The two-storey building, which was formerly a supermarket and restaurant, became available and at a stroke and for £25,000 we acquired two large and well fitted halls and a large store, plus a catering-sized kitchen. This building now houses many activities and meetings, including a Christian Literature Centre.

The church has always been evangelistic in outlook but, like many other churches in industrial areas, has gone through difficult times. Northern towns are dotted with warehouses, stores, and workshops which used to be church buildings, housing congregations of Christians. In the goodness of God, the Tabernacle survived and grew. Today there are three full-time staff. As well as a Senior Pastor there is a Minister for Youth and a Minister of Evangelism. In addition a salaried administrator mans the church office.

The present ministry

The ministry of the present pastor began in 1969. At that time the church had five members serving on the overseas field. One family was serving in Uganda, while a second family and a single lady missionary were at work in Brazil. There was a fair missionary interest on the part of many in the congregation and a strong interest from the usual nucleus of enthusiasts. The church giving for overseas work in 1968 was £500, though at that time individuals often sent gifts direct to Missionary Societies. The church had no record of such gifts and was not in a position to know what the total missionary giving of the whole church amounted to. It would be fair to say that much of the giving was a spasmodic 'event' type of giving rather than a systematic week-by-week commitment. A special appeal for a specific need would produce generous giving, but the 'bread-and-butter' regular support was not systematised as it might have been. For some at least the 'ship-ha'penny' and 'missionary box' mentality of another age prevailed. It was not so much a lack of interest in overseas work – rather it was a need to build a greater vision and organise a systematic support scheme. We will return to the subject of finance later.

The present situation

Four of the original five missionaries came home in the early seventies. One family came home because of illness and could not return to the field. Another family with teenage children returned home to meet the educational needs of those children. The 'single girl' is now a 'single lady missionary' – she is still there after twenty years' excellent service with WEC International. Since 1978 eight others have been commissioned to the field. Some of our most inspiring services are when a missionary is commissioned, or recommissioned.

We now have a single girl in the Upper River Region of Zaïre. She is involved with Regions Beyond Missionary Union in health clinics, delivering babies, and doing church work. In Britain she would be simply an occupational therapist, the profession in which she was trained.

We share a family who serve with the United Mission to Nepal. The husband is one of our members while his wife is a member of a church in southern England. A young family, at present on their first furlough, return to Bangladesh with BMS this summer. They are involved in village work. Another family are doing a specialist work in Gospel broadcasting and follow-up in a Muslim country.

In 1981 our latest missionary family began work in Spain. They are church-planting in a pioneer area and serve with ECM.

In addition to these, a number of our young people have been involved in short-term work overseas. We hope to expand this aspect, thus exposing young people to the needs of the world and producing a continuing missionary vision. In some cases the short-term work may lead to permanent overseas missionary service.

We try constantly to encourage our fellowship to see these people as an extension of our own outreach. They are part of our church family. The work they do is regarded as our work, albeit in another land and in partnership with other Christians of another nation.

We do not send our missionaries to a missionary society feeling that it is now the society's responsibility to look after them and support them. The society is regarded as a necessary channel working in partnership with the home church. We see the accumulated expertise of the society as being at the service of the sending church and the national church overseas. It is also the channel of contact from home church to missionary and vice versa. Our missionaries are not sent by the society, they are sent by the local church. The society facilitates the sending. This is in no way to demean the work of the societies, for we have the highest regard for what they are doing. We would be unhappy if our missionaries did not serve with a society, except in very special circumstances. (Only one of our families is serving independently of a missionary society. Certain aspects of their specialist work demand that they do this. However, they do not regard themselves as 'freelance'. We support them and our elders and deacons act as an Advisory Board when necessary. We are in regular contact with them).

Building the missionary church

The key to missionary expansion is the local church. Churches with missionary vision produce missionary candidates, as well as missionary support in terms of prayer and finance. They are also involved on the home front in missionary work. However many-sided the work of a missionary society, in the end it is concerned with the salvation of the lost and the discipling of the redeemed. This is equally true of the church on the mission field at home. Christians should learn to think of one world mission on two fronts, home and abroad. Despite many cultural differences, the basic need of salvation through Christ is the same on any field in the world.

The key to producing such Christians and such churches must lie with the pulpit and the leadership. It is very difficult to create a missionary vision without leadership from the pulpit. The missionary challenge is presented regularly as part of the whole counsel of God from the pulpit at Stockton Tabernacle. Regular pulpit prayer reminds the people of their missionary commitment.

Deacons and elders share the vision: missionary features appear regularly in the church magazine, and each missionary sends a newsletter, which is circulated by one of the church members as part of their Christian service. Usually the letters are reproduced on the church's offset printing machine. For fifteen years an Annual Missionary Convention, usually lasting four days, has been part of our church programme. All these factors help to inspire a missionary concern.

Once the vision begins to take hold, it must be kept alive and renewed. In any given year forty to fifty new members will join our church. Many of these will be brand-new Christians. They too need to be educated and inspired. The missionaries will be only names to them at first; later they will become friends.

The fact that we have members overseas makes it much easier to build the vision. It is now unlikely that any year will pass without some of our missionaries being home. New Christians have opportunity to meet people who have, up to now, been names in a pulpit prayer or a prayer letter. Now they become real people.

We make a big thing of the 'welcome home'. The missionary is introduced from the pulpit and, usually, briefly interviewed. A fellowship meal and reception is organised. We make an equally big thing of a missionary commissioning, or recommissioning when they return to the work overseas. Our missionaries are seen as very special people, and our church is encouraged to feel very privileged to have them and to support them.

Whilst at home, the missionaries will have opportunity (after adequate rest), to share details of their work and of what God is doing in their particular area. For the weeks or months of furlough, they will visit our many home groups with visual aids. There will be opportunity for questions and discussion. In addition, opportunity will be given to visit all the departments of the church, including Sunday school. Missionary concern needs to begin young. In this way personal links are maintained and deepened, and new links are established with new members.

Furlough should be primarily a time for *rest* and *re-establishment* of home church links. We realise the need of missionary societies for deputation workers. We also are aware that many churches, especially the smaller ones, want and need to have the ministry of missionaries. However, as a church, we are unhappy about some of the demands made upon our missionaries to travel long distances for one-off deputation meetings. This would seem to us to be an unreasonable demand to make of a missionary on furlough, unless there are very extenuating circumstances. Missionaries usually return home from the field tired, and often shattered. A heavy deputation programme, often entered into much too early, does not help to prepare them for the time when they return to the demanding work of the field.

Missionary magazines, regular newsletters and church magazine features all help to play a part in developing a 'missionary minded' church. Twice yearly frugal meals, with audio-visual aids, highlight the work of TEAR Fund and BMS Operation Agri. All these things help to educate and stimulate missionary vision.

Prayer backing

Regular prayer letters are circulated for each of our missionaries. Sections of the letters, or items from the letters, are often published in the church magazine. There are a number of monthly missionary prayer meetings supporting the work of various societies. Once a month the church prayer meeting is largely given to missionary matters. The Secretary of our Missionary Council is responsible for bringing up-to-date matters to that meeting for prayer. He is also responsible for the church magazine missionary articles.

Some of our people have an occasional telephone link with some missionary families. Obviously STD does not reach to the Upper River area of Zaïre, nor the mountains of Nepal. However, a telephone call where possible is an excellent way of reminding our missionaries that they are not forgotten, and an excellent way also of gaining up-to-date information for prayer and interest.

Financial support

At the beginning of the present ministry the financial system was revamped. It was felt that we needed a practical workable system which would encourage *regular* support for overseas work. Most churches have a methodical stewardship system to ensure support for the work here at home, and the same approach ought to be taken for overseas work.

Furthermore, we felt a system was required which would channel all our missionary giving through the church. It would then be possible to know whether the missionary giving of the whole church was worthy or not. An intelligent and informed assessment of our financial stewardship could be made. At that time money was being sent directly by individuals to missionary societies. This was commendable, but we had no idea how we *as a church* were facing up to our financial responsibilities.

At the same time we did not want a system in which the church designated the gifts. Numbers of people had supported a society, or missionary family, for years. Some were involved in team support systems with missionaries from other churches – perhaps personal friends of many years. We wanted a system which would enable them to continue their commitment as they felt right, *but through the church*. The scheme we devised was quite simple. We ordered three sets of ordinary stewardship envelopes, in pink, blue and white. Each member automatically received these three sets. Any non-members who worshipped regularly with us and regarded the 'Tab' as their church, could also have sets of envelopes on request and thus share in the scheme. The pink envelope we would use for the needs of the home fellowship. The white one was marked 'Evangelism in Britain' – this would cover our commitment to the Baptist Home Mission fund, and other gifts we might wish to make to other evangelical causes in the U.K. The blue envelope would be for overseas missions. It could be used to designate the gift by marking it with the name of any evangelical missionary society. The church undertook to forward all designated gifts, on a monthly basis, though we particularly encourage our people to designate gifts to 'Tab missionaries'. It was a complicated task for the treasurers but it has worked out well. Most of our people use the scheme though increasingly people are beginning to give by monthly Banker's Order.

In the beginning of the scheme, in 1970, a large number of

societies were supported; however, the number has now been considerably reduced since we have concentrated our efforts on those societies with which our own missionaries serve. Nevertheless, if even a small gift comes in and is designated for another society, it is always sent as the donor indicates.

We teach tithes and offerings as a desirable practice. It is taught once a year as part of the whole counsel of God. In 1984 our budget for *outside* causes is around £44,000 – almost £38,000 of this is for overseas work. The greater part of that amount is for the support of 'Tab missionaries'. Our goal for each of our missionary families is £6,600 per annum. The target is reviewed annually. This will certainly not keep them in luxury, but will give them a firm financial base of support. The giving usually runs under budget target for the first half of each year; however, missionary gifts are sent monthly to budget, any shortfall in missionary income being supplied from the General Account.

Our total commitment as a church is large. In fact in total we support seven families and two singles in whole-time work home and abroad. This does not include office staff and caretaking. In a recession area this is a constant test of faith. However, it is our corporate faith rather than the missionaries' individual faith.

In addition to our regular stewardship system, we tithe our annual 'Thanksgiving Gift Day' total for overseas missions. We also tithe our covenant monies (the Chancellor is good to us – we received £12,000 from him last year in recovered tax. Next year the figure will be £14,000, but it still ought to be more. Our treasurers regard a Christian taxpayer as a bad steward if he doesn't covenant his gifts).

Of course, we are aware that missionary needs vary from country to country and from time to time. A gift may be worth much more in real terms in one country than in another. Similarly it may be worth more this year than next year (or last year); inflation plays havoc in some areas. We have considered this at great length but feel it best to send equal amounts to each country. It would be impossible to take every eventuality into account.

When our missionaries are on furlough a special offering is made for any project they wish to name.

Our primary emphasis then is support for the *missionary*

rather than the *society*. This works for us at the present time. It gives our people a link with their friends on the field – the church helped to 'buy that car', 'pay for those air tickets', 'stock that dispensary', 'provide that broadcasting equipment', etc. Of course, if we didn't have missionaries on the field we would still be involved in missionary giving. In such a situation support would probably involve giving to societies rather than individuals, although it is possible that we would try to sponsor missionary families. We are aware that numbers of missionaries come from small churches which would perhaps be unable to support them fully. Our scheme would not perhaps work in those situations. We are conscious of the fact that the system which best suits our church family may not work for others. Each church must work out its own system.

Financially the cost is high. There are many things we would like to do with our own church premises, but we prefer to emphasise personnel rather than buildings.

Practical approach

We have tried to take a practical and down-to-earth approach to our missionaries and their needs, but to bear in mind also the need for flexibility. Societies operate in different ways. Some societies make provision for their personnel by retaining monies, for example, towards furlough air fares; others have different methods. In one instance our treasurers, after consultation with the missionary concerned, agreed to hold a small proportion of the monthly support in account for furlough air tickets when the time for furlough arrived. The particular mission in which our missionary was serving did not make such a provision.

If accommodation is needed for a family on furlough, we rent a home for them. At some point in the future we may buy a missionary home, but at present it would be under-used and superfluous for periods of time. If any unforeseen or urgent need arises we expect our missionaries to feel free to share it with us. If specific needs arose we would always be willing to give extra help.

Another practical need is with regard to the education of the children of missionaries. At present we have two young people from one of our missionary families living with church families. This we feel is better than a boarding school situation and enables the young people concerned to be involved in the youth activities of our church.

Visits to the field

In these days of rapid travel, many new possibilities are opening up for church members and elders to visit the overseas field. Of course some fields are more accessible than others, and, in all honesty, some fields are more attractive than others! Numbers of our people have visited the missionary work in Southern Spain. In total four of our fields have been visited by church members at some point; however, up to now this has been at the initiative of individuals rather than as a church-sponsored venture. This may well be an idea we can expand in the future.

One of our young people has just returned after six very useful months with one of our families abroad. The missionary family are very keen to have someone else join them on a similar venture as soon as we have a suitable young person available to go. Perhaps the best way to create missionary concern is to see the field at first hand.

In conclusion

We have seen a great deal accomplished in the past few years but there is no room for complacency – the Great Commission still stands. Missionary concern for the foreign field must be built into the mind of every new Christian. The fires must continually be stirred or they become smouldering ashes. The greatest vision can fade. The most dedicated and spirit-filled life can drift from high dedication to low mediocrity.

At present we have a large number of young people in our church. Many are keen Christians. It is a matter for concern that we have none in training for the overseas field at the moment. Of course, that could change rapidly and we pray that it will. However, the point remains: vision has to be continually given and maintained. To rejoice in what God has done is one thing, to rest on our laurels is another. We wish to remain a 'sending' church.

Chapter 3

Gold Hill Baptist Church, Gerrards Cross, Bucks

Jim Graham

Gold Hill Baptist Church serves the village of Chalfont St. Peter near Gerrards Cross in London's commuter belt, an area which contains a higher-than-average proportion of executives. Its proximity to Heathrow also makes it a popular area for international businessmen. The community tends to be a mobile one with many families moving away within two or three years. The church is situated in a residential area which has two council estates and large number of private houses. On an average Sunday around 600 people attend the services.

Gold Hill Baptist Church has an active interest in the work of the Overseas Missionary Fellowship, WEC International and Wycliffe Bible Translators. The church supports sixteen missionaries and has several members in training.

The Rev. Jim Graham was born into a Christian home in the town of Airdrie in Lanarkshire where he was later baptised as a teenager following his conversion. After studying for his Master's Degree in Philosophy and History at Glasgow University, he was called to the ministry. He continued his studies at the Baptist Theological College of Scotland and Trinity College, Glasgow. Jim Graham's first appointment was as a student pastor at East Kilbride Baptist Church.

His wife Anne is a doctor and they have one married daughter and three sons.

The background

Our church, originally a small country chapel, is twenty-three miles north-west from Central London. The records show that a Free Church came into being in 1774 and was established on its present site by 1792 as part of the Countess of Huntingdon's Connexion. It was greatly influenced by Baptist teaching and by 1807 was organised on principles similar to Calvinist and Strict Baptist churches. 1922 saw a further change when the membership was widened to include all evangelicals, and this continues to this day. Although still affiliated to the Baptist Union of Great Britain and Northern Ireland, the strong traditional denominational emphasis has gone and the concern of the church centres around six main principles:

1. The centrality of Christ
2. The authority of Scripture
3. The practical outworking of biblical teaching
4. The significant movement of the Holy Spirit in renewal
5. The importance of fellowship
6. The plurality of leadership

The growth in the local population in the earlier part of the twentieth century was not mirrored in marked congregational growth, as might have been expected, but membership remained over 100 from 1929; over 200 from 1966; and over 300 from 1973. Now the membership is just over 500, with about 690 adults meeting in fellowship in any given week. A large youth section, divided into three age groups, has a total of 500 names on its books.

Until the last twenty-five years the church's attitude to and involvement in mission was dutiful, traditional and denominational – like the majority of churches throughout the United Kingdom. It is hard to say what effect two large interdenominational and international missionary societies, which moved their headquarters into the area, had on the life and thinking of the Fellowship during this time. At an official level in the beginning, apparently, no effect at all, but on a personal level it would be very much more difficult to assess. It is impossible to be in fellowship with the Lord's servants and remain impervious to their vision, faith and obedience.

The call to mission

Most people would consider that much of the reason for the growth of the Fellowship lies in the quality of its teaching, its worship and member care. The most powerful creative force, however, in terms of mission and evangelism – as well as many other aspects of our lives both personally and corporately – was, and is the insistence that the Word of God has not only to be heard in a meaningful way, but also understood, put into practice and then shared with confidence and authority. Anything which has happened among us over these past years can be traced in its origins to that fundamental conviction. It is not enough for the people of God to say that they believe the Word of God – they need to go on to say that we *believe* the Word of God *works* (because we have proved and demonstrated that it is so!).

Most Christians know of the Great Commission of Christ, 'the marching orders of the Christian Church': 'I have been given all authority in heaven and on earth. Go, then, to all peoples everywhere and make them my disciples: baptise them in the Name of the Father, the Son, and the Holy Spirit, and teach them to obey everything I have commanded you. And I will be with you always to the end of the age.' (Matt. 28:18–20; Mark 16:15). This is his great mandate to us, signed and sealed. G.K. Chesterton once said: 'It is not the parts of the Bible which I do not understand which bother me, but the parts which I do understand' – just so! Our first concern is not compassion for those who are living as guilty men and women aware that they have not lived up to the light they have received – whatever 'light' that has been – and so desperately need to know the nature and reality of forgiveness. It is not even compassion which is stirred in our hearts when we recognise that countless millions are going to a Christless eternity. Our first concern is obedience to the clear directive of Jesus, who is Lord, and gives us his Word, not so that we can discuss it or debate it and decide thereafter whether we like or not, but who gives his Word so that we will respond to it.

The call to mission, evangelism and witness is not dependent on isolated texts, scattered sparingly throughout the Bible and quoted often at random and out of context, but is to be found consistently and undeniably on every page of the New Testament. Compassion for the lost is important, but obedience to the Lord is much, much more so. We have allowed the Gospel to become so man-centred that sometimes it is hardly God-honouring. We need to get our perspective right. God is a sending God, and Jesus unequivocally draws us into his purposes: 'Peace be with you', he says; 'As the Father sent me, so I send you'.

Compassion is not absent, however, in all of this – it is there aching and yearning in the heart of Jesus. 'The harvest is large', he says, 'but there are few workers to gather it in. Pray to the owner of the harvest that he will send out workers to gather in his harvest'. (Matt 9:37–38). Perhaps it is needless to say that more people are alive today than the total number of people who have ever lived on earth in all of human history! But it is not needless to point out that there are over 2,700,000,000 of these living people who have never heard the Gospel. There are over 16,000 different and distinct people-groups and even whole countries where not one single living church is in existence. There are 7,000 distinct living languages and 5,200 of them still have no Bible or Scripture translations available in their own language. It is estimated that 80,000 unsaved people die every day (approximately 3,300 every hour – 55 people every single minute!) and go out to stand one day before the Great White Throne. It is awesome to remember that Hell is not for the weekend, but for eternity! Hell is not simply a theological concept, but a stirring and desolating reality.

At this time *worldwide* there are only 85,000 workers on the mission field – mainly among those who have heard the Gospel before. Only 9 per cent of the world's population speak English, and yet 94 per cent of all the preachers in the whole world minister to them. In that enormously generous country, the United States, 96 per cent of all Christian finances are spent on 6 per cent of the world's population. Only 4 per cent of all Christian money is spent on missionary efforts to reach the other 94 per cent of the world's population! There are over 1,000,000 full-time Christian workers in the United States; whilst one half of the world's population (three major groups – Muslim, Hindu and Chinese), 2,200,000,000 people, have only 2,417 full-time

Christian workers. It is estimated that those who have never even heard the Gospel once have one worker for 450,000 persons.

Many have heard the unequivocal statement by Oswald J. Smith, now dated and often disregarded, that 'No one has the right to hear the Gospel twice, while there remains someone who has not heard it once.' In other words, if you had twenty children to feed and plenty of food with which to feed them all, could it ever be right to give three of the children ten meals a day, seven of them only one meal, and the remaining ones nothing at all – and so cause them to die of starvation? Yet we do this with the Gospel, which has an eternal significance, and not just a temporal one!

Biblically it seems that God's anointing in a special way is on those who leave home and native land to share the Gospel with others. From Noah to Abraham, from Moses to Jonah and from Daniel to Paul this is the message. The great romance of the Acts of the Apostles is that in one generation the Gospel went from the religious capital of the world to the political capital of the world, and this through ordinary people who had come to appreciate what it meant to be crucified with Christ; buried with him in baptism; raised to new life under his Lordship; baptised in the Holy Spirit; aware that Christ had ascended to the place of the authority and power from whence one day he would return in glory to judge the living and the dead. In the radiant joy of the Resurrection and in the irresistible power of the Holy Spirit they went out confidently, not only to declare God's Word, but to display and demonstrate it with signs and wonders.

It is this biblical perspective which has captivated our hearts and lives as well as our minds within the Fellowship here. Added to this has been a very clear prophetic word (i.e. God's Word for *us* at this *time* and in this *place*!) which has come in a number of circumstances. This has emphasised what God has to say in a more general way through his written Word. So the new emphasis on mission has come as a result of our taking the Word of God seriously. In the light of the revelation of God's Word and the confirmation of God's Spirit certain practical steps had to be taken. I well remember one of the most dramatic church meetings I have ever been part of, when, as a Fellowship, we were convinced that if God would honour us by calling men and women out from our church to serve him, we would be responsible to supply the resources, both spiritual, material and financial to maintain them in the ministry to which God would call them. Excitement mingled with faith in the light of reality!

Principles for a missionary church

However, such a faith-declaration was bound to be significantly far-reaching at every level. It was clearly necessary to establish certain principles on which we as a church would operate. God gave us seven very clear principles.

1. *Mission needed to be removed from the periphery of the church's life and put at the heart of our life together.* Involvement and responsibility had to be moved from the 'enthusiast' to the 'ordinary' church member. This was achieved – at least in part, because we have so much ground yet to possess – firstly teaching the principle of mission and evangelism regularly, consistently and clearly from the Word of God. Secondly, by making it known – certainly to those who join us here in the commitment of membership (and that has been a considerable number in recent years) – that to be involved in this part of the local Body of Christ requires taking seriously the last words that Jesus spoke on earth before his Ascension that the Gospel is to be taken 'to the ends of the earth'. There was a warm corporate response from the Fellowship to devote a large proportion of our effort and money in the support of mission work at home and overseas.

This first principle is so strategically important that it really set the scene for the other six. To fail to establish this principle is to fail. To return to this principle again and again is much more significant than setting up missionary meetings, weekends and the like to which a disappointing number would inevitably respond. How much embarrassment I have felt over the years to have to be a part of, and sometimes to lead, such gatherings.

2. *Money is a key.* That needs to be stated clearly, since Jesus taught more about money than about any other single

subject – even more than he taught about prayer or about heaven! Practically it meant for us breaking new ground by establishing a faith budget. This meant that we did not have the funds, but by faith we trusted God to release from among us, and to us, such funds as would be necessary for the encouragement, maintenance and support of people and projects which we believed the Lord had given us specifically. This is done on a calculated basis which is designed to honour God and so to be honourable to those we support. Careful attention is given to the situation in which a person is working (for example, the cost of living in some South American countries is much higher than it is in the United Kingdom), and to the needs of the individual concerned. We are concerned that there should be no geographical demarcation of mission, and anything reasonably considered to be outside our own immediate borders would be regarded as such.

Our commitment to people is primary and our support of them is on the basis that their 'call' to some specific aspect of mission has been recognised and then ratified by the local church. This is done through the eldership and the Mission Board, set up within our local church, 'examining' the potential missionary with a view to commending him or her to the church corporately for its confirmation. Such a confirmation by the church carries with it full support in every area. Candidates with neither involvement by the leadership nor ratification by the Fellowship would have no grounds for any expectation of support, although each would be considered on the basis of individual merits.

Our support of projects is on the basis of a deep spiritual kinship and vision for what is being done rather than on a personal or denominational basis. It has been necessary to limit the number of these projects so that our commitment and involvement could be relevant and significant. This has meant 'screening', and inevitably turning away requests to which we cannot respond.

3. *Many missionaries, both individually and corporately, fail because spiritual supplies are not getting through to them from the base.* Our concern was to ensure, with clinical precision, that effective prayer and the widest possible support was given to individual missionaries whom God has

given to us to care for. In practice each missionary has a prayer-cell which is called into being around him or her on the basis of personal relationship, the geographical area where the missionary is serving, or the specific work that he is doing. This is voluntary and is at the discretion of the individual responding to the leading of God. This in effect becomes the core-group for effective prayer. In addition, however, each missionary is assigned to a house fellowship attached to the church under the pastoral care of an elder and two house fellowship leaders. The responsibility of the house fellowship is to relate to the missionary in the widest possible way: to express the love and concern of the whole Fellowship in correspondence, in sending teaching and worship tapes, in responding to domestic and personal needs, and in surrounding the missionary with live fellowship and being sensitive to his or her needs on returning for leave.

4. We constantly recognise that *our first priority is to support to the full extent of our vision those who have been called out from the Fellowship and those projects which have come within the orbit of the Fellowship's concern.* Whatever remains financially after this has been done is allocated on an agreed percentage basis to other specified missionary activities. This forms a clear guide for handling 'emotion' giving and denominational 'duty' giving. Earmarked gifts, of course, are allocated according to the expressed wishes of the giver.

5. Unquestionably many missionary 'breakdowns' have occurred as a result of insufficient *pastoral care on location*. Distance, shortage of manpower, lack of gift, internal loyalty to the mission's policy, all make it very difficult to pastor *in situ*. Although it can never be regarded as the final or the fullest answer to this issue, the Fellowship has accepted as a significant responsibility the need to promote missionary pastoral visits by the pastoral team and the church leadership to stimulate, nourish and encourage missionaries overseas from wherever they have come, and in particular those we support from our own Fellowship. Although it has not been specifically laid down, we attempt to ensure that each missionary sent out from us is 'visited' pastorally at least once

during any given period of service between furloughs. In this way an understanding is gained at first hand of the spiritual pressures and the material needs of those who have gone out from us. Another, and a complementary way of achieving this is to be financially responsible for bringing a missionary home during his or her holiday break. Few missionary locations are now more than forty-eight hours' journey away. We have found that in some situations more can be achieved in doing this than by someone visiting 'on the field'. Sensitivity and understanding needs to be exercised in this regard, as well as close co-operation with the missionary society to which the individual is attached and committed.

6. *In order to carry out our responsibility before God with honour, a new, realistic structure had to be found.* This was called the Mission Board. It includes an elder and a missionary secretary and treasurer who serve on the diaconate. Other specifically called members within the Fellowship are part of the Board. The task of the Mission Board is to develop missionary interest and support within the church. It co-ordinates all the various activities involved including prayer groups, missionary evenings, the despatch of tapes and letters, and giving missionary reports when the committed membership of the local Body of Christ meets monthly. It also acts as an advisory body to the elders on the changing pattern of missionary work, and actively formulates specific missionary proposals each year to be approved by the elders and then by the church. The Mission Board, of course, is also involved in assessing and encouraging individuals with a view to the calling of God on their lives and how best they may honour that and prepare to respond to it.

7. In order to maintain continuity, momentum and reality, *it is necessary to set aside time each year for a review of the achievements and failures of the previous year* and to agree proposals for the following year initiated by the Mission Board and the elders.

Inevitably in all of this there is a constant need for adjustment since un-thought-of details arise and new circumstances emerge. For example, two of our missionaries are planning to return to the area where they have been working – but this time with a new ministry and without the 'institutional' commitment where they were formerly involved. Again, with the rapid development of a 'home' ministry from the Fellowship, it has been necessary to call into being a new board called 'Gold Hill United Kingdom.' Nevertheless, in spite of the fact that change is here to stay, these general principles remain to channel the life God has given us, to widen the horizons, and to extend the borders of the local church.

Principles in practice

Since what we are concerned with here is people rather than principles, I felt it right to ask one of our missionaries to respond to me as one who had been among us and had been sent out by us. I think you will discern some interesting features in what she writes.

If you are unable to fulfil the ministry to which God has called you in the Philippines we are at fault; we have failed!' were the firm words of one of our pastors before I left England, and that sentiment has been reiterated during the past seven years. Recognising that the prayer support and loving interest and concern of my church were vital to my being an effective missionary has meant taking the Fellowship into my confidence – honestly sharing my joy and grief and pain through sending letters and tapes to my prayer cell and house fellowship and other prayer partners in the church, as well as talking things through with church members who visited me.

Because God's call to missionary work came after I was a church member, and was confirmed by the elders, most of the church knew me in all my weakness and shortcomings. Sometimes that was embarrassing, but it also gave me courage: since they knew me they knew how to pray, could anticipate needs, etc. The Fellowship collectively had become my family even before my parents died, and instead of that link wasting away over years of physical separation, it is stronger today than ever before. Often during the early years of language learning and cultural adjusting I felt my most effective ministry was praying for all God was doing at Gold Hill as his Spirit was poured out and so much was happening there. Because our relationship is bathed in God's love and communication channels have been kept open; prayer-support and commitment have been two-way. I'm proud of the way the church has risen to the challenge of being personally committed to me and it is a tremendous privilege to be equally committed to them.

Imperfect as they are, the principles given are not for writing about in order to be read, discussed and even criticised, but to be put into practice and made to work not according to a slavish legalism, but with the joyful liberty and sense of privilege which comes through the precious ministry of the Holy Spirit. The keynote to it all is *partnership* – with God; with those called and commissioned by Him; and with the local church.

Already a plurality of leadership has been established and accepted within the church. Five of the eldership have been released by the church to serve the Lord, depending on the church to supply their daily needs, whilst the remaining seven are either retired or earn their living in 'secular' jobs. This has been necessary because of the different functions each has been called to fulfil. I regard those who serve the Lord elsewhere – and certainly overseas – from the Fellowship as much on the church's 'payroll' as those of us who are centrally based. I have a burning vision on my heart (which I believe to be from the Lord!) that ten per cent of our total membership will be so released to serve him as he directs – either at home or abroad. After all, on the day of Pentecost, when the Holy Spirit was first poured out on the church, and the church was born and blasted into orbit, ten per cent of the 120 believers were *supported* by them. There is a key here which I believe to be significant!

How this will be achieved must be under God's hand, and yet practical procedure needs to be recognised. I can well remember how two of our members returned from abroad deeply burdened about a specific place and particularly concerned about a godly work which was being carried out there. I had gone out with them and identified the need and also the opportunity. They returned to share their burden with the elders. Subsequently the elder unanimously came to feel that they themselves were to be God's answer to the problem. This was difficult in view of the husband's business involvement, and also because of their very natural ties to house, family and the local fellowship.

The elders' conviction was shared with them and they were invited to consider it together before the Lord. No pressure would be exerted on them, and they were assured of our loving and prayerful concern, and urged that they, too, must feel comfortable in their own spirits. They would have access to those of us in the leadership to discuss and pray through any matters. That was shared with them one Sunday morning in my office. On that same day, in the evening service, someone who knew nothing whatever of the situation, but whom we trust, had a very specific word of knowledge from the Lord which fitted precisely into the situation which confronted them – it even specified that a couple were being called by the Lord.

They were among the first that night to come to the front of the church at the end of the service. In their case the initiative came from God through the leadership. More recently, however, another couple presented themselves to the eldership to share a conviction in their hearts that God was calling them to some specific service which necessitated their release from 'secular' employment. The implications for them were far-reaching in terms of security, lifestyle, career advancement (and this man had been well recognised for his ability in his profession in the commercial world over twenty years) and so on. The elders gave certain directives to ensure the reality of their call and also to give more exposure to the ongoing life of the local church. In the event the elders came unanimously to the conclusion that their call was certainly of God and last Easter they launched out on their new calling.

To write about these four people makes me aware that there is so much more to be shared that is deeply significant in their personal lives, but the principle of the calling of God upon them is well illustrated by them.

Sharing in mission

Our concern at this time is to co-operate with existing missionary societies where that seems appropriate. We feel a spiritual kinship with many and would feel it arrogant on our part to disregard their experience, fellowship and ministry.

However, as the scene both at home and abroad changes so rapidly – not least the relationship of the local church to missionary societies – new ground will have to be explored in the light of the urgency of the world situation and the new and glorious outpouring of the Holy Spirit. Our involvement with a missionary society inevitably demands that we recognise its policy and practice financially and in other ways. Our membership is encouraged to do this in order to avoid any conflict of loyalties. In the event of such a clash, the first loyalty of our missionaries would be to the local church and our Mission Board, however, rather than to the missionary society. We have found thus far that co-operation and sensitivity by the historic missionary societies has been humbling, and for that we have been profoundly grateful. Certain tensions are inevitable, since changes and developments occur so rapidly within the local church situation while comparable changes must inevitably take so much longer within the historic missionary situation for a whole variety of perfectly understandable reasons. How patient we need always to be with one another, and how concerned we must be never to lose sight of what it is we are involved in.

We are grateful to God for all that he has shown us and for all he has enabled us to do. Anything that has been accomplished has been evidence of his grace. For that we want humbly to give thanks. But there is so much more to be explored and done – and all the while time runs out on us! How can we more clearly hear what God is saying to us? How can we, as a church, release more and more resources into the harvest fields of the world? How best can we call and prepare both old and young for the work of Christian service – since what is being done is good, but not good enough? How can we be sure that the children of the Lord's servants will be properly cared for according to their individual needs? How best can the time of our missionary brethren be used when they are at home on furlough? How should we act when we are aware of an area to which God has called some of our members, where the resources of a missionary society are not available and the ministry of a missionary society is not adequate to meet the need? How can the fundamental importance of mission be shared with home churches?

Douglas Webster says somewhere that we need to make the local church aware of the total church. Maybe the local church needs to become more aware of itself – its nature and purpose. Were we truly to discover that, maybe we would be more equipped to deal with some of these questions which are easy to ask, but difficult to answer.

Chapter 4

Charlotte Baptist Chapel, Edinburgh

Ian Finlayson

Charlotte Baptist Chapel is surrounded by the shops, offices and older residential properties in the centre of Edinburgh. Around 800 people attend the morning service and in the evening there is an average congregation of 500.

Charlotte Baptist Chapel has had a long-standing interest in Christian work overseas, and today supports twenty-two missionaries. There are strong links with the Overseas Missionary Fellowship and the Africa Inland Mission.

The Minister is the Rev. Derek J. Prime who has spent much of his life south of the border. He was ordained in 1957 and for twelve years was minister of Lansdowne Evangelical Free Church, West Norwood. He has been minister of Charlotte Baptist Chapel since 1969.

Ian Finlayson, the author of this chapter, is the Missionary Convener and an elder at Charlotte Baptist Chapel. In 1973 he and his wife Sheila, a midwife, returned from Nigeria after eight and a half years' service with the (then) Sudan Interior Mission. Ian now teaches in an Edinburgh school. He has four grown-up sons and he relaxes by maintaining his car and playing tennis and badminton.

Charlotte Baptist Chapel has been involved in mission since the days of its first pastor, the Rev. Christopher Anderson, in the early part of the last century. He was a close friend of

William Carey and wanted to accompany Carey on his mission to India, but ill-health prevented him from doing so. Interest in mission at Charlotte Chapel evolved from then. In the first hundred years from 1821 to 1921 about twenty missionaries were commissioned. Half of these went to India and the others were more or less equally divided between Africa and China. During the next twenty years from 1921 to 1941, thirty-five more missionaries were sent out, mostly to Africa, then China and India, but also to the Middle East and even to the New Hebrides. An additional thirty-five missionaries went abroad from 1941 to 1961, mostly to Africa and the Indian sub-continent; and over the last two decades a further twenty missionaries have gone to a wide variety of places: from Europe to the Philippines, and from Central Africa to Brazil.

At present there are some twenty-two members of Charlotte Chapel serving as missionaries and supported by the church, nineteen of whom are linked to one of twelve interdenominational societies.

Although none of our present missionaries is working with the Baptist Missionary Society many of our members have maintained a strong personal link with BMS and contribute regularly to the society through its many supporting schemes.

Three of our missionaries receive support personally rather than through a formal mission channel, because their particular missions place the onus on the individuals to raise their own finances. While one understands the underlying principle of this system, it does mean that those who have the ability to 'sell' their projects tend to get more support. Others who for many reasons do not market a good claim for support, may well be under-financed, though their effective work may not be any less.

The primary emphasis at present is on the support of individuals mainly through interdenominational societies. All of these missionaries are full members of the church before being considered for support. Many members give to other missionaries and societies not directly linked with Charlotte Chapel.

Most of our own missionaries were either brought up in the church or have families within the membership. A few became members during their training years while studying in

Edinburgh and formed their links in that way.

The New Testament pattern

The church emphasises mission fundamentally because Jesus
did. Christ's commission to the early church in Matthew 28
and Mark 16 was 'to all the world', to 'teach all nations' and to
bring the message of the Gospel 'to every creature', and this is
still the charge to the church today.

In New Testament times the early church was led by the
Spirit to set aside gifted members of their community to
engage in missionary work. From those days until the present
the mark of a healthy, growing church has been its
involvement in mission. When the church ceases to be
involved in mission, whether it be 'to the ends of the earth' or
in the immediate locality, it begins to die.

The New Testament pattern is clearly that the local church
has the responsibility for sending out missionary personnel.
In practice, we have found that the challenge to commitment
to missionary work is presented to the whole church. Rarely,
to my knowledge, has the pastor or the Missionary Committee
presumed to suggest that a particular individual prepare for a
life of missionary service abroad: rather the initiative lies with
the applicant. One young nurse felt God calling her to
missionary service and applied to a well-known Bible college
to train. She was turned down after her interview because
they did not consider her suitable. One of the reasons given
appeared to be that she had not read missionary books!

For a time she was bewildered and disillusioned, but the
conviction remained, and a while later she applied direct to a
missionary society for an urgent need in a missionary
hospital. She was accepted by the society despite her lack of
Bible school training, and proved to be a most excellent
member of staff and an effective missionary, respected by
staff and patients alike.

This nurse gained further qualifications during furlough
and has studied Arabic. She is still a most valuable member of
that missionary team.

Someone intending to apply for overseas service is
encouraged to bring the matter initially to the pastor, elders
and missionary committee before applying to the society. We

then encourage the individual to spend about six months, ideally, working as an integral part of the Chapel team, preferably engaging in part-time employment to provide personal support. At the end of this period the pastor, elders and Missionary Committee consider whether they will recommend that such a person should receive the church's confirmation and seal of their call. Normally, only if this pattern is followed can the Missionary Committee consider recommending such a person to the members for financial and prayer support.

Encouraging prayer support

The whole church is encouraged to support mission in prayer in a number of ways. The pastor regularly features a letter received from a missionary during a Sunday service. In fact, most weeks we receive one or more letters from various members of our missionary family. Usually at the earliest opportunity the pastor shares the fact of the letter with the congregation and highlights perhaps one or two of the points raised in an intercessory prayer. Regular letters from one particular missionary have kept us so well informed about the local church in southern Kenya that we feel we know the pastor well, the problems he faces and the encouragements experienced. The local headmaster is almost as well known to our missionary prayer supporters as any of the headmasters in our own congregation. At the beginning of each month we publish an insert in our church magazine containing a digest of all the letters received from our own missionaries since the last edition (usually between four and twelve). We find that our missionaries tend to plan their writing home to meet the deadlines for inclusion in the *Missionary Record*. One missionary, in fact, rarely misses a month!

Once a month we have a Missionary Prayer Meeting when additional topics may be shared. Often missionary speakers are invited. In other weeks the regular church prayer meeting takes place, when particular missionary topics are frequently included. There are also many prayer groups linked to particular societies – these tend to be house meetings in various members' homes, but are conducted independently of the church and are under the auspices of the societies. We hold an Annual Missionary Conference in November. Any of our own missionaries who are on furlough at that time are automatically involved and, in addition, we invite a particular missionary speaker for the weekend as well as a variety of missionary societies. The make-up of the conference varies from year to year and usually lasts three days, Saturday to Monday. There is normally an exhibition providing displays from the participating societies and also a selection of audio-visual presentations.

That personal touch

All members are encouraged to write directly to individual missionaries or missionary families, and many do. Each new member is given a prayer card and is encouraged to 'adopt' a missionary by prayer and correspondence. One missionary couple working in the Far East had two children attending the nearest school for missionaries' children. The time came for the elder child to pursue further education in the U.K. Where could she go? With whom would she stay? Her mother planned to return with her to this country, and when the daughter had settled down she would return to her husband and son in the Far East. The need was shared with the congregation. Immediately there were two responses. One young lady had two spare rooms which were available for the two women until the daughter found more permanent accommodation. Secondly, a family were considering opening their home to a student wanting to study in Edinburgh and offered to take the girl to stay with them. They live just over a mile from the college where she will be studying.

Mother and daughter spent two weeks in the first home and were able to adjust well to the different lifestyle in this country, enrol in the college and generally prepare for the new term. Now at the time of writing the daughter has completed her first week at college, and is comfortably settled with the family who are looking after her. Mother is preparing to return to the rest of her family, happy in the knowledge that God has provided for her daughter and has confirmed that they were doing the right thing.

Birthdays are noted: the primary Sunday School sends birthday cards to children of missionaries, and auxiliaries take special interest. The missionary secretary acknowledges all letters sent directly, in the first instance sending a picture post-card. Then each is followed up with a proper letter. All missionaries receive a monthly cassette and recordings of special events, e.g. Missionary Conference, New Year Text, special visits of notable Christian leaders, etc.

Gifts are received by regular covenanted contributions, designated Sunday offerings, Welcome Home offerings, and through the annual Thank-offering. Occasionally a special appeal may be made to meet an emergency. From time to time we receive legacies which are designated for missionary work.

Relating to the missionary society

As far as the activities of the missionary on the field are concerned, the home church has confidence in the expertise of the field councils of the respective missionary societies. Generally speaking, churches in this country are not sufficiently aware of all the implications of the local parameters affecting the missionary on the field to presume to determine mission priorities. If several missionaries from different church backgrounds are working together on any project, it is surely the responsibility of the mission under whose umbrella the team is working to dictate policy, to define principles and to determine objectives. For the sending churches to do this would result in chaos! The Lord is not the author of confusion and the way to avoid it is to respond to the leading of the Spirit through the Mission Boards. Only when the sending church is aware of a particular problem or burden relating to its own sent missionary would there be a need to intervene and suggest action.

Prayer is a particularly strong weapon in influencing events abroad. One of our members had been involved in church-planting in the Philippines. He had seen a growing church established in a large city situation. There was a strong national leadership who had been trained as deacons and also to preach at Sunday services. All were lay members in secular jobs.

There was a growing need to appoint a national pastor. The problem was made known to us and for nearly two years this had been a priority in prayer. Only *this week* we heard that a national pastor – working in another area, with a sizeable church in a larger city, with a bigger salary – had asked to be considered, as he felt God calling him to this particular need. He went to the church, met the members, preached at the services and received a unanimous call which he accepted.

Many had said 'It is impossible. He will not consider it. It is too big a sacrifice to expect him to make.' But God had other plans! Here was another miraculous answer to our prayers!

It is most important that each home church is aware of what is expected of it by each Mission Board, and also that each Mission Board is aware of what the home church expects. In particular we felt in Charlotte Chapel that occasional misunderstandings had occurred in the past as far as furlough obligations were concerned, and we recently circulated each of the societies represented by our own missionaries with a copy of the following letter:

> We recommend that it is the responsibility of both the local church and the missionary to keep in closest possible touch so that there can be the maximum support and fellowship in the Gospel. We recognise, too, that financial support alone is insufficient. There must also be intelligent prayer partnership and involvement. One of the obvious needs is that of renewing links with the congregation and fellowship during times of furlough, especially as the membership of the church is always changing and, for many new members, some of the missionary family are inevitably just names. The times of furlough are, therefore, of strategic importance in meeting the need.
>
> It is the conviction of the church that missionaries on furlough should be expected to spend part of their furlough in the church, participating in its everyday life, with the purpose, amongst others, of getting to know those who have come into membership since the missionaries were last on furlough. This period should be free of deputation demands, and the church is prepared to make this request of each missionary society. The period of time spent in the church would be subject to mutual agreement, of course, and the church is sensitive to the varying circumstances of each missionary, only desiring to be of the maximum help to the whole missionary family.
>
> Where the opportunity of spending time with the church

is not made and taken, the Missionary Committee must feel its responsibility to review the relationship of the missionary concerned and the missionary commitments of the church, and to raise the matter with the individual missionary.

Financial gifts

Charlotte Chapel does not have a missionary budget as such at present. Having said that, at our Annual General Business Meeting, in response to an earlier proposal from the membership, our Church Treasurer presented one for this present year. So perhaps next year we will have our first missionary budget!

A complete financial statement of missionary funds is given to all church members each year along with the treasurer's statement of the general church funds immediately prior to the Annual General Business Meeting. The church is informed, by means of graphs and visual presentations, about the level of giving during the previous year and comparisons are made with the giving of the church over the past three years or so. There may not be an official budget but a target is set for the next year in terms of the level of support we wish to provide for our own missionaries.

Those members who pay income tax are encouraged to covenant their gifts and an increasing number are doing so. Members who do not covenant are given a set of fifty-two specially designed envelopes for weekly giving throughout the year. Each week's unit is subdivided into two compartments marked 'General Fund' and 'Missionary Fund'. In this way members can determine their own priorities and apportion their gifts. In practice about two-thirds of the total giving is allocated to general church funds and about one-third to the missionary fund.

The total missionary giving for 1983 was in excess of £40,000 from a membership of 850, partially supporting twenty-two missionaries. Five of our own missionaries are married to partners who are members of some other church. They, of course, receive support from their home churches and have obligations towards them in terms of furlough and deputation commitments, etc.

As a matter of principle we divide the total amount donated to the missionary fund equally among the twenty-two missionaries we support, and send such amounts to the societies every three months. It is our custom to send four-fifths of each quarterly disbursement direct to the missionary society towards 'support' and the remaining one-fifth direct to the missionary as a personal gift. Often this is channelled through the mission's home office as the most convenient way to transfer gifts.

Linking and liaising

Our Missionary Committee consists of twelve members and is appointed immediately after the election of elders and deacons which takes place every five years. The committee is made up as follows:

1. Convener (elder)
2. Treasurer (elder or deacon)
3. Four court members (elders or deacons)
4. Secretary (church member)
5. Minute secretary (church member)
6. In addition there is a representative from each auxiliary of the church. Some of these may serve for two years, others serve for only one year.

The elders and deacons are appointed on election to the respective courts. The secretaries are co-opted by the committee and approved by the Deacons' Court and the convener is recommended by the committee and appointed by the Elders' Court. In practice the office-bearers of the Missionary Committee tend to hold office for more than five years: the secretary has in fact held the post for sixteen years! The principle of re-election every five years does give the opportunity to achieve change without causing offence or hurt to any replaced.

Each member of the committee is given the responsibility to link and liaise with either a couple or two single missionaries, or perhaps a couple and a single missionary. In this way each committee member is expected to take a particular prayer interest and practical interest in two or three missionaries. Especially at furlough times they ensure that adequate provision is made in terms of furlough accommodation, meeting at the airport or station and generally keeping in personal touch with the missionaries. If special needs arise, e.g. a 'cri de coeur' from the missionary, they are expected to bring this to the attention of the Missionary Committee who will act appropriately. External pressures were really bearing down heavily on one single lady missionary working in a particularly sensitive area of the Asian continent. She had reached a point where she could go no further. She had had enough! Then, for no apparent reason, a peace came to her that enabled her to rise above the situation and God gave her the strength to fight through.

Two weeks later, she received a letter from one of our retired members who had been engaged in missionary support for a number of years. He wrote, 'For some strange reason I feel a particular need to pray specially for you today. I don't know why – but I am writing to assure you of our prayers and to encourage you to remember amongst other things that God has said in his Word, "I will fight for you and you have only to be still". She looked at the date on the letter and – you have guessed it – it coincided exactly with the time when that peace calmed her fears! This kind of prayer link is vital, real and effective.

Furlough needs

Where missionaries do not have a family home in the city, then accommodation is sought usually amongst the membership or through furlough houses belonging to the Church of Scotland or Overseas Missionary Fellowship which may be available locally.

We do not have a 'missionary car', but Icthus Motor Services, run voluntarily by Catford Hill Baptist Church, South London, is made known to missionaries who need transport. The only problem for us in Edinburgh may be that the car has to be collected from and returned to London. However, this was no problem to one of our missionary families who obtained the use of a car in this way last year. It was simply collected on their way home and returned on their way back to the field. Most travel tends to be via London anyway. This service was much appreciated – only the insurance and petrol was paid for by the missionary. Catford insurance and petrol was paid for by the missionary. Catford Hill Baptist Church are to be commended for their initiative and commitment.

Mission begins at home

In our church we have at present two separate committees involved with mission at home and abroad. The Evangelistic Committee is concerned primarily with outreach locally, while the Missionary Committee is involved specifically in overseas outreach. There has recently been a certain amount of discussion about the logic of such a division. It may well be that in the future mission will be defined in terms that compass both the home and overseas aspects. This is certainly relevant in the sense that for each of us as individual members of the Church of Christ our own 'mission field' begins at our front doorstep. Also, in the church context, our missionary responsibility is towards all of the 'lost', and that includes the environs of the local church. However, for the present, the Missionary Committee does concern itself primarily with overseas missions although this remit does necessarily overlap that of the Evangelistic Committee. For example, there is much excellent work done amongst overseas students and workers in the city. This at present is not the primary concern of the Missionary Committee though it could be argued that it ought to be!

It is significant that it tends to be those members who have a commitment to missionary involvement, who are also those involved with overseas students in Edinburgh, and also with outreach at home. It is also from those who are busy in the work of the church at home that the Lord calls individuals to serve him abroad. God does not call missionaries from the spiritually unemployed.

Maintaining communication with the missionary

One of the results of maintaining good regular correspondence with missionaries is that the home church quickly becomes aware of specific needs. If an emergency arises on the field, any major calls for help tend to go in the first instance to the pastor, who incidentally does a sterling job in corresponding regularly with all who write to him. The pastor then informs either the convener, the elders or the membership at the earliest opportunity. If the problem is a spiritual or personal one the pastor, elders or Missionary Committee will act. If it is a financial problem the missionary treasurer and the church treasurer will confer. A special church offering may be received.

In addition to such major concerns, other matters (which missionaries may not want to 'trouble' the pastor or Missionary Committee with) may become apparent to individuals, either on the committee or amongst the membership, for instance from a member of the missionary's family. It is then the responsibility of the Missionary Committee to deal with the matter or refer it to someone who can.

In our case in Charlotte Chapel we do not have direct links with the local churches to which our missionaries are attached. That responsibility lies with the Mission Boards. However, in some cases through the correspondence with missionaries, the home church knows the local pastors and even elders by name and meaningful prayer links are maintained.

So far we have not sent our present pastor to visit our missionaries. We did, in fact, encourage a previous pastor to do so, with excellent results both for him, the missionaries visited and the church as a whole. However, our present pastor did visit the Indian sub-continent at the request of the Baptist Missionary Society and visited those of our missionaries who were there at the time. On another occasion the chapel sent the pastor to visit a church in Bratislava, Czechoslovakia, with whom we had build a significant link by sending a gift of money to enable them to purchase an organ. That link has been maintained and two of their elders have visited us recently. Several individual members of the Chapel have, in the course of overseas visits, either on holiday or through business, visited a wide variety of missionary situations and have reported back to the fellowship.

It is quite possible that a more comprehensive tour of some of our missionaries' spheres of service is something we ought to consider.

It is most important to maintain good and frequent

communications between missionaries and the home church. It is just as important to have good relationships with the Missionary Societies involved. Recognising that administrative staff of Mission Boards do move on, or hand over to others, we try to keep in regular touch with the home office staff. In this way we endeavour to ensure that we understand what they expect from us and that they understand what we expect from them.

Chapter 5

St. George's, Leeds

Michael Botting

St. George's is an Anglican Church in the centre of Leeds. As an inner-city church, it tends to draw its number, largely families and single people, from all over the area. On an average Sunday there are around 350 adults and 80 children in the congregation.

St. George's Church supports fifteen missionaries, some of whom are currently serving with the South American Missionary Society, the Church Missionary Society, BMMF International and the Overseas Missionary Fellowship. The church keeps in regular contact with the OMF through John Wallis, its Home Director and a former curate at St. George's.

The Rev. Canon Michael Hugh Botting was born in Maidstone, Kent and educated at Sutton Valence School and Edinburgh Academy. Following his four years in the Army and a course of study at King's College, London, he taught at Croftinloan Boys' Preparatory School. In 1954 he went to Ridley Hall Cambridge to train for the ministry. Michael Botting became Vicar of St. George's, Leeds in 1972. He is now Joint Director of Training in the Diocese of Chester.

He and his wife Mary have a son and a daughter. He has written several books on Family Worship, and has recently promoted city-wide campaigns with David Watson and Luis Palau. His leisure interests are reading, gardening and music.

Historical Background

The year 1930 was probably one of the most significant for

St. George's Church this century, because the Simeon Trustees, who had recently accepted the patronage from the local trustees, appointed the Rev. Don Robins as vicar. He was only thirty years old, had been an officer in the Royal Flying Corps and was greatly influenced by the work of St. Martin-in-the-Fields, London. Appalled at the conditions under which the unemployed were living in the depression of the thirties, he took the bold step of opening up the crypt as a place for shelter and providing somewhere dry and warm, with cocoa and friendship for those who cared to come. The cholera epidemic of the 1850s had led to the crypt being filled with some 750 coffins, the doors shut and the dead left undisturbed till Don's dramatic action.

The curate in those days was the Rev. Arthur Bagshaw, who is now St. George's senior missionary, because in those early days he went from the parish to serve Christ in India under the auspices of the Church Missionary Society. Apart from Arthur there was little other prominent missionary work from the church, except for a teacher, Miss Effie Colbeck, who became Head of a CMS school (one of her head girls later worshipped at St. George's as a student).

It was during the fifties and sixties that overseas missionary interest broadened. Staff like Tom Overton and John Wallis went to join the Overseas Missionary Fellowship for work in the Far East. Students and younger members of the church like Joyce Illingworth went to the South American Missionary Society and are on our missionary lists now. In this period people have also served with the Sudan United and Sudan Interior Missions, (now SIM International), and the North Africa Mission. The church has had a long-standing interest in the Ruanda Mission which was visited by Raymond Turvey (vicar 1958–1972) as part of a sabbatical leave in East Africa, but no one has actually served there.

The first person to set the trend was Hester Quirk, who in September 1952 went to Pakistan under the auspices of the Bible and Medical Missionary Fellowship: our first link with an interdenominational society. Hester was a teacher at Lawnswood High School for Girls and a leader of a Girls' Crusader class. She normally brought a number of her girls down to St. George's each Sunday for worship and they became a natural prayer-support group for her when she left for the Asian mission field.

Hester's call may well have arisen out of a change of theological emphasis at St. George's. From 1930 to 1948, a period which covered the incumbency of Don Robins, life at the church had been dominated by the development of the crypt; spare money and time would have been channelled there. From 1939 everything was overshadowed by the Second World War and its aftermath. However, following the death of Don Robins in early 1948, the Rev. Tony Waite became vicar, and though the work of the crypt continued unabated, there was a much greater evangelical thrust in the ministry above the crypt. The 'Key' Campaign of 1954 led by the Rev. L.F.E. Wilkinson, Principal of Oakhill Theological College, assisted by students like young Michael Baughen and David Bubbers, brought many in the congregation to a personal awareness of Jesus Christ as Saviour and Lord.

In 1958 Tony Waite was followed by the Rev. Raymond Turvey, who soon developed a considerable ministry amongst students from the expanding University and Polytechnic. From such students came men and women who heard the call of God to the foreign mission field. Some had links with churches outside Leeds, but wanted St. George's to be their primary 'sending' church, though other churches often helped with prayer, finance and interest.

The mission of the church is one

One of the more recent missionaries from St. George's was the Rev. Christopher Sugden, who was curate from 1974 to 1977. Rightly, he wanted the church to recognise that the whole world needed the Gospel, so to think that the mission field was beyond the shores of Great Britain was misleading. This change of emphasis is reflected in the name for our annual missionary Sunday, which is now called 'World Church Sunday', and 'World Church Spot', our recently introduced missionary comment in our evening services. There is a sense in which the distinguishing between home and abroad is quite understandable. In one of the Servant Songs in Isaiah 49:1–6, the prophet sees Israel personified as the Servant of the Lord, called to glorify God (vs.1, 3), called suffer (v.4), but in vs 5, 6a there is an apparent contradiction,

contradiction, because Israel is called to be a servant 'that Israel might be gathered to him'. The explanation would seem to be that the servant here is the *spiritual* remnant returning to Palestine from Babylon, whose mission is in the first place to those *nominal* Israelites dispersed abroad, who have no vital living faith in God. The Lord Jesus Christ, the true Servant of Israel, went first to his own people, the lost sheep of the house of Israel. Peter and Paul proclaimed the Gospel message first to their own people. The complaint often levelled against the local evangelistic enterprises and the somewhat larger crusades is that so many people who respond to the appeal to receive Christ have previous church backgrounds. But this is totally predictable. Jesus has said that 'One sows, another reaps' – the faithful sowing of a local minister to nominal worshippers prepares the ground for the incoming evangelist to reap, that both sower and reaper may rejoice together.

However, the Servant in Isaiah was also given a much wider call. 'It is too light a thing that you should be my servant to raise up the tribes of Jacob and to restore the preserved of Israel; I will give you as a light to the nations, that my salvation may reach to the end of the earth.' (Isa.49:6) Before his earthly ministry closed, Jesus commanded the church to go into all the world to preach the gospel (Matt. 28:18–20). He promised his disciples the power of the Spirit for a universal proclamation of the message (Acts 1:8). When the Apostle Paul despaired of his own people, because they opposed the Gospel, it was to this scripture he turned to support his change of direction and become primarily a missionary to the gentiles.

So this distinguishing between home and abroad, natural and understandable as it is, at the end of the day is artificial. The spiritual needs of the world are the same everywhere – 'all have sinned and fall short of the glory of God' (Rom.3:23). 'But how are men to call upon him in whom they have not believed? And how are they to believe in him of whom they have never heard? And how are they to hear without a preacher?' (Rom.10:14-15) Could it be true that those churches that are especially aware of the need to bring the Gospel to those on their own doorstep will have a much greater concern for those who need the Gospel way beyond those doorsteps, than those who have no such concern?

The missionary committee

In the 1950s there was a rather large missionary coucil, but this was reduced to the present missionary committee in July 1971. The hub of St. George's missionary concern is this small committee, which is a sub-committee of the Parochial Church Council. Its chairman, secretary and treasurer are all appointed, or more often re-appointed, by the PCC at the first meeting following the Annual Church Meeting. The other four or so members have especial interest in and links with overseas mission. The committee seeks to include within its number those with actual experience on the field: the present chairman was a medical missionary in Kenya for over twenty years. The vicar is automatically ex-officio. The committee meet normally three times a year unless there is an especial emergency or a potential missionary candidate to interview. It plans the World Church Sunday and generally initiates and monitors all aspects of World Church outreach of the church, about which more is said below. From time to time it will invite a missionary society representative to come to one of its meetings to discuss his or her work and ways in which the church can be more involved. Missionary accounts are presented at the ACM.

How is missionary work supported?

It is said that it is an ill wind that blows nobody any good. In February 1962 a freak gale dislodged masonry from St. George's steeple, which crashed through the roof of the church, causing damage that cost £25,000 (in 1962!) to put right. One of the bonuses was an area created at the back of the church, free from pews, where the congregation mill around before and after services. Here a large blackboard, four feet high and over ten feet in length, displays a large map of the world, with the word 'together ...'. On the board there is a little detail about the work of the crypt and the parish, but most of it is taken up with pictures and potted details about our present missionaries.

Every month two pages of our twenty-page magazine are devoted to 'The Internationals', being either a specially written article by one of our congregation (usually our Missionary Secretary) on a topic of general interest, or news of the work of one of our missionaries, with quotations from their letters.

Every year a long-standing member of our congregation writes the *Friends of St. George's* newsletter, which has quite a wide circulation and includes news of our missionaries over the past year.

Being an eclectic church with families travelling several miles on a Sunday to worship, our main weekday ministry is in area groups, apart from a monthly central prayer meeting when any recent prayer requests from missionaries will be mentioned. John Wallis, Home Secretary of the OMF, keeps the vicar regularly supplied with his own needs for prayer. If a missionary is home on furlough he or she is asked to speak and possibly show slides. Anne White, whose dramatic story comes later, was given a major section of our monthly central prayer meeting. A special meeting was laid on for Dr. Ruth Coggan.

When missionaries do return to this country we much prefer them to stay around for a week or more rather than just for one-night stands. Tom Overton actually stayed for a month and shared in ministry over that period to help people get to know him and his family, because many had not been members of the church when Tom first left England.

However, the area groups take a much more personal interest in individual workers and as far as possible the Missionary Committee has encouraged each area group to be responsible for at least one missionary each. This has not been too difficult because often missionaries are particular friends of those in the group. This means that there is regular communication by letter and from time to time by cassette, to which the vicar is also asked to add a few words. When the missionary is home on leave the area group makes him or her especially welcome, perhaps attending to special needs like temporary accommodation and even provision of a car for deputation work. Groups have also become aware of a particular person's need, such as a cassette player for Dr. Ruth Coggan in Bannu, or a generator to provide power for audio-visual aid equipment, which was the urgent requirement of Joyce Illingworth in Salta, Northern Argentina, with SAMS.

Every month there is the meeting of the International

Fellowship, normally in the home of the Missionary Committee secretary and his wife, where there is either a speaker, possibly a missionary on leave, or slides of some part of the missionary work we especially support, all concluding with prayer. On another side of Leeds the committee chairman and his wife occasionally throw their home open for a missionary evening.

On Sundays in church during morning worship one of our missionaries will be remembered by the person leading the intercessions. To assist the mechanics of this week by week, there is a special envelope for each of our missionaries with a brief biography typed on the front. Recent needs, quotations from letters, etc. are enclosed in the envelope. The person responsible for the intercessions on any given Sunday receives this envelope in advance and incorporates the information in his prayers. The missionary secretary keeps the envelope up to date for each missionary. Much as we should like to have extempore prayer in our public worship the size and acoustics of the building make it quite unrealistic.

In the evening, when there is more time because young children are not present, we have a 'World Church Spot' when different people report on some area of the world, normally, but not exclusively, where one of our missionaries is working.

Just occasionally we have a missionary slant to our Wednesday lunch-hour programme. Recently the Rev. Humberto Axt and his wife Iris spoke through an interpreter (Miss Barbara Kitchen, SAMS Area representative) about their five years' work in Salta. Humberto is Chairman of the Urban Pastoral Committee, which is responsible for the development of the church life in the Spanish-speaking churches. He is also Pastor-in-Charge of a new, but growing congregation in Pinca Independencia, a new housing estate in Salta.

The main event of the year is World Church Sunday. The planning for this usually starts immediately the previous one is over, sometimes before. It is almost invariably held in the autumn, normally in November close to St. Andrewtide. We usually invite a speaker from one of the main missionary societies with whom our missionaries are working: CMS, BMMF International, OMF or SAMS. However, this is not an invariable rule, and one year when Chris Sugden and Vinay

Samuel were doing a tour round Britain we incorporated them into our programme. Our most recent missionary candidate, Charles Montagu, is to serve Christ in North Africa, so in 1984 we invited Sir Norman Anderson as our speaker, in view of his extensive knowledge of that area.

The speaker preaches morning and evening. We lay on an inexpensive lunch on church premises for those who would like to hear more from our visitor than can be worked into a sermon. Sometimes we also have a short meeting after the evening service for slides and/or questions. In order to involve those actually on the field, if they cannot be present on the Sunday, we either interview them on tape when they are around, or get them to send us slides and a cassette recording to be used in the services. We also plan that our missionaries read the lessons. We ask the weekend speaker to provide us with his lessons well in advance, and we inform the missionaries selected to read the set passages including the page numbers in the pew Bibles in our church. Our amplification system is of high quality and we can easily play cassettes through it, which means the sound comes from the same loudspeakers as those actually using microphones in church. The effect is quite moving – there is a real sense that our missionaries are with us, even though we know they are thousands of miles away and the recordings made weeks before.

Financial support

We have a separate missionary fund. A few people still use missionary boxes and a number of people contribute by means of the free-will offering scheme, which has two envelopes, one for Christ's work overseas. Some people give to the fund by regular cheques and banker's orders and take advantage of covenants, so that missionary societies benefit from refund of income tax. On the weeks before World Church Sunday, and for a few weeks afterwards, there are special envelopes in the pews for the missionary fund. The total money received for the year is divided out amongst the missionary societies in proportion to the number of accredited missionaries we have linked with the societies.

We have no really accurate figure about the extent of our

missionary giving. Some years ago there was a 'threat' that the missionary giving that passed through our church treasurer's hands would be subject to 'quota', that is the money that Anglican Churches pay to dioceses to fund a wide range of expenses including clergy salaries. Because of this, the vicar at the time very understandably encouraged church members to support missionary societies direct, without the money passing through the church accounts. We now have no idea of the extent to which this happens. From time to time members of the congregation tell us they have sent so much to an overseas mission or special scheme, and that amount is reckoned into our missionary fund total.

We do of course support missions financially in other ways. Sometimes our annual gift day will include something for overseas work. We always reckon to put a contribution into a contingency fund for emergencies and this has been used, for example, to pay the air fare for one of our missionaries, Anne White, who had to come home when her mother was seriously ill and not expected to live. We are aware that missionary societies are not keen on direct giving to their staff because the practice can be invidious, some coming from wealthy parishes, others not. However we feel that helping in emergencies is different.

Then we have had special projects, sometimes in Lent, for a missionary cause. We also support TEAR Fund, which provides a great deal of aid to missionary societies. Recently our teenagers raised £300 in Lent for TEAR Fund simply by persuading members of the congregation to fill Smartie tubes with pennies (or 20p pieces). Donors enjoyed the smarties, but were surprised to find they had to part with 70p (or £14)! The whole congregation collected £12 in ½p pieces before they ceased to be legal tender, which was sent to Michael Cassidy for African Enterprise.

How do people become St. George's missionaries?

Clearly the world-wide church is never far from our thoughts and prayers. Because of our unique position in Leeds, so central that the town hall, City station and main coach terminal are actually within our parish boundaries, people look to us to provide the leadership for big evangelistic

events, so evangelism generally is likewise in our thinking and
praying. We also have a continuous ministry amongst
students and from that body have come a number of our
overseas missionaries. Our pressure on people to respond to
the call overseas has been low-key. We have not especially
preached on the needs of the overseas field, though on World
Church Sunday or at a valedictory service, or even during the
weekly World Church Spot, the call will be there. We have
occasionally included 'Missions and Missionaries' as one of of
the ten week courses availabe in our Sunday Morning
Christian education programme (similar to the American all-
age Sunday School). Nor do we especially 'buttonhole' people
and ask if they have considered going abroad to serve Christ.
For these reasons, therefore, when people do approach the
vicar as a first tentative move towards enquiring about
serving Christ abroad, it is felt that it is more likely to be the
genuine prompting of the Holy Spirit.

The usual procedure, then, is to talk about how the Lord
may guide in such matters. Suggestions are made where more
specific help could be obtained. The vicar put Charles
Montagu directly in touch with Sir Norman Anderson,
because of his particular knowledge. If the call becomes loud
and clear then the candidate meets the Missionary
Committee, who decide if it feels able to recommend his or
her acceptance as an official St. George's missionary
candidate. Having an ex-missionary of considerable
experience as Chairman is an enormous help. If the
Missionary Committee recommend a person, the matter is
reported to the next meeting of the P.C.C.

It is not uncommon for a member of the congregation to
take on the responsibility of prayer secretary for the potential
missionary concerned. Quite often a valedictory service is
planned when the candidate is actually leaving the church for
his first tour of duty, though he may already have spent time
away at college for missionary training. If the candidate is
supported by a missionary society, then a representative of
the society is normally involved in this service. The vicar, on
behalf of the church, will hand the candidate over to the care
of the society in much the same way that a father hands over
his daughter to her husband at a wedding. The service also
includes a particular opportunity for the congregation to

promise its support by prayer, finance and interest.

The missionaries we currently support

Occasional references to individuals have already been given to illustrate points being made. The following is a very brief outline of some of those whom we regard as St. George's missionaries in 1984.

1. NORTH AND SOUTH AMERICA

Canon Roger and Mrs. Carole Briggs work in Ottawa where Roger is 'Chaplain to Native Peoples' and his pastoral responsibility is for Eskimos and Indians who have migrated from the north. He says that these are deeply complicated pastoral situations and that the ministry is bound to lead into the political arenas if they are to care for people in every area of life.

Miss Joyce Illingworth (SAMS) has been working in Salta for sixteen years. She was the only British missionary to remain in Argentina throughout the Falklands war, and with the withdrawal of many expatriates her responsibilities inevitably increased. In a letter written on her return to Argentina after leave in 1983, she indicates that St. George's care for her has been about right:

> Life is full of surprises, the majority of which are often pleasant, especially if one belongs to St. G's. Even after sixteen years away in Salta I still feel that I do belong, which is all credit to all of you, and not least the staff and missionary committee. There are so many things that I want to thank you for: friendship, prayer, financial support, phone calls during the War, visitors (only one has gone as far as Salta so far), the preparation and distribution of my newsletter, and more recently, a car. Very many thanks to those who contributed as it certainly makes travelling much less wearing! It was great to be back in Leeds to see you, if only at brief intervals in between the 'grand tour' of the British Isles.

Joyce has moved location to Buenos Aires to be responsible for the Provincial Christian Education programme.

2. INDIA, PAKISTAN AND NEPAL

The Rev. Arthur Bagshaw (ex-CMS) we mentioned briefly

at the very beginning of this account. Though now retired from CMS, he is still active as vicar of St. Peter's Church, Kodaikanal, a hill resort in South India, where he ministers largely to retired folk and holiday visitors. The congregation have a lively interest in social and educational work amongst the under-privileged in the area. Earlier this year Arthur wrote:

> On February 2nd I shall, D.V., have completed fifty years of ministry in India. Now in my seventy-seventh year I have much to be thankful for, and by dint of consuming many pills on medical orders I keep in reasonably good health and usually manage nine holes of golf twice a week. You are all very good in remembering me after so many years.

Miss Hester Quirk (BMMF) went to Pakistan in September 1952. After serving successfully as a teacher and headmistress of the Kinnaird High School, she became Associate Field Director of the Mission with a special responsibility for personnel. She has now just returned to England and will be spending her last year before retirement on the home staff of BMMF, visiting churches. As an exception we have agreed to continue to finance her, though she is in the U.K.

Dr. Ruth Coggan (CMS) was a student in Leeds and still returns from time to time for further study. She specialises in gynaecology and obstetrics at Pennell Memorial Hospital, Bannu, in N.W. Pakistan, where she has many opportunities to witness to women. She was awarded the O.B.E. in the 1984 New Year Honours list for medical services.

The Rev. Christopher and Dr. Elaine Sugden (BCMS) Chris was curate at St. George's from 1974 to 1977 before going to India, where he spent most of his time as Assistant Presbyter at St. John's Church, Bangalore, South India. He is now Registrar of a new centre for mission studies based initially at Westminster College, Oxford. Elaine was able to practise as a medical doctor in India, and hopes to continue to do so in Oxford.

Mr. Ian Kerr (BMMF) has been in Nepal for a period of service to the United Mission to Nepal as an accountant. His work includes auditing, advising and assisting in the financial aspect of the Mission. He returned to the U.K. in the summer of 1984 and was recently welcomed to a meal by his area group.

3. AFRICA

Miss Sheila Harrison receives financial support from St. George's, but works independently as an optician, travelling in South and Central Africa to provide optical services which would not otherwise be readily available to churches and missions in remote areas. Much of her work relies upon a supply of second-hand spectacles which are received at St. George's and passed on to her.

4. UNITED KINGDOM AND EUROPE

Mr. Bob and Dr. Margaret Lunt had to leave Argentina at the time of the Falklands Crisis, but at the time of writing there is hope that visas will be obtained for their return, so that Bob can complete his translation work of the Mataco New Testament. During his time in Britain (Durham) he has had to work by correspondence with his colleague Isidro in Argentina. St. George's has provided a small amount of financial support. Margaret used to worship at St. George's before her marriage. They both hope to go to Salta City in the north of Argentina, with support from SAMS.

The Rev. John and Mrs. Kathleen Wallis. As already mentioned, John was a curate at St. George's before serving with the OMF in Korea. Kathleen's ill-health forced them to return to the U.K. John worked in Scotland for a while, before he was made Home Director, working from Sevenoaks in Kent. In addition to his staffing responsibilities and routine administration he seeks to make the spiritual needs of East Asia more widely known by preaching, speaking and writing.

Mr. Charles Montagu (North Africa Mission) came to Leeds from university to teach Classics at Leeds Grammar School, which is in St. George's parish, and has other members of the congregation on the staff. Charles has gone through all the stages mentioned earlier to discover his vocation to work overseas. After studying at All Nations Christian College he is now at the NAM training centre in Montpellier, France, learning Arabic, and hopes to take a teaching post in one of the countries of North Africa.

This is not all. I correspond regularly with a former student at the University who is serving Christ in India for a year with Operation Mobilisation. This could lead to more specific service overseas. No doubt other members of the

congregation will be in touch with him, or with others who
worshipped with us for a while and are now witnessing for
Christ abroad.

The world is one, and the Lord's commission is universal.
This is especially brought home to us in these days of easy
travel. We have not felt the expense for special trips to our
missionaries justified, but one member of our congregation
deliberately took part of her holiday to South America to see
Joyce Illingworth. Likewise a visit to Anne White in Iran
before the revolution was undertaken by members of the
church at their own expense as part of a holiday.

Anne White's name has occurred several times in this
chapter. Like others she is no longer one of our serving
overseas missionaries, but the circumstances that led up to
her return home to us, help to underline the vital importance
of the home church constantly bearing up their missionaries
in prayer. Anne writes of her experience:

> I should not really be alive. Eighteen months before my
> release from Iran I had fallen 150 feet, and had not only
> lived to tell the tale, but been teaching in the midwifery
> school within two months! However with three limbs in
> plaster I obviously could not live on my own. So when the
> hospital was expropriated by the Revolutionary
> Committee I was already living in the Gini Blind Institute.
> This, plus the fact that I had the Diploma in ophthalmic
> nursing, meant that when the expatriate hospital staff
> (now out of work) left the country, I obtained a new work
> permit, so I jointed Margaret and Libby in caring for the
> blind girls and women at the Institute!
>
> For over a year we were there together. Other church
> institutions were expatriated. Bishop Hassan Dehqani-
> Tafti, Anglican Bishop in Iran, was arrested and released,
> and an attempt made on his life. Jean Waddell, his
> secretary, was shot, a national pastor was murdered. Yet
> through it all was the sense that we were where the Lord
> wanted us.
>
> August 1980 and things suddenly changed. First the
> impression through daily readings that we would be
> leaving Iran. Then Margaret and Libby were summoned to
> Teheran about the renewal of their work permits. They
> were told to return a couple of days later when all the ex-

patriates working in the diocese should report with them. So all six of us presented ourselves on the Tuesday. Our papers were retained, the borders closed to us and we were instructed to return to Isfahan and await news of whether our permits would be renewed or cancelled. Wednesday evening we heard that Jean had been arrested. Thursday brought a 'phone call summoning us back to Teheran.

Because the church cared about us, once again the administrator travelled with us, knowing that in so doing he was putting himself at risk. I have a vivid memory of him singing 'When I feel the touch of his hand upon my life', as we made the eight-hour journey through the heat. He was taken in first to see the official next day and we didn't see him again. He had been arrested. Hours later four of us went in. (A Dutch fellow, Yan, who had done all our maintenance was with us, but we didn't see the Colemans who were travelling from Yazd in the east. When they arrived they, too, were arrested.) Eventually we were handed our passports back complete with exit visas and given seventy-two hours in which to leave the country. Then began the series of amazing details which emphasised to us that God wanted us back in the U.K.

1. Letters were written to the police department to expedite the granting of official papers; the department was requested to remain open until we arrived (!) and transport was provided across the city.

2. Tax clearance was a problem as there was no one available of the church leaders to sign the papers. Yet officialdom was prepared to accept a letter from the Roman Catholic Archbishop. This most gracious and godly man not only provided the necessary letters in both languages at the request of someone he had never met before, but stamped them with the Vatican seal which would remain valid even if he himself had to leave the country. In addition he personally loaned us money and air fares, because our finances were in Isfahan.

3. Flights were leaving the country full. A friend's father had a friend in a travel agency who had a friend working for British Airways. The result? On Sunday afternoon when three cancellations came through on the computer

Margaret, Libby and I obtained tickets for Heathrow. (Yan had earlier reserved a flight to Europe.)

4. Despite advice to leave the capital, we felt we must return to see the church again, give them any news and information possible, and hand over the work we had been doing. Yet again we made the eight-hour journey to Isfahan, and amazingly were not held up at any road blocks nor noticed by the Revolutionary Committees. The courage shown by the church leaders that night, and next morning as they took far-reaching decisions, remains a vivid memory and inspiration.

5. The last night was spent in Teheran, because customs formalities required three hours and the flight was at eight a.m. Finally at eight-thirty a.m. we had only one more formality left: passport control. The official took them, looked and said 'You can't leave, you're blacklisted.' All of us had very mixed feelings about leaving anyway. We were stunned – what was God doing? A few minutes later the official reappeared and without comment stamped our passports and returned them. We boarded the plane.

Arriving at Heathrow we were very 'high'. CMS had a thanksgiving service arranged. Within a couple of hours the press and media were on to the story and it was headlines the next day. But the whole thing has left a very strong awareness that the imprisonment of some and the release of others was God's doing and no accident, and that he is able to look after us and control circumstances.

Chapter 6

Selly Oak Methodist Church, Birmingham

Donald Knighton

The Methodist Church at Selly Oak is in 'a very mixed but primarily residential' part of Birmingham. Among the 250 people who attend the Sunday services are a number of students. The church also enjoys the opportunities it has to utilise the talents of the overseas members.

Mission plays a large part in the lives of all the members at Selly Oak, as every one automatically joins the Methodist Missionary Society on membership. Missionaries are supported through the Methodist Church Overseas Division which sends out workers on behalf of the whole church.

The Rev. Donald George Knighton was minister of Selly Oak Methodist Church for ten years until August 1984 and was also Superintendent of the Birmingham South-West Circuit. Originally from Penarth in South Wales, Donald Knighton read Modern History at Oriel College, Oxford, following National Service in the Royal Air Force. He trained for the Methodist ministry at Wesley House, Cambridge. He is now Chairman of the Cardiff and Swansea District of the Methodist Church.

His wife, Anne, has a background in domestic science and they have three teenage children. His interests include church history and the sociology of religion and he also enjoys walking, gardening 'when there is time' and being with his family.

A receiving church

At the back of Selly Oak Methodist Church there is a world map. Marked on it are the names of regular worshippers from overseas and the countries from which they have come.

On the first few Sundays of each term, one of our church families – a father, mother and two daughters – stand by the world map at the end of each service, and welcome overseas friends, inviting them to give their names and details. We are a *receiving* church, and our geographical knowledge, as well as our vision and understanding of the world church, has been immensely improved: some of us are beginning to master the geography of Africa with its new names and boundaries, as distinct from our school geography, and to pray with a new interest and knowledge. In this we are aided by the Methodist Church Overseas Division Prayer Manual, which is issued annually and is often used in public worship as well as private devotion. (A specific area with people and concerns, issues and opportunities is cited for each day of the month.)

Most of our overseas worshippers belong to Selly Oak Colleges, the University of Birmingham and the local hospitals, especially Selly Oak Hospital; there is also a small but strong nucleus of overseas people who are permanently resident in the area. They all greatly enrich our worship, ministry and fellowship, bringing in fresh and stimulating insights, understanding and knowledge. A preacher has only to mention a country or a specific area or town and several people in the congregation will have come from there, or know it well. Somebody probably flew in from there last night! Such immediacy makes a great deal of difference to our awareness and to the meaningfulness of our concern and prayer.

Overseas people regularly share in the leading of worship and prayer; in the teaching and supervision of Junior Church and other young people's activities, and in the whole range of fellowship and ministry. At the time of writing, the world map has eighty people's names from twenty-five countries written in, and when a count was taken in an ordinary morning service several years ago, twenty-eight different countries were represented. Following the service, one lady commented – not seriously – 'You don't count if you come from Selly Oak!'

The congregation rejoices in its geographical, ecumenical and cultural variety. We have people in the congregation preparing for service overseas, those on furlough and those retired after service abroad. The much-loved Dr. Fred Milson, who died in 1983, used to say, 'The back pews of Selly Oak Methodist Church are in Africa.'

A strong tradition

Selly Oak Methodism has had a long tradition of links with the world church, and a strong sense of belonging to and sharing in a church which is global in its strategy and which transcends all cultural and geographical boundaries. These links and belonging applied to both traditions, the Wesleyan and Primitive Methodist, which came together into Selly Oak Methodist Church. St. John's and St. Paul's, the original churches, both sent people overseas and welcomed people from foreign shores. They were both *receiving* and *sending* churches. Methodist Union happened in 1932 – the year of the author's birth, so he claims to be a plain Methodist – but union between St. John's, ex-Wesleyan, and St. Paul's, ex-Primitive Methodist, came in 1956 after long negotiation and growing together.

After ten years of worshipping in the old St. Paul's on the Bristol Road at the heart of Selly Oak village, the united and growing Selly Oak Methodist Church moved up to the new church building, on a new site, in September, 1966. The position is very near the Selly Oak Colleges and we became in many ways their local church.

An ecumenical church

We are an ecumenical church in ourselves, although we are playing a growing part in developing Selly Oak Council of Churches. Many traditions are represented in our congregations. To name a few of the regular worshippers in the recent past: A Mennonite from the U.S.A.; a member of the Remonstrant Church from the Netherlands; a Syrian Orthodox Priest; several Anglican Priests; a Lutheran Evangelical Pastor from South India; a family belonging to an Evangelical Church in Egypt; and so the list could go on. 'Names and sects and parties fall, Thou, O Christ, art all in all' (Charles Wesley).

We worship together round the Cross, which is in a central position at the front of the church. A Mexican straw crucifix is at the side – the empty Cross and the crucifix speak clearly and cogently of the total work and ministry of Christ. The batik picture of 'Christ, the Teacher' by the Reverend Dr. Solomon Raj, who worshipped with us and taught us so much for many years while he was on the staff of Selly Oak Colleges, reminds us of the teaching ministry in which we all share. The Egyptian tapestry, 'The Flight to Egypt' on the other side of the church near the organ reminds us of the vulnerability of Christ and of his people – 'the exposed nerve of humanity'. In Word and Sacrament we experience as one what it means to be part of the company of the people of God and to be involved in the great commission of Jesus Christ: 'Make all nations my disciples'.

The world is our parish

Ever since its foundation, the basis of the Methodist Missionary Society, now the Methodist Church Overseas Division, is that every member of the Methodist Church is automatically a member of the Society. Mission and all that it means is not just for the enthusiasts – it is not an optional extra, tacked on for those who choose it – it is for everybody. Every Christian is called to mission in various directions through different means. We are all caught up, or ought to be caught up, in this tremendous enterprise: the spreading of the good news of Jesus Christ throughout the world. This is not a duty or a burden, to be shouldered with grim determination, but rather a being caught up in the ongoing tide of God's love in Jesus Christ through the power of his Holy Spirit. 'We love, because he first loved us'. The initiative is always God's and he will empower, inspire and enable us as a Christian community and as individuals in the work of mission and ministry: 'Yet the power to do all these things is given us in Christ, who strengthens us', (The Covenant Service, *Methodist Service Book*).

John Wesley declared, 'The world is my parish', and from their origins Methodists have been brought up to have a world vision and to think on a large map. In the United Methodist Church Minutes of Conference earlier in the century, the preaching station, China, appears between Chesterfield and

Chorley. We belong to a world church in Jesus Christ. Charles Wesley's hymns, beloved of Methodists, stress time and again the universality of the Gospel: 'For all my Lord was crucified, For all, for all my Saviour died' 'To praise the Lamb who died for all, the general Saviour of mankind'. Congregations, particularly Methodist ones, learn their theology as much from hymns as from sermons. The *Methodist Hymn Book* and now *Hymns and Psalms* are also being used by many Methodists in their private devotions as well as for public worship.

A sending and receiving ministry

These convictions and insights are informed and illuminated in Selly Oak Methodist Church by preaching, not only from ministers and local preachers in the Birmingham South-West Circuit, to which the church belongs, but also by the preaching and teaching of missionaries returned from overseas and of members and ministers of the overseas churches themselves. 'Come over and help us,' the cry of the people in Macedonia to Paul and his colleagues, is still put into practice and people go out to share in the spreading of the Gospel in all sorts of ways.

The dictum is also implemented the other way round, and Selly Oak Methodist Church is immeasurably enriched by the ministry of people from overseas. One Caribbean couple, the Rev. Dr. George and Mrs. Elaine Mulrain, who for a number of years were on the staff of Kingsmead College, ran the Nightgroup (for young people over fourteen) in a highly effective way for a considerable time and gave the members a world vision and awareness. Overseas people naturally and happily hold office and responsibility within the church and make a distinctive and much valued contribution. Until recently one of the stewards, the leading office within the church, was a South African black lady doctor, Dr. Eugenia Jolobe. This sharing at a deep level is of great importance to the whole life and ministry of the church.

Keeping in touch

The Methodist Church Overseas Division is the agent of mission overseas for the Methodist Church. It acts in all respects, and money and support are channelled through the

Division. Individual churches and circuits do not sponsor and support missionaries and projects. There are strong links, however, with missionaries overseas and with members and ministers of overseas churches, both Methodist and others. A monthly church newsletter is published and forty copies are sent out each month to people overseas by a lady who keeps in touch personally with quite a number of recipients. (When they come back to Selly Oak they always ask to see her!) A considerable correspondence is carried on between members of the church, including the minister, and missionaries and people overseas. This is invaluable in terms of knowledge and awareness, contact and concern. Different members over the years have been most perceptive in seeing, settling and welcoming people, particularly from overseas. This tradition continues and many people have testified to the warm welcome they have found in Selly Oak Methodist Church. The welcome does not stop at the church door – hospitality is freely offered in people's homes, and lunches, teas and cups of coffee or tea are the modern equivalent of Christ's 'cup of water'. Many people overseas, including missionaries and others under great pressure, regard Selly Oak Methodist Church as their spiritual home and base and return gladly and eagerly again and again.

Local colleges

We are fortunate in having several colleges and hostels nearby. Kingsmead College plays an important part in the life of the church. It was originally a Quaker foundation, and was then shared with the Methodists. It is the main Methodist training centre for mission and service overseas. The range of service involved has extended far beyond the original vision of the founders but it is all part of the work of Jesus Christ. The members of the college come from many countries and cultures; it is a rich and diverse community and its members greatly enrich our life and worship.

The Methodist Overseas Guest House in College Walk was founded fifty-five years ago, by the Cadbury family, for missionaries of all denominations on furlough. The Methodist Church Overseas Division took over control about fourteen years ago. Because there are fewer missionaries on the field, the house now caters for overseas students as well. Normally it accommodates about eighty-five people. The ministers and members of Selly Oak have strong pastoral links with the residents and many of them come to worship Sunday by Sunday.

The Methodist International House in Oakfield Road came into being through the vision, faith and sheer determination of two men: the Rev. J.J. Whitfield (a much-loved worshipper and worker at Selly Oak who quite often preached in the church, and who for many years did pioneer work among overseas people in Birmingham) and the then Chairman of the Birmingham District of the Methodist Church, the Rev. W. Russell Shearer. It has about fifty residents from many countries and the University Chaplain does excellent pastoral work there.

The Wardens of both the Overseas Guest House and of the International House are members of the Church and many of the officers and committee members, with all the work and caring that such responsibilities involve, are provided by the church and the circuit. The links between both communities and the church are close and strong.

Kingsmead College works within the Federation of Selly Oak Colleges, an ecumenical and multi-cultural enterprise, with rich resources and considerable facilities. Centred on Selly Oak are the Multi-Faith Resource Unit, accommodated in the Gemeindehaus, a Lutheran student hostel; the Black/White Partnership, an imaginative and exciting enterprise to train pastors in a series of week-ends; the Christian-Islam Dialogue; the Centre for the Study of Primal Religions; and the departments of Selly Oak Colleges based on Central House – the Department of English, the Department of Social Work and the Department of Mission. Mission is central to the life of the Selly Oak Colleges and imaginative research as well as teaching is happening within the Department.

Equipment for the work of ministry and mission is provided in terms of work both overseas and at home. A succession of distinguished teachers and missionary statesmen from all the colleges, particularly from Kingsmead (and St. Andrew's Hall when it still had a Methodist component), have contributed a great deal to the thinking and awareness of the church over the years. The presence of students and staff from overseas, playing a full part in the life and worship of the church, continues to be a living demonstration of a belonging to and sharing in a world church.

A mission awareness at many levels

Every Methodist member belongs to a class, a small informal group for caring, study, prayer and fellowship. Selly Oak Methodist Church has twenty-nine classes, most of which meet regularly each month. Overseas people frequently share in the life of these classes and other activities. They also often speak to classes and other groups and share their insights and concerns. The Tuesday Fellowship, formerly the Women's Fellowship but now thrown open to men as well – two or three men come each week – has a monthly missionary meeting, described as the Women's Work afternoon. Missionary and overseas people speak each month and share knowledge, experience and insight. Missionary concern and world vision are developed, as indeed they are in all the groups of the church. The Junior Missionary Association consists of young people who collect for the work of the church overseas week by week – a fifth of the amount raised goes to Home Missions. It is not just a matter of raising money but also very much a matter of education. The Inters Department of the Junior Church has a missionary morning at least every other month and missionary education is regularly given throughout the Junior Church and indeed the whole church.

The Guides, Rangers and Brownies have a world vision within their own movement, as indeed have the Scouts and Cubs; the Guides remember this dimension very clearly and imaginatively in their 'Thinking Day' celebrations each February on our church premises. Many Guides work hard for their 'Commonwealth Badge' and draw on the knowledge and insight of missionaries and overseas people who make themselves readily and helpfully available. Alice Jones, a stalwart and wonderful Ranger, Guide and Brownie Leader as well as church member, worker and pastor, laid the foundations for this world vision among the Guides and other young people. I remember a family and parade service a number of years ago when I witnessed a most effective presentation of the world-wide nature of the Guide movement. Wishing to make the point that the church is even more universal and more comprehensive, the preacher asked, 'What is an even wider family than the Guide movement?' A diminutive Brownie put up her hand and said, 'The human race,' and, of course, she was right!

The Wives' Group and Open Circle (formerly Young Wives) have speakers on overseas and missionary subjects and concerns regularly and every so often have projects for raising money for urgent needs abroad. Recently it was Nigeria and Ghana for the Open Circle, and Sri Lanka for the Wives. The projects always include plenty of information so that the members can understand and be intelligently aware. Similarly, the Guild has a missionary dimension in its balanced and varied programme. *The missionary theme in all these programmes is not just tacked on but is an essential dimension.*

Birmingham University and Colleges Methodist Society is based on Selly Oak Methodist Church and caters for students and nurses. The ministers are the chaplains. The main meeting of the society is at Selly Oak after the evening service, and there are four or five fellowship groups which meet for study, prayer and sharing each week. The bulk of the members belong to the groups and the average attendance at the meeting of the Methodist Society is between forty and fifty, though the society is in touch with up to eighty or ninety students. The topics of both society and group meetings include missionary and overseas themes and the society has a strong tradition of world vision and missionary concern. The members are equipped and challenged to be committed Christians with a world vision: citizens aware of, and deeply concerned about world issues. The Methodist Society has sent out generations of students and nurses with a strong sense of the urgency of mission, service and ministry to society and the world, and a passion for peace, justice and spreading the good news of Jesus Christ.

During the Easter vacation students share in missions in local churches throughout the country – in 1984 they were at Bromsgrove, Walsall and Wolverhampton. Careful preparation and planning are carried out with the local church and there is follow-up. This experience is formative in

the life and faith of many students, who then proceed to
explore how their faith can be expressed in life-long vocation
and ministry. They learn how to articulate and share their
faith in a new way, different from their usual kind of
communication in their own groups, among their fellow
students and in society as a whole.

Formal support for mission

The missionary dimension of church life is handled and led by
the World Service and Mission Committee, which meets
about twice a year, and is responsible to the Church Council
which has oversight of the whole life, ministry, mission and
worship of the church. It includes not only Overseas Missions
and Home Missions, but also World Service projects like
Christian Aid, Oxfam, the World Development Movement,
Amnesty International and a host of other concerns with
world dimensions.

At least once a year, and sometimes more often, the church
has an exhibition and display of the whole range of issues
represented on the World Service and Mission Committee. It
is usually held in the church hall; coffee is served and people
have time and opportunity to browse and ask questions. The
members take part enthusiastically in the Christian Aid door-
to-door collection and are quite often asked questions
themselves. A number are involved in Oxfam, running the
shops and other activities, while others are interested in the
work of the Development Education Centre at the Charles
Gillett Centre in Selly Oak Colleges.

The specifically Overseas Missionary concerns are dealt
with in detail in the Overseas Missionary Sub-Committee.
This body plans events, including international lunches and
evenings, which arouse much interest and enthusiasm;
overseas people are fully involved, and it is an excellent way
of learning more about them, their churches and countries in
depth.

Each autumn there is a Missionary Lunch (Women's Work
Lunch traditionally) with a speaker, and this is well supported
and much enjoyed. It is an ideal way of comunicating and
sharing new ideas and insights about mission. Each year there
is within the church calendar – usually in March or May – the

World Church Sunday (formerly known as Overseas Missionary Anniversary) when all the worship, thinking and concern are focussed upon the mission of the world church. A succession of distinguished preachers – some of them from our own congregation! – have come to challenge, enthuse and inspire us.

Self-denial envelopes are distributed near Christmas for the work of the church overseas, and Women's Work self-denial envelopes at Easter, and the response is generous. The World Development Appeal, with plenty of preparation in terms of background information and education provided beforehand, is linked with the Harvest Festival and usually this dimension of world need is included within the harvest decoration.

Mission through the year

Missionary education and growth in world vision go on throughout the year and in all the groups and aspects of church life. The weekly notices each Sunday include a list of concerns suggested for our prayers each day at 7.00 a.m. and 10.30 p.m., and these concerns usually include an overseas dimension. For the Sunday of the week of writing the concerns include, 'for Chile and for peace and justice in that country and other South American countries'. The preacher for the Sunday morning is a Methodist Minister from Chile who is living in Kingsmead College and studying for his Ph.D. at the University of Birmingham. He will bring recordings of a psalm and a song in Spanish, as used in worship in his own country, and members of the congregation are provided with the words in Spanish and English. Hymns, music and other forms of worship are often used from other cultural traditions, often in other languages, and greatly enrich our worship. The monthly newsletter also regularly includes articles of missionary and world concern.

The Methodist Church Overseas Division monthly magazine, *Now* , with its supplement *Facets* for missionary workers, is well and imaginatively produced and provides information, ideas and indispensable facts. A great number of people in the church take *Now* regularly and pass on the information it contains.

A commitment at circuit level

Methodist churches always belong to and operate in circuits. Selly Oak Methodist Church belongs to the Birmingham South-West Circuit, a group comprising eleven very different churches, including four ecumenical projects. The Mission Committee of the circuit oversees the missionary dimension of work and ministry in the circuit and each year organises a Circuit Consultation on Mission, alternating between Home and Overseas Missions. This present year the consultation looked at Kenya and the Caribbean, and it was followed by a United Circuit Service at which the preacher was a young man from the Caribbean, training at Cliff College. The previous consultation focussed on South Africa under the leadership of the Rev. Dr. Theo Kotze from South Africa, a Research Fellow of Selly Oak Colleges, and the Rev. Dr. Bongani Mazibuko, the new Director of the Black/White Partnership programme and another South African Methodist Minister.

The Birmingham District of the Methodist Church has an Overseas Missionary Committee which superintends the missionary education and work throughout the twenty-six circuits of the Birmingham District. At the Central Hall this year, the district welcomed the May meetings of the Methodist Church Overseas Division and there were many excellent speakers, including the Rev. Dr. Colin Morris of the BBC, a former General Secretary of the division. The event included a steel band and Asian dancing. The Methodist Church is a 'connexion' – Methodist preachers were first in connexion with the Rev. John Wesley – and we are in connexion with the whole of the Methodist Church at home and overseas and indeed with the whole of the world church in all its richness and variety. We belong together and share together in Jesus Christ.

Selly Oak Methodist Church is a microcosm of that world church and we are privileged to have such variety and richness. We welcome people from overseas and send them out in the name of Jesus Christ. The Commissioning Service is usually held at or near the Methodist Conference, which is the highest authority within the Methodist Church. The service is an impressive event. We had one in the church a few years ago, and most of the people were being trained at Kingsmead and were well known. It will long be remembered.

The rhythm of *sending* and *returning* is basic to the Christian strategy and life and we are privileged and proud at Selly Oak Methodist Church to be *sending* and a *receiving* church. Mission is basic to our life and ministry as it is to that of the whole church, and it is Christ who calls and sends, empowers and enables: 'Yet the power to do all these things is given us in Christ, who strengthens us.' Christ is always present and active and his strength and grace are always sufficient.

Chapter 7

St. John and St. Germain, Harborne, Birmingham

Tom Walker

St. John's is an Anglican church in one of Birmingham's older suburbs, Harborne. The parish emphasises praise and prayer and runs a full programme of evangelism and training for lay leadership. On an average Sunday, the congregation totals 1,000.

The church's interests extend worldwide through the work of thirty-two missionaries whom it supports. The Bible Churchmen's Missionary Society, the South American Missionary Society and the Wycliffe Bible Translators have special links with St. John's.

The vicar is the Rev. Canon Tom Walker who was appointed to St. John's Church, Harborne in 1970. Tom Walker grew up in Dorking, Surrey and then studied Music and English at Keble College, Oxford. After training for the ministry at Oak Hill College, he returned to his native county where he was ordained priest at the very first ordination service held in Guildford Cathedral. Following curacies in the south of England, he spent three years as a Travelling Secretary through the Inter-Varsity Fellowship and then joined the staff at Birmingham Cathedral as Succentor.

He is married to Molly Anne and they have two married daughters and one teenage son. Tom Walker has led a number of missions in this country and has undertaken extensive preaching tours in Scandinavia and also a study tour in South America.

St. John's, Harborne, was established in the middle of the
nineteenth century to cope with the dramatic expansion of
Birmingham's population in the Industrial Revolution. It had
an avowedly evangelical foundation and when the new
Victorian mock-Gothic building was completed in 1858, it was
used as a 'preaching shop'. That is not to deny its real, local
and parochial identity, but because of the emphasis on
unashamed Gospel preaching, crowds were drawn from miles
away. There are accounts of people walking over ten miles
each way to church on Sunday. The pioneer of this Gospel
work was the Rev. T.S. Smith, who was so anxious to preserve
the distinctive evangelical nature of the church that his own
son later became the vicar.

A growing missionary vision through individuals

Members of today's congregation tell of the strikingly
authoritative ministry of the Rev. Isaiah Siviter from 1917 to
1925, when one hundred men gathered each Sunday
afternoon. Here was the grounding for the missionary zeal
which has characterised the congregation from that day to
this. The parish was composed mainly of working people such
as coachmen, nailsmiths, harness makers and clerks, as the
parish registers record, and a notable feature of the local
community is that it had been remarkably static since the
First World War. Even today we have eighty-year-olds in our
parish who meet in the 'village' High Street of Harborne, and
who remember sitting next to each other in their days in the
kindergarten. When I arrived as vicar in 1970, several
members of the Church Council had experience of no other
church than St. John's.

This gave the church a tight-knit, inward-looking feel, but
not at the expense of an outward-looking missionary vision.
If, because of the local nature of the community, it was
unlikely that many would be called either to old-fashioned,
pith-helmeted missionary endeavour or to more modern jet-
setting Gospel ministry, it did not mean that there was no
commitment to the world-wide missionary task. The
commitment was in the prayer meeting and in the back-up
letter writing to encourage those who were called abroad.

And it was in the tremendous enthusiasm for parochial evangelism that has always characterised the life of St. John's. One former churchwarden, Sidney Smith, was renowned for his hair-raising feats in transporting visiting evangelists around Birmingham. He was nicknamed Jehu because he drove 'furiously' on all his Gospel engagements (2 Kings 9:20). Furthermore he was ahead of his time in using Christian films and slides, projected on what would seem in our video age to be the most primitive equipment. For this he was strongly criticised by his contemporaries for partaking in 'the works of darkness'.

Another key figure in the development of missionary concern in the church was also for many years a churchwarden. Ernest Rowley achieved renown for entering the old church building over the Easter weekend of 1941, to rescue the lecterns, the Holy Table and the church safe, after the building was blown up by a delayed-action bomb. The explosion took place on Good Friday, mercifully without damage to life or limb.

Missionary giving like a fetish

Ernest was so emphatic in his missionary support because as a young man his application for missionary service with the then China Inland Mission had been turned down on health grounds. He suffered from defective hearing, and this disqualified him from going abroad. However, all his energies were spent in parish evangelism and in supporting the missionary cause through prayer and generous giving. Indeed, it was largely through his influence, whilst treasurer of the church, that nearly fifty per cent of the annual income was given away to missionary and charitable causes. It was with great reluctance that I had to urge that a larger proportion of our income should be invested in staff salaries and improvement of our parochial resources in terms of equipment and buildings. This was in order to stimulate afresh our house-to-house evangelism so that a new generation of potential missionaries could be won to the Lord. It seemed to me that we were dangerously near to making the high level of missionary giving a fetish. It seemed so much wiser to give even a smaller percentage of a much larger income through church growth and tithed giving. As more and more have been won to the Lord over the years, and the total giving has increased by well over twenty-five times, this has in fact happened.

Ernest Rowley was also used under God to ensure the continuing existence of St. John's as a separate parish, when it was proposed by the diocesan authorities to split the parish into three after the Second World War. Because the church building had been destroyed it was thought reasonable to divide the area among three neighbouring parishes, and St. John's would have lost its separate existence altogether. Canon Leathem the vicar shared in this task and he was involved in church politics too, so he was able to fight tooth and nail to guarantee that the evangelical witness of St. John's should not be lost.

Perhaps it was because of a rather distinctive and strident note to the Gospel testimony of St. John's that some of the powers-that-be wanted it closed down. In the earlier years of this century, St. John's was not renowned for an attitude of warm co-operation with the Church of England at large, and the local diocese in particular. The sense of independence from diocesan life was highlighted in the 1920s, when St. John's was deeply involved in the national controversy over prayer-book revision, culminating in the appearance of the 1928 Prayer Book. A national prayer meeting was held at St. John's at the time of the parliamentary debate, and the church register records a list of names of those present that reads like an evangelical *Who's Who*. That particular controversy was linked with the differences of theological emphasis that led to the formation of the Bible Churchmen's Missionary Society and its training colleges at Bristol that were ultimately incorporated into Trinity College. St. John's members were deeply committed to this new missionary initiative and felt completely at one with the desire to 'guard the truth' entrusted to them (2 Timothy 1), and to proclaim it vigorously and in a sacrificial way.

Looking back to the idiom of independent, protestant proclamation, it is not surprising that in a totally well-meaning, but rather isolationist way, St. John's has banged the Gospel drum to good effect both in its local evangelism and in its world-wide missionary endeavour. My impression is that in earlier days, missionary interest in the church was stimulated and sustained by the enthusiasm of certain key members of the church who were 'missionary-minded'. Support was given to particular missionary societies because of their firm evangelical stance or because they were favoured by the vicar or by the keenest missionary supporters in the church.

Rethinking the issue of missionary support

This rather 'ad hoc' policy worked well until so many missionary candidates were coming forward, associated with different societies, that we had to rethink the whole question of missionary support. It was quite clear that our call was to be a 'sending church'. We had a large number of students in our congregation, who were from local colleges or who had grown up as members of our own young people's organisations. The potential was considerable once the missionary vision was caught, and young lives began to be offered in the service of Christ. However, as a church we were already committed to support certain missionary societies, and it did not seem right to withdraw money from these societies in order to give it to candidates going out with organisations of their own choice.

Several decisions had to be made. We decided that our primary call was to back Anglican evangelical societies. Other, quite splendid, missionary organisations had much wider support on an interdenominational basis. We felt that it was our task to help those societies which had limited financial support from Anglican evangelical churches. We do not remotely begin to pay the salaries and expenses of all those who have gone into full-time service from our congregation. If the English set-up for missionary support demanded that, we should have to budget accordingly. Some of our candidates would be accepted as a financial obligation, and others would not. However, because of the existence of missionary societies, it is possible for one church to provide workers, and for other churches throughout the country to share in their support. It has been pointed out to us that this can sometimes raise some difficulty because it is not always easy for other churches to get to know the new missionary who is to be linked to them. Consequently, they do not become involved in making significant financial contributions towards the upkeep of the missionary on the field as the sending society would like. However, if we have a world view of mission, it does not seem unreasonable that one church should have a sending role, and others a supporting role. That does not mean that the one will not give generously as well, to help those who have been sent out from its congregation, nor that the other will not seek to provide missionaries from its congregation as well as giving financial help.

In practice, this is not necessarily a hard and fast rule. For example, one missionary from our congregation was called to a work which involved raising her own finances before she was accepted by the society concerned. Many in our congregation provided this support, quite apart from normal giving for other societies. Such giving does not appear in the church accounts and does not establish a precedent for helping future candidates in the same way, but illustrates our freedom in Christ to break our own rules.

However, at a later stage, there was a request from this same missionary, Kath, to provide a Land-Rover-type vehicle in order to make the journey into a remote part of the Cameroon where, with a missionary friend, she was engaged in translating part of the New Testament into the language of the Baka tribe. The thought of a former Birmingham University student driving for days across rutted, muddy tracks and then building her own house in a pygmy village clearing, helped only by pygmies with whom she had no effective language communication at that time, filled many of our comfortable Birmingham Christians with horror, and they were stirred to give generously to meet the transport need.

Furthermore, we do feel it right to give special support to our 'own' missionaries over and above the ruling of their sending society. We realise this can create a problem on the field if some colleagues are not helped to the same degree by their home churches. We seek therefore to be discreet and disciplined in giving some help. It is normally in the case of illness or some other emergency that special assistance is given, and in particular we want to help with accommodation or transport when one of our missionaries is on furlough.

Building a solid wall of prayer

Missionary support means, of course, much more than money. The importance of prayer backing, letter writing, caring for children of missionaries and maintaining friendship links is fully appreciated. Prayer groups are established for individual missionaries – especially those in notably dangerous situations, and prayer groups for particular societies are also organised. This stems from the initiative of individuals in the congregation and does not have to be organised by a committee. However, to make sure that no one is forgotten there is a system for linking our missionaries to different Home Groups. Inevitably this works better in some cases than in others, but some groups are given a real 'burden' for their link person both in prayer and in other forms of co-operation. If the missionary has an urgent prayer need, the Home Group can be relied upon to bring the problem to the attention of the whole church. This was the case when one of our number who was serving with the Church Missionary Society had to leave Iran at a time of difficulty. Often in the main services on Sunday, there is a time of open prayer when individuals are mentioned by name, and missionaries are prayed for by different members of the congregation. Again, it is noticeable that the church feels a special sense of prayer responsibility towards some missionaries more than others. This is sometimes due to human factors, such as the apparent glamour of the task to which they are called, but more often than not it depends on the amount of involvement that the missionary had in the congregation before being called abroad. In several cases a worker was delayed in going abroad, so the church took that person on to the staff on a salaried basis until it was possible to fulfil the missionary call. In such instances the delay was usually out of the person's control and was due to lack of space on a language course, or some other unavoidable factor. The opportunity for developing the loving, pastoral relationships that this afforded led in every instance to a very committed prayer support from the church.

Pursue the 'call' through the church family

Another significant reason for the notable backing of some missionaries is that as a pattern of eldership developed in the church, some candidates have pursued their sense of call to God's work by seeking advice from the elders at every phase, whilst others have bypassed the eldership in order to do their own thing. It is still possible to work the system and to approach a missionary society without seeking references from the current local congregation or its pastor. Some have been known to use their home church to provide these references, even though they left it before student days. In our experience the person who presents a *fait accompli* to their current local church never enjoys the same sort of warm support as the person who is sent out with a sense of responsibility on the part of the whole congregation.

The ministry of the elders of the church is for us a vital factor in discerning a true sense of call and in commending the person concerned to the missionary society or missionary training college to which they feel called. Previously this could be a tremendous responsibility on the shoulders of the vicar who had to recommend or reject candidates virtually single-handed. Now we find that some enquirers are urged to delay their approach to a missionary society or college until personal and spiritual problems are sorted out. The elders offer counsel and continuing help to such a person, and there is great rejoicing when eventually he or she goes abroad healed, trained and clearly called to a particular missionary task.

The positive results of a mission-minded church

The challenge to consider missionary work is often given at a tea meeting for those considering full-time Christian service during the church's main missionary weekend. Sometimes an exhibition is arranged at which a number of different missionary societies provide information for those who are enquiring about the possibility of service abroad. Over recent years, scores of people have left our church to serve either in the ordained ministry at home or as missionaries overseas. We have church planters in Peru and Bolivia, laboratory workers in Tanzania, a secretary waiting to return to the Province of the Southern Cone in South America, a potter in the Seychelles, a teacher of the blind in Central Asia, another teacher preparing to go to Peru, a senior nurse in Kenya, a

TEAR Fund worker in the Sudan, a Bible translator in the Cameroon, a chiropodist in India, dentists in Central Africa and a bishop and his wife in Uganda. A teacher is training in preparation for work in France and in addition to these there are many who have been abroad and returned after their short terms of service have been duly completed. Others are in secular jobs abroad, but have a sense of God's call to their tasks. Some have returned from missionary work, and still continue working for their missionary society here at home. One such is in a senior position with the Mission Aviation Fellowship. Some, wondering about a possible call to work for God abroad have ended up in the ordained ministry at home, still open to a call overseas at some later time.

In a city like Birmingham, people can join our church at varying stages of their Christian development. Some have been open to a missionary call for a number of years, but find that it crystallises during their time with us. Some come to train at a missionary college in Birmingham with little support from their home church, which may not be missionary-minded, and find that they become adopted as 'our' missionaries. Others grow up through our Sunday schools and youth organisations and find their call to full-time ministry either within our own fellowship, or away at college or some other church.

When I first arrived as vicar of St John's in 1970, there was a regular meeting after church on Sundays when slides of missionary work would be shown, and time was given to pray for missionaries in various situations of need. I was quite misunderstood at first, because I was not willing to attend such a meeting on a regular basis. I argued that it was quite vital to *do* missionary work at such a key time after the evening service. This seemed almost unspiritual to those who were called to prayer, but in the long run it was proved to be the correct priority. Some of those who found deep Christian fellowship and instruction at those meetings after church eventually became missionaries themselves. The lesson is that different Christians have different calls. For some it is quite right to stay on the church premises and pray. For others it is vital to get out into the world, where people are, and to win them for Christ. Clearly, those who have been won to Christ through our own organisations are well known to us as a church, and their call is confirmed by clergy and other leaders.

Counselling from a distance

If a missionary is accepted by a society and has the full recommendation of our own elders, and goes for training with the total good will of our Parochial Church Council and congregation, we feel responsible as far as the candidate is concerned. We also feel that in some sense the missionary is also accountable to us. It is perfectly possible that emotional problems or difficulties of relationships can occur on the field, either with other workers or with those in authority in the missionary society. As a church, we are always glad to be consulted in the case of such difficulties, and often exercise a counselling role from a distance. We then count it to be our responsibility to help as much as we can during a furlough period. Sometimes this help takes the form of the vicar working in conjunction with the missionary society in counselling or decision-making; sometimes the elders are involved in giving corporate advice and counsel. In some cases, the missionary concerned feels the need to 'present' strongly and successfully to the vicar, and he will then prove to be the last person who can solve the problem. The image of the nearly perfect, super-successful Christian worker dies hard, and one of the most difficult lessons for some missionaries to learn is that they are truly human, and that sometimes 'vessels of clay' can be somewhat brittle. When the defences are down it is possible for honest sharing to begin, and the vicar or some other counsellor can start to exercise the loving care that is the true responsibility of the local church.

Visiting the missionary on the field

On one occasion I was given time off by the church to visit those members of the congregation who were serving God in South America. The visit was also sponsored by the Bible Churchmen's Missionary Society, so that it was seen to be a joint caring initiative on the part of the local church and the home missionary society. It is true to say that the vicar was more in need of a sabbatical break than the missionaries concerned needed pastoral attention, but the tour gave a sense of mutual responsibility in God's work. Returning home, it was evident that the visit had an enormously beneficial effect in subsequent prayer backing, and in knowing how to decide matters of practical help. The whole church could identify with the workers abroad, and the missionaries who were visited had an opportunity to show immense kindness to their vicar. Some of the local customs seemed gruesome to a casual visitor, not least drinking 'maté' out of a shared pot, in unhygienic surroundings. Maté is a form of tea which even the average South American missionary enthuses about so strongly, that the visitor feels duty bound to partake. The only consoling thought in attempting to swallow the foul liquid is that none of the other participants have died of it – yet!

There were other hazards too. I arrived at the airport at Buenos Aires to be greeted with a bear hug by Alan Hargrave, who was working in Northern Argentinian on an agricultural project among the Indians of the Chaco, and John Ellison who was attached to the chaplaincy church in the capital city. Driving out of the airport car park at a very modest speed, we were suddenly confronted by an irate policeman who showed us at pistol point into the police station. It was evident that they were having a purge on everyone in order to pass the time in the small hours of the morning, but the studied cleaning and clicking of pistols was guaranteed to intimidate the casual visitor more used to the ways of the friendly British Bobby. In the end it turned out that we were being accused of exceeding the speed limit, and with some embarrassment they eventually released the motley collection of English missionaries and their guest from Birmingham. An hour or so in custody was not the expected Argentinian welcome.

As my visit progressed, it was common to see road blocks with attendant snipers, and Virginia Patterson, one of the missionaries with the South American Missionary Society, told a hair-raising story of how she drove straight though one of these blocks because of brake failure, and the sniper only refrained from shooting when he saw that there were children in the car with the group of English women missionaries. In Buenos Aires itself, the atmosphere was oppressive, and John

Ellison warned me at all costs to keep my camera out of sight as we approached the main government buildings. The sad stories of women whose husbands and sons had been kidnapped at dead of night, never to be heard of again, were experienced at first hand. The victory of Christ in the lives of those who had turned to him in their desolation was a remarkable testimony to the healing power of the Gospel of Reconciliation proclaimed though missionary endeavour.

Another positive aspect of the tour was the opportunity to study Liberation Theology in the countries of origin. It was also a stimulating experience to discover the dignity of those surviving, and indeed growing in Christian faith, in the unpromising circumstances of a Peruvian shanty town. Others in the congregation have from time to time been in the fortunate position of having a holiday with one or another of our missionaries, and this again has had a beneficial effect for all concerned.

Gaining a vision through local evangelistic outreach

The flow of missionaries and candidates for the ordained ministry began when the church established a programme of local evangelism. A number of our key workers found their call confirmed by engaging in the regular evangelistic visiting in the parish which began as long ago as 1971. Some of our number were praying together to find out God's way to tackle the mammoth task of evangelising thousands of disinterested residents. They realised that this was not a task for a few enthusiasts, but was something to be faced by the whole church. Consequently, as many as were willing formed Home Groups, with the intention of sharing the things of Christ together so that each person would be better equipped to share his faith with outsiders. It was planned that after six months a team of evangelistic visitors would be called out from among those who belonged to the Home Groups. These would be given training, and would be backed by the continuing prayer support of those who remained behind. The Home Groups thus became missionary prayer groups and the visitors became missionaries, taking the Gospel from door-to-door.

The gift of evangelism – not just for the young

Over the years, hundreds have been trained and have gained experience in this form of evangelism. A number have found their call to full-time Christian work confirmed through these visitations. Indeed, some who have remained in our own church rather than going out to serve God in the wider church, have discovered and developed a remarkable evangelistic gift. This gift has continued to be exercised not only in our local church, but also in missions in other parts of the country too, as teams have been sent out from St. John's. In a recent mission at Bradford Cathedral, Joan Phillimore, who came to Christ in middle age, was giving powerful testimony of the power of Christ to deliver her from a strongly occult background. The confidence gained in local church evangelism in Harborne helped her in ministering to large and small groups of solid Bradford citizens, who listened, open-mouthed, to the story of Christ's power to change a human life. Margaret Hopkinson, also on the team, spoke from her experience of our own parish evangelism. Her story had quite a different emphasis, since she was brought up in a sheltered Christian home, but the transformation that came to her life as she was freshly filled with the Spirit in her middle years was a striking one. Testimony from older Christians is so pertinent to the lost generations to whom we are called to minister today. Part of the church's missionary task is undoubtedly to train its older members for effective evangelism. Joan and Margaret's witness was marvellously balanced by the more youthful contribution of Jeff Cuttell, who with a Ph.D. in radioisotope hydrogeochemistry, proved to have a remarkable skill in communicating the Gospel to old and young alike, in simple, everyday terms. He is now training for the ordained ministry.

The important thing about this system of evangelism is that it is undertaken not by a team of specialists, but with many people in the church contributing their gifts. Some pray, some offer administrative and secretarial help, some give hospitality, some baby-sit, and as far as possible people with different abilities throughout the whole range of church life are used. This destroys any sense of superiority that can sometimes spoil well-meaning evangelistic enterprise. The door-to-door witness team is not considered superior to those

who offer their services for other tasks. The fact that they
have received training does not give them the edge over other
Gospel workers. And above all, the team does not witness to
parishioners with any sense of condescension or pride. Each
member goes out with an honest desire not to win arguments
and debates, but to offer love and care to those who live in our
parish. The questionnaire we have devised asks if there is
anything that our church can do for the local community that
is not already being done, and in that spirit of service we seek
to commend Christ. Some years ago we were taken up on that
offer, as many young housewives expressed the need for a
playgroup in Harborne, so we appointed a new staff member
in order to provide that facility. It has in fact proved a
continuing means of evangelism as well as social outreach,
and we are grateful to those who first asked for it to be
provided.

Social work alongside evangelism

Interestingly, a number of those who have been called abroad
have found themselves involved in a combination of
evangelistic and social work, especially when working in
needy areas such as the shanty towns of Lima, or the Chaco in
northern Argentina. In this country with our developed social
services, we have found that our call has often been to fill in
the gaps of care not covered by other statutory bodies. If the
playgroup is one illustration of this, another is the series of
afternoon Home Groups for older women, which meets the
tremendous needs of the lonely. In the central part of our
parish, the statistic from the last census which shocked us
into action was that we have twenty-five per cent above the
national average of retired people living within a very small
geographical area. In the past we have linked our parish
evangelists to each of these Home Groups in order to bring a
sense of fellowship in evangelism. This has also had the effect
of bringing some of the older people in our parish to faith in
Christ as visiting links have been established with them. In
turn, they too have become effective prayer partners for our
missionaries as they have gone abroad.

The reality of prayer

Lessons have been learned not only from the structure of this evangelistic scheme, but also from some of the direct and rather startling answers to prayer that have occurred. For example, at one point we were puzzled about finding a way to break through the considerable apathy that the visiting team encountered in the parish. Waiting upon God, the answer eventually came through one of those present in the praying group. He said: 'We must pray for people in our parish to become more and more miserable, so that realising that they are miserable sinners, they will turn to God.' This was an unexpected prayer topic for us to be given, but obediently we prayed along those lines. One evening, shortly after that, two burly men in our evangelistic team called rather late one night on an elderly lady. She was expecting a visit, because a preliminary letter sent by me, distributed by yet another team of people, had prepared the way.

'Come in', she said. 'I don't know why, but just recently I have been feeling more and more miserable, and I am sure that you have the answer to my problem.' Normally, of course, a frail, elderly person would not even have opened the door that late in the evening, and it seemed to be a direct answer to prayer that that door was 'open for the Gospel'. On other occasions, the reality of prayer on the part of the team was so considerable, that one of my colleagues felt that he was being physically knocked backwards through the door, when he tried to enter the room whilst the team was at prayer.

These lessons of prayer have been valued by many called into full-time service as a result of participating in our own local missionary efforts. Furthermore, the reality of prayer support from the congregation has been enormously enhanced because those who have gone out in Christian service have been co-workers in past days. Also, many who have gone out from us have had considerable help and ministry in order to bring them to a deep inner healing. This sense of identifying with them in need and seeing their growth through afflictions, has integrated them strongly into the prayer life of the church.

Our common 'skunkhood'

Sometimes the most surprising people have been called out in God's service – humanly surprising, that is. It is not always the outwardly strong, or confident, or brilliantly communicative people who have been called. But the dedication of their lives and gifts to the Lord has meant that God has honoured their obedience, and a marvellous and effective work for God has been accomplished through them. This makes sense of the missionary call in Luke 10. Jesus said to his seventy disciples, appointed to go on ahead of him to prepare the way in the places he intended to visit: 'The harvest is plentiful, but the labourers are few; pray therefore the Lord of the harvest to send out labourers into his harvest. Go your way . . . ' He did not say, 'look for the strong, and obvious, and humanly outstanding people to do the missionary task.' He urged his followers to get praying, and then be the answer to their own prayer in fulfilling the missionary tasks themselves. The former Archbishop of Capetown, the Rt. Rev. Bill Burnett, uses a vivid illustration to describe our qualification to be called by God to know Jesus as our Saviour, and to serve him in his world. He speaks of our common 'skunkhood'. Our smell is not too good, and we may not be the most popular creatures, but we know that God loves skunks, and he wants to take us just as we are, with strengths and weaknesses, with our part-healed wounds, so that as wounded healers in his world we can take his grace to others in the fellowship of our common need and in the fellowship of God's grace.

Chapter 8

Alton Evangelical Free Church, Alton, Hants.

Barrie Taylor

The Evangelical Free Church (FIEC affiliated) is situated in the rural town of Alton in Hampshire. Many of the working inhabitants either commute to London or are in local industrial or agricultural employment. New housing estates have sprung up in the town over the past few years to cater for a growing population. The church is also seeing an increase in numbers and is currently looking for new premises. On an average Sunday there are around 230 people at both services.

Alton Evangelical Free Church sees overseas mission as an extension of mission at the local level. The members support three full-time workers; a family in Bible college training and two who are working with SIM International.

The pastor is Barrie Taylor, a former sales representative and evangelist among Merchant Seamen in Southampton. He serves on the Board of Governors at Moorlands Bible College and has been pastor of the church at Alton since 1972.

He is married to Sandra, a part-time secretary, and they have two teenage sons. He enjoys walking and is a 'fairly serious bird-spotter'.

'The farthest limits will be yours'

The question came about ten minutes into our conversation, just five words that went like a sword to my heart, making me wish the ground would open up and hide me. We had been talking together about God's graciousness to us in the church at Alton and the measure of growth he had brought by His Spirit, and then came the question – 'What is your mission strategy?'

The problem was not so much that there was no mission interest in the church, for following in the steps of many other evangelical churches, one-tenth of the church's income was given to mission, four societies each receiving one-quarter of that tenth! Further, there were to be found in the church some missionary prayer warriors who actually believed in the power of prayer to affect and change things anywhere in the world. The problem right then was in my own heart, a heart cold towards mission, lacking in biblical perception, vision and zeal in this vital area.

Twenty-two months later, surrounded by the evening chorus of crickets, frogs and lizards, I sat alone on the verandah of a missionary's house in Northern Liberia. My heart welled up, my throat tightened around the lump forming in it, and through my closed eyes came a trickle of hot, anguished tears. I could still hear the words spoken to me earlier that evening by the young Gbandi Christian who had been my interpreter as I preached in a village home. He had interpreted with power under a real anointing of God's Spirit, and I later asked him, 'With such a gift of communication, do you think one day God might have you become a preacher to your own people? He replied, 'I need help to read and understand. Who will help me, who will help me?' I thought of all the hoarded spiritual resources back home in the United Kingdom, my heart melted, and a tear reached the verandah floor.

A lot had happened in those twenty-two months in my own heart, and also in the heart of the church.

Stirrings amongst the leaders

Being challenged by those five simple words,'What is your mission strategy?' I had begun to search the scriptures for a biblical understanding of mission. In addition to this I read as widely as possible on the theology of mission, approached SIM International for input and stimulation, and acquired

information from churches where God was blessing their
response to mission. With a mind beginning to be informed
and a heart beginning to be warmed I was looking forward
eagerly to the church's forthcoming joint elders' and deacons'
retreat in which we were to examine our response to mission.
As this group of leaders met, the church prayed.

God met with us that day and we were conscious of his
mercy towards us amidst all our shortcomings and failures,
but we were conscious also of that gracious ministry of
encouragement he exercised towards us, as he showed us
how things might be. Four things he bore in upon us that day
were to subsequently become the foundation pillars upon
which our mission response was to be based.

Firstly, we needed to realise afresh that the grand purpose
of mission is to save perishing souls and see them established
as disciples. Writing many years ago, Dr. Robert E. Speer, then
Secretary of the American Presbyterian Board of Missions,
had this to say:

> The founders of modern mission were men to whom
> eternity was awful and who could not play lightly with the
> everlasting fortunes of the soul. They believed Christ is the
> only Saviour and that without Him men could have no
> hope . . . these early missionaries saw only the future doom
> of the souls of the heathen and went solely to save them
> from Hell. They did not hold the shallow tinsel views on
> these questions so glibly rolled out by many today. Hell was
> a reality to them.

Secondly, we needed to re-educate ourselves to think big.
This is one of the reasons why our mission forebears saw such
large success. They thought big. Prayed big. Gave big.
Believed big, and all because they saw a big God! C. T. Studd
put it perfectly: 'Let us ever see the impossible, the utterly
impossible, and then get to God and ask Him to do it. That
glorifies Him, magnifies Him, and gives Him a chance to
magnify Himself which is best of all.'

Thirdly, we needed to re-examine whose responsibility it
was to identify, select, and send out missionaries. There are
many individuals and churches in our land who have reason
to thank God for that pertinent and inspired booklet, *Get Your
Church Involved in Missions* (Michael Griffiths, OMF

Books). His opening heading comes straight to the point: 'Ministers and congregations have the chief responsibility for the selecting and sending of new missionaries. How grateful we were for insights into the selection of potential missionaries, insights like this one gleaned from the booklet: 'The most an individual can do is to express his willingness. Others must determine his worthiness. The individual may be free to go but only his church knows if he is really fitted to go.'

Fourthly, we needed to re-evaluate the levels of missionary support, personally, practically and pastorally. We were astonished to see how much we spent on ourselves in the local church in relationship to what we were giving to mission. The treasurer's pie chart read 'local 83.5%, national missions 5.3%, overseas missions, 11.2%'. We envisioned the day when by God's grace we would give more away to mission than we would spend on ourselves.

And so we returned to the church to share with them what God had shown us.

Sharing with the church

The over-riding need was to educate biblically so the church might see that mission was rooted in the Word of God, felt in the heart of God, and carried out by the Spirit of God through men and women in the hands of God. The preaching, taking the form of systematic exposition, now drew attention to mission theology and application. Formerly these aspects had been neglected.

The very first such sermon God winged to the ears and hearts of a young couple in the congregation. It was to be a link in the chain that led them to dedicate and offer their lives in missionary service. Beware if you start preaching mission. God does not hang about – you may well lose your best members to the mission field!

Mid-week meetings were given over to missionary biographies, introducing our people to the giants of world mission, but more importantly to the God behind them who called, motivated and equipped them. That God was our God too. He who lit up the lives of those great men and women of mission was longing to do the same in our lives also! Visitors from the church overseas and visitors from the mission field were interviewed in the pulpit. We began to see beyond the parochial blinkers that only took in Alton. All over the world God's Spirit was moving: there were needs to be met, situations to be prayed for, personnel to be found, and praise to be given.

We sought next to explain to the church what steps individuals should take if they felt that God might be calling them to mission service at home or overseas. After all, if we believed God's word concerning mission and regularly preached mission, then we should expect a response, for God's Word never returns empty. It was necessary, therefore, for those sensing a call to know that the church leaders would receive them sympathetically and do everything possible to surround them with local opportunities to identify and develop their potential for the church to see. In other instances the elders might initiate an approach, so challenging an individual to think through the whole area of his or her gifts and service.

Finally, we shared with the church our concept of mission response. It now stands today as our Mission Policy. It is stated in terms of principles which we believe to be biblical, rather than stating individual names. People change; they come, they live, they serve, they remove, they die. The principles of God's Word stand as timeless guidelines.

So we made our commitment before the Lord – it reads, and looks like this: (The capitals highlight the pertinent factors).

OUR MISSION RESPONSE

1. Recognising the GREAT COMMISSION, Matthew 28:17–20, we resolve to respond UNDER THE GUIDANCE OF THE HOLY SPIRIT, as fully as we are able, LOCALLY, NATIONALLY AND INTERNATIONALLY. (Acts 1:8).

2. Support will be channelled into PEOPLE (missionaries) and PROJECTS, needs being evaluated regularly and priorities assessed in context of the whole.

3. A MISSION COMMITTEE* will regularly review and make recommendations through the elders to the church. They will be responsible for the flow of information, and arranging of missionary meetings.

   * Comprising: one elder, one deacon, and three church members, with power to co-opt if specialised input is needed.

At the time of our responding to mission in this way our membership numbered about 140 people, with an adult Sunday morning attendance of around 190. The full-time staff of the church consisted of myself, a lady worker, and an assistant pastor, whom we had just called. Within the next months we were to face exciting new challenges in respect of both people and projects.

People in mission

By and large, the church in our land today is missionary-society orientated rather than missionary orientated. Failure at local church level to think biblically and act boldly has resulted in the abdication of missionary responsibility to the missionary societies, who today are seen by many as the sole agents of missionary work. This situation is biblically untenable, a disgrace to the local church and a source of grief to many missionary societies. The days of either the church or the society going it alone are over. We need each other. The church's task is to provide fully supported people, proficient spiritually, theologically, pastorally, evangelistically. The society's task is to provide the specialised training that may be needed, for example, linguistic and cultural training. The joint task is to ensure under the guidance of the Holy Spirit a correct placement, and adequate support within it, both on the mission field and during furlough.

But what if a church has no missionary of its own – where on earth does it begin? That was precisely the situation we were faced with in Alton. The solution for us was two-fold: adoption and asking.

Joan was already a missionary and known to us, when during one furlough she started attending the church. For various reasons it was not possible for her to continue in the supportive relationship she had enjoyed some years before with her sending church. She arrived as it were on our doorstep as one of God's special gifts – a missionary orphan! What adoption meant to her is perhaps best described in her own words:

> The most exciting facet of adoption is that it involves a
> deliberate choice, and it was a precious blessing when the
> Lord forged a love-link for me with Alton E.F.C. After my
> first term in Nigeria I returned home for furlough to
> discover I needed a caring home fellowship. Although I had
> not grown up with, or served in, that particular church, I
> was welcomed into their midst with a real warmth, and the
> ties developed and deepened over the years. Regular
> support was a part of the commitment, but the real
> strength of our relationship lay in the bond of love and
> prayer concern which sealed our partnership in our mutual
> missionary call.

Today Joan is regarded as one of the church staff and fully
supported financially and prayerfully in her role with SIM
International. Maybe adopting a partly supported missionary
could be a starting place for mission response in your church
that will give you immediate involvement with a missionary.
Limit adoption perhaps to just one person, because if you
start asking God to raise up missionaries in your church as
you preach and teach mission, believe me, he is going to
answer!

'My husband's a donkey's jaw-bone!'

Doug and Chris, with their family of three children, had been
in the church for some time, having moved to us from an
adjacent town. Christine, a trained nurse, was the stronger of
the two spiritually. Doug was the quieter, introspective,
depressive, and always struggling as a Christian to keep his
head above water. We were about to learn that God chooses
the most unlikely people to work through! In his own way, in
his own time, and in many different ways God began to break
into Doug's life – freeing him, filling him, forming him for the
future he had already planned for him. It was whilst they were
away at a Christian camp that God shared with Christine a
glimpse of what her husband would become.

When they returned from the camp she shared her new
insight. 'Pastor, I do hope you will not misunderstand what I
am saying, I can only put it this way, God has shown me from

his word – my husband's a donkey's jaw-bone!' Together we
turned to Judges 15 and read the account of Samson using a
most unlikely object to do battle with – 'Finding a fresh
jawbone of a donkey, he grabbed it and struck down a
thousand men. Then Samson said, "With a donkey's jaw-bone
I have made donkeys of them. With a donkey's jaw-bone I
have killed a thousand men".' God used a most unlikely
instrument – and so it was to be with Doug. His wife was right!

God took Doug, filled him with his Spirit and called upon
him and his wife to lay their lives on the altar of full-time
Christian service. They shared their sense of call with the
elders. The church tested the call as Doug, for nine months,
engaged more publicly in service in the church, and gave
himself to a guided study course in theology. His wife also
engaged in service and committed herself to study in a Bible
Survey course. It was a new experience not only for Doug and
Christine, but also for the church (we made mistakes from
which we have learnt) and God has brought us through.

Today, fully supported by the church financially and
prayerfully, Doug and Christine are at Moorlands Bible
College equipping themselves further. And God, just as he
always does, has the crowning word – for, four months after
we had committed ourselves to support them fully in a
financial way, the Sovereign Lord disposed the heart of the
Local Authority to give them a grant retrospectively, and
Doug and Christine returned a good measure of their support
to the church! God knew what we didn't know – that we were
to be stretched yet further financially as another couple
responded to the call to Christian service – but then God had
computed that before the world began.

Computing possibilities

Steve, of course, had not computed that possibility, even
though he was a computer team leader with a nationally
known organisation. Neither was it to take a long time for God
to call Steve and Judi into the place where he wanted them to
be. Within three months, through preaching, personal contact
with a missionary, and a letter, God had convinced them that
Steve's computing skills were needed by SIM International.
Today, supported fully by the church, Steve oversees the

computer operations in Europe. At home Judi brings up the
two boys. Together they are looking forward to the day when
the computer installations in Europe are settled and running.
Then together they can go to Africa and serve the Lord there.

Projects

Each quarter of the year, in addition to supporting our
members in full-time Christian service, a project is presented
to the church. We look to the Holy Spirit to lead us so that we
can be responsive to his calls upon us. The last eighteen
months have seen some exciting ventures begun and
completed.

The church in East Africa had need of the advisory services
of a forestry expert. Such a man was to be found in our
fellowship. By circumstances and timing which only God
could bring about, Dr. Julian Evans, in conjunction with the
Africa Inland Mission and TEAR Fund, was enabled to meet
the need of the hour. God allowed us the privilege of sharing
in the cost of his travel and the production of a slide-tape
programme.

Little did I know that I, too, would soon visit Africa: the
word 'sabbatical' is like music to any pastor's ears, and the
church in Alton made that a reality for my wife and myself in
giving us a four-month break. This gave me the opportunity to
respond positively to the invitation of SIM to visit, as one of
their Council members, the missionaries in West Africa. God
provided through the church the means for my wife to
accompany me on our first and unforgettable trip to the
African mission field.

Meanwhile, another country was laid on our hearts, this
time Poland, and the plight of our Christian brothers and
sisters as they faced yet another hard winter. Over £10,000
was raised, goods were given in kind, and gifts received from
other churches, raising the overall value to about £18,000.
Every department of the church was involved, from the
Sunday school to the adults. Skills were employed in
producing clothing and woollens, and many saw for the first
time that their talents could be used in the Lord's service. And
so it was that three of our members drove the largest lorry we

could lay our hands on into Southern Poland.

Back in the United Kingdom, mission was not being neglected as a further five members visited the north-east of England to help in a church planting situation, using their gifts in door-to-door visitation, speaking in schools, video meetings and preaching.

An educational project to acquaint us with the missionary potential of radio work was undertaken in yet another quarter. Our first attempts were made in producing on tape a programme suitable for hospital radio. In the summer months a team of people visited Valencia in Spain, not to holiday, but to help in putting the finishing touches to a new church building.

The lesson that God taught us as we enlarged the staff, supported missionaries and students, and undertook projects, was that with God nothing is impossible. It is so exciting helping God to build his Kingdom!

Mission news and prayer support

The Sunday services provide a regular opportunity to convey up-to-date news and to pray for our mission outreach. Overseas visitors, students, and pastors are interviewed, and so our world vision is broadened. Mid-week meetings either centrally or in house groups (both operate on alternate weeks) offer opportunity for part or all of the meeting to be given to mission matters.

All this is supplemented by our own bi-monthly mission broadsheet *Impact*, where space is given to news of missionaries, projects, educational snippets, and a competition for children.

Someone once asked, 'How do you operate the budget for missionary support, and how is it presented to the church for approval?' Ministers are notorious for being naïve in practical areas, but my answer is not meant to be. Money has never been the prime concern. If you ask God to raise up from amongst yourselves servants for the mission field, and he answers and leads the church to recognise, set apart and send out those people, it is inconceivable that he will not provide for them fully through the church. It may hurt to give, but no Christian has ever yet died through over-giving! Incidentally, if you preach and practice tithing, ten people tithing can virtually raise one extra salary. If your church is short of money for mission, start praying for ten souls to be saved. Ten converts convinced of tithing can increase your effectiveness in mission considerably. The same criterion applies to the mission projects God's Spirit lays on our hearts. The dictum is this, 'Faithful is He who calls you – who also will do it.'

Preparing God's people for works of service

The great aim of the church after worship and evangelism must surely be 'to prepare God's people for works of service' (Eph. 4:12). That should be the aim of every pastor and mission-minded church. The local church is God's hatchery on earth, where he desires to incubate the gifts of new-born Christians, until they are developed for service anywhere in the world. A critical factor for incubation is the right environment, which must be warm and encouraging. This has been the hardest thing for our local churches to develop, for far too often as church leaders we have appeared 'severe professionals' who expect an immediate and incredibly high standard from anyone who may respond to calls for works of service. Similarly, the corporate membership itself can often seem less than sympathetic to someone making mistakes in early days as gifts are tentatively exercised. Yet nature itself teaches us that first steps are faltering steps.

A second factor in preparing God's people for works of service is to provide the right food to strengthen their growth and develop their 'muscle' for service. A typical local church teaching menu – supplementing the main preaching ministry – might look something like this:

STARTER:	Discipleship Training (How to disciple new converts)
	A Survey of the Bible (Through every book)
MAIN COURSE:	A Christian Studies Course
	(The first year could give introduction into Christian beliefs, church history, mission, organisation and administration, public speaking, visiting, media, etc.)
DESSERT:	Leadership Training.

More specialised courses could form the core of a second year in the Christian Studies area.

A further factor in preparing God's people for works of service is exercise. Just taking in food and not expending the energy generated in practical exercise leads to a fat, inactive body. This principle holds true in the spiritual realm. Our people need training as well as teaching. They need to serve as well as to be spoon-fed. The church is too full of fat lambs in its crêches and bloated sheep in its pews! To change the metaphor – the great task of mission-minded leadership is to create such a warm, encouraging practical environment that the church's frozen assets will be thawed, and blessing flow to a needy world.

I thank God for those five questioning words laid at the door of my mind and heart. I lay them now before you. What is your mission strategy? You may reply, 'Your church seems larger than mine and gifted.' I say, forget the present size of your church, its present mission response, and your personal capabilities, and remember:

> But God chose the foolish things of the world to shame the wise; God chose the weak things of the world to shame the strong. He chose the lowly things of this world and the despised things – and the things that are not – to nullify the things that are, so that no one may boast before him. (1 Cor. 1:27–29)

Your church may be big and already engaged in mission. How exciting! Then you will surely be wanting to ask God, 'What next, Lord?' Our God is always the God of the regions beyond, calling us on to new ground and fresh endeavour.

The words spoken to the house of Joseph still speak to us today:

> You are very numerous and very powerful. You will have not only one allotment, but the forested hill country as well. Clear it, and its farthest limits will be yours; though they are strong, you can drive them out. (Joshua 17:17,18.)

If the Panama Canal builders, hacking their way through the dense forests, could sing their song with anticipated triumph, then so will we the Lord's people. We borrow their song with alterations, that the glory may be given where it is due:

Got any rivers you think are uncrossable?
Got any mountains you can't tunnel through?
God specialises in things thought impossible,
For HE can do what no other can do.

In the field of mission, why not try believing that, and act as
though you do believe it – 'the farthest limits will be yours!'

Chapter 9

Cranleigh Chapel, Bournemouth, Dorset

Derek Copley

Cranleigh Chapel (Open Brethren) is situated in a residential area of Bournemouth in Dorset. On a typical Sunday, around 200 people attend each service.

Of the nine members who are working overseas, seven are missionaries who are being supported by Cranleigh Chapel. Echoes, the New Tribes Mission, BMMF International and Christian Nationals are the societies in which the Chapel takes a keen interest.

Dr. Derek Copley, a former Research Scientist, is an elder of Cranleigh Chapel, in which Mr. Elfed Godding is a full-time elder. Derek Copley has undertaken church planting in this country and in the United States, and has been Principal of Moorlands Bible College since 1970.

He is married with two teenage children. His hobbies are cycling, jogging and volleyball, and he enjoys cultivating orchids. Derek Copley is the author of several books including Building with Bananas.

Cranleigh Chapel was founded in 1930 as the result of a tent campaign in the Southbourne area of Bournmouth. The membership grew steadily until 1948 when there was a serious decline which almost forced its closure. After a rescue operation by several local Christians, numbers rose to 100 by

1971. During those first forty years the church was generally regarded as a fairly typical Open Brethren Assembly. The fields on which the tent stood have long since disappeared, and the church is now in the heart of a residential area consisting of council housing, bed-sitters, flats and owner-occupied homes.

Until 1971, mission interest focused on three families and a number of societies with which the church had connections. In 1943, Mr. and Mrs. Meadows (now deceased) were commended by the church to full-time evangelism in the United Kingdom with a special concern for youth camps and children's work. Mr. and Mrs. James became part of the fellowship after being forced out of China while they were working with the China Inland Mission (now Overseas Missionary Fellowship). Mr. James continued his work among the Chinese by visiting ships docking in London. Finally there was Tony Poulson who left for training in the U.S.A. with New Tribes Mission in 1957; there he met Mary who became his wife, and together they went to Brazil.

With two missionary homes nearby, a steady stream of missionaries visited the church, and of course members who met them continued to pray for them when they went overseas. Prayer by the whole church was more or less limited to the monthly missionary prayer meeting which replaced the usual ministry and prayer time. Through the visits of missionaries, the prayer times and deputation meetings on behalf of societies like Wycliffe Bible Translators, Scripture Gift Mission, Scripture Union and the British and Foreign Bible Society, a reasonable degree of interest was generated.

On the money side, a monthly collection provided some support for individual missionaries and societies. As the years went by, many more names were added to the list of those supported and the total resources were spread thinner and thinner. The special position of Mr. Meadows and his contribution to the church was officially recognised by specified regular gifts from the General Fund, while the James family were given just small gifts twice a year. Eventually, gifts for societies were donated from the General Fund and numerous missionaries shared the proceeds of the monthly collection.

Who is where?

The church has a current membership of about 170. If we exclude those who have done only short-term service overseas, like Andrea Johanson (Indonesia with OMF), there are twenty-three members in full-time service at present. Looked at statistically, it works out at fifteen per cent, or one person in seven. Nine are actually living abroad, and a further two couples are concerned with sponsorship and training for overseas service. It means that about half are promoting mission in other countries.

1. OVERSEAS
Here is a list of church members who are currently serving God in other countries:

Tony and Mary Poulson are with the New Tribes Mission in Brazil doing pioneer work among unreached tribes. This involves language learning and putting into writing a previously unwritten language. Because Tony was a carpenter he is also able to teach crafts and skills. Both he and Mary have been house parents at a mission station in Manaus. They lost one of their children, Tim aged 11, in 1973.

Steve and Moira Poulson are with New Tribes in Senegal, reducing a language to writing among a local tribe. Moira, a qualified nurse whom Steve met during training, does dispensing and nursing. Steve has had seven years' training! Three at Moorlands Bible College, one at horticultural college, one at boot camp, one at the mission headquarters in Matlock, one in French language study, and has spent two summers on Wycliffe linguistics courses.

Marie Poulson is with New Tribes in Columbia as a house grandma, looking after children whose parents are missionaries. Now in her late sixties, she was commended to overseas service at the age of sixty-five! She is Tony and Steve's mum.

Deryck and Sandra Jones work with Echoes (a Brethren missionary agency) in Zimbabwe. Their work is mainly among the blacks and involves preaching, youth work, women's ministry, Bible studies, army work and Emmaus courses. Deryck comes from a missionary family: his parents worked in Zaïre and Zimbabwe. Both were trained at Moorlands Bible College.

Rodney and Ruth Dibden. Rod is doing secular work to support the family while they work for God in Spain by helping a local church. During the summer months they are involved in the distribution and translation of literature with the Gospel Literature Outreach.

2. AT HOME

Derek and Esther Redpath work with Lindley Training, whose aim is to witness to young people while providing them with courses designed to help them with their personal development. Derek is involved in marketing the courses and Esther is Financial Administrator and Secretary to the Director.

Stuart Redpath works with Lindley Training as an instructor to sixteen- to eighteen-year-olds, helping them to understand themselves better and to be more effective in their day-to-day relationships.

Elfed and Jackie Godding. Elfed is a full-time elder. Along with Jackie, his main task is to co-ordinate the pastoral work of the church. He does about twenty per cent of the church's teaching and preaching. They also lead Koinonia, a fellowship group for people in their twenties, and the team which disciples new converts. Both trained at Moorlands Bible College.

Mary Austin works at Pilgrim Hall as Conference Secretary. Mary is qualified in hotel work and catering and has completed a three-year course at Moorlands Bible College. She followed college with three years' teaching at a Christian English language school.

John and Kim Oliver. John has worked since 1980 with Frontier Youth Trust in London. After training at London Bible College, he worked with the YMCA, then a Christian-sponsored open club in London, the Mayflower Centre, and The Newham Local Authority Youth Club.

Bill and Gladys Cotton returned in 1983 from missionary work with Echoes in Bolivia and Argentina. Bill is a tutor in Old Testament Studies at Moorlands Bible College.

3. AT HOME WITH OVERSEAS LINKS

David and Rowena Holt. David, formerly a long-distance lorry driver, works with Christian Nationals, an organisation specialising in sponsoring the training of nationals overseas. His particular area of responsibility is the promotion of theological training. Rowena is a qualified chef, and works at a local school. David spent three years at Moorlands Bible College.

Derek and Nancy Copley are both working at Moorlands Bible College which prepares pastors, evangelists, and missionaries. Derek is the principal and Nancy teaches English. Both are active at Cranleigh: Derek is an elder and Nancy is leader of the Junior Church. Derek is also on the Executive Committee of the Evangelical Alliance and the Personnel Committee of BMMF International.

'Home grown' or adopted?

If we look at the twenty-three people in full-time service, about half are 'home grown'. By that we mean they came up through the Sunday school and youth work, or their conversion as adults took place through the witness of the church.

Marie Poulson and her two sons have been closely involved in the church since the early 1950s and both Tony and Steve became Christians at an early age. Rodney and Ruth Dibden, John Oliver and Deryck Jones were converted as teenagers. Derek and Esther Redpath became Christians in 1979 as a result of the changed life of their teenage daughter Nicky. The fourth member of the family, Stuart, came to know Christ at a youth camp where I was the padre in 1980.

Of the thirteen 'adopted' people, Moira, Mary, Sandra and Kim's connections are through their husbands. The rest have transferred membership from other churches – Mary Austin from a URC church in Kingston, the Holts from an Assembly in Dorchester, the Goddings from an Assembly in Greenford, and the Copleys from an FIEC church in Manchester. The Cottons came to us from Argentina but were not originally commended by us.

Choosing the right people

In the past, entry into full-time service was much more of an individual affair, without the elders or church playing a really significant role. The same was true generally – people became involved in church activities as they 'felt led'. For example, the recognition of the missionary call to Tony and Mary Poulson came *after* they had left for Brazil and had returned on furlough.

Although the 'waiting for volunteers' procedure still applies to some extent, it is now being replaced by more positive action by the elders. Over the past few years, they have begun to recognise in practical terms that every Christian has at least one spiritual gift to be used in God's service. So they try to guide individual members towards the discovery of their gifts and then to locate the appropriate sphere of service.

Church members who want guidance about their futures may ask to talk to one or two elders, or even the whole group of seven. We feel that it is especially important for those considering full-time service to discuss it with the elders at an early stage rather than presenting them with a *fait accompli* before any advice and direction has been given. At various points along the way, the church is usually asked to pray concerning God's will for the prospective candidates. Since 1970, there has been some form of commissioning service for all those entering short- or long-term service at home or overseas.

Sometimes this process may take a year or two, because the candidate may not yet be sufficiently mature or experienced. The question of training must also be considered. About half our group of twenty-three have been through two or three years of formal Bible College training. (Others have either been given specific preparation by their missionary society or have not trained at all except through their work in the church.) Will Ross is an example. He is now twenty-four years old. Several years ago he was gently approached by an elder and asked to consider the possibility of giving up his job to go to Bible College. Today he is a student at Moorlands.

Who looks after the missionaries?

On average, our missionaries receive two or three letters a month. Mr. and Mrs. Nash are officially responsible for writing regularly, often when missionaries need to be informed about gifts being forwarded. They hear from other people too, like Sunday Takeaway (a group of younger teenagers). We try to make sure they get plenty of news about church life. This is especially valuable because it ensures that when missionaries come home on furlough they don't feel too left out. And the more we tell them, the more effectively they will be able to pray for us too.

To Steve and Moira we send tapes of the ministry of Derek Stringer who visits us once or twice a year for several weeks. On the first Monday of each month one of the elders, Colin Richards, talks to them on the telephone. Steve keeps in radio contact with his base during that particular day to make sure that the news is up-to-date.

The information missionaries send us for prayer is channelled through to the prayer meetings, family services, and youth groups. Their prayer letters are distributed by Mr. and Mrs. Nash. Occasionally they send us tapes and slides, which we find very helpful because these enable us to see and hear what they are doing.

We are especially fortunate with furloughs because there is a missionary home next door but one to the church. This is administered by the Bournemouth Missionary Homes Trustees, two of whom are from Cranleigh. A deacon and his wife (Reg and Eileen Cook) get the home ready when it is needed; this includes stocking the larder with food. The missionaries pay only the day-to-day running costs of heat, light and telephone calls.

The missionaries' diaries are organised by Colin Richards in advance of their arrival. This not only introduces them to other churches who might not know of their work, but also guarantees that our own church gets plenty of their time, and ensures that they have real opportunities to visit friends and relatives as well as taking time off for rest and relaxation.

Money

During the five years 1971-5 out of a total church income of around £3000, an average of £500 a year (i.e. seventeen per cent) was divided between our missionaries and ten societies. It meant that the missionaries received only tiny gifts. A church meeting in 1975 approved two dramatic changes of policy. Firstly, all our missionary money would go to our own people (and none to the societies) and secondly, our overseas giving would be increased by 300 per cent over the next year. To achieve that faith target, two offerings were taken each Sunday. One was for the running of the church and the other for the missionaries. The 1975 figure of £643 jumped to £1916 the following year. In percentage terms it rose from seventeen per cent to thirty-five per cent!

Since then, we have taken the decision to support Derek Stringer for two or three months a year and Elfed and Jackie full time. The result is that we now give about forty per cent to those in full-time service, but the proportion going to those overseas has dropped back to fifteen per cent. In cash terms the total of £1,916 in 1976 has only grown to £4,500 in 1983. On the other hand, we musn't forget that large sums of money have been channelled elsewhere. In 1979, the house next door was purchased for £20,000, and in 1983, the seating capacity of the church was increased from 200 to 300 at a cost of £50,000.

Our missionary support is undoubtedly in decline compared to the cost of living. But we must also bear in mind that last year, for example, we donated £1,000 to Steve and Moira to help them build their home, £175 to the missionary homes, £304 to David and Rowena (Christian Nationals), £300 to Andrea in Indonesia, £339 to TEAR Fund and £51 to Steve and Moira on a recent visit to the U.K.

What influenced people to go overseas?

Past influences. Meeting lots of missionaries has clearly made a big impact over the past fourteen years. Some have been missionaries sent out by us and who have come back for home leave. Others were not 'our' missionaries at all, like Colin and Cynthia Tilsley. Colin was the director of Gospel Literature Outreach and for several years, until 1974, had his headquarters only a few streets away from the church. Cynthia did an enormous amount of entertaining of church members in their home. As a result they generated considerable interest in mission, and quite a number of Cranleigh people became involved in GLO projects in France.

Although they lived locally for rather shorter periods of time, the Joneses senior (parents), ı Colin and Hazel Phillips (Columbia), and Mr. and Mrs. Pratten (India) rubbed shoulders with us enough to impart significant missionary vision.

The monthly visits of missionary speakers have contributed to our knowledge of what God is doing overseas. During my time as the missionary secretary I invited a number of overseas nationals to address the church (most were students at Moorlands). We have also 'adopted' Teklu Tesso (who can't easily return to Ethiopia) after finishing at College and we look forward to his visits.

The Tilsleys were especially influential because they were with us for several years. We still benefit enormously from having several ex-missionaries permanently with us. I have worked among American Indians and spent time in Europe and Asia. Muriel Chalkley served God in Kenya until her retirement. Jennie Steggles had previously been in India. On the U.K. side we have Mr. Chapman and Mr. and Mrs. Cleave who formerly worked with the London City Mission.

Present influences. I have to admit that our missionary teaching is really quite weak. At present it does not form a substantial proportion of the time allotted, compared to doctrine and Bible exposition. It tends to be arranged only on a one-off basis, when someone suitable is available. Fortunately this weakness is counteracted to some degree by a considerable number of formal and informal activities which generate interest in mission, and so the church has a missionary atmosphere.

One mid-week meeting in four is allocated to missionary speakers. This is followed by a prayer time which focusses mainly on our members living overseas. As a result, I would say that most of the congregation have some knowledge and interest in several areas of the world. Recent visits have included Cecil Sirwardene (with Christian Nationals in Ceylon), Dan Pastie (Pocket Testament League in Russia) and Mike Donovan (Africa Inland Mission). On the whole, our intercessory prayer times have not been particularly intensive or dynamic in recent months. Some people undoubtedly pray privately for our missionaries but it is difficult to tell whether most people do so.

Information on mission reaches people from several sources like the church library, the bookstall, the noticeboard, magazines such as *Echoes*, and *Brown Gold*, as well as prayer letters. Items of special interest are often selected from these and inserted in the weekly newsheet. Often, when a letter has just reached us, items for praise and prayer are read out at any of the normal services.

As well as officiallly organised activities related to mission, there are several initiatives such as the sponsoring of orphans in India by the Junior Church children. One of the teenagers, Andrew Green, has recently been promoting interest in a Scripture Union project in Peru. And there are individuals who give money and pray for the work of Christian Nationals. Although few in number, there are some who attend missionary conventions.

We must also include Moorlands Bible College as a past and present influence. The involvement of staff and students in the life of the church has increased steadily since the college was re-established locally in 1970. At present about ten students and several staff families regularly worship with us, and a number of third-year students have been allocated to us in order to gain practical Christian service experience under the supervision of elders.

To sum up

Clearly the sovereign God has touched the hearts of those now involved in full-time service. Yet it would not be unspiritual to try to work out logically why so many have been sent out. There are probably four key factors leading to the rapid increase from 1980 onwards.

1. A deepening of church life began in the late seventies. This was caused by the gentle breeze of the Holy Spirit combined with systematic teaching on the need to serve God using the service gifts provided by him.

2. What followed were more open and loving relationships within the fellowship. The gradual releasing of love for God and his people led to a desire to reach out to the unconverted living locally and overseas. In 1981 there were nineteen adult conversions.

3. There was an improvement in pastoral care leading to

greater personal growth and consecration. The appointment of Elfed Godding as pastoral co-ordinator made it possible for members to be cared for and built up far more effectively. The quality and scope of teaching steadily improved as more gifts developed among the elders, deacons and others. As people grew and were encouraged to discover God's will for their lives, those who were called by God to do so left their jobs.

4. The unusually large number of missionary influences over the last fourteen years have made a major impact. People were affected more by those they rubbed shoulders with than by words from the pulpit. To some extent this has compensated for the weak missionary teaching programme.

Where now?

There are three areas which need strengthening: our giving, teaching and praying. Taking on several large commitments has forced us to hold missionary giving at a level well below what it should be compared to the cost of living. Since we have been willing to aim at huge faith targets for other personnel and buildings, maybe we need to re-examine how much goes overseas.

Our teaching has improved beyond all recognition in the past ten years. Around 1975 I drew up a five-year plan to cover the whole Bible, the major doctrines and practical subjects like evangelism, ethics and Christian lifestyle. What I didn't do was to include a syllabus on the principles and practice of mission. Soon we are due for some major re-organisation of leadership responsibilities and the new pulpit committee will undoubtedly put mission high on the agenda.

Few churches find intercessory prayer easy. You can't whip people into being enthusiastic about the kind of praying which is costly. Yet our missionaries and those whom they are serving need that kind of commitment from us. The appointment of an elder to promote overseas service and prayer concern will be made later this year. It won't guarantee that we will have a burden to pray but it will begin to move us in the right direction.

Chapter 10

Elim Church, Portsmouth

Susan Jones

The Elim Church in Portsmouth's City Centre is situated opposite the main shopping precinct. In total there are about 450 people who attend the services on an average Sunday.

The church does not support individual missionaries, as all funds allocated to overseas work are channelled through the Elim Missionary Society.

Len Cowdery has been the pastor of the Elim Church in Portsmouth since 1977. He is married to Bridget and they have three grown-up sons and four grandchildren.

Mrs. Susan Jones, the author of this chapter, is a member of the Elim Church and is a journalist by profession. Until 1981 she was the local government reporter for Portsmouth's local newspaper. She now works from home.

Susan and her husband Graham have two young children and they are expecting a third child. When she has time, Susan enjoys relaxing with a good book.

This chapter is included to show how an individual church can take the initiative and make a major impact by concerted effort.

Terry was horrified. Flashing up on his television screen were scenes of unimagined deprivation. The sorry tale of the Polish people's struggle for survival against the daily threat of food shortages and the associated problems of a floundering economy was being unfolded. Now political unrest was throwing up a new threat. The Soviet Union, undoubtedly disturbed by the activities of the free trade union, 'Solidarity', was closely monitoring that part of its bloc – presumably with a view to intervention.

These were not the problems of a remote African state. This was Europe, and the scenes contained in the late-night documentary were enough to move anyone to prayer. But for Terry Wiseman, the church secretary, it was more than just moving. For the people being subjected to this hardship were his friends. Just seven months earlier, he had organised a ministry trip to Poland from Portsmouth's Elim Pentecostal Church. The gospel singing group, 'Sons and Daughters', was asked by the denomination's European Missions Director, Brian Edwards, to tour Poland. In April 1981, armed with some extra chocolate supplies and some fairly vague notions about how expensive everything would be, a coach-load of youngsters set off.

What they found was eye-opening. A shop the size of an average British supermarket might be chock-full with row upon row of pickles, for instance, or vinegar. The hostesses who threw open their homes to 'Sons and Daughters' spent hours queuing for more basic essentials. But at least then a patient wait outside a shop was likely to be rewarded by a loaf of bread. What was being shown on the November documentary was far, far worse.

Seven miles away, Terry's lifelong friend, David Keeping, was watching the same programme. He, too, was stunned by the scenes, and dogged by the same feeling of being powerless to help his Polish friends.

He telephoned Terry and found he shared his conviction that they had to do something, however small, to help. Launching a mercy mission into a foreign country would be a new experience for them both. But they were convinced it was right – and so began the start of a modern-day missionary work which was to spread rapidly over the following three years. It was to provide the strife-torn Polish people with hundreds of thousands of pounds' worth of vital food and medical supplies.

Food collection in the precinct

The first step, though, was to get the full backing of the

ministry team and eldership of the Portsmouth church. Terry and David outlined their proposal to remove the seats of the church coach, cram it with food and clothing, and make what they presumed would be a one-off mercy-dash to the Polish towns they had visited the preceding Easter. With the blessing of the church authorities, Terry, David and Assistant Minister John Harris with a team of workers embarked on an intensive three-week programme of fund-raising, sorting, buying, contacting local companies for provisions, and sifting through the necessary paper-work. It seemed a monumental task to fill a coach. But the money came in steadily. Church members manned the coach for two Saturdays, offering information to harrassed shoppers in Portsmouth's shopping precinct. Some people took out an extra supermarket trolley and wheeled one load to the coach to give to the Polish mission. Others gave the odd tin or packet. Altogether the general public gave £2,200 in cash and a quarter of a ton of food over those two days.

Terry, David and the organising team had envisaged taking up to six tons of food to Poland on the first trip. Two days before they were due to leave they loaded up for the trial run. As the coach chugged through the side-streets round the inner-city Portsmouth church, its exhaust pipe dragging on the ground, it was obvious the supplies were too abundant. The vehicle would never make the 1,600 mile trip weighed down as it was. At the last minute, Dave Elmes, a church member with a greengrocery business, kindly agreed to part with a precious van and some of the boxes were off-loaded.

Two more volunteers were quickly drafted into the 'mission team' to drive the van. Eight men left Portsmouth for Poland, including the Minister of the church, Len Cowdery. At the East German border, they were held up for four hours while guards examined their load to ensure it tallied with what they had declared. It was here that they encountered their first snow – and it did not stop until they arrived back in Hampshire, twelve miles from home, eight exhausting days later. One morning in Poland, one of the team went to the back of the coach to cook some eggs for breakfast and found they had frozen. The temperature was minus 22 degrees.

First impressions of Poland

That previous visit by the 'Sons and Daughters' group had at least given the team some inkling of the financial straits of the Polish people. Barely had the coach gone through the checkpoint on that earlier Easter trip, when they reached a railway crossing. At their approach the barrier descended and the driver paused waiting for the train to come. Almost immediately a small boy appeared from the signalman's house and began cleaning the coach windows. He was followed by his father who asked for money for the work, and then for English or American money in exchange for his Polish zlotys. These are practically worthless compared, say, to the dollar with which people could, at that stage, buy imported goods in the city's dollar shops. When the man and his son had left, the railway barrier was raised and the group continued on their way. No train ever appeared.

Another insight into the make-up of the Polish people was gleaned by the group when they visited Auschwitz, the infamous Prisoner of War camp. Without exception they were deeply moved by the visit. As Terry Wiseman observed, up to that point they were all quite ignorant about the nation they were visiting, and the people whom they were later to be called by God to help. To pass through those grim gates, and head towards the building where thousands of Poles and people of other nationalities were tortured and butchered during the Second World War was a chastening experience. Hearing about the various forms of horrible, agonising death suffered by so many people at Auschwitz (those who had carbolic acid injected straight into their hearts, or the pregnant women 'experimented' on without anaesthetic) deepened the youngsters' awareness of the nation's recent past, and explained something about the people's national characteristics. The fact that it was the Russians who liberated them then, and the same country suppressing their freedom forty years later, struck the group as an irony.

Arguably the most successful stop-off in the 'Sons and Daughters' tour of 1981 was their last, in a place called Nysa, in the south-west of Poland. Here in the United Evangelical Church of Poland, where Janek Cieslar was minister, the group sang to a packed hall with an overflow of eager people outside. One of the group, Nigel Fisher, recorded that people were open to the Word of God. There were marvellous worship and prayer times, tears flowed and more than forty hands were raised by people asking for prayer. A young man who was due to go into a mental hospital was prayed over and delivered from his problem, and a member of the church commented that it was some while since the Holy Spirit had moved as he did during that meeting.

Janek Cieslar – or 'Pastor Jan' as he became known to the Portsmouth church – was to become a vital link in the mission to Poland. He spoke fluent English, which was a definite advantage as he was able to organise the distribution of food in the other towns, and deal with the minsterial side of the work. So strong were the links forged between Portsmouth Elim and Jan's church, that it thrilled the congregation to welcome him and his wife and family to England in May 1983. This was a miracle in itself, since the authorities are extremely reluctant to allow a whole family to leave the country, for fear that they will defect.

On the first food-carrying trip to Poland, Terry Wiseman and his team revisited the towns toured by 'Sons and Daughters'. This included Nysa where they sought out Jan to renew his friendship and get some direction from him. Communications between England and Poland were bad and there had been no chance to let Jan know they were coming. As the Portsmouth coach and van drew up outside his house, Jan was driving in from the opposite direction. He was bringing a visiting American preacher back from Opole, a nearby town, and as they travelled, Jan recounted to the visitor the good time his church had during the 'Sons and Daughters' tour the previous Easter. He was still in the middle of the story of his Portsmouth friends' visit as he rounded the corner – and stared in amazement at the English coach standing outside his front door. They were back!

The team had quite an itinerary to get through, so once they had unpacked and rested for a while, they were back on the road. Unloading for all the nine trips to Poland followed the same pattern. A church base was used, and workers from the church helped to sort the goods into parcels in quantities suitable for the family for whom they were intended – larger amounts for families, smaller packages for single people.

Despite the desperate shortages of basic necessities, the teams never once witnessed any shows of greed or panic in the distribution. Everything was carried out in an extremely ordered way, and no matter how unexpected the visitors from the West were, there were always church volunteers available to sort out the provisions.

Pictures that will always remain

Some of the sights witnessed at the distribution points were very moving. Soap is a rare commodity in Poland, and even if someone is fortunate to come by a bar, at £7 a time, it will not be the sweet-smelling article we are used to. It is more likely to resemble the hardware soap with which our mothers used to scrub floors.

One Portsmouth lad has a picture printed indelibly on his mind of a young girl's face as she lifted up a bar of scented soap to smell its perfume. The look of wonder crossing her features as she handled and smelled what to him was a mundane object, almost moved him to tears. Learning what goods cost in Poland was an object lesson to everyone. Shampoo was on sale for £15 a bottle, eggs were £3 each and coffee, a much-prized article, was an astonishing £20 for a two-pound jar. It was coffee which smoothed the way through many a border barrier, since the team did not have the other highly-prized beverage – whiskey – on board. Many a British housewife would find it difficult to make the house-keeping money stretch to these sky-high prices. Imagine, then, the plight of the Polish housewife, surviving on the average wage of £45 a month.

Literally most of a Polish housewife's day is spent in queueing outside any shop where it is rumoured that a new influx of provisions is expected. She has to rack her brains to stretch what few resources she has to hand. The results can be pretty bizarre to pampered British palates. Without exception the Polish people gave their best to their visitors from Portsmouth. Nevertheless, there were some memorable meals for the team on various occasions. Ravenous after a long journey, Dave Keeping once bit into a 'sausage' he was given, only to find to his horror that it was skin filled with pearl barley! The 'coffee' served up in the poorer homes was sometimes boiling water poured over brown rice, and 'tea' could be brewed from celery.

At one point, bread had become virtually unobtainable, and David Keeping's wife, Rene, thought it would be a sensible move for him to take over bread mixes from Britain. Naturally, the instructions on the packet were not bi-lingual, which resulted in Dave, an elder of the Portsmouth church, giving an impromptu late-night cookery demonstration to a pastor's wife – a scene he has not repeated at home!

For the sake of the children

For parents in the midst of the kind of privation which Poland is undergoing, it is far more painful to see the children having to go without than to miss out on luxuries themselves. During the December 1981 trip, the team got lost looking for the pastor's house in Lublin and by 'chance' drew up outside a mother and baby welfare clinic. A Hampshire company, John Wyeth, had given a large consignment of S.M.A. baby milk and other food and goods to the Portsmouth church for distribution. Some of the team went inside the building to ask directions, and came across the mothers and their babies and toddlers queueing to see a doctor. It was the work of a moment for them to go back to bring in some supplies of baby food, and the look of gratitude on the faces of the doctor and mothers may be imagined. Malnutrition is becoming a prevalent threat in a country starved of resources, and as always it is the very young and the old who are most at risk.

Outside, a young mother was making her way along the road to the clinic, pulling a sleigh through the thick snow with her year-old baby on it. Drawing up alongside the coach she caught sight of the team unloading the baby food and clothing, and gasped audibly. She was invited to board the coach and asked to pick out what she needed for her baby. She was not able to speak English but communicated that she needed food and clothes. Again the vivid image imprinted on the memory of a team-member is of a young woman pulling her sleigh with her child and a precious load of goods back down the road.

It was children who were responsible for the near-arrest of two of the Portsmouth men on a subsequent visit to Nysa in February 1982. The lorry had stopped and some curious youngsters came up to take a peep. Brian Hanley and Barry Martin gave them some chocolates, and soon many more children magically appeared, until a crowd of fifty or more surrounded the vehicle. One of the team began to take some pictures of the delighted young faces – and in a trice the police were on the scene. The 'offenders', Barry and Brian, were taken into the police car and their passports were removed. It seemed the authorities were concerned that the photographs would be used for propaganda purposes, casting a slur on the lifestyle in this small corner of the Soviet bloc. Happily, at this juncture, the pastor of the church they were heading for appeared and explained what the English team was doing and they were released. There were a few other occasions when the team had near misses with the authorities. But they always came through unscathed and felt that they were travelling with God's loving protection around them.

Brian Hanley recalled one other occasion on which he was struck forcibly by the effect of Poland's hardship on the children. He was staying with a family in Bielsko-Biala. By comparison his hosts were well off, since it is a rural area with more scope for bartering. At the home where he was staying was a small girl, about the same age as his own three-year-old, Emma-Sue. After giving her a lollipop which she savoured with a relish rarely seen in the more blasé children of Western Europe, Brian produced a pair of slippers with clowns' faces on. She wore her prized possessions non-stop from then on. Said Brian, 'She was so happy to have a pair of slippers. It made me think that if such a small thing could cause a child so much happiness, the whole trip must be worthwhile'.

Confirmation of the call

The circumstances surrounding the first food team's departure from Poland, in December 1981, were perhaps what singled out the work as being a mission from God, and confirmed in the hearts of the Portsmouth congregation their belief that the church had been called to this work. The evening before the team was due to leave, the weather was extremely inclement.

Huddled in Pastor Jan Cieslar's cosy home, they watched the snow building up outside as the barometer fell. Poised over their maps, Terry and his friends were asking Jan's advice on the best way back to the border. It was eleven p.m. and looking at the thick pelt of snow outside, Jan begged his friends to stay overnight and leave the next day. It was a tempting proposition, but the team agreed that they should leave as planned in order not to worry their families at home.

They left Poland on December 11th. Next day martial law was declared. Had the Portsmouth folk stayed for an extra night, they would have certainly been caught up in the early days of imposition of martial law, because for the first three weeks there was a complete curfew.

Terry Wiseman recalled the amazement he and the others shared when they arrived home and first heard about the declaration of martial law on television news flashes:

'We couldn't believe it,' he said. 'We had noticed a military presence as we made our way out of Poland, and we had wondered whether the troops were Russian or General Jarulsewski's. When we got back and heard the news, though, we knew why we had been called to go to Poland at that particular time. While the curfew was in force, people couldn't go out, even to get shopping. You have to bear in mind that this is a country where it is impossible to build up a store cupboard of food, as housewives would in Britain. Polish women spend hours queueing for that day's food. So many would have been confined to their homes with little or no food to see them through the curfew.'

Generosity in the face of hardship

Because a core of people in a church far away from Poland had been tuned in to the will of God, some of his people in that strife-torn country had enough supplies to see them through the period. For some of those Christians, too, their food parcels were a means of testifying to their Christian faith. Pastor Jan had a neighbour who was a devout member of the Communist Party. Party membership is not compulsory in Poland (though of course, the people live according to Soviet dictate) and it is only a small minority of political activists who join. As a gesture of good will, Jan shared some of his food with his neighbour. He was astonished. In Jan's position, he remarked, he would not have shared food with him. All the same, he was grateful for it.

By no means was the sharing one-sided, though. Whatever the Polish Christians had, they shared with their friends from England – to the point of embarrassment. In the end, trip organisers had to warn those going on the food trips not to admire openly any ornament, picture or household article. No sooner would they have uttered the words, than the host removed the article and gave it to his visitor. Generosity abounded in other ways, too. The first time 'Sons and Daughters' toured Poland, lines were down and it was impossible to communicate from one county to another. The people of Lodz did not even realize the group was coming. Yet enough people, not all of them young, willingly slept on the floor to give 30 youngsters a bed for the night. On another occasion, two of the girls were staying in a house with Polish Christians, and early one morning one got up to go to the bathroom. Taking a wrong turn, she wound up in the kitchen and stumbled on the whole family sleeping on the floor. They had all forsaken their beds to give their tired young visitors a good night's sleep.

Poland's old people seem particularly hardy. Possibly the war years helped to cultivate their attitude. Travelling towards Lodz one night, the coach stopped to pick up an elderly man making his way towards the town in quite thick snow. He was about fifteen miles from his destination, and told the team he was setting off at that time of night to be in time for work next morning. But for their lift, he would have walked all the way. There are no concessions for women, either. Equal rights is in force with a vengeance, so that an all-women workforce repairing the roads is not an unusual sight.

Day-to-day miracles

Once they had made a few trips to Poland with 'hauls' of food and clothing, God opened up a way for the Portsmouth Christians to take over a consignment of sorely-needed medical supplies. There is a shortage of even the most basic equipment – bandages, disinfectant and plaster for example – in the country. Trip organisers were to witness many miracles in the way the supplies came pouring in for them to take across Europe. Local firms were incredibly generous in giving to the cause, so that an estimated £110,000 worth of medicines went to Poland on one trip.

A straightforward telephone call from Terry Wiseman to a medical company's public relations department produced hundreds of pounds' worth of paediatric suspension, antibiotics and syringes. The Gosport company, Cyanamid, donated £40,000 worth of medical supplies and there was more S.M.A. baby milk from Johnson and Johnson.

A massive consignment of vitamin tablets – more than a million of them – were given to the Polish cause. The firm concerned had accepted an order from a West African country, which then could not afford to buy the tablets; rather than waste them, they gave them to Terry for distribution. It seemed they were just waiting for his call. In a country where citrus fruits and vegetables are a rare sight indeed, vitamin tablets can make all the difference to people's health.

But one of the biggest miracles was the team's acquisition of some breathing apparatus. During the first trip carrying medical supplies, Polish doctors told David Ford, a general practitioner in Portsmouth and a church elder, that respirators were desperately needed for children. It seemed like a tall order. David Ford got the church praying and began his search for the apparatus. His first setback was to find that British hospital authorities regarded as obsolete the type of equipment needed by their counterparts in Poland. In Britain, respirators are powered by compressed air which is unavailable to the Poles who operate their machines by means of a small motor. Even if the respirators were available they would cost £5,000 each, David discovered. Undeterred, he pursued his inquiries with the Area Health Authority and tracked down two of the type of machines the Poles required. They had stood idle, though in perfect working condition, in a Portsmouth hospital for eighteen months, ousted by more modern equipment. The authority named an extremely reasonable price.

David helped to take the medical supplies, including the precious respirators, in April 1983. He presented one to Nysa Hospital – an event which was televised and reported in the State-controlled papers. Hardship was evident at the hospital. Apart from the lack of supplies, the building was in a bad state of repair with falling plaster and tatty paintwork. Dr. Ford had expected Nysa hospital to take charge of both respirators, but the Regional Director of the Health Service asked if the team would mind taking one on to Opole. Here David was met by a doctor who presented him with a previously prepared comprehensive list of medical requirements. Right at the bottom she recorded the item she told David he would have the most difficulty in obtaining. It was a respirator – the exact make the team had brought with them.

The experience astonished David. He was stunned by the Lord's attention to detail. And the repercussions were great. The ability of the Portsmouth church to meet some of Poland's crushing medical needs was to contribute to the opening of the door to evangelism on a mass scale as 'Sons and Daughters' toured the country a second time. This, David felt, was surely God's direct response to the Polish churches' fervent prayers for a new outpouring of his Spirit, just before Portsmouth Elim was formulating its plans to make the first visit to the country. Poland proved again to Dr. Ford that his Lord, while working on a large scale, has an absorbing interest in individual people. On one winter trip, David met a woman who had undergone an operation for cataracts, but could not subsequently get the right lenses for her glasses. He brought back the appropriate prescription and the glasses were made up in Britain. On a return visit he had the great joy of fitting the glasses on the woman, enabling her to see for the first time in many years.

From the beginning of Portsmouth Elim's mission to Poland, the prime movers in the work had felt that their calling was to meet the prevalent physical needs of their brothers and sisters in Christ. As a by-product of that there were, of course, spiritual blessings – but the team and the church were united first in their efforts to get provisions to Poland. As Terry Wiseman put it:

> The Polish venture has brought a lot of people together in the church and given them the opportunity to minister, perhaps in a small way, such as sorting through clothes to send. I believe it has given us all the first tangible evidence that there is a social aspect to the Gospel, that there is more to our faith than merely preaching the Word and where we are able to give physical help we must.
>
> I didn't think at the beginning that I would see some of

the things I have. And the absolute miracles we have seen
would not have happened unless God wanted us in the
work we are doing. At one stage, for example, two of the
team were issued with visas for Poland in ninety minutes –
which is unheard of. God has prompted us to do this work.

A time of blessing and spiritual enrichment

Despite the emphasis of the mission being on the practical,
there have been times of great blessing and many spiritual
lessons were learned. Perhaps this was particularly so when
'Sons and Daughters' made their second tour in April 1983,
taking along some of the medical equipment, and during
another singing tour by Canadian Gospel singer Ginny
Ambrose-Bridle, accompanied by Portsmouth people and
supported by the church, in the following September.

The two years between the two 'Sons and Daughters' tours
made a world of difference to the reception the group were
given, both by the authorities and by the general public. As far
as the Polish authorities were concerned, it seemed that the
trips to bring food and medical supplies paved the way for a
smooth passage for the singing group and some extremely
civil gestures. 'Sons and Daughters' were the first group of
their kind to be allowed into the country after the imposition
of martial law. And there were some more pretty significant
'firsts' to follow.

As usual, the Portsmouth crowd stopped off first at Pastor
Jan's church in Nysa, where they discovered the authorities'
first gesture of kindness had been to allow them use of the
town's social club to share their meals with their Polish
friends. Secondly, the group was allowed to perform in Nysa
Theatre. When Jan was in Britain shortly after their visit, he
told the Portsmouth church that it was the first time since the
Second World War that the Gospel had been publicly
proclaimed in the town. Inside the church, he is free to preach
salvation through the cross of Jesus Christ. Outside, however,
there must be no advertising to indicate what is going on in
the church, or its beliefs.

This, then, was a tremendous opportunity. Of the 700
people crammed into the theatre, an estimated 400 were non-
Christians. Many surged forward after the concert to talk to

the group and members of the Nysa church, for as long as they would stand with them.

There was a similar scene at Cieszin on the Czechoslovakian border, the next town where the group performed. As they arrived they were greeted by large posters in the town square advertising the Gospel concert – the first ever to be held in the public hall, a converted cinema. Here the people began queueing outside the hall an hour and a half before the concert was due to begin. About 350, many of whom were not Christians, managed to cram into the hall and it was packed to capacity.

In Bielsko-Biala another 300 curious Poles turned up at the Cultural Building concert hall on the first night – again a very public place – to hear the group. It was yet another indication of the spiritual thirst among the people of that highly religious country.

The second evening in Bielsko was a great time of blessing. This time there were an estimated 500 people in the hall, who were immensely receptive to the Word given by Dr. David Ford on the subject of divine healing. All those taking part were conscious of the close presence of God. Nigel Fisher recorded in his daily note-book:

Many came forward for salvation, to receive gifts of the Spirit and prayer for release from drug addiction. This part of Poland is the worst for drug pushing and many came forward asking for prayer to kick the habit.

One Polish brother spent time in prisoner of war camp during the Second World War and someone had fired a gun near his eyes, so that he suffered from the appearance of eleven spots before his eyes. He was at the concert the first night and Ginny Ambrose-Bridle said she would pray for him the following night. He stepped out in faith and on his way to the meeting God took away nine of the spots. We are trusting that the other two spots will also be removed. Praise the Lord for miracles!

Terry Bridle was praying for a Polish lady who was due to go into hospital to have an operation. As Terry and others prayed with her, she experienced a warm sensation where her illness was. God had started to work in this person.

On their last night in Bielsko, 'Sons and Daughters' were

asked to do two concerts and there were audiences of between 800 and 1,000 at both houses. People came forward freely for salvation, healing and prayer, and during the second concert many Christians raised their hands as a signal that they wished to rededicate their lives to Christ.

Opole was the last venue on the tour, and as a conciliatory and friendly gesture, the Party official who was to take David Ford round the hospital later and take delivery of the respirator, offered to show the group round the town. He even arranged a special horse-riding expedition for a couple of the girls who expressed interest and laid on a horse-drawn carriage to take the group round Opole's open-air museum. That night more than 600 residents poured into the concert hall to hear the singing, while others grouped round the exits or listened outside in the reception area, as the concert was taped for a radio broadcast. The tour ended on a spiritually high note; only the illness of two of the group, who had to drop out of the concert, marred it.

Trials

Illness was just one of the problems to dog the tour carried out by Ginny Ambrose-Bridle, her husband Terry and assorted musicians and friends in September 1983. But when the problems were overcome, the group enjoyed such a powerful time of blessing with the Polish people that they knew their difficulties were brought about by being caught up in the middle of some spiritual warfare, and praised God that he had gained the glory rather than the enemy.

Trouble began shortly after the group set out in a Mercedes coach loaded with food and medical supplies. Almost as soon as they had crossed the Channel the coach began to play up. Several times the group stopped to pray over the vehicle. But just as they approached the West German border with Holland the engine died. The coach was towed to Venlo in Holland, from where they made some SOS calls back to England, to no avail. Eventually they contacted Terry Wiseman and asked whether he could make arrangments for them to go on to Poland. Within twenty-four hours he had organised a rescue party with a car and a hired minibus, sorted out the various insurance transactions, including that for the recovery of the coach, and the group was on its way again.

Travelling in a twelve-seater minibus mile upon mile was extremely cramped and uncomfortable and to add to the problems, one of the team had his coat stolen, with the minibus keys in the pocket. They had to break in and rig the leads with a screwdriver as a makeshift ignition device. Another of the lads lost his passport.

On top of all this, Ginny contracted a virus. She carried on with the concert tour until their last night, when just as the audience was clamouring for an encore, she collapsed in the wings and was carried to her dressing room. There was general agreement that she was too ill to stand the drive home – so husband Terry was forced to leave his wife in a foreign country to be flown home when she was strong enough. Happily, they were reunited shortly afterwards.

There have been other problems involved with Portsmouth's mission to Poland. On one recent trip, Terry Wiseman and John Harris were held for some hours by the East German authorities – a terrifying experience – but allowed to go unscathed. But in one sense the church would be worried if there was no evidence of opposition, and start to question whether they were still in the will of God, since the enemy was showing no interest in thwarting them.

As it is, they have that evidence, and also the encouragement of seeing many other churches and organisations heeding the call to take essential supplies to God's people in Poland. And the Portsmouth work will continue for as long as the church senses that they are doing God's perfect will in retaining the link with the Poles.

Appendix 1
Mission Policy, Gold Hill Baptist Church

Introduction

Gold Hill Baptist Church is administered by elders, five of whom are full-time pastors. The spiritual direction of the church is the responsibility of the eldership while practical matters are administered by the diaconate. The eldership has delegated much of its responsibility for overseas mission to the Overseas Mission Boad. The Board itself is therefore responsible to the elders for its spiritual direction, and to the diaconate for its financial accountability.

Gold Hill's present significant involvement in mission began in the mid 1970s, when a working group was established to oversee Gold Hill Mission Policy. At that time there was only one church member on the mission field, and she had come to join the church late in her missionary career. In 1977, this group presented their first mission policy, a document which was to be of crucial importance. It emerged from a growing and deepening interest by various members of the church, and the desire to find a God-honouring framework within which to support, encourage and care for our missionaries.

The original document differentiated three different types of missionary within our fellowship, since two major missionary societies, WEC International and the Wycliffe Bible Translators, have centres close to the church. Because of the nature of the church's life, missionaries on furlough or those working on the home staff often take up membership in the church. To have assumed a financial responsibility for all these members right at the commencement would have been very difficult, so the first policy distinguished 'homegrown' missionaries, who would have first priority; those who became members of the church following their joining a missionary society, with second priority; and finally, those who might proceed to missionary work without the backing of the leadership of the church, with third priority. This differentiation has been helpful to us, and enabled us to make decisions based on principle rather than individual cases.

By the early eighties the number of missionaries and candidates under the Mission Board had grown rapidly enough to put the existing structure under severe strain; the Board was enlarged and in 1983, mainly for the benefit of the new members of the Board and eldership, work began on a statement of policy. The statement was therefore not intended to be a restrictive document, but merely to indicate our present mode of operation and plans for the future. We do not hold to it quoting paragraph and verse in our meetings: it is merely there as a point of reference; a reminder of decisions we have made, as we have sought the mind of the Lord in individual situations.

The following table attempts to indicate the number of personnel with whom the Board has been involved over particular (irregular) time periods, and also the type of involvement.

| Date | Sponsored missionaries | | | Associate missionaries | | Candidates | | Total people involvement by Board |
| | Full-time | | Short-term | Over-seas based | U.K. based | Under super-vision | With-drawn appli-cations | |
	Over-seas based	U.K. based	Total					
1977	6	1	2	-	-	-	-	9
1982	7*	6*	2†	-	-	8	9	41†
1983	7	6	3	-	-	19	-	35
1984	6	7	2	11	7	25	2	60

* Eight full-time missionaries joined and two left during this period.

† Seven short-term missionaries joined and seven left during this period.

The present Mission Board consists of about ten members, and meets monthly in full session. In addition, three subcommittees deal respectively with candidates, members and administrative details. They meet as needed during the month and present their findings to the main Board Meeting. The purpose of the main Board Meeting is to resolve difficult issues requiring the attention of the whole Board and to spend time in prayer.

The Mission Board is privileged to have amongst its members: two retired missionaries with experience in different parts of the Far East; one businessman with missionary experience in South America; two other missionaries who have served in South America (at present working in the U.K.) and other church members with a real desire to see the Lord's Kingdom extended overseas.

Concerning the actual policy document below, it needs to be said that:

1. *It was not written for publication;* merely for informal use within the church, by new members of the Mission Board, by the elders, the deacons and the missionaries themselves, so that all concerned would have a clear idea of the way the Mission Board was moving.

2. *The document is not intended to be legislative or restrictive in any sense of the word.* Rather, it is a statement of the way the Mission Board has operated up to the present or intends to operate in the future (e.g. retirement provision).

3. *A separate committee, the Gold Hill Home Mission Board, has recently been inaugurated.* Originally, the Mission Board was responsible for both the Home and Overseas Mission, but as the tempo of work increased, this rapidly became impossible. The new committee is in its early stages and has so far produced only a brief guide to its method of operation.

4. *The division between the Overseas Board and the Home Mission Board* is not one of geography, but of culture; that is cross-cultural evangelism compared with intracultural evangelism. (The cross-cultural evangelism within the U.K. would come under the Overseas Mission Board).

5. *The Mission Board seeks to discern from individual situations which are presented to us, the way that the Lord is leading us as a Board.* In large measure therefore, the document results from the decisions made or precedents set when facing those individual situations.

6. *We recognise that there are a number of insights into missionary work which are not included in this document.* But it should be remembered that this is not intended to be a statement of how missionary work should be done – merely a statement of how we are at present operating or intending to operate in Gold Hill.

The following statement is a summary of the way in which Gold Hill Baptist Church seeks to approach its missionary work, at home and overseas. This is not a blueprint, only a guideline. We hope that it will be a useful tool for churches which are seeking to formulate their own policies.

Gold Hill Home Mission Board
An interim policy statement

1. *Intention and General Aims*

1.1 As the Body of Christ at Gold Hill, we recognise our responsibility to fulfil the Commission of Christ (Acts 1: 8), not only in overseas mission, but also in the evangelisation and building up of those with whom we are in contact in our own locality and in the rest of the United Kingdom.

1.2 We willingly accept, therefore, the cardinal principle that we have an obligation, both individually and corporately, to share the good things which God has given us and done for us in our Fellowship.

1.3 In consequence we seek to express our life together in Gold Hill in such a way that there will be blessing for others, particularly by working, largely if not exclusively, within fellowships associated with the historic Churches and in partnership with interdenominational agencies.

1.4 We furthermore intend to confirm and strengthen the gifts and ministries of other fellowships, encouraging them to develop their own individual insights and understanding of the full Gospel of Christ.

1.5   We would normally respond to invitations from other fellowships, but may, if necessary, take the initiative, sensitively and courteously, in seeking to share the life which God has given us.

1.6   Within these parameters, and with regard to Gold Hill's involvement in evangelism, faith-sharing and discipling in the United Kingdom, we would identify the following general aims:

1.6.1   To maintain a Home Mission Board which will provide a prophetic vision for the development of these aspects of the church's life, by co-ordinating all home mission activity and acting as an advisory body on home mission policy to the eldership and the church.

1.6.2   To confirm and authenticate the Lord's call upon individuals or groups from amongst our membership who are and will be involved in these activities.

1.6.3   To instigate and establish new gifts and ministries, thus ensuring a dynamic and not a static concept of the church's role.

1.6.4   To inspire, maintain and encourage existing gifts and ministries, particularly by creating an atmosphere of faith, prayer and fellowship in which they will flourish.

1.6.5   To inform and educate the church in all aspects of evangelism and faith-sharing in the United Kingdom, but especially in the activities of our own members.

1.6.6   To evaluate and assess the progress of our total programme in this area, recognising our accountability to God and to the leadership and Fellowship of the Body of Christ at Gold Hill.

Gold Hill Overseas Mission Board

1.   *Preamble: statement of general aims*

1.1   To devote a large proportion of our effort and money to the support of missionary work overseas.

1.2   To fix an annual missionary budget as an agreed percentage of the total annual church budget.

1.3   To organise effective financial and prayer support, fellowship and pastoral care for missionaries in membership of the church.

1.4   To recruit and encourage the training of missionary candidates from amongst our own membership.

1.5   To support, where appropriate, the work of other missionaries and missionary societies which may have no direct personal links with the church.

1.6   To maintain Mission Board which will develop missionary interest and support, coordinate all overseas missionary activity and act as an advisory body on missionary policy to the eldership and the church.

1.7   To initiate a regular survey and review of missionary achievement and policy.

2.   *Introduction*

2.1   *A Definition of Mission: its Biblical Basis*

The Body of Christ at Gold Hill seeks to appropriate the authority of the Lord Jesus and to fulfil the great commission which he gave to his church:

> Go therefore and make disciples of all nations, baptising them in the name of the Father and of the Son and of the Holy Spirit, teaching them to observe all that I have commanded you. (Matt. 28: 19,20; cf. Mark 16: 15–18; Luke 24: 46–9; Acts 1: 7, 8)

In the context of these verses, every member of the Body at Gold Hill is called and trained to be a missionary, seeking to share the good news of Jesus Christ with those who are lost. Thus, though caring ministries are not ignored, we emphasise direct evangelism and encourage ministries and gifts which, when exercised in the power of the Holy Spirit, facilitate evangelisation, church planting, teaching and discipling. For the purposes of this document, however, a 'missionary' is defined more specifically as a member of this Body who exercises these gifts and ministries after receiving a call to full-time service with a society involved in cross-cultural work (generally overseas) where such a call is confirmed and accepted by the church.

2.2 *Extent of responsibility*

God's people are commanded by the Lord Jesus to be witnesses 'in Jerusalem and in all Judea and Samaria and to the end of the earth' (Acts 1:8). The church is concerned, therefore, to enable and encourage its members to witness to the saving power of Christ in all places where they are called to live and work. Ultimate responsibility for this task resides spiritually with the eldership and financially with the diaconate. However, for reasons of effective administration and organisation, and to ensure the efficient allocation and distribution of funds, responsibility for crosscultural mission, including mission home bases, is delegated to the Overseas Mission Board. Responsibility for other geographical ares of missionary activity, particularly in the locality of the church and in the United Kingdom as a whole, is vested elsewhere (in the Gold Hill Home Mission Board). The Board is thus concerned largely, but not exclusively, with the enabling of missionary members who, in the traditional manner, are prepared in faith to look to the Lord for their support.

2.3 *Intention*

This policy statement is designed to ensure that the Great Commission is carried out by establishing a clear sense of direction, maintaining momentum and acting as a framework within which decisions can be made. It is intended to be flexible and adaptable so that changes can be effected as the Board would agree under the guidance and control of the Holy Spirit. The document will be received annually and reviewed and revised at least once every five years.

3.   *Composition of the Board*

3.1   *Membership*

The Board comprises approximately ten members, according to need, and includes the following:

3.1.1   Chairman (elder)

3.1.2   Vice-Chairman

3.1.3   Secretary (ex-officio deacon)

3.1.4   Treasurer (ex-officio deacon)

Other members will assume responsibility for areas such as prayer, information, display and communication, assisted by a sub-committee where appropriate.

The appointment of a full-time chairman and member of the pastoral staff may eventually be envisaged with the growth of the Board's activities.

3.2   *Appointment and term of office*

Appointment of members is made by a recommendation of the Board to the eldership, subject to ratification annually by the church meeting, from among church members with a proven interest and involvement in the missionary life of the church. The term of office should be for three years in the first instance and may be renewed.

3.3   *Responsibilities of members*

3.3.1 To attend Board meetings (usually monthly).

3.3.2 To maintain viable links with the missionaries and candidates assigned to them.

3.3.3 To be familiar with Board policy.

3.3.4 To spend between five and ten hours a month in mission business.

3.3.5 To attend Board occasional days in order to consider mission strategy and pray for missionary work.

4.   *Responsibilities of the Board*

The Board's responsibilities include the following:

4.1   To act as the church's executive arm with regard to mission and to keep abreast of missionary matters, giving advice on all aspects of missionary activity and formulating specific proposals for the consideration and approval of the eldership and the church meeting, particularly those involving an extension of our missionary outreach.

4.2   To take the initiative in challenging those within our Fellowship, particularly young people, with the need for a full-time missionary commitment.

4.3   To be responsible for the recruitment, selection and advice about training and placement of our members who have received a missionary call.

4.4.   To organise effective prayer support for all our missionaries by encouraging prayer for them by individual members and by prayer cells and during House Fellowship meetings and church services.

4.5   To give spiritual, mental and physical support to our missionaries in the field by correspondence, video and audio cassettes, pastoral visits and short furloughs at Gold Hill where it is considered necessary.

4.6   To encourage the House Fellowships to undertake their responsibilities to their missionaries and their families, including missionaries not sponsored or funded by the church.

4.7   To care for our missionaries when on furlough or in retirement and to offer help and succour to missionaries visiting from outside the Fellowship.

4.8   To serve as a liaison between the church, the missionaries and their missionary organisation.

4.9   To educate the Body of Christ at Gold Hill in mission, in its wider sense, and including evangelism, in the conviction that a renewed church must have a world concern.

4.10   To establish an annual mission budget and to administer and distribute the funds allocated.

5.   *The preparation of missionaries*

In fulfilling the Great Commission, it is a prime responsibility of the Board that it should prayerfully identify those who have the call of God upon them and present them with the challenge of this call upon their lives, preferably before they have become well settled in a secular career or in marriage. They will then require training, within and outside the church, careful counselling and pastoring and placement in a suitable work, usually with a missionary society. The Fellowship is looking for its most gifted members for the Lord's work of mission.

5.1   *Recruitment and selection procedures*

The following procedures will normally be followed:

5.1.1   Candidates should have been in membership for a sufficiently long time to ensure that their spiritual integrity is unquestioned. They should be aware of the importance of body life through attendance at their House Fellowship.

5.1.2   They will normally seek the recommendation of their elder, House Fellowship leader and youth leader. There will be a recognition of their spiritual gifts and clear evidence of the Lord's blessing upon their services in the church in addition to any personal desire they may have to serve the Lord. They should normally have reached the age of eighteen years before going through the formal procedures.

5.1.3   Candidates will be interviewed by members of the Board and will be counselled and pastored by the member or members to whom supervision of their progress is entrusted.

5.1.4   Candidates should be in agreement with the doctrinal basis of the church and have our understanding of the full Gospel of Christ.

After recommendation from the Board, a candidate's call will be confirmed by the eldership and the church meeting.

5.1.6   Where an applicant's approach to the Board is

considered, after interview, to be premature, for reason of age, lack of spiritual maturity or for any other reason, he or she will be encouraged to take up some form of active service in the church and to become (or remain) committed to his or her House Fellowship. The application to the Board will be reported to the candidate's elder and House Fellowship leader who will pay particular attention to his or her spiritual progress. Such applicants will not be included upon the Board's *Candidates' List*, but rather upon the *Potential Candidates' List*. They will not therefore be pastored and counselled by the Board until such time as their condidature is renewed upon the recommendation of their elder and leaders.

5.2   *Training*

The church expects our missionaries to move under the direction of the Holy Spirit, to grow steadily in spiritual maturity, to be equipped to handle spiritual warfare and to be effective in service. Therefore, before a candidate's call can finally be confirmed, he or she must submit to some or all of the following forms of practical and formal training:

5.2.1   Service in some area of the Gold Hill Fellowship.

5.2.2   Experience in some evangelistic work in another area of the United Kingdom.

5.2.3   Short-term service overseas (specifically as a preparation for long-term service).

5.2.4   Formal training in a recognised Bible College or Missionary Training College.

5.3   *Members serving abroad*

Where members or associates wish to serve abroad for shorter or longer periods, either in their normal professional capacity, or in V.S.O.-type schemes, or in short-term missionary activity which is not seen as part of our training programme, they may apply to the Board for advice and counselling. They would then be included on the *Church Members Serving Overseas*

List. Responsibility for their pastoral care and prayer support would remain with their House Fellowship elder and leaders.

These arrangements will not preclude the Board from inviting a member to proceed abroad for a period of short-term service outside the training programme if it so wishes.

6.   *Placement of missionaries*

The Board recognises its responsibility to advise candidates upon the choice of the society to which they will commit themselves. They will be encouraged to investigate the potentialities of as many societies as are appropriate to their call.

Criteria for the evaluation of a society would include the following:

6.1   A general doctrinal agreement and unity in the Spirit with the church at Gold Hill.

6.2   It must be properly directed, organised, administered and financed.

6.3   Its goals and objectives should be clearly articulated and be approved by the church. It must be of sufficient size to ensure that its goals and objectives can be effectively realised.

6.4   Its missionary methods should be appropriate to its fields of activity and to its size.

6.5   The general welfare of the missionary should be seen to be a matter of partnership with the church.

6.6   A sympathetic attitude to the missionary's family responsibilities.

6.7   The Board will not confine our involvement entirely to societies with which we already have close relations. We will always be guided by the witness of the Spirit. However, candidates will be carefully counselled to ensure that they do not commit themselves to ineffectual or unsuitable societies.

7.   *The development of prayer support*

This is the most important aspect of missionary support

and requires the energetic commitment of the Board and the church.

It may be encouraged by the following means.

7.1   One Board member will be responsible for the promotion of prayer for our missionaries.

7.2   Prayer needs will be publicised in the *Bulletin* and *Messenger*, by prayer letters, by prayer times in Sunday services, especially mission services and communions, and during church meetings.

7.3   A commitment to pray regularly and consistently for at least one missionary, both privately and corporately, will be seen as a normal requirement for a church member and will be stressed in commitment classes.

7.4   House Fellowships will develop prayer for their missionary or missionaries normally by supplying a prayer cell leader and by encouraging their members to develop a gift for intercession by attendance at the cell, as well as by prayer during normal Fellowship meetings. The role of the House Fellowship leadership in setting an example is essential.

7.5   Prayer cells will provide for in-depth intercession in the power of the Holy Spirit for individual missionaries and should meet at least once a month. They may be convened independently or form part of grouped missionary prayer cell evenings.

7.6   Each missionary should be encouraged to ensure that there is an adequate communication of prayer needs by letter or tape.

8.   *Pastoral care of missionaries*

Pastoral care for the missionary does not end with his or her departure overseas. Though missionaries in the field will always be in submission to their mission leaders, we will continue to offer them pastoral care in consultation with the Society and in the following ways:

8.1   Every missionary will be firmly linked with a House Fellowship and will receive comfort and succour of both a practical and spiritual nature from this group. This will supplement the mainly prayer support offered by his other prayer cell and will ensure that he or she continues to experience life in the Body of Christ.

8.2   Every missionary should be adopted by a family, preferably chosen from the House Fellowship, which will encourage pastoral support.

8.3   The Board will endeavour to ensure that a missionary receives at least one pastoral visit during each term or has a mid-term short-stay furlough at Gold Hill, whichever is more appropriate to need. Pastoral visits may be made either specifically by pastors, elders or Board members or more incidentally by members visiting the missionary's field of service.

8.4   The church will endeavour to provide, and the Board or its representative will administer, a mission house in the immediate locality of Gold Hill. It will serve as a home and base for the spiritual and physical refreshment of our own missionaries and of missionaries and Christian workers from outside our Fellowship. No missionary should be unable to use the house through lack of finance, though the house should be largely self-financing.

8.5   The society will be encouraged to allow the missionary on furlough to spend as much time as possible at Gold Hill, so that relationships may be renewed and support built up, church instructed and informed about work in the field, and the missionary refreshed physically, mentally and spiritually.

8.6   Missionaries will be encouraged to undertake periods of inservice training and refresher courses either in the field or during furlough. Books and cassette recordings of church services and teaching sessions may also be regularly purchased and distributed to them through their House Fellowships.

8.7   The Board will maintain close links with the

sponsoring society, thus ensuring that we receive regular reports upon the missionary's progress and situation for which it is totally responsible through the field director.

However, the Board may, on occasions, initiate dialogues with the society, where pastoral concern indicates that our missionary is unable to function under scriptural principles in the situation or circumstances to which he or she is posted.

8.8   Our responsibility for the reasonable educational, welfare and pastoral needs of our missionary families is also recognised by the Board.

8.9   Pastoral care for missionaries will not cease with retirement or cessation of missionary service overseas. They will be encouraged to resettle near Gold Hill where they can remain under the care of the Fellowship and where it may be possible to make accommodation available.

9.   *The education of the church in mission*

Teaching on mission should be an integral part of the church's educational programme.

It may be encouraged by the following means:

9.1   One Board member will be responsible for the development of educational programmes upon mission, assisted by a committee where necessary.

9.2   Educational programmes will be organised to instruct and inspire the church through the House Fellowships, youth organisations and the Bible School.

9.3   Regular reports will be presented to church meetings, particularly as a stimulus for prayer.

9.4   Mission will feature regularly in Sunday services, normally in the evening, but, where appropriate, and as guided by the Spirit, in the morning teaching programme.

9.5   All available forms of educational technology will be used to communicate information about mission and about our missionaries. Use will be made of programmes and materials produced by missionary agencies and societies.

9.6 Experienced missionaries and missionary 'statesmen' will be invited, from time to time, to speak to the church. Missionary conferences may be organised.

9.7 Members, particularly young people, will be encouraged to attend missionary conferences.

10. *Missionary finance*

10.1 *The missionary budget*

The budget is the mechanism used by the Mission and the Finance Boards to ensure that, as far as possible, all Gold Hill missionaries are supported according to their needs. It also serves to present the outworkings of the Board's strategy in a form which is easily understood by the church and to demonstrate practically the principles governing our financial allocation to missionaries, thus encouraging sacrificial giving and demonstrating how our involvement in mission is bearing fruit.

The Mission budget is set as a percentage of the total church budget and is normally not less than thirty per cent of that total. It is authorised by the church meeting after consideration and adoption by the Mission Board, the Finance Board, the diaconate and the eldership.

10.2 *Budget distribution*

Budget headings cover all areas of our missionary activity, i.e.:

Missionary preparation and training
Missionary support
Missionary pastoral care, including pastoral visits, etc.
Missionary education and in-service training
Church education in mission
Contingency

However, the main emphasis of funding policy lies in

the direction of the preparation and training of new missionaries and the continuing support of missionaries already in service. No specific support level is guaranteed, but the church sees the provision of funds adequate to the needs of the missionary as its responsibility before the Lord, and as one of the most important faith dimensions of life in the Body of Christ.

We give priority to the support of missionaries who are in membership at Gold Hill rather than to societies, agencies or specific projects whether denominational or inter-denominational. Furthermore, stress is laid upon the support of loving evangelistic outreach rather than programmes involving mere social action. Within these parameters, priorities for funding are established and three categories of missionary are identified:

10.2.1   *Gold Hill 'sponsored' missionaries.* Substantial support is offered to members in training or in service who have been called of the Lord and set apart by the church in accordance with the procedures described above (para. 5: 1,2) or who have been invited by the church to join the 'sponsored' category.

10.2.2   *Gold Hill 'associate' missionaries.* Some support may be offered to those who have been accepted into membership after their call to missionary service. Support for these may develop as they become more known to the Fellowship and it may well be organised initially through their House Fellowship.

10.2.3   *'Other' missionaries.* No support will normally be offered through the budget to missionaries who have no direct connection with the church except by specific extra-budgetary designations by individual church members which may be distributed by the mission treasurer.

Church members who proceed to missionary service

without the agreement and recommendation of the Board and the eldership may expect no support other than personal gifts of this kind. In the case of extreme hardship, grants may be made as an expression of our love and concern.

Members going out to normal secular employment or to V.S.O.-type short-term commitments (para. 5.3 above), will not normally receive any financial support. Members specifically guided and encouraged by the Board to undertake short-term service may be assisted financially.

10.2.4 Well-defined finance-intensive 'aid' ministries such as TEAR Fund, UBS and FEBA Radio, even where we have no personnel actively in service with them, may receive support (normally by means of special offerings). Other societies and agencies may not, however, expect support except by specific extra-budgetary designations by individual church members which may also be distributed by the mission treasurer.

10.3 *Level of support*

Support will provide a standard of living appropriate to the area where the missionary is serving, as determined by the society or agency. At present, support for 'sponsored' missionaries (para. 10.2.1 above) is allocated at eighty per cent of need according to family size and any other relevant factors. Our aim is to increase this to one hundred per cent. Allocations are adjusted annually in line with increases in the cost of living and inflation as recommended by the society and also in accordance with changes in family circumstances.

'Associate' missionaries may initially expect little or no direct financial support. However, after a suitable period of membership, and at least one furlough spent largely in the Fellowship, and at the discretion of the Board, they may be placed in the 'sponsored' category of support.

10.4 *Duration of support*

Full missionary support will normally begin with departure to the field and continue throughout service, as long as there is need. Special requirements for equipment may be met by love gifts from the missionary's House Fellowship or by grant from the Board.

Support may be withdrawn for any of the following reasons:

10.4.1 The missionary is no longer in membership at Gold Hill and has alternative sources of support.

10.4.2 He or she no longer agrees with the doctrinal basis of the church.

10.4.3 He or she is no longer in submission to the leadership of the church.

10.4.4 He or she has returned home and is able to accept responsibility for his or her own support.

10.5 *Insurance and retirement policy*

Where a missionary's society expects payment of National Insurance contributions and/or retirement fund payments this is effected by the Board through normal support channels.

Where there is no retirement provision or where pension payments are voluntary, the provision of a Gold Hill pension scheme through private insurance will ensure that all our missionaries can expect similar provision upon retirement. In the case of premature termination of service, missionaries should then be able to take over payment of premiums themselves if they so wish.

Older missionaries for whom there is no such provision will require continued support in retirement to ensure an adequate standard of living.

10.6 *Support for candidates in training*

10.6.1 *Short-term workers.*

An important feature of short-term work in a training programme is to give candidates experience of living by faith. They should therefore, normally seek their own support for short-term projects. However, if they have already funded their short-term experience in the United Kingdom themselves (see para. 5.2.2 above), the Board will consider making a substantial grant as a contribution to their travel and living expenses for their short-term experience abroad (see para. 5.2.3 above). Such grants would depend upon costs and each case would be considered upon its merits.

10.6.2   *Bible and Missionary College students.*
Where the Lord's call is upon a candidate's life and he or she has completed the preparatory stages of the Board's selection and training programme (see para. 5.2.1–3 above) and proposes to undertake formal training, he or she should seek to obtain Local Government or other grants. However, where such grants are unavailable, the Board may make interest-free loans to cover fees and living costs. Repayment of these loans will be waived in the event of the candidate's completion of four years of missionary service (or equivalent). Any special difficulty of repayment would be treated sympathetically.

10.6.3   *National or international conferences.*
Some help may be offered to young people, when suitably recommended, so that they may attend such conferences. Criteria for grant aid would include potential for missionary service as well as financial need.

10.7   *Contingency Fund*

This serves as a source of funding for unforeseen emergencies. All other financial needs are met under the appropriate headings (see para. 10.2 above).

10.8   *Allocation of surpluses*

At the end of the financial year, any surpluses in the mission account may, according to need and as the Board determines, be distributed in any of the following ways:

10.8.1   Allocation by gift to our 'associate' missionaries.

10.8.2   Allocation as a grant to special projects, normally associated with one of our own missionaries.

10.8.3   Allocation to approved mission agencies and societies.

10.8.4   Appropriation for the same or other headings in the following years's budget.

10.8.5   Virement to the Contingency Fund.

10.9 *Legacies and special gifts*

Legacies and gifts are distributed according to the wishes of the legator or donor. Where there is no designation, the Board will make an allocation by the normal fund mechanism, reserving the right to carry over money into subsequent financial years or to allocate it, with eldership approval, to some special unbudgeted project.

10.10 *Funding of deficits*

When any mission budget heading (see para. 10.2 above) is in deficit at the end of the financial year, the shortage will normally be offset either by virement from other budgetary headings or from the Contingency Fund. However, if there is likely to be an overall deficit at the end of the financial year, on the advice of the Mission and the Finance Boards, the eldership may recommend any of the following steps:

10.10.1   An appeal be made to church members encouraging them to increase their weekly giving as a token of their responsibility before the Lord to provide for those he has called.

10.10.2   Virement be effected from the Church General Fund to the Mission Fund.

10.10.3   A special Gift and Self-denial Day, with prayer and fasting, be called.

10.10.4   A reduction be made in giving to approved agencies.

10.10.5   *In extremis*, an across-the-board percentage reduction be made in missionary allowances.

11. *Review and survey of missionary achievement and policy*

The Mission Board recognises its accountability to the Lord, to the church at Gold Hill and to its leadership. Monitoring of missionary policy and activity will, therefore, be effected by the Board in the following manner:

11.1 This policy document will be received annually and reviewed and revised at least once every five years (see para. 2.3 above).

11.2 The need for the recruitment and rotation of Board members will be kept constantly in mind.

11.3 Board members will report informally to the Board at the monthly meetings on any contacts they have had with missionaries or candidates in their pastoral care. There will, in consequence, be a continuing process of monitoring and evaluation of progress.

11.4 Lists of missionaries in service, of candidates considering service or in training and of members working abroad will be compiled and will appear on the agenda of monthly meetings to assist report and review. These lists include the following:

'Sponsored' missionaries (para. 10.2.1)
'Associate' missionaries (para. 10.2.2)
'Other' missionaries (para. 10.2.3)
Members serving overseas (para. 5.3, 10.2.3)
Candidates (paras. 5.1,2)
Potential candidates (para. 5.1.6)

11.5 Our missionaries and candidates in training are expected to help in the process of evaluation by reporting regularly to the Board either by letter or when they are on furlough or vacation.

11.6 Field leaders will be requested to make brief occasional reports on the missionary's service if this is appropriate (para. 8.7).

11.7 Pastors or representatives of the Board will be invited to report when they have participated in a pastoral visit (para. 8.3).

11.8   The Chairman will make regular brief reports informally to the eldership and the church meeting whenever it is appropriate.

11.9   There will be a formal annual review and survey of missionary achievement and policy, conducted concurrently with the establishment of the Budget. A brief formal report will be presented to the eldership and the church meeting.

11.10   The mission budget will be established by the treasurer and the Board, scrutinised by the Finance Board, the diaconate and the eldership and presented for approval to the church meeting. It will be audited by the church auditors (see para. 10).

Appendix 2

Ideas for Getting Your Church Involved in Missions

1. *World map* displayed with church missionaries marked (and visitors?)

2. *World awareness quiz* in church magazine occasionally.

3. *World prayer focus files* for magazines for prayer group leaders.

4. *World awareness conference* for the church each year.

5. *World awareness noticeboard.*

6. *OHP transparencies* for missionary 'spots'. (Available from WEC)

7. *Mission teaching* part of pulpit ministry.

8. *Winter midweek course* on mission.

9. *Bookstall and book review* of good missionary books.

10. *Church members'* reports back on summer visits.

11. *Use audio-visuals and films* with discussion.

12. *Public prayer* – include world events and missionary news.

13. *Missionary focus* for house groups.

14. *Missionary challenges and prayer target* – don't leave this to visitors, but make it central to the church.

15. *Realistic budget* for outside giving.

Bibliography:
Books on World Mission

Turning the Church Inside Out. H.R. Rowden   (*BMMF*)

The Christian at Work Overseas. Ed. I. Prior.
   (*TEAR Fund*)

What on Earth Are You Doing? M. Griffiths. (*IVP*)

Don't Just Stand There. M. Goldsmith. (*IVP*)

Going Places. E. Goldsmith. (*IVP/STL*)

Love Your Local Missionary. Ed. M. Goldsmith.
   (*EMA/MARC*)

Move Out. M. Duncan. (*MARC/STL*)

A Hitch-hikers Guide to Mission. A. Lum   (*IVP/STL*)

The Eleventh Commandment. P. Cotterell   (*IVP*)

Christian Mission in the Modern World. J. Stott.   (*Falcon*)

Also from MARC Europe

EDDIE GIBBS
(Editor)

Ten Growing Churches

Ten ministers tell how their churches are growing in numbers and vitality.

Eddie Gibbs has chosen ministers from the Anglican, Church of Scotland, Methodist, Baptist, United Reformed, Elim, Free Evangelical and the House Churches. They come from the inner city, suburbia, industrial and rural areas. Together they offer a range of encouraging models, illustrating how God is at work in *ordinary* churches today.

With honesty and courage each has described both successes and failures. There are no check lists or patterns to be slavishly followed – but here is evidence, often dramatic, of God present in power.

Eddie Gibbs has conducted many Church Growth courses for Bible Society and is author of several books including *I Believe in Church Growth*. He is Assistant Professor of Church Growth at Fuller Theological Seminary.

'This book . . . offers no facile prescriptions. It is about ministers taking risks, about people being open to God, about churches responding to the wind of change.'
Methodist Recorder

Published jointly with the British Church Growth Association.

MARTIN GOLDSMITH
(Editor)

Love Your Local Missionary

Missionaries are front-line troops: how can we best support them?

Christians pay lip service to the goal of mission, but commit little money or time. Yet many are called to the mission field: over 5,500 from Britain alone are serving with different societies. How can the churches help?

Love Your Local Missionary explains how Christians can understand the vital importance of mission and offer friendship, prayer and support where it is most needed.

Martin Goldsmith, lecturer at All Nations Christian College, writes on the biblical basis of mission; the **Rev. Stanley Davies**, General Secretary of the Evangelical Missionary Alliance, surveys missionary outreach today; the **Rev. John Wallis**, Home Director of the Overseas Missionary Fellowship, describes how to back the missionary abroad; and **Dr Anne Townsend**, Director of CARE Trust, shows how local Christians can offer help where it is needed to the missionary at home.

'You will find not only some useful theology but also a great many practical hints.'
Church Times.

Published jointly with STL Books and the Evangelical Missionary Alliance.

MICHAEL DUNCAN

Move Out

Taking your place in God's world.

Michael Duncan is a young New Zealand Baptist Minister who has caught a vision for the needs of the world. He and his family are currently preparing for a ministry in Asia amongst the urban poor.

'An excellent introduction to becoming a world Christian. A thoughtful response to the practical teaching provided could well add a new dimension to your Christian service.'
John Wallis, British Director, OMF.

'I am impressed! You have researched well . . . the issues of the day – it is relevant.'
C. Peter Wagner, Fuller School of World Mission.

'Filled with practical help for a person thinking of a cross-cultural ministry . . . lots of helpful direction for a church developing a world mission programme.'
Rev. Murray Robertson, New Zealand.

Published jointly with STL Books.

DATE DUE

"The only thing which will stop me is you," he continued, his voice a deep silken purr. **"So stop me, Molly. Turn away and walk out right now and do us both a favor, because something tells me this is a bad idea."**

He was giving her the opportunity to leave but Molly knew she wasn't going to take it—because when did things like this ever happen to people like her? She wasn't like most women her age. She'd never had sex. Never come even close, despite her few forays onto a dating website, which had all ended in disaster. Yet now a man she barely knew was proposing seduction and suddenly she was up for it, and she didn't care if it was *bad*. Hadn't she spent her whole life trying to be good? And where had it got her?

Her heart was crashing against her rib cage as she stared up into his rugged features and greedily drank them in. "I don't care if it's a bad idea," she whispered. "Maybe I want it as much as you do."

Sharon Kendrick once won a national writing competition by describing her ideal date: being flown to an exotic island by a gorgeous and powerful man. Little did she realize that she'd just wandered into her dream job! Today she writes for Harlequin, and her books feature often stubborn but always *to-die-for* heroes and the women who bring them to their knees. She believes that the best books are those you never want to end. Just like life...

Books by Sharon Kendrick

Harlequin Presents

A Royal Vow of Convenience

Conveniently Wed!

Bound to the Sicilian's Bed

One Night With Consequences

The Pregnant Kavakos Bride
Secrets of a Billionaire's Mistress
Crowned for the Prince's Heir
Carrying the Greek's Heir
The Greek's Bought Bride

Wedlocked!

The Sheikh's Bought Wife
The Billionaire's Defiant Acquisition

The Billionaire's Legacy

Di Sione's Virgin Mistress

Visit the Author Profile page
at Harlequin.com for more titles.

Sharon Kendrick

—

THE ITALIAN'S CHRISTMAS HOUSEKEEPER

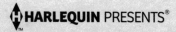

HARLEQUIN PRESENTS®

Recycling programs
for this product may
not exist in your area.

ISBN-13: 978-1-335-41980-4

The Italian's Christmas Housekeeper

First North American publication 2018

Copyright © 2018 by Sharon Kendrick

Printed in U.S.A.

THE ITALIAN'S CHRISTMAS
HOUSEKEEPER

To Maura Sabatino, who is funny and beautiful and whose help for this book was invaluable.

Grazie mille for bringing Naples alive with your words—and for helping me to create a Neapolitan Christmas!

CHAPTER ONE

SALVIO DE GENNARO stared at the lights as he rounded the headland. Flickering lights from the tall candles which gleamed in the window of the big old house. They made him think of Christmas and he didn't want to think about it—not with still six weeks left to go. Yet here in England the shops were already full with trees and tinsel and the kind of gifts surely no sane person would want for themselves.

His mouth hardened as the dark waters of the Atlantic crashed dangerously on the rocks beneath him.

Christmas. The *least* wonderful time of the year in his opinion. No contest.

He slowed his pace to a steady jog as dusk fell around him like a misty grey curtain. The rain was heavier now and large drops of water had started to lash against his body but he was oblivious to them, even though his bare legs were spattered with mud and his muscles were hot with the strain of exertion. He ran because he had to. Because he'd been taught to. Tough, physical exercise woven into the fabric of his day, no matter where in the world he was. A discipline which was as much a part of him as breathing and which made him hard and strong. He barely noticed that his wet singlet was now clinging to his torso or that his shorts were plastered to his rocky thighs.

He thought about the evening ahead and, not for the first time, wondered why he had bothered coming. He was here because he wanted to buy a prime piece of land from his aristocratic host and was convinced the deal could be concluded more quickly in an informal setting. The man he was dealing with was notoriously difficult to pin down—a fact which Salvio's assistant had remarked on, when she'd enquired whether she should accept the surprise invitation for dinner and an overnight stay.

Salvio gave a grim smile. Perhaps he should have been grateful to have been granted access to Lord Avery's magnificent Cornish house, which stood overlooking the fierce midwinter lash of the ocean. But gratitude was a quality which didn't come easily to him, despite his huge wealth and all the luxury it afforded him. He wasn't particularly looking forward to dinner tonight. Not with a hostess who'd

been eying him up from the moment he'd arrived—
her eyes lit with a predatory hunger which was by
no means unusual, although it was an attitude he inevitably found tedious. Married women intent on seduction could be curiously unattractive, he thought
disdainfully.

Inhaling a lungful of sea air, he grew closer to the
house, reminding himself to instruct his assistant to
add a couple of names to the guest list for his annual Christmas party in the Cotswolds, the count-
down to which had already begun. He sighed. His
yearly holiday celebration—which always took place
in his honey-stone manor house—was one of the
most lusted-after invitations on the social calendar,
though he would have happily avoided it, given the
opportunity. But he owed plenty of people hospitality and you couldn't avoid Christmas, no matter how
much the idea appealed.

He'd learnt to tolerate the festival and conceal
his aversion behind a lavish display of generosity.
He bought expensive gifts for his family and staff
and injected yet more cash into the charitable arm
of his vast property empire. He took a trip to his native Naples to visit his family, because that was what
every good Neapolitan boy did, no matter how old
or successful he was. He went back to the city which
he avoided as much as possible because it was the

home of his shattered dreams—and who liked to be reminded of those? For him, home would always be the place where he had been broken—and the man who had emerged from the debris of that time had been a different man. A man whose heart had been wiped clean of emotion. A man who was thankfully no longer at the mercy of his feelings.

He increased his pace to a last-minute sprint as he thought about Naples and the inevitable litany of questions about why he hadn't brought home a nice girl to marry, nor produced a clutch of bonny, black-haired babies for his mother to make a fuss of. He would be forced to meet the wistful question in her eyes and bite back the disclosure that he never intended to marry. *Never.* Why disillusion her?

He slowed his pace as he reached the huge house, glad he had declined his hostess's invitation to accompany her and her husband to the local village that afternoon, where a performance of Cinderella was taking place. Salvio's lips curved into a cynical smile. Amateur dramatics in the company of a married woman with the hots for him? Not in this lifetime. Instead, he intending making the most of the unexpected respite by trying to relax. He would grab a glass of water and go to his room. Listen to the soothing soundtrack of the ocean lashing hard against the rocks and maybe read a book. More likely still, he would chase up that elusive site in New Mexico which he was itching to develop.

But first he needed to dry off.

Sinking her teeth into a large and very moist slice of chocolate cake, Molly gave a small moan of pleasure as she got her first hit from the sugary treat. She was starving. Absolutely starving. She hadn't eaten a thing since that bowl of porridge she'd grabbed on the run first thing. Unfortunately the porridge had been lumpy and disappointing, mainly because the unpredictable oven had started playing up halfway through making it. Not for the first time, she wondered why her bosses couldn't just have the kind of oven you simply switched on, instead of a great beast of a thing which lurked in the corner like a brooding animal and was always going wrong. She'd been working like crazy all morning, cleaning the house with even more vigour than usual because Lady Avery had been in such a state about their overnight guest.

'He's Italian,' her employer had bit out. 'And you know how fussy they are about cleanliness.'

Molly didn't know, actually. But more worrying still was Lady Avery's inference that she wasn't working hard enough. Which was why Molly dusted the chandeliers with extra care and fastidiously vacuumed behind the heavy pieces of antique furniture. At one point she even got down on her hands and knees to scrub the back door porch—even if she did manage to make her hands red raw in the process. She'd put a big copper vase of scented eucalyptus and dark roses in the guest bedroom and had been baking biscuits and cakes all morning, so that the house smelt all homely and fragrant.

The Averys rarely used their Cornish house— which was one of the reasons why Molly considered being their resident housekeeper the perfect job. It meant she could live on a limited budget and use the lion's share of her wages to pay off her brother's debt and the frightening amount of interest it seemed to accrue. It was the reason she endured the isolated location and demanding attitude of her employer, instead of spreading her wings and finding some- where more lively.

But the winter had made her isolation all the more noticeable and it was funny how the approach of Christmas always reminded you of the things you didn't have. This year she was really missing her brother and trying not to worry about what he was doing in Australia. But deep down she knew she had to let go. She *had* to. For both their sakes. Rob- bie was probably having the time of his life on that great big sunny continent—and maybe she should count her blessings.

She took another bite of chocolate cake and did exactly that, reminding herself that most people would revel in the fact that when the Averys *were* around, they entertained all kinds of amazing people. Guests Molly actually got to meet—even if it was only in the context of turning down their beds at night or offering them a home-made scone. Politicians who worked with Lord Avery in the Palace of Westminster, and famous actors who spouted Shakespearean sonnets from the stages of London's theatres. There were business people, too—and sometimes even members of the royal family, whose bodyguards lurked around the kitchen and kept asking for cups of tea.

But Molly had never heard Lady Avery make such a fuss about anyone as she'd done about the impending arrival of Salvio De Gennaro, who was apparently some hotshot property developer who lived mostly in London. Earlier that day she had been summoned into her boss's office, where the walls were decked with misty photos of Lady Avery wearing pearls and a dreamy expression, in those far-off days before she'd decided to have a load of extensive work done on her face. A bad idea, in Molly's opinion—though of course she would never have said so. Lady

Avery's plump lips had been coated in a startling shade of pink and her expression had been unnaturally smooth as she'd gazed at Molly. Only the hectic flicker in her pale eyes had hinted how excited she was by the impending visit of the Italian tycoon.

'Everything is prepared for our guest's arrival?' The words were clipped out like tiny beads of crystal.

'Yes, Lady Avery.'

'Make sure that Signor De Gennaro's bed linen is scented with lavender, will you?' continued her boss. 'And be sure to use the monogrammed sheets.'

'Yes, Lady Avery.'

'In fact...' A thoughtful pause had followed. 'Perhaps you'd better go into town and buy a new duvet.'

'What, *now*, Your Ladyship?'

'Yes. Right now.' A varnished scarlet fingernail began tracing a circle on the sheet of blotting paper on the desk and an odd, trembling note had crept into her employer's aristocratic voice. 'We don't want Signor De Gennaro complaining about the cold, do we?'

'We certainly don't, Lady Avery.'

The last-minute purchase of the new duvet had been the reason why Molly hadn't been on hand to greet the Italian tycoon when he'd arrived. And when she'd returned from her shopping expedition— gasping under the bulky dimensions of a high-tog goose-down duvet—there had been no sign of him. Only his open suitcase and a few clothes strewn around his room indicated he was somewhere in the vicinity, although he was nowhere to be seen in the house. Which at least meant Molly had been able to make up his bed in peace—though her heart had started racing when she'd spotted the faded denims slung carelessly over a stool. And when she'd picked up the dark sweater which lay crumpled beside it, she had been startled by the softness of the cashmere as she'd automatically started to fold it. Briefly, her fingertips had caressed the fine wool before she had taken herself downstairs for tea and some restorative cake and she was just on her third mouthful when the kitchen door opened then slammed shut with a rush of icy air and Molly looked up to see a man framed in the doorway who could only be the Italian billionaire.

Her heart crashed against her ribcage.

The most perfect man she could have imagined.

Her mouth opened slightly but she clamped it shut and the chocolate fudge cake she'd been eating suddenly tasted like glue against the roof of her mouth.

Mud-spattered and windswept, he was standing perfectly still—his singlet and shorts surely the craziest choice of clothes he could have selected for the bitter winter day, although a fleecy top was knotted around his narrow hips. His olive skin was silky-smooth and his body was... Molly tried not to shake her head in disbelief but it took some doing, because his body was sensational—and she was certainly not the kind of woman who spent her time analysing men's bodies. In fact, her interest had never really been sparked by anyone.

Until now.

She swallowed, the cake she was holding suddenly forgotten. It took a lot for Molly to disregard the sugar craving which had always been the bane of her life, but she forgot it now. Because she'd never seen a man like this. Not someone with a rocky torso against which his wet top clung to every sinew, as if it had been painted on with a fine-tipped brush. Nor such narrow hips and sculpted thighs whose glorious flesh was exposed by the shorts he seemed to wear so comfortably. Her eyes moved up to his face. To eyes as black as one of those moonless nights when you couldn't ever imagine seeing daylight again. And his lips. Molly swallowed again. Oh, those lips. Sensual and full, they were hard and unsmiling as they looked at her with something it took a moment for her to recognise. Was it...*disdain*? Her heart pounded uncomfortably. Yes, of course it was. Men with whiplike bodies which didn't carry an ounce of extra weight would be unlikely to approve of an overabundant female who was bulging out of her ugly uniform and stuffing a great big fix of carbohydrate into her mouth.

Flushing to the roots of her hair, she put down the half-eaten cake and rose to her feet, wondering why the ground beneath them suddenly felt as if it were shifting, the way she'd always imagined standing on quicksand might feel. 'I'm...' She blinked at him before trying again. 'I'm so sorry. I wasn't expecting anyone...'

His voice was sardonic as his gaze met hers for one heart-stopping moment, before dropping briefly to the crumb-laden plate. 'Clearly not.'

'You must be...' *A dark angel who has suddenly fallen into my kitchen? The most gorgeous man I've ever seen?* Her chest felt tight. 'You must be Signor De Gennaro?'

'Indeed I am. Forgive me.' Jet eyebrows were raised as he unknotted the warm top from his hips and pulled it over his head before shaking out his damp, dark curls. 'I seem to have disturbed your snack.'

Her *snack*? Although his English was faultless, his richly accented voice was nearly as distracting as his body and Molly opened her mouth to say it was actually a late lunch because she'd been rushing around all morning preparing for *his* arrival, but something stopped her. As if someone like Salvio De Gennaro would be interested in her defence! As if he would believe her making out she was a stranger to cake when her curvy body told an entirely different story. Smoothing her uniform down over her generous hips, she tried to adopt an expression of professional interest, rather than the shame of being caught out doing something she shouldn't. And he was still staring at her. Making her aware of every pulsing atom of her body in a way which was making her feel extremely self-conscious…but strangely enough, in a *good* way.

'Can I get you anything, Signor De Gennaro?' she questioned politely. 'I'm afraid Lord and Lady Avery have gone to the village pantomime and won't be back until later.'

'I know,' he said coolly. 'Perhaps some water. And a coffee, if you have one.'

'Of course. How do you take your coffee?'

He flickered her a smile. 'Black, short, no sugar. *Grazie.*'

Of course not, thought Molly. No sugar for someone like him. He looked as if he'd never been near anything sweet in his life. She wished he'd go. Before he noticed that her brow had grown clammy, or that her nipples had started to push distractingly against the unflattering navy-blue uniform Lady Avery insisted she wore. 'I'll do that right away,' she said briskly. 'And bring them up to your room.'

'No need for that. I'll wait here,' he said.

She wanted to tell him he was making her feel awkward by standing there, like some kind of brooding, dark statue—just *staring* at her. As if he had read her thoughts, he strolled over towards the window and she became aware of an almost imperceptible limp in his right leg. Had he injured himself when out running and should she ask him whether he needed a bandage or something? Perhaps not. Someone with his confidence would be bound to ask for one.

She could feel a stray strand of hair tickling the back of her neck and wished she'd had time to fix it. Or had been sitting reading some novel which might have made her look interesting, instead of scoffing cake and emphasising the fact that she was heavy and ungainly.

'I'll try to be as quick as I can,' she said, reaching up into one of the cupboards for a clean glass.

'I'm in no hurry,' he said lazily.

Because that much was true. Salvio had decided that he was enjoying himself though he wasn't quite sure why. Maybe it was the novelty factor of being with the kind of woman he didn't come across very often—at least, not any more. Not since he'd left behind the backstreets of Naples, along with those women whose curves defined fecundity and into whose generous flesh a man could sink after a long, hard day. Women like this one, who blushed alluringly if they caught you looking at them.

He had waited for a moment to see if she would recognise him. If she knew who he was—or, rather, who he *had* been. But no. He was familiar with recognition in all its forms—from greedy delight right through to feigned ignorance—but there had been no trace of any of those on her face. And why should there be? She was much younger than him and from a different country. How would she have known that in his native Italy he had once been famous?

He watched her busying herself, her curvy silhouette reminding him of the bottles of Verdicchio which used to line the shelves of the city bar he'd swept as a boy, before the talent scouts had discovered him and ended his childhood. She turned to switch on the coffee maker and a sudden dryness turned his throat to dust because...her breasts. He swallowed. *Madonna mia*—what breasts! He was glad when she turned away to open the fridge door because his erection was pressing uncomfortably against his shorts, though, when she did, he then became mesmerised by her shapely bottom. He was just fantasising about what her shiny brown hair would

SHARON KENDRICK 21

look like loose when she turned around and surveyed
him with eyes as grey as the Santissima Annunziata
Maggiore—that beautiful church in Naples, which
had once been an orphanage.

Their gazes clashed and mingled and something
unspoken fizzled in the air as Salvio felt a leap of
something he couldn't define. The hardness in his
groin was familiar but the sudden clench of his heart
was not. Was it lust? His mouth twisted. Of course it
was lust—for what else could it be? It just happened
to be more powerful than usual because it had taken
him by surprise.

Yet there was no answering hunger in her quiet,
grey gaze—something which perplexed him, for
when *didn't* a woman look at him with desire in her
eyes? She was wary, he found himself thinking, with
a flicker of amusement. Almost as if she were silently reproaching him for his insolent appraisal—
and maybe that sentiment was richly deserved. What
was he doing surveying her curvy body, like a boy
from a single-sex school who was meeting a beautiful woman for the first time?

'You're the cook?' he questioned, trying to re-
deem himself with a safe, if rather banal question.

She nodded. 'Sort of. Officially, I'm the housekeeper but I do a bit of everything. Answer the door
to guests and make sure their rooms are serviced, that

sort of thing.' She pushed the coffee towards him. 'Will there be anything else, Signor De Gennaro?'

He smiled. 'Salvio. And you are?'

She looked taken aback, as if people didn't ask her name very often. 'It's Molly,' she answered shyly, in a voice so soft it felt like silk lingerie brushing against his skin. 'Molly Miller.'

Molly Miller. He found himself wanting to repeat it, but the conversation—such as it was—was terminated by the sudden sweep of car headlights arcing powerfully across the room. As he heard the sound of a large car swishing over gravel, Salvio saw the way she flinched and automatically tugged at her drab dress so that it hung more uniformly over her wide hips.

'That's the Averys.'

'I thought it must be.'

'You'd better… You'd better go,' she said, unable to keep the waver of urgency from her voice. 'I'm supposed to be preparing dinner and Lady Avery won't like finding a guest in the kitchen.'

Salvio was tempted to tell her that he didn't give a damn what Lady Avery would or wouldn't like but he could see the fear which had darkened her soft grey eyes. With a flicker of irritation he picked up his espresso and water and headed for the door. *'Grazie mille,'* he said, leaving the warm and steamy kitchen and walking rapidly towards the staircase, reluctant to be around when the Averys burst into the hallway.

But once back in his own room, he was irritated to discover that the low burn of desire was refusing to leave him. So that instead of the hot shower he'd promised himself, Salvio found himself standing beneath jets of punishingly cold water as he tried to push the curves of the sweet little housekeeper from the forefront of his mind and to quell the exquisite hardness which throbbed at his groin.

CHAPTER TWO

'MOLLY, THESE POTATOES are frightful. We can't possibly ask Signor De Gennaro to eat them. Have they even *seen* an oven? They're like rocks!'

Molly could feel herself flushing to the roots of her hair as she met Lady Avery's accusing stare. Were they? She blinked. Surely she'd blasted them for the required time, carefully basting them with goose fat to make them all golden and crispy? But no. Now she stopped to look at them properly—they were definitely on the anaemic side.

She could feel her cheeks growing even pinker as she reached towards the table to pick up the dish. 'I'm so sorry, Lady Avery. I'll pop them back in the—'

'Don't bother!' snapped her employer. 'It will be midnight before they're fit to eat and I don't intend going to bed on a full stomach. And I'm sure Salvio won't want to either.'

Was it Molly's imagination, or did Lady Avery

shoot the Italian a complicit smile from the other
side of the table? The way she said his name sounded
unmistakably predatory and the look she was giving him was enough to make Molly's stomach turn.
Surely the aristocrat wasn't hinting that she intended
ending up in bed with him, not with her husband sitting only a few feet away?

Yet it had struck her as odd when Sarah Avery
had come down for dinner wearing the tightest
and lowest-cut dress imaginable, so that the priceless blaze of the Avery diamonds dazzled like stars
against her aging skin. She'd been flirting outrageously with the Italian businessman ever since
Molly had served pre-dinner drinks and showed no
sign of stopping. And meanwhile, her husband—
two decades older and already a quarter of the way
through his second bottle of burgundy—seemed
oblivious to the undercurrents which had been
swirling around the dinner table ever since they'd
sat down.

The meal had been a disaster from the moment
she'd put the starters on the table and Molly couldn't
understand why. She was a good cook. She knew
that. Hadn't she spent years cooking for her mother
and little brother, trying to produce tasty food on a
shoestring budget? And hadn't part of her job interview for Lady Avery consisted of producing a full

afternoon tea—including a rich and rather heavy fruit cake—within the space of just two hours… a feat she had managed with ease? A simple meal for just three people should have been a breeze, but Molly hadn't factored in Salvio De Gennaro, or the effect his brooding presence would have on her employer. Or, if she was being honest, on her.

After he'd swept out of the kitchen earlier that afternoon, it had taken ages for her heart to stop thumping and to be able to concentrate on what she was supposed to be doing. She'd felt all giddy and stupidly…*excited*. She remembered the way he had looked into her eyes with that dark and piercing gaze and wondered if she'd imagined the pulsing crackle of electricity between them before telling herself that, yes, of course she had. Unless she really thought a man who could have his pick of any woman on the planet would have the slightest interest in a naïve country girl who was carrying far too much weight around her hips.

In her dreams!

But there was no doubt that Salvio's unexpected trip to the kitchen had rocked Molly's equilibrium and after he'd gone, all the light had seemed to disappear from the room. She'd sat down at the table feeling flat, which was unusual for her because she'd always tried to be an optimist, no matter what life threw at her. She was what was known as a glass-half-full type of person rather than one who regarded the glass as half empty. So why had she spent the rest of the afternoon mooching around the kitchen in a way which was completely out of character?

'Molly? Are you listening to a word I'm saying?'

Molly stiffened as she saw the fury in Lady Avery's eyes—but not before she'd noticed Salvio De Gennaro's face darken with an expression she couldn't work out. Was he wondering why on earth the wife of a famous peer bothered employing such a hapless housekeeper?

'I'm so sorry,' said Molly quickly. 'I was a bit distracted.'

'You seem to have been distracted all afternoon!' snapped Lady Avery. 'The meat is overcooked and the hors d'oeuvres were fridge-cold!'

'Come on, Sarah. It's no big deal,' said Salvio softly. 'Give the girl a break.'

Molly's head jerked up and as she met the under-standing gleam of Salvio De Gennaro's ebony eyes, she felt something warm and comforting wash over her. It was like sitting beside a fire when snow was falling outside. Like being wrapped in a soft, cash-mere blanket. She saw Lady Avery appear momen-tarily disconcerted and she wondered if Salvio De Gennaro's silky intervention had made her decide that giving her housekeeper a public dressing-down wouldn't reflect very well on *her*. Was that why she flashed her a rather terrifying smile?

'Of course. You're quite right, Salvio. It's no big deal. After all, it's not as if we're short of food, is it? Molly always makes sure we're very well fed, but— as you can tell—she's very fond of her food!' She gave a bright, high laugh and nodded her head towards the snoring form of her husband, who had now worked his way through the entire bottle of wine and whose head was slumped on his chest as he snored softly. 'Molly, I'm going to wake Lord Avery and guide him to bed and then Signor De Gennaro and I will go and sit by the fire in the library. Perhaps you'd like to bring us something on a tray to take the place of dinner. Nothing too fussy. Finger food will do.' She flashed another toothy smile. 'And bring us another bottle of the Château Lafite, will you?'

'Yes, Lady Avery.'

Salvio's knuckles tightened as he watched Molly scuttle from the room, though he made no further comment as his hostess moved round the table to rouse her sleeping husband and then rather impatiently ushered him from the room. But he couldn't shake off the feeling of injustice he had experienced when he'd seen how the aristocrat treated the blushing housekeeper. Or the powerful feeling of identification which had gripped him as he'd witnessed it.

Was it because he'd known exactly how she would be feeling? His mouth hardened. Because he'd been where she had been. He knew what it was like to be at the bottom of the food chain. To have people treat you as if you were a machine, rather than a person.

He splayed his fingers over the rigid tautness of his thighs. He would wait until his hostess returned. Force himself to have a quick drink since she'd asked for one of the world's most expensive wines to be opened, then retire to his room. He glanced at his watch. It was too late to go back to London tonight but he would leave at first light, before the house was awake. All in all it had been a wasted journey, with Lord Avery too inebriated to talk business before dinner. He hadn't even been able to work because the damned Internet kept going down and because his thoughts kept straying to the forbidden... And the forbidden had proved shockingly difficult to erase from his mind. He sighed. How crazy was it that the wholesome housekeeper had inexplicably set his senses on fire, so that he could think of little but her?

He'd walked into the orangery before dinner to see her standing with a tray of champagne in her hands. She had changed into a simple black dress which hugged her body and emphasised every vo-luptuous curve. With her shiny brown hair caught back at the nape of her neck, his attention had been

caught by those grey eyes, half concealed by lashes
like dark feathers, which were modestly lowered as
she offered him a drink. Even that was a turn-on. Or
maybe especially that. He wasn't used to modesty.
To women reluctant to meet his gaze, whose cheeks
turned the colour of summer roses. He'd found himself wanting to stand there studying her and it had
taken a monumental effort to tear his eyes away. To
try to make conversation with a host who seemed to
be having a love affair with the bottle, and his disen-
chanted wife who was almost spilling out of a dress
much too young for a woman her age.

'Salvio!' Sarah Avery was back, a look of determination on her face as she picked her way across the
Persian rug on her spiky black heels. 'Sorry about that.
I'm afraid that sometimes Philip simply can't hold his
drink. Some men can't, you know—with predictable
effects, I'm afraid.' She flashed him a megawatt smile.
'Let's go to the library for a drink, shall we?'

There had been many reasons why Salvio had left
Naples to make his life in England and he had absorbed the attitudes of his adopted country with the
tenacity he applied to every new challenge which
came his way. These days he considered himself ur-
bane and sophisticated—but in reality the traditional
values of his Neapolitan upbringing were never far
from the surface. And in his world, a woman never

criticised her husband to another person. Particularly a stranger.

'Just one drink,' he said, disapproval making his words harsher than he intended. 'I have a busy schedule tomorrow and I'll be leaving first thing.'

'But you've only just arrived!'

'And I have back-to-back meetings in London, from midday onwards,' he countered smoothly.

'Oh! Can't you cancel them?' she wheedled. 'I mean, I've heard that you're a complete workaholic, but surely even powerhouses like you are allowed to slow down a little. And this is a beautiful part of the world. You haven't really seen any of it.'

With an effort, Salvio forced a smile because he found her attitude intensely intrusive, as well as irritating. 'I like to honour my commitments,' he observed coolly as he followed her into the firelit library, where Molly was putting cheese and wine on a table, the stiff set of her shoulders showing her tension. He wasn't surprised. Imagine being stuck out here, working for someone as rude and demanding as Sarah Avery. He sank into one of the armchairs, and watched as his hostess went to stand by the mantelpiece in a pose he suspected was intended to make him appreciate her carefully preserved body. She ran one slow finger over the gleaming curve of an ancient-looking vase, and smiled.

'Are you looking forward to Christmas, Salvio?' she questioned.

He was immediately wary—recoiling from the thought that some unwanted invitation might soon be heading his way. 'I am away for most of it—in Naples,' he said, accepting a glass of wine from Molly—ridiculously pleased to capture her blushing gaze before she quickly turned away. 'I'm always glad to see my family but, to be honest, I'm equally glad when the holiday is over. The world shuts down and business suffers as a result.'

'Oh, you men!' Sarah Avery slunk back across the room to perch on a nearby chair, her bony knees clamped tightly together. 'You're all the same!'

Salvio managed not to wince, trying to steer the conversation onto a more neutral footing as he sipped his wine, though all he could think about was Molly hovering nervously in the background, the black dress clinging to her curvaceous figure and a stray strand of glossy brown hair dangling alluringly against her pink cheek. He cleared his throat. 'How are you and your husband planning to spend Christmas?' he questioned politely.

This was obviously the opportunity Sarah Avery had been waiting for and she let him have the answer in full, telling him how much Philip's adult children hated her and blamed her for ending their parents' marriage. 'I mean, I certainly didn't set out to get him, but I was his secretary and these things happen.' She gave a helpless shrug. 'Philip told me he couldn't help falling in love with me. That no power on earth could have stopped it. How was I supposed to know his wife was pregnant at the time?' She sipped a mouthful of wine, leaving a thin red stain above the line of her lip gloss. 'I mean, I really don't care if his wretched kids won't see me—it's Philip I'm concerned about—and I really think they need to be mindful of their inheritance. He'll cut them off if they're not careful!'

Salvio forced himself to endure several minutes more of her malicious chatter, his old-fashioned sensibilities outraged by her total lack of shame. But eventually he could stand no more and rose to his feet and, despite all her cajoling, she finally seemed to get the message that he was going to bed. Alone. Like a child, she pouted, but he paid her sulky expression no heed. He felt like someone who'd just been released from the cage of a prowling she-cat by the time he escaped to the quietness of the guest corridor and closed the door of his room behind him.

A sigh of relief left his lips as he looked around. A fire had been lit and red and golden lights from the flames were dancing across the walls. He'd been in these grand houses before and often found them unbearably cold, but this high-ceilinged room was deliciously warm. Over by the window was a polished antique cabinet on which stood an array of glittering crystal decanters, filled with liquor which glinted in the moonlight. He studied the walls, which were studded with paintings, including some beautiful landscapes by well-known artists. Salvio's mouth twisted. It was ironic really. This house contained pictures which would have been given pride of place in a national gallery—yet a trip to the bathroom required a walk along an icy corridor, because the idea of en-suite was still an alien concept to some members of the aristocracy.

He yawned but didn't go straight to bed, preferring to half pack his small suitcase so he was ready to leave first thing. Outside he could see dark clouds scudding across the sky and partially obscuring the moon, turning the churning ocean silver and black. It was stark and it was beautiful but he was unable to appreciate it because he was restless and didn't know why.

Loosening his tie and undoing the top button of his shirt, Salvio braved the chilly corridor to the bathroom and was on his way back when he heard a sound from the floor above. A sound which at first he didn't recognise. He stilled as he listened and there it was again. His eyes narrowed as he realised what it was. A faint gasp for breath, followed by a snuffle.

Someone was crying?

He told himself it was none of his business. He was leaving first thing and it made sense to go straight to bed. But something tugged at his... He frowned. His conscience? Because he knew that the person crying must be the little housekeeper? He didn't question what made him start walking towards the sound and soon found himself mounting a narrow staircase at the far end of the corridor.

The sound grew louder. Definitely tears. His foot creaked on a step and an anxious voice called out.

'Who's there?'

'It's me. Salvio.'

He heard footsteps scurrying across the room and as the door was pulled open, there stood Molly. She was still wearing her black uniform although she had taken down her hair and removed her sturdy shoes. It spilled over her shoulders in a glorious tumble which fell almost to her waist and Salvio was reminded of a painting he'd once seen of a woman sitting in a boat, with fear written all over her features. He could see fear now, in soft grey eyes which were rimmed with red. And suddenly all the lust he'd felt from the moment he'd set eyes on her was replaced by a powerful sense of compassion.

'What's happened?' he demanded. 'Are you hurt?'

'Nothing's happened and, no, I'm not hurt.'

Quickly, she blotted her cheeks with her fingertips. 'Did you want something?' she asked, a familiar note of duty creeping into her voice. 'I hope… I mean, is everything in your room to your satisfaction, Signor De Gennaro?'

'Everything in my room is fine and I thought I told you to call me Salvio,' he said impatiently. 'I want to know why you were crying.'

She shook her head. 'I wasn't crying.'

'Yes, you were. You know damned well you were.'

An unexpected streak of defiance made her tilt her chin upwards. 'Surely I'm allowed to cry in the privacy of my own room.'

'And surely I'm allowed to ask why, if it's keeping me awake.'

Her grey eyes widened. 'Was it?'

He allowed himself the flicker of a smile. 'Well, no—now you come to mention it. Not really. I hadn't actually gone to bed but it's not a sound anyone particularly wants to hear.'

'That's because nobody was supposed to. Look, I'm really sorry to have disturbed you, but I'm fine now. See.' This time she gritted her teeth into a parody of a smile. 'It won't happen again.'

But Salvio's interest was piqued and the fact that she was trying to get rid of him intrigued him. He glanced over her shoulder at her room, which was small. He hadn't seen a bedroom that small for a long time. A narrow, unfriendly bed and thin drapes at the window, but very little else. Suddenly he became aware of the icy temperature—an observation which was reinforced by the almost imperceptible shiver she gave, despite the thickness of her black dress. He thought about the fire in his own bedroom with the blazing applewood logs which she must have lit herself.

'You're cold,' he observed.

'Only a bit. I'm used to it. You know what these old houses are like. The heating is terrible up here.'

'You don't say?' He narrowed his eyes speculatively. 'Look, why don't you come and sit by my fire for a while? Have a nightcap, perhaps.'

She narrowed her eyes. 'A nightcap?'

He slanted her a mocking smile. 'You know. The drink traditionally supposed to warm people up.'

He saw her hesitate before shaking her head.

'Look, it's very kind of you to offer, but I can't possibly accept.'

'Why not?'

'Because…' She shrugged. 'You know why not.'

'Not unless you tell me, I don't.'

'Because Lady Avery would hit the roof if she caught me socialising with one of the guests.'

'And how's she going to find out?' he questioned

with soft complicity. 'I won't tell if you won't. Come on, Molly. You're shivering. What harm will it do?'

Molly hesitated because she *was* tempted—more tempted than she should have been. Maybe it was because she was feeling so cold—both inside and out. A coldness she'd been unable to shift after the telling off she'd just been given by Lady Avery, who had arrived in the kitchen in an evil temper, shaking with rage as she'd shouted at Molly. She'd told her she was clumsy and incompetent. That she'd never been so ashamed in her life and no wonder Signor De Gennaro had cut short the evening so unexpectedly.

Yet now that same man was standing in the doorway of her humble room, asking her to have a drink with him. He had removed his tie and undone the top button of his shirt, giving him a curiously relaxed and accessible air. It was easy to see why Lady Avery had made a fool of herself over him during dinner. Who wouldn't fall for his olive-dark skin and gleaming ebony eyes?

Yet despite his sexy appearance, he had looked at her understandingly when she'd messed up during dinner. He'd come to her rescue—and there was that same sense of concern on his face now. He had an unexpected streak of kindness, she thought, and kindness was hard to resist. Especially when you weren't expecting it. An icy blast of wind rushed in through the gap in the window frame and once again Molly shivered. The days ahead didn't exactly fill her with joy and her worries about Robbie were never far from the surface. Couldn't she loosen up for once in her life? Break out of the lonely mould she'd created for herself by having a drink with the Italian tycoon?

She gave a tentative shrug. 'Okay, then. I will. Just a quick one, mind. And thank you,' she added, as she slipped her feet back into the sensible brogues she'd just kicked off. 'Thank you very much.'

He gave a brief nod, as if her agreement was something he'd expected all along, and Molly tried to tell herself that this meant nothing special—at least, not to him. But as he turned his back and began to walk she realised her heart was racing and Molly was filled with an unfamiliar kind of excitement as she followed Salvio De Gennaro along the narrow corridor towards his grand bedroom on the floor below.

CHAPTER THREE

'Here.'

'Thanks.' Molly took the brandy Salvio was offering her, wondering if she'd been crazy to accept his invitation to have a drink with him, because now she was in his room she felt hopelessly embarrassed and out of place. She noticed his half-packed open suitcase lying on the far side of the room and, for some stupid reason, her heart sank. He obviously couldn't wait to get away from here. Awkwardly, she shifted from one foot to the other.

'Why don't you sit down over there, beside the fire?' he suggested.

Lowering herself into the chair he'd indicated, Molly thought how weird it was to find herself in the role of visitor to a room she had cleaned so many times. Just this morning she'd been in here, fluffing up the new duvet and making sure the monogrammed pillowcases were all neatly facing in the right direction. Over there were the neat stack of freshly ironed newspapers Lady Avery had insisted on, and the jug of water with the little lace cover on top. Yet it was funny how quickly you could get used to the dramatic change from servant to guest. The soft leather of the armchair felt deliciously soft as it sank beneath her weight and the warmth of the fire licked her skin. She took a tentative sip from her glass, recoiling a little as the powerful fumes wafted upwards.

'Not much of a drinker?' observed Salvio wryly, as he poured his own drink.

'Not really.' But even that minuscule amount of liquor had started to dissolve the tight knot of tension in the pit of her stomach, sending a warm glow flooding through her body. Molly stared out of the windows where clouds were racing across the silvery face of the moon. Outside the temperature had plummeted but in here it felt cosy—in fact, she might even go so far as to say she was starting to feel relaxed. Yet here she was in a strange man's bedroom in her black uniform and heavy-duty shoes as if she had every right to be there. What on earth would Lady Avery say if she happened to walk in? Anxiety rippled through her as she glanced at Salvio, who was replacing the heavy stopper in the bottle. 'I really shouldn't be here,' she fretted.

'So you said,' he drawled, his tinge of boredom

implying that he found repetition tedious. 'But you are here. And you still haven't told me why you were crying.'

'I...' She took another sip of brandy before putting the glass down on a nearby table. 'No reason really.'

'Now, why don't I believe you, Molly Miller?' he challenged softly. 'What happened? Did you get into more trouble about dinner?'

Her startled expression told Salvio his guess was correct. 'I deserved it,' she said flatly as she met his gaze. 'The meal was rubbish.'

Briefly he acknowledged her loyalty. She would have been perfectly justified in moaning about her employer but she hadn't. She was a curious creature, he thought, his gaze flickering over her dispassionately. Totally without artifice, she didn't seem to care that the way she was sitting wasn't the most flattering angle she could have chosen. Yet her abundant hair glowed like copper in the firelight and as she crossed one ankle over the other he was surprised by how unexpectedly erotic that simple movement seemed. But he hadn't brought her here to seduce her, he reminded himself sternly. Tonight he had cast himself in the role of the good Samaritan, that was all. 'And that's the only reason for your tears?'

Molly gave an awkward wriggle of her shoulders. 'Maybe I was feeling sorry for myself,' she admitted, shifting beneath his probing gaze. Because no way was she going to tell him the real reason. He wouldn't be interested in her wayward brother or his habit of accumulating debt, but more than that—she was afraid of saying the words out loud. As if saying them would make them even more real. She didn't want to wonder why Robbie had rung up just an hour ago, asking her if she had any spare cash for a 'temporary' loan, despite his promises to find himself some sort of job. Why hadn't he got any money of his own? Why was he asking her for more, after all his tearful promises that from now on he was going to live his life independently and free of debt? She swallowed. She couldn't bear to think that he'd got himself into that terrible spiral yet again—of playing poker and losing. Of owing money to hard-faced men who wouldn't think twice about scarring his pretty young face…

'Call it a touch of self-pity,' she said, meeting the black fire in his eyes and realising he was still waiting for an answer. 'Not something I imagine you have much experience of.'

Salvio gave a mirthless smile. How touching her faith in him! Did she think that because he was wealthy and successful, he had never known pain or despair, when he had been on intimate terms with both those things? His mouth hardened. When his life had imploded and he'd lost everything, he remembered the darkness which had descended on him, sending him hurtling into a deep and never-ending hole. And even though he'd dragged himself out of the quagmire and forced himself to start over—you never forgot an experience like that. It marked you. Changed you. Turned you into someone different. A stranger to yourself as well as to those around you. It was why he had left Naples—because he couldn't bear to be reminded of his own failure. 'Why do you stay here?' he questioned quietly.

'It's a very well-paid job.'

'Even though you get spoken to like that?'

She shook her head, her long hair swaying like a glossy curtain. 'It's not usually as bad as it was tonight.'

'Your loyalty is touching, *signorina*.'

'I'm paid to be loyal,' she said doggedly.

'I'm sure you are. But even taking all that into account, this place is very *isolato*…isolated.' He gave a flicker of a smile, as if begging her to forgive his sudden lapse into his native tongue. 'I can't imagine many people your age living nearby.'

'Maybe that's one of the reasons I like it.'

He raised his eyebrows. 'You don't like to socialise?'

Molly hesitated. Should she tell him that she always felt out of place around people her own age? That she didn't really do the relaxed stuff, or the fun stuff, or the wild stuff. She'd spent too many years caring for her mother and then trying to keep her brother from going off the rails—and that kind of sensible role could become so much a part of you that it was difficult to relinquish it. And wouldn't that kind of admission bring reality crashing into the room? Wouldn't it puncture the slightly unreal atmosphere which had descended on her ever since she'd walked in here and settled down by the fireside, allowing herself to forget for a short while that she was Molly the housekeeper—so that for once she'd felt like a person in her own right?

'I can take people or leave them,' she said. 'Anyway, socialising is expensive and I'm saving up. I'm intending to put my brother through college and it isn't cheap. He's in Australia at the moment,' she explained, in answer to the fractional rise of his dark brows. 'Doing a kind of…gap year.'

He frowned. 'So you're here—working hard—while he has fun in the sun? That's a very admirable sacrifice for a sister to make.'

'Anyone would do it.'

'Not anyone, no. He's lucky to have you.'

Molly picked up her glass again and took another sip of brandy. Would Salvio De Gennaro be shocked if he knew the truth? That Robbie hadn't actually got a place at college yet, because he was still 'thinking about it', in spite of all her entreaties to get himself a proper education and not end up like her. She licked her lips, which tasted of brandy. She didn't want to think about Robbie. Surely she could have a night off for once? A night when she could feel young and carefree and revel in the fact that she was alone with a gorgeous man like Salvio—even if he had only invited her here because he felt sorry for her.

Putting her glass down, she stared at him and her heart gave a sudden lurch of yearning. He hadn't moved from his spot by the window and his powerful body was starkly outlined by the moonlight.

'What about you?' she questioned suddenly. 'What brought you here?'

He shrugged. 'I was supposed to be discussing a deal with Philip Avery.' He twisted his lips into a wry smile. 'But that doesn't look like it's going to happen.'

'He'll be much more receptive in the morning,' said Molly diplomatically.

'It'll be too late by then,' he said. 'I'm leaving as soon as it's light.'

Molly was aware of a crushing sense of disappointment. She'd wanted… She stared very hard at her brandy glass as if the dark amber liquid would provide the answer. What had she wanted? To see him at breakfast—their eyes meeting in a moment of shared complicity as they remembered this illicit, night-time drink?

'Oh, that's a shame,' she said, sounding genuinely disappointed.

He smiled, as if her earnestness had amused him. 'You know, you're far too sweet to be hiding yourself away somewhere like this, Molly.'

Sweet. Molly knew it was a compliment yet for some reason it offended her. It made her sound like the cake he'd caught her eating. Because sweet wasn't sexy, was it? Just as *she* wasn't sexy. 'Am I?' she questioned tonelessly.

He nodded, walking over to the desk and writing something on the back of a business card before crossing the room and handing it to her. 'Here. Take this. It will get you straight through to my assistant. If ever you decide you want a change, then give her a ring. She knows plenty of people, and domestic staff are always in short supply.' He met her eyes. 'You could always find something better than this, you know.'

'Despite dinner being such a disaster?' She tried to sound jokey even if she didn't feel it, because she realised she was being dismissed. Getting up from the comfort of her fireside seat, Molly took the card and slid it into the hip pocket of her dress.

'Despite that,' he agreed, his words suddenly trailing away as his gaze followed the movement of her hand.

Molly became aware of a subtle alteration in the atmosphere as Salvio lifted his eyes to her face. She'd wondered if the attraction which had sizzled between them earlier had been wishful thinking, but maybe it hadn't. Maybe it had been real. As real as the sudden thrust of her nipples against the soft fabric of her dress and the distracting heat between her thighs. She held her breath, waiting, instinct telling her that he was going to touch her. Despite him being who he was and her being just Molly. And he did. Lifting his hand, he ran the tips of his fingers experimentally over her hair.

'*E capelli tuoi so comme a seta,*' he said, and when she looked at him in confusion, he translated. 'Your hair is like silk.'

It was the most beautiful thing anyone had ever said to her and when she heard it in Italian it made her want to melt. Was that why he did it, knowing it would push her a little further beneath his powerful spell? Molly told herself to move away. She should thank him for the drink, for his kindness and for giving him his card and then hurry back to her little room to mull over her memories and hug them to her like a hot-water bottle. But she didn't move. She just carried on gazing up into the rugged perfection of his looks, praying he would kiss her and make the fairy tale complete—even if that was all she was ever going to have to remember him by. 'Is—is it?' she questioned.

Salvio smiled, letting his thumb drift from the fire-warmed strands, to hover over the unmistakable tremble of her lips. He felt a tightness in his throat as he realised what he was about to do. He had invited her here because he sensed she was lonely and unhappy—not because he intended to seduce her. Because there were rules and usually he followed them. He no longer took physical comfort just because it was available—because it was pretty much always available to a man like him. Just as he no longer used sex to blot out his pain, or his anger.

But the little housekeeper had touched a part of him he'd thought had died a long time ago. She had stirred a compassion in his soul and now she was stirring his body in a way which was all too obvious, if only to him. He could feel the aching hardness at his groin, but the urge to kiss her was even more overwhelming than the need to bury himself deep inside her body. He told himself he should resist— gently shoo her out of the door and send her on her way. And maybe he would have done—had she not chosen that moment to expel a shaky breath of air, the warmth of it shuddering softly against his thumb.

How could something as insignificant as a breath be so potent? he marvelled as he stared down into her wide grey eyes. 'I want to kiss you,' he said softly. 'But if that happens I will want to make love to you and I'm not sure that's such a good idea. Do you understand what I'm saying, Molly?'

Wordlessly, she nodded.

'And the only thing which will stop me, is you,' he continued, his voice a deep silken purr. 'So stop me, Molly. Turn away and walk out right now and do us both a favour, because something tells me this is a bad idea.'

He was giving her the opportunity to leave but Molly knew she wasn't going to take it—because when did things like this ever happen to people like her? She wasn't like most women her age. She'd never had sex. Never come even close, despite her few forays onto a dating website, which had all ended in disaster. Yet now a man she barely knew was proposing seduction and suddenly she was up for it, and she didn't care if it was *bad*. Hadn't she spent her whole life trying to be good? And where had it got her?

Her heart was crashing against her ribcage as she stared up into his rugged features and greedily drank them in. 'I don't care if it's a bad idea,' she whispered. 'Maybe I want it as much as you do.'

Her response made him tense. She saw his eyes narrow and heard him utter something which sounded more like despair than joy before pulling her almost roughly into his arms. He smoothed the hair away from her cheeks and lowered his head and the moment their lips met, she knew there would be no turning back.

At first his kiss was slow. As if he was exploring her mouth by touch alone. And just when she was starting to get used to the sheer dreaminess of it, it became hard. Urgent. It fuelled the hunger which was building inside her. He levered her up against him, so that her breasts were thrusting eagerly against his torso and she could feel the rock-hard cradle of his pelvis. She should have been daunted by the unmistakable bulk of his erection but she wasn't, because her hungry senses were controlling her now and she didn't feel like good, rule-following Molly any more. She felt like wanton Molly—a victim of her own desire.

And it felt good.

More than good.

His laugh was unsteady as he splayed his fingers over one of her breasts, the nipple instantly hardening against his palm. 'You are very passionate,' he murmured.

Molly gave a small gurgle of pleasure as he found the side zip of her dress because suddenly she *felt* passionate. As if she had been waiting all her life to feel this way. 'Am I?'

'I don't think you need any reassurance on that score, *bedda mia.*'

He was wrong, of course—but he wasn't to know that and Molly certainly wasn't going to tell him. She felt breathless as he peeled the plain black dress away from her body and let it fall to the ground before stepping back to survey her. And wasn't it funny how a look of admiration in a man's eyes could be powerful enough to dispel all a woman's instinctive insecurities? Because for once Molly wasn't thinking that her tummy was too plump or her breasts unfashionably massive. Or even that her bra didn't match her rather functional pants. Instead she was revelling in the look of naked hunger which made his eyes resemble black fire as they blazed over her.

And then he picked her up. Picked her up! She could hardly believe it. He was carrying chunky Molly Miller towards the bed as if she weighed no more than a balloon at a child's birthday party, before whipping back the brand-new duvet she'd purchased that very morning and depositing her beneath it. It was the most delicious sensation in the world, sink-

ing into the mattress and lying beneath the warmth of
the bedding, her body sizzling with a growing excitement—while Salvio De Gennaro began to undress.
She swallowed, completely hypnotised as she watched
him. The shoes and socks were first to go and then
he unbuttoned his shirt, baring his magnificent chest
before turning his attention to the zip of his trousers.
But when he hooked his thumb inside the waistband
of his boxers, Molly squeezed her eyes tightly closed.

'No. Not like that. Open your eyes. Look at me,'
he instructed softly and she was too much in thrall
to disobey him.

Molly swallowed. She couldn't deny that it was
slightly daunting to see just how aroused he was and
as she bit her lip, he smiled.

'Me fai asci pazzo,' he said, as if that explained
everything.

'Wh-what does that mean?'

'It means you make me crazy.'

'I love it when you talk Italian to me,' she said
shyly.

'Not Italian,' he said sternly as he slipped into bed
beside her. 'Neapolitan.'

She blinked. 'It's different?'

'It's dialect,' he said and she noticed he was placing several foil packets on the antique chest of draw-
ers beside the bed. 'And yes, it's very different.'

The appearance of condoms somehow punctured some of the romance, but by then he was naked beside her and Molly was discovering that the sensation of skin touching skin was like nothing she'd ever known. It was *heaven*. Better than chocolate cake. Better than…well, anything really.

'Salvio,' she breathed, trying out his name for the first time.

'*Sì, bedda mia?* Want me to kiss you again?'

'Yes, please,' she said fervently, and he laughed.

His kisses were deep. It felt as if he were drugging her with them, making her body receptive to the caress of his fingers. And, oh, those fingers—what magic they worked as he tiptoed them over her shivering flesh. He massaged her peaking nipples until she was writhing with pleasure, and when he slid his hand between her thighs and discovered how wet she was, he had to silence her instinctive gasp with another kiss.

And because she didn't want to be passive, Molly stroked him back. At first she was cautious—concentrating on his chest and ribcage, before daring to explore a belly which was far flatter than her own. But when she plucked up the courage to touch the unfamiliar hardness which kept brushing against her quivering thigh, he stopped her with a stern look. 'No.'

She didn't ask him why. She didn't dare. She was

afraid of doing anything which would shatter the mood or show how inexperienced she really was. Which might make Salvio De Gennaro bolt upright in bed and incredulously question what the hell he was doing, being intimate with a humble house-keeper. But he didn't. In fact, he seemed just as in tune with her body as she was with his. Like greedy animals, they rolled uninhibitedly around on the bed, biting and nipping and stroking and moaning and there was only the briefest hiatus when Salvio reached for one of the foil packets.

'Want to put this on for me?' he questioned pro-vocatively. 'Since my hands are shaking so much I'm beginning to wonder if I can manage to do it myself.'

Some of Molly's composure left her. Should she say something?

Salvio, I've only ever seen a condom in a biology class at school. I've never actually used one for real.

Mightn't learning that send him hurtling out of bed in horror? Yes, he might be as aroused as she imagined any man *could* be, but even so…mightn't it be a bit heavy if she burdened him with a piece of knowledge which wasn't really relevant? After all, it wasn't as if she was expecting this…interlude to actually go anywhere.

And maybe he read her thoughts because he

brought his face up close to hers and surveyed her with smoky eyes. 'You know that I—'

'Yes, I know. You're leaving in the morning,' she said. 'And that's okay.'

'You're sure?'

'Quite sure. I just want…'

'What do you want, Molly?' he questioned, almost gently.

'I just want tonight,' she breathed. 'That's all.'

Salvio frowned as he stroked on a condom. Was she for real, or just too good to be true? He kissed her again, wanting to explode with hunger but forcing himself to move as slowly as possible as he pushed inside her molten heat, because he was big. He'd been told that often enough in the past but he had never felt bigger than he did tonight.

But size had nothing to do with her next reaction. The tensing of her body and her brief grimace of pain told their own unbelievable story. Confusion swirled his thoughts and made him momentarily still. With an almighty effort he prepared to withdraw, but somehow her tight muscles clamped themselves around him in a way which was shockingly new and exciting, making him dangerously close to coming straight away. He sucked in a raw breath, trying desperately to claw back control. Trying to concentrate on not giving in to his orgasm, rather than on the unbelievable fact that the housekeeper was a virgin. Or rather, she *had* been.

But stopping himself from coming was the hardest sexual test he'd ever set himself. Maybe it was her tightness which felt so delicious. Or the uninhibited way she was responding to him. She was a stranger to all the games usually played in the bedroom, he realised—and her naivety made her an unmatchable lover, because she was a natural. She hadn't learnt any tricks or manoeuvres. The things she was doing she hadn't done with any other man before and somehow that turned him on. He revelled in the way she squirmed those fleshy hips as he drove into her. The way she thrust her breast towards his lips, so that he could tease the pointing nipple with first his tongue and then his teeth. He sensed the change in her—the moment when her orgasm became inevitable—and he watched her closely, seeing her dark eyelashes flutter to a close. Triumph washed over him as she made that first disbelieving choke of pleasure and a rosy flush began to blossom over her breasts. And only when the last of her violent spasms had died away did he give in to his own need, unprepared for the power of what was happening to him. It felt like the first time, he thought dazedly. Or maybe the only time.

And then he fell asleep.

CHAPTER FOUR

IT WAS STILL dark when Salvio awoke next morning—
the illuminated dial of his wristwatch informing him
it was just past six. He waited a moment until his
eyes became adjusted to the shadows in the bedroom. In the heat of that frantic sexual encounter
which had taken him almost by surprise last night,
he hadn't bothered to close the drapes and outside
it was still dark—but then, sunrise came late to this
part of the world in the depths of an English winter.

He glanced across at the sleeping woman beside
him, sucking in a slow lungful of air as he tried
to get his head around what had happened. Trying
to justify the fact that he'd had sex with the innocent housekeeper, when deep down he knew there
could be no justification. Yet she had wanted it, he
reminded himself grimly. She had wanted it as much
as him.

They had been intimate again during the night—

several times, as it happened. His stretching leg had encountered the voluptuous softness of her warm flesh, making him instantly aroused. There had been a stack of questions he'd been meaning to ask, but somehow her touch had wiped them from his mind. The second time had been amazing—and so had the third. She was so easy to please. So grateful for the pleasure he gave her. He'd expected her to start bringing up tricky topics after orgasm number five, but his expectations hadn't materialised. She hadn't demanded to know if he had changed his mind about seeing her again, which was fortunate really, because he hadn't. His eyes narrowed. He couldn't. She was too sweet. Too naïve. She wouldn't last a minute in his world and his own cynical nature would destroy all that naïve enthusiasm of hers in an instant.

Leaning over, he shook her bare shoulder—resisting the desire to slip his hand beneath the duvet and begin massaging one of those magnificent breasts.

'Molly,' he murmured. 'Wake up. It's morning.'

It was a shock for Molly to open her eyes and realise she was staring up at the magnificent chandelier which hung from the ceiling of the guest bedroom. In this faint light it twinkled like the fading stars outside the window and she forced herself to remember that in several hours' time she would be attacking it with her feather duster, not lying beneath the priceless shards of crystal, with the warm body of a naked man beside her.

A shiver ran through her as she turned her head to look at Salvio, her heart punching out a violent beat as she realised what she'd done. She swallowed. What *hadn't* she done? She had let him undress her and explore every inch of her body, with his tongue and his fingers and a whole lot more beside. When he'd been deep inside her body, she had choked out his name over and over again as he had awoken an appetite she hadn't realised she possessed. Somehow he had waved a magic wand and turned her into someone she didn't really recognise and she had gone from being inexperienced Molly Miller, to an eager woman who couldn't get enough of him. Briefly she closed her eyes.

And she wasn't going to regret a single second of it. Because you couldn't turn the clock back—and even if you could, who would want to?

She yawned, stretching her arms above her head and registering the unfamiliar aching of her body. How many times had he made love to her? she wondered dazedly, as she recalled his seemingly insatiable appetite and her own eager response.

She forced herself to ask the question she didn't really want to ask. 'What time is it?'

'Just after six.' There was a pause. His eyes became hooded. 'Molly—'

'Well, you'd better get going, hadn't you?' Her breezy interjection forestalled him because she'd guessed what he was about to say—the heaviness of his tone warning her that this was the Big Goodbye. And he didn't need to. He had to go and she was okay with that. Why ruin everything by demanding more than he'd ever intended to give? She pinned an efficient smile to her lips. 'You did say you wanted to get away early.'

He frowned, as if her response wasn't what he'd been expecting, but Molly knew there was only one way to deal with a situation like this, and that was by being sensible, the way she'd been all her life. She had to face facts, not mould them to suit her fantasies. She knew there could be no future between her and the billionaire tycoon because their lives were too different. Last night the boundaries had become blurred—but one night of bliss didn't change the fundamentals, did it? She was employed as a housekeeper—and lying in an honoured guest's bed was the very last place she should be.

'You're sure you're okay?' he growled.

She wondered where the rogue thought came from. The one which made her want to say, *Not really, no. I wish you could take me with you wher-*

ever you're going and make love to me the way you did last night.

But fortunately, the practical side of her character was the dominant one. As if Salvio De Gennaro would want to take her away with him! She tried to imagine cramming herself into that low-slung sports car—why, her weight would probably disable the suspension! 'Why wouldn't I be okay?' she questioned breezily. 'It was great. At least, I think it was.' For the first time, a trace of insecurity crept into her voice as she looked at him with a question in her eyes.

'Oh, it was more than "great",' he affirmed, reaching out to trace the tip of his finger over the quiver of her bottom lip. 'In fact, it was so good that I want to do it all over again.'

Once again Molly felt her stomach clench with desire and a rush of heat tugged deep inside her. 'But…' she whispered as he moved closer.

'But what, *mia bedda*?'

'There isn't…' She swallowed. 'There isn't time.'

'Says who?'

He slipped his hand between her legs. Molly wondered what had happened to the sensible part of her now. Forgotten, that was what. Banished by the first lazy stroke of his finger over her slick heat. 'Salvio,' she moaned, as his dark head moved down and his tongue found her nipple.

He lifted his head from her breast, dark eyes gleaming in the half-light. 'You want me to stop?'

'You know I don't,' she gasped.

'So why don't you show me what you *would* like?'

Maybe it was the knowledge that this was the last time which made her so adventurous, because Molly suddenly found her hand drifting over his taut belly to capture the rocky erection which was pressing so insistently against her thigh. 'This,' she said shakily. 'This is what I want.'

'And where do you want it?'

'In me,' she breathed boldly. 'Inside me.'

'Me, too,' he purred, reaching out to grab a condom from the sadly diminished pile on the bedside cabinet.

Molly was aware of being warm and sticky as he moved over her. Of her hair all mussed and her teeth unbrushed—but somehow none of that seemed to matter because Salvio was touching her as if she were some kind of goddess. His fingers were sure and seeking and goosebumps rippled over her skin in response as he smoothed his hand over her belly. She felt as if she were *soaring* as she wrapped her thighs around his hips and gave herself up to the exquisite sensation of that first sweet thrust and then the deepening movements which followed.

She loved the way they moved in time. The way

she felt as if she were on a fast shuttle to paradise when another orgasm took her over the top. And she loved his almost helpless expression as his face darkened and he pumped his seed inside her. The way his tousled head collapsed onto her shoulder afterwards as he uttered something intently in what she presumed was more Neapolitan dialect. His breathing was warm and even against her neck and, terrified he would fall asleep and delay his departure, she shook him. 'Salvio,' she whispered. 'Don't go to sleep. You'd better go. Before anyone wakes up.'

'Then you'd better get out of here, too,' he instructed, pushing aside the rumpled duvet. 'Right now. Before anyone sees you.'

For some reason his remark dispirited her and brought her crashing back to earth, allowing reality to puncture her little bubble of happiness. But despite the insecurities which were bubbling up inside her, Molly managed to retain her cheery smile, enjoying the sight of Salvio pulling on his jeans and sweater and quietly opening the door as he headed for the bathroom.

Once he'd gone she got out of bed and pulled on her discarded underclothes—pulling a face as she smoothed her crumpled work dress over her hips and rolled her black tights into a little ball, which she gripped in her hand. She'd be able to do something with her appearance once Salvio had left, she reasoned—glancing up as the door opened as he came back into the bedroom, his dark hair glittering with tiny drops of water from the shower.

In silence he dressed before snapping his over-night case closed, his expression very serious as he walked towards her. For a moment he just stood in front of her, his gaze sweeping over her like a dark spotlight, as if he were seeing her for the first time.

'So why?' he questioned simply. 'Why me?

Molly expelled a shuddered breath, because in a way she'd been waiting for this question. He hadn't asked her last night and she'd been glad, because she hadn't wanted the mundane to spoil what had been the most fantastic night of her life. In a way, she would have preferred it if he hadn't brought it up now—but he had, and she needed to answer in a way designed to keep it light. Because she didn't want a single thing to tarnish the memory of how glorious it had been. She shrugged. She even man-aged a smile. 'I don't meet many men in this line of work,' she said. 'And certainly none like you. And you're...you're a very attractive man, Salvio—as I expect you've been told on many occasions.'

He frowned, as if her honesty troubled him. 'I want you to know that I didn't invite you in here in order to seduce you,' he said slowly. 'I'm not saying the thought hadn't crossed my mind earlier, but that wasn't my intention.'

She nodded. 'I know it wasn't. You were being kind, that's all. Maybe that's why I agreed to have a drink with you.'

He gave an odd kind of laugh. 'You had a very profound effect on me, Molly.'

There was an expression in his dark eyes which Molly couldn't work out but maybe it was best that way. She didn't want him telling her it had been an inexplicable thing he'd done. She wanted to hang onto what had happened between them—to treat it as you would one of those precious baubles you hung on the tree at Christmas. She didn't want to let the memory slip from her fingers and see it shatter into a million pieces.

'I'm glad,' she said, holding onto her composure only by a thread, her heart pounding frantically beneath her breast. 'But time's getting on. You'd better go.'

He nodded, as if being encouraged to leave a bedroom was a novel experience for him, but suddenly he turned and walked towards the bedroom door without another word, and Molly's heart twisted painfully as he closed it quietly behind him. She stood there framed in the window, watching as he emerged from the house, his dark figure silhouetted against the crashing ocean, and for a second he looked up, his black gaze capturing hers. She waited for him to smile, or wave, or something—and she told herself it was best he didn't, for who knew who else might be watching?

Throwing his bag inside, he slipped into the driver's seat, the closing door blotting out her last sight of him. His powerful car started up in a small cloud of gravel before sweeping down towards the coastal road and she watched until it was just a faint black dot in the distance. As sunrise touched the dark clouds with the first hint of red, Molly wondered if Salvio's life was a series of exits, with women gazing longingly out of windows as they watched him go.

Her cheeks were hot as she whipped the bottom sheet from the bed and removed the duvet cover. She would come back later to collect the linen and clean the room from top to bottom. But first she needed a hot shower. The Averys had plenty of events coming up and Molly had a long list of things to do today. Perhaps it was good that the weeks ahead were busy during the run-up to Christmas. It would certainly stop her from dwelling on the fact she would never see Salvio again. Never feel his lips on hers or his powerful arms holding her tight. Because this was what happened in the grown-up world, she told herself fiercely. People had fun with each other. Fun without expectations, or commitment. They had sex and then they just walked away.

Quietly, she closed the guest-room door behind her and was creeping along the corridor with the exaggerated care of a cartoon thief, when she became aware of someone watching her. Her heart lurched with fear. A shadowed figure was standing perfectly still at the far end of the guest corridor.

Not just anyone.

Lady Avery.

Molly's footsteps slowed, her heart crashing frantically against her ribcage as she met the accusing look in her boss's pale eyes.

'So, Molly,' Lady Avery said, in a voice she'd never heard her use before. 'Did you sleep well?'

There was a terrible pause and Molly's throat constricted, because what could she say? It would be adding insult to injury if she made some lame excuse about why she was creeping out of Salvio's room at this time in the morning, carrying a balled-up pair of tights. And now she would be sacked. She'd be jobless and homeless at the worst possible time of year. She swallowed. There was only one thing she *could* say. 'I'm sorry, Lady Avery.'

Her aristocratic employer shook her head in disbelief. 'I can't believe it!' she said. 'Why someone like him could have been interested in someone like you, when he could have had…'

Her words trailed away and Molly didn't dare fill the awkward silence which followed. Because how could Lady Avery possibly finish her own sentence without losing face or dignity? How could she possibly admit that *she* had been hoping to end up in Salvio's bed, when she was a married woman and her husband was in the house?

Molly's cheeks grew hot as she acknowledged the shameful progression of her thoughts. Behaving as if the Neapolitan tycoon were some kind of prize they'd both been competing over! Had the loneliness of her job made her completely indiscriminate, so that she had been prepared to leap into bed with the first man who had ever shown her any real affection? 'I can only apologise,' she repeated woodenly.

Once again, Lady Avery shook her head. 'Just get back to work, will you?' she ordered sharply.

'Work?' echoed Molly cautiously.

'Well, what else did you think you'd be doing? We have ten people coming for dinner tonight, in case you'd forgotten. And since this time I'm assuming you won't be obsessing about one of the guests, at least the meat won't arrive at the table cremated.' She gave Molly an arch look. 'Unless no man is now safe from your clutches. I must say you're the most unlikely candidate to be a *femme fatale*. Just get back to work, will you, Molly, before I change my mind?'

'Y-yes, Lady Avery.'

Unable to believe she hadn't been fired on the spot, Molly spent the next few weeks working harder than she'd ever worked before. She went above and beyond the call of duty as Christmas approached and she tried to make amends for her unprofessional behaviour. She attempted ambitious culinary experiments, which thankfully all turned out brilliantly. She baked, prodded, steamed and whipped—to the fervent admiration of the stream of guests which passed through the mistletoe-festooned hallway of the house. And if Lady Avery made a few sarcastic digs about Molly hanging around hopefully beneath the sprigs of white berries, Molly was mature enough not to respond. Maybe her boss's anger was justified, she reasoned. Maybe she would have said the same if the situation had been reversed.

And it didn't matter how busy she was—it was never enough to stop her thoughts from spinning in an unwanted direction. She found herself thinking about Salvio and that was the last thing she needed. She didn't want to remember all the things he'd done to her. The way he'd stroked her face and lips and body, before pushing open her thighs to enter her.

Just as she didn't want to think about the way he'd whispered *'bedda mia'* and *'nicuzza'* in that haunting dialect when they'd both woken in the middle of the night. Because remembering that stuff was dangerous. It made it all too easy to imagine that it mattered. And it didn't. Not to him. He'd been able to walk away without a second glance and Molly had told him she was able to do the same.

So do it.

Stop yearning.

Stop wishing for the impossible.

It was four days before Christmas when two bombshells fell in rapid succession. Molly had just been about to drive to the village, when she came across Lady Avery standing in the hallway—a full-length fur coat swamping her fine-boned frame. Her face looked cold. As cold as the wintry wind which was whistling outside the big house and bringing with it the first few flakes of snow.

'Molly, don't bother going to the shops right now,' she said, without preamble.

Molly blinked. She'd made the pudding and cake and mince pies, but she still had to pick up the turkey and the vegetables. And hadn't they run out of satsumas? She looked at her boss helpfully. 'Is there something else you would rather I was doing?'

'Indeed there is. You can go upstairs and pack your things.'

Molly stared at her boss in confusion. 'Pack my things?' she echoed stupidly. 'I don't understand.'

'Don't you? It's really quite simple. Surely there's no need for me to spell it out for you. We no longer require your services.'

'But…'

'But what, Molly?' Lady Avery took a step closer and now Molly could see that all the rage she'd been bottling up since Salvio's departure was about to come spilling out. 'I hope you aren't going to ask me why I haven't given you more notice, because I really don't think the normal rules apply when you've abused your position as outrageously as you have done. I really don't think that *sleeping with the guests* ever made it into your job description, do you?'

'But it's just before Christmas!' Molly burst out, unable to stop herself. 'And this…this is my home.'

Lady Avery gave a shrill laugh. 'I don't think so. Why don't you go running to your boyfriend and ask if he wants you over the holiday period? *Because it's not going to happen, that's why.* Salvio will have moved on to the kind of women he's more usually associated with by now.' Her pale eyes drilled into Molly. 'Do you know, they say there isn't a supermodel on the planet he hasn't dated?'

'But why…why wait until now?' questioned Molly in a low voice. 'Why didn't you just fire me straight away?'

'With wall-to-wall engagements planned and Christmas just over the horizon?' Lady Avery looked at her incredulously. 'I was hardly going to dispense with your services and leave myself without a house-keeper at such a busy time, now, was I? That's what's known as cutting off your nose to spite your face.' There was a pause. 'You'll find you've been paid up to the end of the month, which is more generous than you deserve. Philip and I have decided to fly to Barbados tomorrow for a last-minute holiday and we're going out for the rest of the day. Just make sure you're gone by the time we return, will you, Molly?'

'But…but where will I go tonight?'

'You really think I care? There's a cheap B&B in the village. You can go there—*if* they'll take you.' Lady Avery's mouth had curved into a cruel smile. 'Just make sure you leave your car and house keys on the hall table before you go.'

And that was that. Molly could hardly believe it was happening. Except that she could. Her heart clenched as her old friend Fear re-entered her life without fanfare and suddenly she was back in that familiar situation of being in a fix. Only this time she couldn't blame her brother, or the vagaries of fate which had made her mother so ill throughout her childhood. This time it was all down to her.

Biting her lip, she thought desperately about where she could go and what she could do, but no instant solution sprang to mind. She had no relatives. No local friends who could provide her with a roof over her head until she found herself another live-in job. Her mind buzzed frantically as some of Lady Avery's words came flooding into her mind. How would Salvio react if she called him up and told him she'd been fired as a result of their crazy liaison? Would he do the decent thing and offer her a place to stay? Yet, despite recoiling at the thought of throwing herself on the mercy of a man who'd made it clear he wanted nothing but a one-night stand, it was growing increasingly clear that she might *have* to. Because the second bombshell was hovering overhead ready to explode, no matter how hard she tried to block it from her mind.

Telling herself it was stress which had made her period so late, she pushed the thought away as she remembered the card Salvio had given her—the one with a direct line to his assistant. What had he said? That his assistant knew plenty of people and could help her find a domestic role if ever she needed one. Molly licked her lips. She didn't want to do it but what choice did she have? Where would she even *start* looking for a new job and a home at this time of year?

Quickly, she packed her clothes, trying not to give in to the tears which were pricking at the backs of her eyes. Carefully she wedged in the framed photo of her mother and the one of Robbie in his school uniform, the cute image giving no hint of the gimlet-eyed teenager he would become. And only when she was standing in her threadbare winter coat, with a hand-knitted scarf knotted tightly around her neck, did she dial the number on the card with a shaking finger.

Salvio's assistant was called Gina and she didn't just sound friendly—she sounded *relieved* when Molly gave her name and explained why she was ringing.

'I can't believe it,' she said fervently. '*You* are the answer to my prayers, Molly Miller.'

'Me?' said Molly doubtfully.

'Yes, you.' Gina's voice softened. 'Are you free now? I mean, as of right now?'

'I am,' answered Molly cautiously. 'Why?'

'Because Salvio is having his annual pre-Christmas party in the Cotswolds tomorrow, just before he flies to Naples—and the housekeeper we'd hired has called to say her mother has fallen downstairs and broken her wrist, and she's had to cancel. If you can step in and

take over at the last minute I can make it very worth
your while.'

Molly pushed out the words from between suddenly frozen lips. 'That's very bad news—about the
broken wrist, I mean, but I don't think I—'

But the tycoon's assistant was breezing on as if
she hadn't spoken.

'Salvio must rate you very highly to have given
you my number,' Gina continued. 'Why, it's almost
like fate. I won't even have to bother telling him
about the change. He doesn't like to be bogged down
with domestic trivia and he's always so busy.'

Molly bit her lip so hard it hurt. This was fast
becoming a nightmare, but what else could she do?
How could she possibly turn down this opportunity
just because she'd had sex with the man who would
now unwittingly be employing her? She would just
blend into the background and pray that the Neapolitan tycoon would be too busying partying to pay her
any attention. And if the worst came to the worst and
he discovered her identity—then she would shrug her
shoulders and tell him it was no big deal.

Realistically, what could go wrong?

But being rumbled by Salvio wasn't the worst
thing which could happen, was it? Not by a long
way. The fear which had been nagging at her for days
came flooding into her mind and this time would not

be silenced, because all her excuses about stress and anxiety were rapidly fading. Because she wasn't sure if anxiety was capable of making your breasts ache and feel much bigger than usual. Or whether it could sap your normally voracious appetite.

She stared at her pale reflection in the hall mirror and saw the terror written in her own eyes. Because what if she was pregnant with Salvio De Gennaro's baby?

CHAPTER FIVE

VISIBILITY WAS POOR—in fact, it was almost non-existent. Salvio's fingers tightened around the soft leather of the steering wheel. Eyes narrowed, he stared straight ahead but all he could see was an all-enveloping whiteness swirling in front of the car windscreen. Every couple of seconds, the wipers dispelled the thick layer of snow which had settled, only to be rapidly replaced by another.

Frustrated, he glanced at the gold watch at his wrist, cursing the unpredictability of the weather. His journey from central London to the Cotswold countryside had been excruciatingly slow and in an ideal world he would have cancelled his annual party. But you couldn't really cancel something this close to Christmas, no matter how preoccupied you were feeling. And he *was* feeling preoccupied, no doubt about it—even though the reason for that was disconcertingly bizarre. An impatient sigh escaped his lungs as he watched another flurry of snow. Because he couldn't stop thinking about the curvy little housekeeper with the big grey eyes, with those luscious breasts, whose tips had fitted perfectly into his hungry mouth. Most of all, he couldn't stop remembering her purity. Her innocence.

Which he had taken. Without thought. Without knowledge. But certainly not without feeling.

Memories of how it had felt to penetrate her beautiful tightness flooded his mind and Salvio swallowed as he touched his foot against the brake pedal. Would he have bedded her so willingly if he'd known she was a virgin? Of course he wouldn't. His desire for the housekeeper had been completely out of character and he still couldn't quite fathom it. He usually enjoyed women who were, if not quite his equal, then certainly closer on the social scale than Molly Miller would ever be.

He thought about Beatriz—the Brazilian beauty with whom he'd been enjoying a long-distance flirtation for the past few months. He had been attracted to her because she'd played hard to get and he'd convinced himself that a woman who wouldn't tumble straight into his arms was exactly what he needed. But as her attitude towards him had thawed, so had his interest waned—and the memory of Molly had completely wiped her from his mind. And although

Beatriz had made it clear she would be happy to share his bed after his Christmas party, the idea had left him cold, despite the fact that most men lusted after her statuesque beauty. He had been wondering about the most tactful way to convey his sudden change of heart, when she'd rung last night to say her plane had been delayed in Honolulu and she didn't think she was going to make his party. And hadn't he been struck by an overwhelming feeling of *relief*?

'*No importa.* Don't worry about it,' he had responded quickly—probably too quickly.

A pause. 'But I'm hoping we can see each other some other time, Salvio.'

'I'm hoping so too, but I'm flying out to Naples for Christmas and I'm not sure when I'll be back.' His response had been smooth and seasoned. And distinctly dismissive. 'I'll call you.'

He could tell from her sharp intake of breath that she understood the underlying message and her goodbye had been clipped and cold. She hadn't even wished him a happy Christmas and he supposed he couldn't blame her.

But his mind had soon moved on to other things and, infuriatingly, he kept recalling the sweet sensation of a naked Molly in his arms. He swallowed. The way her soft lips had pressed into his neck and her fleshy thighs had opened so accommodatingly.

There were a million reasons why he shouldn't be thinking about her but she was proving a distractingly difficult image to shift. Was that because she hadn't put any demands on him? Because she'd been okay about him walking out of her life? Most women hung on in there, but Molly Miller was not among their number. And hadn't that intrigued him? Made him wonder what it might be like to see her in a more normal setting. Perhaps even take her out to dinner to see how long it would take for her allure to fade.

He'd thought a few times about contacting her—but what could he say, without falsely raising her hopes? No. He was doing her a favour by leaving her alone—that was what he needed to remember. Breaking hearts was his default mechanism—and no way would he wish that kind of pain on the passionate little housekeeper.

It was the most beautiful house Molly had ever seen. Pressing her nose against the icy-cold glass, she peered out through the taxi window at the sprawling manor house, whose gardens were a clever combination of wild and formal and seemed to go on for ever. Although the sky was pewter-grey, the light was bright with snow and everything was covered in white. Fat flakes tumbled like giant feathers from the sky, so that the scene in front of her looked like one of those old-fashioned Christmas cards you couldn't seem to buy any more.

But Molly's emotions were in turmoil as the cab inched its way up the snowy drive. She had underestimated the impact of leaving Cornwall because even though the job had left a lot to be desired, it had still been her home and her security for the last two years. More than that, her departure had been forced upon her in the most dramatic and shameful of ways. Suddenly she felt rudderless—like a leaf caught up by a gust of wind being swirled towards an unknown destination.

But even worse than her near-homelessness was the confirmation of her worst fears. That it hadn't been stress or anxiety which had made her period so late. That the weird tugs of mood and emotion—like wanting to burst into tears or go to sleep at the most inopportune times—hadn't been down to the *worry* of getting pregnant. She couldn't even blame the sudden shock of losing her live-in job, or the corresponding jolt to her confidence. No, the reason had been made perfectly clear when she'd done not one, but two pregnancy tests in the overcrowded bathroom of the little boarding house she'd stayed in last night. With growing horror and a kind of numb disbelief she had sat back on her heels and stared at the unmistakable blue line, shaking with the shock of realising that she was pregnant with Salvio's baby.

And wondering what the hell she was going to do about it.

But she couldn't afford to think about that right now. The only thing she needed to concentrate on was doing her job—and as good a job as possible. She was going to have to tell him, yes, but not yet. Not right before his party and the arrival of his presumably high-powered guests.

She paid the driver and stepped out of the cab onto a soft blanket of snow. There were no other tyre marks on the drive and the only sign of life was a little robin hopping around as she made her way to the ancient oak front door, which looked like something out of a fairy tale. She knocked loudly, just in case—but there was no answer and so she let herself in with the keys she'd picked up from Salvio's assistant, along with a great big wodge of cash for expenses.

Inside, everything was silent except for the loud ticking of a grandfather clock, which echoed through the spacious hallway, and the interior was even more beautiful than the outside had suggested. It spoke of elegance and money and taste. Gleaming panelled walls carved with acorns and unicorns. Huge marble fireplaces and dark floorboards scattered with silk rugs were illuminated by the sharp blue light which filtered in through the windows. Yet the beauty and the splendour were wasted on Molly. She felt like an outsider. Like the spectre who had arrived at the feast bearing a terrible secret nobody would want to hear. She felt like curling up in a ball and howling, but what was the point of that? Instead she forced herself to walk around the house to get her bearings, just as she would with any new job.

A quick tour reassured her that the cupboards and fridge were well stocked with everything she could possibly need, the beds all made up with fresh linen and the fires laid. She lit the fires, washed her hands and started working her way through the to-do list. Barring bad weather cancellations, twenty-five guests would be arriving at seven. Gina had informed her that there were plenty of bedrooms if bad weather prevented some of the city guests getting back to London, but Salvio would prefer it if they left.

'He's a man who likes his own company,' she'd said.

'Does he?' Molly had questioned nervously, as an image shot into her head of a crying baby. How would he ever be able to deal with *that*?

Maybe he wouldn't want to.

Maybe he would tell her that he had no desire

for an unplanned baby in his life. Had she thought about *that*?

A local catering company were providing a hot-buffet supper at around nine and wine waiters would take care of the drinks. All Molly had to do was make sure everything ran smoothly and supervise the local waitresses who were being ferried in from the nearby village. How difficult could it be? Her gaze scanned down to the bottom of the list.

And please don't forget to decorate the Christ-mas tree!

Molly had seen the tree the moment she'd walked in—a giant beast of a conifer whose tip almost touched the tall ceiling, beside which were stacked piles of cardboard boxes. Opening one, she discovered neat rows of glittering baubles—brand-new and obviously very expensive. And suddenly she found herself thinking about Christmases past. About the little pine tree she and Robbie used to drag in from the garden every year, and the hand-made decorations which their mother had knitted before the cruel illness robbed her of the ability to do even that. It had been hard for all of them to watch her fading away but especially tough for her little brother, who had refused to believe his beloved mother was going to die. And Molly hadn't been able to do anything to stop it, had she? It had been her first lesson in powerlessness. Of realising that sometimes you had to sit back and watch awful things happen—and that for once she couldn't protect the little boy she'd spent her life protecting.

Didn't she feel that same sense of powerlessness now as she thought of the cells multiplying in her womb? Knowing that outwardly she looked exactly the same as before, while inside she was carrying the Neapolitan's baby.

Her fingers were trembling as she draped the tree with fairy lights and hung the first bauble—watching it spin in the fractured light from the mullioned window. And then it happened—right out of nowhere, although if she'd thought about it she should have been expecting it. If she hadn't been singing 'In The Bleak Midwinter' at the top of her voice she might have heard the front door slam, or registered the momentary pause which followed. But she wasn't aware of anything until something alerted her to the fact that someone else was in the room. Slowly she turned her head to see Salvio standing there.

Her heart clenched tightly and then began to pound. He was wearing a dark cashmere overcoat over faded jeans and snowflakes were melting in the luxuriant blackness of his hair. She thought how tall and how powerful he looked. How his muscular physique dominated the space around him. All these thoughts registered in the back of her mind but the one which was at the forefront was the expression of disbelief darkening his olive-skinned features.

'You,' he said, staring at her from between narrowed eyes.

Molly wondered if the shock of seeing her had made him forget her name, or whether he had forgotten it anyway. In either case, he needed reminding—or this situation could prove even more embarrassing than it was already threatening to be. 'Yes, me,' she echoed, her throat dry with nerves. 'Molly. Molly Miller.'

'I know your name!' he snapped, in a way which made her wonder if perhaps he was protesting too much. 'What I want to know is what the hell you're doing here.'

His face had hardened with suspicion. It certainly wasn't the ecstatic greeting Molly might have hoped for—if she'd dared to hope for anything. But hope was a waste of time—she'd learnt that a long time ago. And at least a life spent working as a servant and having to keep her emotions hidden meant she was able to present a face which was perfectly calm. The only outward sign of her embarrassment was the hot colour which came rushing into her cheeks, making her think how unattractive she must look with her apron digging into her waist and her hair spilling untidily out of its ponytail. 'I'm just decorating the Christmas tree—'

'I can see that for myself,' he interrupted impatiently. 'I want to know *why*. What are you doing here, Molly?'

The accusation which had made his mouth twist with anger was unmistakable and Molly stiffened. Did he think she was stalking him, like one of those crazed ex-lovers who sometimes featured in the tabloids? Women who had, against all the odds, come into contact with a wealthy man and then been reluctant to let him—or the lifestyle—go.

'You gave me your assistant's card, remember?' she reminded him. 'And told me to ring her if I needed to find work.'

'But you already have a job,' he pointed out. 'You work for the Averys.'

Molly shook her head and found herself wishing she didn't have to say this. Because wasn't it a humiliating thing to have to admit—that she had been kicked out of her job just before Christmas? 'Not any more, I don't,' she said. She met the question which was glittering from his black eyes. 'Lady Avery caught me leaving your bedroom.'

His eyes narrowed. 'And she *sacked* you because of that?'

Molly's colour increased. 'I'm afraid so.'

Beneath his breath, Salvio uttered some of the words he'd learnt in the backstreets of Naples during his poverty-stricken childhood. Words he hadn't spoken in a long time but which seemed appropriate now as remorse clawed at his gut. It was his fault. Of course it was. Was that why she was looking at him with those big grey eyes, like some wounded animal you discovered hiding in the woods? Because she blamed him and held him responsible for what had happened? And it never *should* have happened, he told himself bitterly. He should never have invited her into his room for a drink, despite the fact that she'd been crying. He'd tried very hard to justify his actions. He'd told himself he'd been motivated by compassion rather than lust, but perhaps he had been deluding himself. Because ultimately he was a man and she was a woman and the chemistry between them had been as powerful as anything he'd ever experienced. Surely he wasn't going to deny *that*.

His eyes narrowed as he studied her. Despite her initial innocence, had she subsequently recognised the sexual power she had wielded over him? It wasn't inconceivable that her sacking had come about as a result of her own ego. She might easily have made a big show of leaving his room, with that dreamy look of sexual satisfaction which made a woman look more beautiful than fancy clothes ever could. And mightn't that have provoked Sarah Avery, whose advances he had most definitely rejected?

Suddenly he felt as if he was back on familiar territory, as he recalled the behaviour of women during his playing days, and one woman in particular. He remembered the dollar signs which had lit up in their eyes when they'd realised how much his contract had been worth. These days he might no longer be one of Italy's best-paid sportsmen, but in reality he was even wealthier. Was that why Molly Miller was here— prettily decorating his tree—just waiting to hit him with some kind of clumsy demand for recompense?

'So why exactly did Gina offer you this job?' he questioned.

She bit her lip. 'Because the woman who was supposed to be doing it had to suddenly go and look after her mother. And I didn't let on that I…' Her words faltered. 'That I *knew* you, if that's what you're worried about. Gina doesn't have a clue about what went on between us. There was a slot to fill, that's all—and I just happened to be in the right place at the right time.'

Or the wrong place at the wrong time. Just like the last time they'd met.

The thoughts rushed into Salvio's head before he could stop them and he felt his body tense as he worked out how best to handle this. Because now he found himself in a difficult situation. He frowned. The amazing night he'd shared with her had haunted him ever since, but nobody was going to deny that it had been a foolhardy action on so many levels. Did she think it was going to happen again? he wondered. Was she expecting to resume her position in his bed? That once all his guests had left, he would be introducing her to another night of bliss?

He raked his gaze over her, unable to suppress the hunger which instantly fired up his blood but resenting it all the same. He shouldn't feel this way about her. He shouldn't still want her. That night had been a mistake and one which definitely shouldn't be repeated. Yet desire was spiralling up inside him with an intensity which took him by surprise and despite his best efforts he was failing to dampen it. With her fleshy curves accentuated by the waistband of an apron, she looked the antithesis of the glamour he'd always regarded as a prerequisite for his lovers. She looked *wholesome* and plain and yet somehow incredibly sexy.

Suddenly he felt a powerful urge to take her in his arms and lie her down beside the Christmas tree. To pull down her mismatched panties and kiss between those generous thighs, before losing his tongue and then his body in all that tight, molten heat. He wondered how she would react if he did. With the same breathtaking eagerness she had shown before—or would she push him away this time? His mouth hardened and so uncomfortably did his groin and, although he was unbearably tempted to test out the idea, he drew himself up, wondering if he'd taken leave of his senses.

He was her boss, for heaven's sake!

Shaking his head, he walked over to the window and stared out at the thick white layer which was coating the lawns and bare branches of the trees. The light was fading from the sky, intensifying the monochrome colours of the garden so that all he noticed was the diamond-bright glitter of the ice-encrusted snow.

His mouth hardened. He'd thought tonight would just be another evening to get through, before flying out to Naples for a family Christmas. Slowly, he turned around. But suddenly everything had changed—and all because of this pink-faced woman who was standing in front of him, nervously chewing her lip.

'How long are you supposed to be working here?' he demanded.

'Just for tonight. And tomorrow I have to supervise the clean-up after the party.'

'And after that?' he probed. 'What then?'

She rubbed the tip of her ugly shoe over the Persian rug as if she were polishing it. 'I don't know yet. I'll just have to find something else.'

'Including accommodation, I suppose?'

She moved her shoulders awkwardly, as if he had reminded her of something she would prefer to forget, and when she looked up, her grey eyes were almost defiant. 'Well, yes. The jobs I take are always live-in.'

His eyes narrowed. 'And how easy will that be?'

Her attempt to look nonchalant failed and for the first time Salvio saw a trace of vulnerability on her face.

'Not very easy at this time of the year, I imagine.'

Salvio felt the flicker of a heavy pulse at his temple as another unwanted streak of conscience hit him and he recognised he couldn't just abandon her to the wolves. He had bedded her and she had lost her job as a result of that—so it stood to reason he must take some of the responsibility. He nodded. 'Very well. Tomorrow, I'll have a word with Gina. See if we can't find you something more permanent.' He saw her face brighten and wondered if he had falsely raised her hopes. 'Not with me, of course,' he continued hastily. 'That isn't going to happen. The night we shared was many things,

Molly, but it certainly didn't lay down a suitable foundation for any kind of working relationship between us.'

Molly flinched. She had thought him kind and that his behaviour towards her in the past had been thoughtful. But he wasn't kind, not really. He'd made it clear she couldn't ever work for him, not now she had been his lover—so, in effect, wasn't he patronising her just as much as Lady Avery had done? Before she thought she'd seen consideration in his face but that had been replaced by a flinty kind of calculation. Because Salvio De Gennaro could be utterly ruthless, she recognised—her heart sinking as she tried to imagine how he was going to react to her unwelcome news.

'Do you understand what I'm saying, Molly?' he continued remorselessly.

'Of course I do,' she said. 'I wasn't expecting to get a job with you. So please don't worry about it, Salv— Signor De Gennaro,' she amended, unable to hide her sudden flash of sarcasm. 'I won't bother you. You won't even know I'm here.'

The look on his face told her he didn't believe her and, despite her inexperience, Molly could understand why. Because how could they remain indifferent to each other when the atmosphere around them was still charged with that potent chemistry which had led to her downfall before? And wasn't she longing for him to touch her again? To trace his fingertip along the edges of her trembling lips, before replacing them with his mouth and kissing her until she capitulated to his every need.

Well, that would be insane.

Molly swallowed as she picked another bauble from its soft nest of tissue paper and the Neapolitan turned away.

'I need to get showered and changed before the party,' he said roughly. 'Just get on with your work, will you, Molly?'

CHAPTER SIX

SHE WISHED HE would stop staring at her.

Liar. Molly shivered as she picked up an empty wine glass and put it on her tray. *Admit it. You like it when he stares at you. Even though his face looks all dark and savage, as if he hates himself for doing it.*

And how much more savage will he look when he discovers the truth? she wondered.

It was the end of a long evening and only a few die-hard guests remained. Contrary to predictions the snow had stopped falling, allowing the chauffeur-driven cars to take the giggling London guests safely back to the capital. Vintage champagne had flowed, delicious food had been eaten and there hadn't been a single crisis in the kitchen, much to Molly's relief. A group of local singers had trudged through the snow and treated the partygoers to an emotional medley of Christmas carols, before being given mulled wine and hot mince pies and sent on their way with a huge donation to rebuild the roof of the village hall. And now Salvio was standing talking to a dark-suited man in the far corner of the huge drawing room—someone had whispered that he was a sheikh—but every time she looked up, Molly could see the hooded black eyes of the Neapolitan trained on her.

She hurried down to the kitchen where at least she was safe from that devastating gaze and the ongoing concern of how exactly she was going to break her momentous news. At least when you were helping stack clean plates and showing the hired help where to put all the silver cutlery, it was easy to forget your own problems, if only for a while. But at twenty past midnight the last of the staff departed and only the sheikh who had dominated Salvio's company for much of the evening was left, the two men deep in conversation as they sat by the fireside.

Molly was in the basement kitchen drying the final crystal glass when she heard a deafening chatter outside and peered out to see a helicopter alighting on the snowy lawn. Moments later the sheikh, now swathed in a dark overcoat, his black head bent against the flattening wind, began to run towards it. She could see the glint of a royal crest on the side of the craft as the door closed and it began its swaying ascent into the sky. Her hands were shaking as she suddenly realised she was alone in the house with

Salvio and she wondered what she should do. She put the glass down. She should behave as she normally would in these circumstances—even if this felt anything like normal.

Taking off her damp apron and smoothing down her black dress, she went upstairs to find Salvio still sitting beside the fire, his stance fixed and unmoving as he gazed into the flickering flames. His long legs were stretched out before him and the rugged perfection of his profile looked coppery in the firelight. Never had he seemed more devastating or more remote and never had she felt so humble and disconnected. How crazy was it that this man had briefly been her lover and would soon be the father of her child?

Molly cleared her throat. 'Excuse me.'

He looked up then, his eyes narrowing as if he couldn't quite remember who she was, or why she was here.

'*Sì*, what is it?' he questioned abruptly.

'I didn't mean to disturb you, but I wondered if there was anything else you'd like?'

Salvio felt his heart slam hard against his chest. If it had been any other former lover asking that question, it would have been coated in innuendo. But Molly's words weren't delivered suggestively, or provocatively. Her big grey eyes weren't slanting out an unspoken invitation. She simply looked anxious to please, which only reinforced the differences between them. Once again he cursed his hot-headedness in taking the curvy housekeeper to his bed.

Even though he could understand exactly why he'd done it.

He'd spent this evening watching her, despite his best intentions. He'd told himself she was strictly off-limits and he should concentrate on his guests, but it had been Molly's wide-hipped sway which had captured his gaze and Molly's determined face as she had scurried around with trays of drinks and food which had captivated his imagination. He had seen the natural sparkle of her grey eyes and had remembered the healthy glow of her cheeks when she had romped enthusiastically in his arms. But her face was pale now, he noted. Deathly pale—as if all the colour had been leeched from it.

'No, I don't think there is,' he said slowly, forcing himself to treat her as he would any other member of staff. 'Thank you for all your hard work tonight, Molly. The party went very well. Even the Sheikh of Razrastan stayed far longer than he intended.'

'You're very welcome,' she said.

'I'm sure we can think about a generous bonus for you.'

'There's no need for that,' she said stiffly.

'I think I'll be the judge of that.' He gave her a benign smile. 'And I haven't forgotten my promise to try to find you some work. Or, rather, to ask Gina to help.' His words were tantamount to dismissal but she didn't move. Salvio saw the faint criss-crossing of a frown over the smooth expanse of her brow and something—he never knew what it was—compelled him to ask a question he usually avoided like the plague. 'Is everything okay?'

Her hands began twisting at the plain fabric of her work dress and he could see the indecision which made her frown deepen.

'Y-yes.'

'You don't sound very sure.'

'I wasn't going to tell you until tomorrow,' she said, her knuckles whitening.

Instinct made Salvio sit upright, his body tensing. 'Tell me *what*?' he questioned dangerously.

Molly licked her lips. She'd thought that a good night's sleep and the addition of daylight might take some of the emotional sting out of her disclosure. But now she could see that any idea of sleep was a non-starter, especially with the thought of Salvio in bed nearby and the heavy realisation that he'd only ever wanted her that one time. But more than that, the news was bubbling inside her, wanting to get out.

She needed to tell someone—and who else was she going to confide in?

'I'm pregnant,' she said bluntly.

There was a moment of silence—a weird and intense kind of silence. It was as if every sound in the room had been amplified to an almost deafening level. The crackle and spit of the fire. The loud thunder of her heart. The sudden intake of her own shuddered breath. And now there was shadow too, as Salvio rose from his chair—tall and intimidating—his powerful frame blocking out the firelight and seeming to fill the room with darkness.

'You can't be,' he said flatly. 'That is, if you're trying to tell me it's mine?'

She met the unyielding expression which had hardened his face and Molly's heart contracted with pain. Did he really think she'd lost her virginity to him and then rushed out to find herself another lover—as if trying to make up for lost time? Or was he just trying to run from his own responsibility? She stared at him reproachfully. 'You know it is.'

'I used contraception,' he bit out. 'You know I did.'

She felt blood rush into her cheeks. 'Maybe you weren't—'

'Careful?' He cut across her words with a bitter laugh. 'I think that's a given, don't you? Reckless might be closer to the mark. On all counts.'

'Don't,' she said quickly.

His eyebrows shot up imperiously, as if he couldn't quite believe she was telling him what to do. *'What?'*

'Please don't,' she whispered. 'Don't make it any worse than it already is by saying things which will be difficult to forget afterwards.'

His eyes narrowed but he nodded, as if acknowledging the sense of her words. 'Are you sure?' he demanded. 'Or is it just a fear?'

She shook her head. 'I'm certain. I did a test.'

Another silence. 'I see.'

Molly's lips were dry and her heart was racing. 'I just want to make it clear that I'm only telling you because I feel duty-bound to tell you.'

'And not because you're after a slice of my fortune?'

Hurt now, she stared at him. 'You think that's what this is all about?'

His lips curved. 'Is it such a bizarre conclusion? Think about it, *mia bedda*. I'm rich and you're poor. What is it they say in the States?' He flicked the fingers of both hands, miming the sudden spill of money from a cash register. 'Ker-*ching!*'

Molly made to move away but his reflexes were lightning-fast and quicker than hers. He reached out to curl his fingers around her arm before pulling her towards him, like an expert angler reeling in their catch of the day. The movement made her breathless but it also made her hungry for him in a way she didn't want to be. Just one touch and her senses had started jangling, as she felt that now familiar desire washing over her. Meeting the gleam of his black eyes, she prayed she would find the strength to pull away from him and resist him. 'What do you think you're doing?' she demanded.

'I'm doing about the only thing which could possibly make me feel good right now,' he grated and brought his mouth down hard on hers.

Molly willed herself not to respond. She didn't have to do this—especially not after those insults he'd just hurled her way, making out she was some kind of gold-digger. But the trouble was that she *wanted* to kiss him. She wanted that more than anything else in the world right then. It was as if the beauty of his touch was making her realise how she'd got herself into this predicament in the first place. His kiss had been the first step to seduction and even now she found it irresistible. Closing her eyes, she let him plunder her lips until there was no oxygen left in her lungs and she had to draw back to suck in a breath of air. She shook her head distractedly. 'Salvio,' she whispered, but he shook his head.

'Don't say anything,' he warned, before scooping her up in his arms and carrying her out of the room.

Molly blinked in confusion because his hands were underneath her bottom and they were caressing it in a way which was making her want to squirm. As if in some kind of unbelievable dream he was carrying her up that sweeping staircase as if she were Scarlett O'Hara and he were Rhett Butler. And she was letting him.

So stop him. Make him put you down.

But she couldn't. Because *this* was powerlessness, she realised—this feeling of breathy expectation bubbling up inside her as he kicked open the door of the master bedroom. The heavy oak door swung open as if it had been made of matchsticks as he carried her effortlessly across silken Persian rugs before depositing her on the huge bed.

And even though Molly could see no real affection on his proud Neapolitan features—nothing but sexual hunger glittering from his dark eyes—that didn't stop her from reciprocating. Was it the delicious memory of his lovemaking which made her open her arms to him and close them around him tightly? Or was it more basic than that? As he peeled her dress, shoes and underclothes from her body before impatiently removing his own clothes she began to wonder if there was some deep-rooted need to connect physically with the man whose seed was multiplying inside her.

Or at least, that was her excuse for what was about to happen.

'Salvio,' she gasped as his finger stroked a slow circle around the exquisitely aroused peak of her now bare nipple. *'Oh!'*

His naked body was warm against hers. 'Shh...'

It was more of a command than an entreaty but Molly heeded it all the same, terrified that words might break the spell and let reality flood in and destroy what she was feeling. His eyes were hooded as they surveyed her body, seeming to drink in every centimetre. Was she imagining his gaze lingering longest on her belly? With her notorious curves, she probably looked pregnant already. But now he was kissing her neck and her eyelids were fluttering to a close so that it became all about sensation rather than thought and that was so much better.

Encouraged by the hand now sliding from breast to thigh, Molly flickered her fingertips over the taut dip of his belly, her touch as delicate as if she were making pastry. And didn't his groan thrill her and fill her with a sense of pride that *she*—inexperienced Molly Miller—could make a man like Salvio react this way? Emboldened by his response, she drifted her hand over his rocky thighs, feeling the hair-roughened flesh turn instantly to goosebumps, and something about that galvanised him into action, because suddenly he was on top of her. He was kissing her with a hunger which was almost *ferocious* and, oh, it felt good. Better than anything had a right to feel. She could feel the graze of his jaw and his lips felt hard on hers, though his tongue was sinuous as it slipped inside her mouth.

She gave a little cry as she twisted restlessly beneath him and he gave a low laugh which was tinged with mockery.

'How quickly my little innocent becomes greedy,' he murmured. 'How quickly she has learnt what it is she wants.'

His words sounded more like insults than observations but by then he was stroking her wet and urgent heat and Molly was writhing beneath his fingers. She moaned as the sensation built and built and she realised what was about to happen. He was going to make her have an orgasm with his...*finger*.

'Salvio,' she cried out in disbelief, but just as she went tumbling over the top he thrust deep inside her. She gasped as he filled her completely—even bigger than she remembered—and he gave a loud moan in response. And so did she. It felt as if her world were imploding. As if a jet-black sky had suddenly been punctured by a million stars. As if the two of them were locked and mingled for all time. Molly clung to him as she felt him momentarily stiffen before thrusting out his own shuddering pleasure.

He stayed inside her for countless minutes and Molly revelled in that sticky closeness because, in a funny sort of way, it felt as intimate as the act of sex had done. Maybe even more so, because now neither of them were chasing the satisfaction which had somehow left her feeling empty and satisfied, all at the same time.

But eventually he withdrew from her and rolled to the other side of the bed. Molly was careful to hide her disappointment as he threw the duvet over them both, quickly covering her up, as if the sight of her naked body offended him. She licked her lips as she waited for him to speak, planning to take her lead from him. It was the habit of a lifetime—of allowing her employer to dictate the conversation—because, technically, Salvio was still her employer, wasn't he? And it seemed vital that she stay quiet for long enough to hear his thoughts. Because what was said between them now was going to determine the rest of her baby's life, wasn't it? His attitude towards her unplanned pregnancy was of vital importance if they wanted to have any kind of amicable future. Not that she was expecting much from him. Not now. She'd thought she could rely on kindness until she'd realised she didn't really know him at all.

And now her heart began to pound with anxiety as she wondered whether she should have given herself so easily to him. Could she really hope for respect in the circumstances?

She found herself studying him from between her lashes as she met the hard glitter of his eyes.

'So now what?' he questioned slowly.

She took him literally, because wasn't it simpler all round if she remained practical and continued to do her job? 'I ought to go down and turn off all the lights—especially the tree lights.'

His face was incredulous. 'Excuse me?'

She pushed her hair away from her face and wriggled into a sitting-up position, though she was careful to keep the top of the duvet modestly covering her breasts. 'I haven't switched off the lights on the Christmas tree—and there's also the fire, which we've left unguarded,' she said. 'I can't possibly go to sleep until all that is in place.'

'The fireguard?' he echoed disbelievingly, looking momentarily bemused before nodding. 'Wait here,' he said, and climbed out of bed.

Quite honestly, Molly didn't feel as if she had the strength or inclination to go anywhere—especially not when an unclothed Salvio was walking towards the door, seemingly unaware of the fact that it was the middle of winter and the snow was thick on the ground outside. She gazed at him as if hypnotised—her eyes drinking in the pale globes of his buttocks, which contrasted so vividly with the burnished olive of his thighs. And then he turned round, frowning with faint concern as he surveyed her, as if he had suddenly remembered that she'd just announced her pregnancy and wasn't quite sure how to deal with her any more.

'Can I get you anything?'

She guessed he was being literal too and that it would have been pointless to have asked for a crystal ball to reassure her about her baby's future. And pointless to have asked for some affirmation that he wasn't planning on deserting his unplanned child, even if he wanted nothing more to do with her. But unlike her brother, Molly had never been a fantasist. She cleared her throat and nodded. 'A drink of water would be nice.'

She waited for him to say something like, *I'll bring it to your room*, but he didn't. Which presumably meant it was okay to stay here.

Of *course* it was okay to stay here—they'd just had sex, hadn't they?

But it wasn't easy to shrug off a lifetime of being deferential and Molly even felt slightly guilty about rushing into the luxurious en-suite bathroom and availing herself of the upmarket facilities. She splashed her face with water and smoothed down her mussed hair before returning to the bed and burrowing down beneath the duvet.

And then he was back and Molly quickly averted her eyes because the front view of the naked Neapolitan was much more daunting than the back had been—particularly as he seemed to be getting aroused again.

Did he read something in her expression? Was that why he gave a savage kind of laugh as he handed her the glass of water? 'Don't worry,' he grated. 'I'll endeavour to keep my appetite in check while we discuss how we're going to handle this.'

The large gulp of water she'd been taking nearly choked her and Molly put the glass down on the bedside table with a hand which was trembling. 'There's nothing to handle,' she said shakily. 'I'm having this baby, no matter what you say.'

'You think I would want anything other than that?' he demanded savagely.

'I wasn't… I wasn't sure.'

Salvio climbed into bed, disappointed yet strangely relieved that her magnificent breasts weren't on show, meaning he'd be able to concentrate on what he needed to say and not on how much he would like to lose himself in her sweet tightness again. He pulled the cover over the inconvenient hardening of his groin. Was she really as innocent as she seemed? Physically, yes—he had discovered that for himself. But was she really so unschooled in the ways of the world that she didn't realise that she was now in possession of what so many women strived for?

A billionaire father for her baby.

A meal ticket for life.

And there wasn't a damned thing he could do about it. Fate had thrown him a curveball and he was just going to have to deal with it.

'Tell me about yourself,' he said suddenly.

She blinked. 'Me?'

The sigh he gave wasn't exaggerated. 'Look, Molly—I think you're in danger of overplaying the wide-eyed innocent, don't you? We've had sex on a number of occasions and you've just informed me you're pregnant. Ordinarily I wouldn't be interested in hearing about your past, but you'll probably agree that this is no ordinary situation.'

Molly's heart clenched as his cruel words rained down on her. Wouldn't another man at least have *pretended* to be interested in what had made her the person she was today? Gone through some kind of polite ritual of getting to know her. Maybe she should be grateful that he hadn't. He might be cruel, but at least he wasn't a hypocrite. He wasn't pretending to feel stuff about her and building up her hopes to smash them down again. At least she knew where she stood.

'I was born in a little cottage—'

'Please. Spare me the violins. Let's just cut to the chase, shall we?' he interrupted coolly. 'Parents?'

Molly shrugged. 'My father left my mother when she was diagnosed with multiple sclerosis,' she said flatly.

She saw a flare of something she didn't recognise in his black eyes.

'That must have been hard,' he said softly.

'It was,' she conceded. 'Less so for me than for my little brother, Robbie. He…well, he adored our mother. So did I, obviously—but I was busy keeping on top of everything so that social services were happy to let me run the home.'

'And then?' he prompted, when her words died away.

Molly swallowed. 'Mum died when Robbie was twelve, but they let us carry on living together. Just me and him. I fought like crazy not to have him taken into care and I succeeded.'

His dark brows knitted together. 'And what was that like?'

She thought she detected a note of sympathy in his voice, or was that simply wishful thinking? Of

"FAST FIVE" READER SURVEY

Your participation entitles you to:
* ✱ 4 Thank-You Gifts Worth Over $20!

Complete the survey in minutes.

Get 2 FREE Books

See inside for details.

Dear Reader,

Since you are a lover of our books, your opinions are important to us... and so is your time.

That's why we made sure your **"FAST FIVE" READER SURVEY** can be completed in just a few minutes. Your answers to the five questions will help us remain at the forefront of women's fiction.

And, as a thank-you for participating, we'd like to send you **4 FREE THANK-YOU GIFTS!**

Enjoy your gifts with our appreciation,

Pam Powers

To get your
4 FREE THANK-YOU GIFTS:

✴ Quickly complete the "Fast Five" Reader Survey
and return the insert.

"FAST FIVE" READER SURVEY

1 Do you sometimes read a book a second or third time? ○ Yes ○ No

2 Do you often choose reading over other forms of entertainment such as television? ○ Yes ○ No

3 When you were a child, did someone regularly read aloud to you? ○ Yes ○ No

4 Do you sometimes take a book with you when you travel outside the home? ○ Yes ○ No

5 In addition to books, do you regularly read newspapers and magazines? ○ Yes ○ No

YES! I have completed the above Reader Survey. Please send me my 4 FREE GIFTS (gifts worth over $20 retail). I understand that I am under no obligation to buy anything, as explained on the back of this card.

❏ I prefer the regular-print edition
106/306 HDL GM3S

❏ I prefer the larger-print edition
176/376 HDL GM3S

FIRST NAME   LAST NAME

ADDRESS

APT.#   CITY

STATE/PROV.   ZIP/POSTAL CODE

READER SERVICE—Here's how it works:

Accepting your 2 free Harlequin Presents® books and 2 free gifts (gifts valued at approximately $10.00 retail) places you under no obligation to buy anything. You may keep the books and gifts and return the shipping statement marked "cancel." If you do not cancel, about a month later we'll send you 6 additional books and bill you just $4.55 each for the regular-print edition or $5.55 each for the larger-print edition in the U.S. or $5.49 each for the regular-print edition or $5.99 each for the larger-print edition in Canada. That is a savings of at least 11% off the cover price. It's quite a bargain! Shipping and handling is just 50¢ per book in the U.S. and 75¢ per book in Canada*. You may cancel at any time, but if you choose to continue, every month we'll send you 6 more books, which you may either purchase at the discount price plus shipping and handling or return to us and cancel your subscription. *Terms and prices subject to change without notice. Prices do not include applicable taxes. Sales tax applicable in N.Y. Canadian residents will be charged applicable taxes. Offer not valid in Quebec. Books received may not be as shown. All orders subject to approval. Credit or debit balances in a customer's account(s) may be offset by any other outstanding balance owed by or to the customer. Please allow 4 to 6 weeks for delivery. Offer available while quantities last.

▼ If offer card is missing write to: Reader Service, P.O. Box 1341, Buffalo, NY 14240-8531 or visit www.ReaderService.com ▼

BUSINESS REPLY MAIL
FIRST-CLASS MAIL   PERMIT NO. 717   BUFFALO, NY

POSTAGE WILL BE PAID BY ADDRESSEE

READER SERVICE
PO BOX 1341
BUFFALO NY 14240-8571

NO POSTAGE
NECESSARY
IF MAILED
IN THE
UNITED STATES

course it was. He was cruel and ruthless, she reminded herself. He was only asking her these questions because he felt he *needed* to—not because he *wanted* to. For a moment Molly was tempted to gloss over the facts. To tell him that Robbie had turned out fine. But what if he found out the truth and then accused her of lying? Wouldn't that make this already difficult situation even worse than it already was?

'Robbie went off the rails a bit,' she admitted. 'He did what a lot of troubled teenagers do. Got in with the wrong crowd. Got into trouble with the police. And then he started…'

Her voice tailed off again, knowing this was something she couldn't just consign to the past. Because the counsellor had told her that addictions never really went away. They just sat there, brooding and waiting for someone to feed them. And wasn't she scared stiff that they were being fed right now—that someone was busy dealing cards across a light-washed table in the centre of a darkened room somewhere in the Outback?

'What did he start, Molly?' prompted Salvio softly.

'Gambling.' She stared down at her short, sensible fingernails before glancing up again to meet the ebony gleam of his eyes. 'It started off with fruit machines and then he met someone in the arcade who said a bright boy like him would probably be good at cards. That he could win enough money to buy the kind of things he'd never had. And that's when it all started.'

'*It?*'

Molly shrugged. 'I think Robbie was still missing Mum. I know he'd been frustrated and unhappy that we'd been so poor while she was alive. Whatever it was, he started playing poker and he was good at it. At first. He started winning money but he spent it just as quickly. More quickly than it was coming in. And the trouble with cards is that the more you want to win—the worse you become. They say that your opponent can smell desperation and Robbie was as desperate as hell. He started getting into debt. Big debt. But the banks didn't want to know and so he borrowed from some pay-day lenders and they…they…'

'They came after him?' Salvio finished grimly.

Molly nodded. 'I managed to use most of my savings to pay them off, though there's still an outstanding debt which never seems to go down because the interest rates they charge are astronomical. I wanted Robbie to have a fresh start. To get away from all the bad influences in his life. So he went to Australia to get the whole gambling bug out of his system and promised to attend Gamblers Anonymous. That's why I was working for the Averys. They were hardly ever in the house so I got to live there rent-free. Plus they paid me a lot of money to look after all their valuable artefacts. They said their insurance was lower if they had someone living permanently on the premises.'

'And then I came along,' he mused softly.

Molly's head jerked back as something in his tone alerted her to danger. 'I'm sorry?'

His bare shoulders gleamed like gold in the soft light from the lamp. 'A young attractive woman like you must have found it incredibly limiting to be shut away in that huge house in the middle of nowhere working for people who only appeared intermittently,' he observed. 'It must have seemed like a gilded prison.'

'I was grateful for a roof over my head and the chance to save,' she said.

'And the opportunity to meet a rich man who might make a useful lover?'

Molly's mouth fell open. 'Are you out of your mind?'

'I don't think so, *mia bedda*,' he contradicted silkily. 'I base my opinions on experience. It's one of the drawbacks of being wealthy and single—that women come at you from all angles. You must have acknowledged that I was attracted to you, and I can't help wondering whether you saw me as an easy way out of your dilemma. Were the bitter tears you cried real, or manufactured, I wonder? Did you intend those sobs to stir my conscience?'

Molly sat up in bed, her skin icy with goose-bumps, despite the duvet which covered most of her naked body. 'You think I *pretended to cry*? That I deliberately got myself pregnant to get you to pay off my brother's debts? That I would cold-bloodedly use my baby as a bargaining tool?'

'No, I'm not saying that. But I do think that fate has played right into your hardworking little hands,' he said slowly. 'Don't you?'

Her voice was shaking as she shook her head. 'No. No, I don't.' Pushing the duvet away, she swung her legs over the side of the bed, acutely conscious of her wobbly bottom as she bent down and started pulling on her discarded clothes with fingers which were trembling, telling herself she would manage. Somehow. Because she had always managed before, hadn't she? Fully dressed now, Molly turned round, steeling herself not to react to his muscular olive body outlined so starkly against the snowy white bedding. 'There's nothing more to be said, is there?'

He gave a bitter laugh. 'Oh, I think there's plenty which needs to be said, but not tonight, not when emotions are running high. I need to think first before I come to any decision.'

Molly was tempted to tell him that maybe he

should have done that before he had taken her to bed and then come out with a stream of unreasonable accusations, but what was the point in inflaming an already inflamed situation? And she couldn't really blame him for the sex, could she? Not when she had been complicit every step of the way. Not when she had desperately wanted him to touch her.

And the awful thing was that she still did.

Tilting her chin upwards and adopting the most dignified stance possible—which wasn't easy in the circumstances—she walked out of Salvio's bedroom without another word.

CHAPTER SEVEN

A COLD BLUE light filtered into the tiny bedroom, startling Molly from the bewildering landscape of unsettled sleep—one haunted by Salvio and the memory of his hard, thrusting body. Disorientated, she sat up in bed, wondering if she'd dreamt it all. Until the delicious aching at her breasts and soft throb between her legs reminded her that it had happened. Her heart began to race. It had actually happened. At the end of an evening's service she had informed her employer she was pregnant with his baby.

And had then been carried up the staircase and willingly had sex with him, despite all the things he'd accused her of.

Did he really believe it was his wealth which had attracted her to him, when she would have found him irresistible if he'd been covered in mud and sweat from working the fields?

Slowly, she got out of bed. She didn't know what

Salvio wanted. All she knew was what *she* wanted. Her hand crept down to cover the soft flesh of her belly. She wanted this baby.

And nothing Salvio did or said was going to change her mind.

She showered and washed her hair—pulling on clean jeans and a jumper the colour of a winter sky before going downstairs, to be greeted by the aroma of coffee. In the kitchen she found Salvio pouring himself an inky cupful, and although he looked up as she walked in, his face registered no emotion. He merely gestured to the pot.

'Want some?'

She shook her head. 'No, thanks. I'll make myself some tea.' She was certain herbal tea was better for babies than super-strong coffee, but mainly she welcomed the opportunity of being able to busy herself with the kettle. Anything rather than having to confront the distracting vision of Salvio in faded jeans and a sweater as black as his hair. She could feel him watching her and she had to try very hard not to appear clumsy—no mean feat when that piercing gaze was trained on her like a bird of prey. But when she couldn't dunk her peppermint teabag a moment longer, she was forced to turn around and face him, glad he was now silhouetted against the window and his features were mostly in shadow.

'So,' he said, without preamble. 'We need to work out what we're going to do about the astonishing piece of news you dropped into my lap last night. Any ideas, Molly?'

Molly had thought about this a lot during those long hours when sleep had eluded her. *Be practical*, she urged herself. *Take the emotion out of it and think facts.* She cleared her throat. 'Obviously finding a job is paramount,' she said cautiously. 'A live-in job, of course.'

'A live-in job,' he repeated slowly. 'And when the baby is born, what then?'

Molly hoped her shrug conveyed more confidence than she actually felt. 'Lots of people don't mind their staff having a baby around the place. Well, maybe not lots of people,' she amended when she heard his faintly incredulous snort and acknowledged that he might have a point. 'But houses which already have children tend to be more accommodating. Who knows? I might even switch my role from housekeeper to nanny.'

'And that's what you want, is it?'

Molly suppressed the frustration which had flared up inside her. Of course it wasn't. But she couldn't really tell him that none of this was what she *wanted*—not without betraying the child she carried. She hadn't planned to get pregnant, but she would

make the best of it. Just as she hadn't planned for
the father of her child to be a cold-hearted billionaire
who right now felt so distant that he might as well
have been on another planet, rather than standing on
the other side of the kitchen. She wanted what most
women wanted when they found themselves in this
situation—a stable life and a man who adored them.
'Life is all about adaptation,' she said stolidly when,
to her surprise, he nodded, walking away from the
window and putting his coffee cup down on the table
before pulling out a chair.

'I agree,' he said. 'Here. Sit down. We need to talk
about this properly.'

She shook her head. 'I can't sit down.'

'Why not?'

'Because I still have to clear up the house, after
the party.'

'Leave it.'

'I can't leave it, it's what you're paying me—'

'I said leave it, Molly,' he snapped. 'I can easily
get people in to do that for me later. Just sit down,
will you?'

Molly opened her mouth to refuse. To tell him that
the walls felt as if they were closing in on her and his
presence was making her jittery. But what else could
she do? Flounce out into the snow, two days before
Christmas Day—with nowhere to go and a child in

her belly? Ignoring the chair he was holding out for her, she chose one at the opposite end of the table and sank down onto it, her mouth unsmiling as she looked at him questioningly.

'I've given a lot of thought to what's happened,' he said, without preamble.

Join the club. 'And did you come to any conclusions?'

Salvio's eyes narrowed as she stared at him suspiciously. She wasn't behaving as he had expected her to behave. Although what did he know? He'd never had to face something like this before and never with someone like her. After her departure last night, he'd thought she might try to creep back into his bed—maybe even whisper how sorry she was for flouncing out like that—before turning her lips to his for another hungry kiss. He was used to the inconsistency of women—and in truth he would have welcomed a reconnection with those amazing curves. Another bout of amazing sex might have given him a brief and welcome respite from his concerns about the future.

She hadn't done that, of course, and so he had braced himself for sulks or tears or reproachful looks when he bumped into her this morning. But no. Not that either. Sitting there in a soft sweater which matched her grey eyes, with her hair loose and shining around her shoulders, she looked the picture of health—despite the shadows beneath her eyes, which suggested her night had been as troubled as his.

And the crazy thing was that this morning he hadn't woken up feeling all the things he was expecting to feel. There had been residual shock, yes, but the thought of a baby hadn't filled him with horror. He might even have acknowledged the faint flicker of warmth in his heart as a tenuous glimmer of pleasure, if he hadn't been such a confirmed cynic.

'Every problem has a solution if you come at it from enough angles,' he said carefully. 'And I have a proposition to put to you.'

She creased her brow. 'You do?'

There was a pause. 'I don't want you finding a job as a housekeeper, or looking after someone else's children.'

'Why not?'

Salvio tensed, sensing the beginning of a negotiation. Was she testing out how much money he was prepared to give her? 'Isn't it obvious? Because you're pregnant with my baby.' His voice deepened. 'And although this is a child I never intended to have, I'm prepared to accept the consequences of my actions.'

'How...how cold-blooded you make it sound,' she breathed.

'Do you want me to candy-coat it for you, Molly?' he demanded. 'To tell you that this was what I always secretly dreamed would happen to me? Or would you prefer the truth?'

'I'm a realist, Salvio,' she answered. 'I've only ever wanted the truth.'

'Then here it is, in all its unvarnished glory. To-morrow, I'm flying home to Naples for the holidays.'

'I know. Your assistant told me when she hired me.'

'I return every year,' he continued slowly. 'To two loving parents who wonder where they went so wrong with their only child.'

She blinked at him in confusion. 'I don't... understand.'

'Who wonder why their successful, handsome son who has achieved so much,' he continued, as if she hadn't spoken, 'has failed to bring home a woman who will one day provide them with the grandchildren they yearn for.' He gave a sudden bitter laugh. 'When, hey, what do you know? Suddenly I have found such a woman and already she is with child! What a gift it will be for them to meet you, Molly.'

She stared at him, confusion darkening her grey eyes. '*Meet* them? You're not suggesting—'

'Like I said last night—it's time to lose all that wide-eyed innocence. I think you know exactly what I'm suggesting,' he drawled. 'We buy you a big dia-mond ring and I take you home to Naples as my fi-ancée.'

'You mean…' She blinked. 'You mean you want to marry me?'

'Let's put it another way. I don't particularly want to marry anyone, the difference is that I'm *prepared* to marry you,' he amended.

'Because of the baby?'

'Because of the baby,' he agreed. 'But not just that. Most women are demanding and manipulative but, interestingly enough, you are none of those things. Not only are you extremely beddable—I find you exceptionally…*agreeable*.' His lips curved into a reflective smile. 'And at least you know your place.'

Molly stared at him, wanting to tell him to stop making her sound like the UK representative for the international society of doormats. Until she realised that once again Salvio was speaking the truth. She *did* know her place. She always had done. When you worked as a servant in other people's houses, that was what tended to happen.

'So what's in it for me?' she asked, thinking she ought to say *something*.

He looked at her in surprise. 'It isn't very difficult to work out. You get financial security and I get a ready-made family. I can pay off your brother's debt in one swoop, on the understanding that this is the only time I bankroll him. And if I were you, I would wipe the horror from your face, Molly. It really isn't

a good look for a woman who's on the brink of getting engaged.' His voice dipped into one of silky
admonishment. 'And it isn't as if you have a lot of
choices, do you?'

Molly felt the sudden shiver of vulnerability rip-
pling down her spine. He didn't have to put it quite
so brutally, did he? She swallowed. Or maybe he did.
It was yet another cruel observation but it was true.
She *didn't* have a lot of choices. She knew there was
nothing romantic about having to struggle. She'd
done all that making-the-best-of-a-bad-situation
stuff—seeing how many meals you could get out
of a bag of black-eyed beans and buying her clothes
in thrift stores. She knew how hard poverty could be.

And this was her baby.

Her defenceless little *baby*.

She was aware of her hand touching her belly and
aware of Salvio's gaze following the movement before
he lifted his black eyes to hers. She searched their
dark gleam in vain for some kind of emotion, and
tried to ignore the painful stab in her heart when she
met nothing but a cold, unblinking acceptance in their
ebony depths. Of course he wasn't going to feel the
same way as she did about their child. Why *wouldn't*
he look sombre? Having his life inextricably linked to
that of a humble little housekeeper was surely nothing
for the Neapolitan billionaire to celebrate.

'Very well. Since—as you have already pointed out—I have very little alternative… I agree,' she said, and then, because subservience was as much a part of her life as breathing and because deep down she *was* grateful to him for his grudging generosity, she added a small smile. 'Thank you.'

Salvio felt his gut clench, knowing he didn't deserve her thanks. Or that shy look which made him want to cradle her in his arms. He knew he could have asked her to marry him in a more romantic way. He could have dropped onto one knee and told her he couldn't imagine life without her. But why get her used to an attitude he could never sustain and raise expectations which could never be met? The only way he could make this work was if he was straight with her, and that meant not making emotional promises he could never fulfil.

But he knew one sure way to please her—the universal way to every woman's heart. 'Go and get your stuff together, *nicuzza*,' he said softly. 'We're going shopping.'

Molly stepped out onto the icy Bond Street pavement feeling dazed but warm. Definitely warm. Who would have ever thought a coat could *be* so warm? Wonderingly she brushed her fingertips over the camel cashmere, which teamed so well with the knee-length boots and the matching brown leather gloves which were as soft as a second skin. She caught sight of her reflection in one of the huge windows of the upmarket department store and stared at it, startled—wondering if that glossy confection of a woman was really her.

'*Sì*, you look good,' Salvio murmured from beside her.

She looked up into his ruggedly handsome face. 'Do I?'

'Good enough to eat,' he affirmed, his black eyes glittering out an unspoken message and Molly could do nothing about the shiver which rippled down her spine and had nothing to do with the icy temperature.

After a slow drive through the snow to London, he had brought her to one of the capital's most famous streets, studded with the kind of shops which were guarded by burly security men with inscrutable expressions. But the faces of the assistants inside were far more open and Molly knew she hadn't imagined the faint incredulity which greeted her appearance, as women fluttered around Salvio like wasps on a spill of jam.

He asked for—and got—a terrifyingly sleek stylist, who was assigned the daunting task of dressing her. Endless piles of clothing and lingerie were produced—some of which were instantly dismissed by an impatient wave of Salvio's hand and some of which were met with a slow smile of anticipation.

'It seems a silly amount of money to spend since whatever I buy isn't going to fit me for very long,' she hissed in a fierce undertone after nearly fainting when she caught sight of one of the price tags.

He seemed amused by her attempt to make economies. 'Then we'll just have to buy you some more, won't we? Don't worry about the cost, Molly. You will soon be the wife of a very wealthy man.'

It was hard to imagine, thought Molly as a featherlight chiffon dress floated down over her head, covering an embroidered bra whose matching panties were nothing more than a flimsy scrap of silk. As she appeared from behind the velvet curtain of the changing room to meet Salvio's assessing gaze, she began to wonder if he'd done this whole transformation thing before. And she wondered whether she should show a little pride and refuse all the gifts he was offering.

But then she thought about the reality. Salvio probably came from an extremely wealthy family who might not take kindly to someone from her kind of background. Wouldn't she feel even more out of place if she turned up looking like a poor relation in her cheap clothes and worn boots? Which was why she submitted to the purchase of sweaters and jeans, jackets and day dresses—and the most beautiful shoes she had ever seen. Gorgeous patent stilettos in three different colours, which somehow had the ability to add precious inches to her height and make her walk in a different and more feminine way.

And when they were all done and the glossy bags had been placed in the limousine which had been slowly tailing them, Salvio guided her past yet another security guard and into a jewellery shop where inside it was all light and dazzle. Locked glass cases contained the biggest diamonds Molly had ever seen—some the colour of straw, some which resembled pink champagne, and some even finer than Lady Avery's vast collection of family jewels.

'So what's your ideal ring? What did you used to dream about when you were a little girl?' asked Salvio softly, his fingers caressing the small of her back as an elegant saleswoman approached them. 'Whatever takes your fancy, it's yours.'

Did he have to put it quite like that? Molly wondered, moving away to avoid the distraction of his touch. The only thing she used to dream about when she was a little girl was making sure there was a hot meal on the table, and wondering if she'd managed to get all Mum's pills from the pharmacy. Yet Salvio was making her sound like someone whose gaze was bound to be riveted by the biggest and brightest ring in the shop.

She could feel her cheeks growing hot, because suddenly this felt like the charade it really was. As if they were going through all the motions of getting engaged, but with none of the joy or happiness which most couples would have experienced at such a time. And while Salvio's handsome face was undeniably sensual, his jet-dark eyes were as cold as any of the jewels on display. Molly lifted her gaze from the display cabinet as a quiet air of certainty ran through her. 'I don't want anything which looks like an engagement ring,' she said.

Hiding her surprise, the assistant produced a ring to just that specification—a stunning design of three thin platinum bands, each containing three asymmetrically placed diamonds which glittered and sparkled in the sharp December sunlight. 'The diamonds are supposed to resemble raindrops,' the young woman said gently.

Or tears, thought Molly suddenly. They looked exactly like tears.

From Bond Street they were whisked to Salvio's home in a fashionable area of London. Molly had heard of Clerkenwell but had never actually been there—just as she'd never been in such a gleaming, modern penthouse apartment before. She wandered from room to room. Everything was shiny and clean, but it was stark—as if nobody really lived there. It was as if some designer had been allowed to keep all décor to a minimum, but its sleek emptiness wasn't her main worry—which was that it was no place for a baby.

What was left of the day rushed past in a whirl of organisation but for once it wasn't Molly doing the organising, since Salvio seemed to have fleets of people at his disposal. People to organise cars and planes. To book hotels and arrange the last-minute purchase of gifts. They ate an early supper, which was delivered and served by staff from a nearby award-winning restaurant who even provided candles and a fragrant floral centrepiece.

'You don't have a chef, or a housekeeper?' Molly asked, as she sat down at the glass dining table and tried not to think about how dangerous a piece of furniture like this might be for a young child.

'I prefer to keep resident staff to a minimum. It optimises my privacy,' Salvio explained coolly, as two delicate soufflés were placed in front of them. 'I hope you're hungry?'

'Very,' she said, shaking out her napkin and trying not to dwell on what he'd just said about privacy—because he was about to have it shattered in the most spectacular way. 'Have you lived here for very long?' she questioned.

'I've had the apartment for about five years.'

'And you're here a lot?'

'No, not really. I have other homes all round the world. This is just my base whenever I'm in London.' He gazed at her thoughtfully. 'Why do you ask?'

She shrugged. 'It's very tidy.'

He laughed. 'I thought, given your occupation, that tidiness might meet with your approval.'

And oddly enough, that hurt. It was yet another reminder of just how far out of her comfort zone she was. A reminder of how he really saw her. She would never be his equal, she thought, as a powerful wave of fatigue washed over her.

'Actually, I'm pretty tired,' she said. 'It's a been a long day and the baby...'

The baby.

Salvio pushed away his wine glass. They hadn't mentioned it all afternoon but the word no longer hit him like a shock. He was slowly getting used to the idea that she was pregnant, even if he wasn't exactly jumping for joy about it. And Molly Miller was proving easier company than he had expected. Undemanding and optimistic. There was something about her quiet presence which made him feel almost *peaceful*. He stared at her washed-out face and felt an unexpected wave of remorse wash over him. Why hadn't he noticed how tired she might be?

'You need to go to bed,' he said resolutely, pushing back his chair.

He saw her throat constrict.

'Where…where am I sleeping?'

'We're supposed to be an engaged couple, Molly,' he said, almost gently. 'Where do you think you'll be sleeping?'

'I wasn't…sure.'

He'd assumed she would be sharing his bed, because why wouldn't he? But something about her pallor and trepidation made him reconsider—for his own sake as well as for hers. Wouldn't a night apart reestablish his habitual detachment—especially since it was obvious neither of them had slept well last night?

He rose to his feet. 'There's no need to sound so fearful, Molly,' he said. 'I'll show you the spare room. You'll have plenty of peace in there.'

He saw the sudden look of uncertainty which crossed her features and then she nodded her head, the way he'd seen her do before.

'That sounds like a good idea,' she said, with what sounded like obedience, and once again he was reminded of the fact that she was, essentially, a servant.

CHAPTER EIGHT

BATHED IN THE bright December sunshine which flooded in through the giant windows of their Neapolitan hotel suite, Molly turned to Salvio, who was just changing out of the jeans and leather jacket he'd worn for the trip over, into something a little more formal.

'We still haven't discussed—' Molly hesitated '—what we're going to tell your parents.'

Pausing in the act of straightening his tie, Salvio turned to look at his fiancée. She looked…incredible, he thought. With her shiny hair scooped on top of her head and her curvy shape encased in a dress the colour of spring leaves, there was no trace of that shy and frumpy housekeeper now. They'd just arrived in his home city—his jet descending through the mountains surrounding the mighty Mount Vesuvius, with all its unleashed power and terrible history. It was an iconic view which took away the breath of the most experienced traveller and he had found himself watching Molly for her reaction. But, oblivious to the beauty which surrounded them, she had seemed lost in thought. Even when the car had whisked them to this luxury hotel overlooking the Castel dell'Ovo and a lavish suite which even *he* could not fault, she seemed barely to register the opulence of their penthouse accommodation.

He wondered if she'd noticed the sideways stares he'd been receiving from the moment they'd stepped off the plane. The double takes and the *'Is it him?'* looks which were as familiar to him as breathing, whenever he returned to his native town. Yet Molly had been impervious to them all.

'We tell them the truth,' he said eventually, giving some thought to her question. 'That you're pregnant and we're getting married as soon as possible.'

She winced a little. 'Do you think we need to be quite so...?'

His gaze bored into her. 'So what, Molly?'

She licked her lips and, mesmerised by the resulting gleam which emphasised their soft beauty, Salvio momentarily cursed himself for not admitting her to his bed last night. Had he really imagined such an action might make him more detached and rational, when he'd been obsessing about her all night long?

'Brutal,' she concluded, pursing her lips together as if it wasn't a word she particularly wanted to use.

'Brutal?'

She shrugged and began walking across the room, pausing only to peer into the elevated stone hot tub which stood at the far end of the enormous suite— an extravagant touch eclipsed only by the tall decorated Christmas tree which was framed in one of the tall windows.

Eventually she came to a halt and perched on an orange velvet chair to look at him. 'You told me you're known as someone who is a commitment-phobe. Someone who doesn't want to get married,' she said.

Salvio gave his tie a final tug. That wasn't the whole story, but why burden her with stuff she didn't need to know? 'What of it?'

'So this sudden marriage is going to come as a bolt out of the blue to your parents, isn't it?'

'And?' he questioned coolly. 'Your point is?'

She studied her left hand warily, as if she couldn't quite get used to the diamond knuckle-duster she was wearing. 'I'd prefer not to say anything about my pregnancy—at least, not yet. It's still very early days. I just thought it might be nice if we could at least *allow* them to think it might be about more than just the unwanted fallout of a…a…'

Her words tailed away and Salvio wondered if, in her innocence, she simply didn't know all the expressions—some of them crude—she could have used to describe what had happened between them that first night. 'A hook-up?' he put in helpfully, before adopting a more caustic tone. 'Are you saying you want to pretend to my parents that this is some great kind of love affair?'

'Of course not.' She flushed before lifting a reproachful grey gaze to his. 'I don't think you're that good an actor, are you, Salvio?'

He inclined his head as if to concede the point. 'Or that good a liar?'

'That's another way of putting it, I suppose.'

He acknowledged her crestfallen expression. 'I don't want to raise your hopes, Molly—or theirs. It's just who I am. And the bottom line is I just don't do emotion. That's all.'

'That's…that's quite a lot,' she observed. 'Do you think…?' She seemed to choose her words very carefully. 'Do you think you were born that way?'

'I think circumstances made me that way,' he said flatly.

'What kind of circumstances?'

Salvio frowned. This was deeper than he wanted to go because he was a man with a natural aversion to the in-depth character analysis which was currently in vogue. But what had he imagined would happen—that he could take an innocent young girl as his wife and present to her the same impenetrable exterior which had made scores of women despair at his coldness in the past? He walked over to the drinks cabinet, ignoring the expensive bottles of wine on display, pouring instead two crystal glasses of mineral water before walking across the room to hand her one. 'You don't know much about me, do you, Molly?'

She shook her head as she sipped her drink. 'Practically nothing. How would I? We haven't exactly sat down and had long conversations since we met, have we?'

He almost smiled. 'You weren't tempted to go and look me up online?'

Molly didn't answer immediately as she met the scrutiny of his piercing black gaze. Of course she'd been *tempted*. Someone like Salvio was high profile enough to have left a significant footprint on the Internet, which she could have accessed at the touch of a computer key, and naturally she was curious about him. But she'd felt as if their lives were unequal enough already. The billionaire tycoon and the humble housekeeper. If she discovered stuff about him, would she then have to feign ignorance in the unlikely event that he wanted to confide in her? If she heard anything about him, she wanted to hear it *from* him—not through the judgemental prism of someone else's point of view.

'I didn't want to seem as if I was spying on you.'

'Very commendable.'

'But it would be useful to know,' she continued doggedly. 'Otherwise your parents might think we're nothing but strangers.'

'And is that what concerns you, Molly?' His black gaze continued to bore into her. 'What other people think?'

Molly bit back her instinctive response to his disdainful question. If she'd been bothered about things like that then she would never have got through a childhood like hers. From an early age she'd learnt there were more important things to worry about than whether you had holes in your shoes or your coat needed darning. She'd learnt that good health— the one thing money couldn't buy—was the only thing worth having. 'I believe it's best to be respectful of other people's feelings and that your parents might be confused and possibly upset if they realise we don't really know one another. But the main reason I need to know about you is because I'm having your baby.' She saw the increased darkening of his eyes—as if she had reminded him of something he would rather forget. But he couldn't forget it, and neither could she. 'I don't know anything about your childhood,' she finished simply. 'Nothing at all.'

He appeared to consider her words before expelling a slow breath of air. 'Very well. First and foremost you must understand that I am a Neapolitan to the very core of my being.' His voice became fierce, and proud. 'And that I have a great passion for this beautiful city of mine.'

So why don't you live here? Molly thought suddenly. *Why do you only ever visit at Christmas?* But she said nothing, just absorbed his words the way she'd absorbed other people's words all her working life.

'I grew up in the Rione Sanità, a very beautiful area, which is rich with history.' There was a pause. 'But it is also one of the poorest places in the city.'

'You?' she echoed disbelievingly, unable to hold back her shocked reaction. 'Poor?'

He smiled cynically as he flicked a disparaging finger towards his sleek suit jacket. 'You think I was born wearing fine clothes like these, Molly? Or that my belly never knew hunger?'

Yes, that was exactly what she'd thought, mainly because Salvio De Gennaro wore his wealth supremely well. He acted as if he'd never known anything other than handmade shoes and silk shirts, and people to drive his cars and planes for him. 'You've come a long way,' she said slowly. 'What happened?'

'What happened was that I had a talent,' he told her simply. 'And that talent was football. The moment my foot touched a ball, I felt as if I had found what I was born to do. I used to play every moment I could. There was nowhere suitable close to my home so I found a derelict yard to use. I marked a spot on the wall and I used to hit that same spot over and over again. Word got out and people used to come and watch me. They used to challenge me to see how long I could keep the ball in the air and sometimes I used to take their bets because many of them thought they could put a ball past me. But I could always score, even if there were two people against me in goal. And then one day the scouts turned up and overnight my whole life changed.'

'What happened?' she prompted as his words faded away.

Salvio stared out of the window, drinking in the sapphire beauty of the bay. Would it sound boastful to tell her he'd been called the greatest footballer of his generation? Or that the superstar lifestyle had arrived far more quickly than expected? 'I trained every hour that God sent, determined to fulfil all that early promise, and very quickly I was signed by one of the country's most prestigious clubs where I scored a record number of goals. I knew success, and fame, and for a while it was a crazy life. Everywhere

I went, people would stop me and want to talk about the game and I don't remember the last time I was made to pay for a pizza.'

'But…something went wrong?' she observed. 'I mean, badly wrong?'

He narrowed his eyes. Was her blithe comment about knowing nothing of his past just another of the lies which slipped so easily from women's lips? 'What makes you ask that?'

She hesitated. 'I'm not sure. Maybe the note of finality in your voice. The look of…'

'Of what, Molly?' he demanded. 'And please don't just give me the polite answer you think I ought to hear.'

She met his eyes, surprised at his perception because she had been about to do exactly that. 'Bitterness, I guess,' she said. 'Or maybe disappointment.'

He wanted to deny her accusations—if that was what they were—but he couldn't. And suddenly he found himself resenting her astuteness and that gentle look of understanding which had softened her face. He'd agreed to tell her the basics—not for her to start peeling back the layers so that she could get a closer look at his damned soul. So why did he continue with his story, as if now he'd lifted the lid on it, he found it impossible to put it back?

'I'll tell you what happened,' he said roughly, becoming aware of the heavy beat of his pulse at his temple. 'My life was a fairy tale. It wasn't just the success, or the money—and the chance to do good stuff with all that money—it was the fact that I loved playing football. It was the only thing I ever wanted to do. And then one day I was brought down by an ugly tackle and tore my cruciate ligament. Badly.' His mouth twisted. 'And that was the end of the fairy tale. I never played again.'

Silence followed his stark statement and then she spoke in that soft voice. 'Oh, Salvio, that must have—'

'Please. Spare me the platitudes,' he ground out, hardening his heart to the distress which had made her eyes grow as dark as storm clouds—because he didn't need her sympathy. He didn't need anything from anyone. He'd learnt what a mistake *that* could be. 'The injury I could have learned to live with. After all, every professional sportsman or woman has to accept that one day their career will end—even if that happens sooner than they wanted. What made it worse was the discovery that my manager had been systematically working his way through my fortune before leaving town.' There was a pause. 'Suddenly, everything I thought I had was gone. No job. No money. My fall from grace was…spectacular.'

'So what did you do?' she whispered.

Salvio shrugged. He had raged for several days and thought seriously about going after his manager and pinning him to the nearest wall until he had agreed to pay the money back. Until he'd realised that revenge was time-consuming and ultimately damaging. That he didn't want to spend his life in pursuit of his broken dreams and to dwell on the glories of his past, like some sad loser. And then had come the final blow. The final, bitter straw which had made him feel a despair he had vowed never to repeat. Resolutely, he pushed the memory away. 'I sold all my cars and the fancy apartment I'd bought in Rome,' he said. 'And gave most of the proceeds to my parents. Then I took what was left and bought a plane ticket to the US.'

'That's a long way from Naples,' she observed slowly. 'Why there?'

'Because it was a big enough place to lose myself in and to start again. I didn't want to be defined by a career which had been cut short and I was young and strong and prepared to work hard.' He'd worked to the exclusion of pretty much everything else in order to get the break he'd needed and, when it had come, he had grabbed at it with both hands. Perceptive enough to recognise that people were starting to move downtown and that run-down areas of the city were potential goldmines, he had started buying up derelict properties and then renovating them. On his Christmas trip back to Naples that first year, he had brought his mother a fancy coat from Bloomingdales. These days he could give her the entire store—and frequently tried—but no amount of material success could ever fill the emptiness in his heart.

He stared at Molly, amazed at how much he had told her. More than he'd ever admitted to anyone, even to Lauren. His gaze raked over her and he thought how different she looked from the first time he'd seen her, eating cake in the kitchen, her ripe body looking as if it was about to burst out of her uniform. Her green dress exuded all the class and sophistication which was an inevitable by-product of wearing designer clothes which had been chosen by an expert. Yet it was the softness of her eyes he noticed most—and the dewy perfection of her creamy skin. She still radiated the same wholesome sex appeal which had drawn him to her in the first place and he wondered why he was wasting time talking like this. What would he be doing with any other woman he was sharing a bedroom with—let alone the one who was wearing his ring?

He felt the erratic hammer of his pulse as he glanced down at his watch. 'I don't want to talk about the past any more.'

'Okay,' she said cautiously. 'Then we won't.'

'And we don't have to be at my folks' place for a while,' he said unevenly. 'Do you want a tour of the city?'

'Is that what you'd like to do?' she questioned, with the compliance which was such an essential part of her nature.

'No. That's the last thing I want to do right now. I can think of a much better way to pass the next couple of hours. Can't you?'

Molly thoughts were teeming as she met his dark gaze. So much of what he'd told her hadn't been what she was expecting, yet now she knew the facts they didn't really come as a surprise. The first time she'd seen him she'd noticed the power-packed body of a natural sportsman and the faint limp which he had all but managed to disguise. The single physical flaw in a man who was looking at her now with a question in his eyes.

She was still a relative novice at sex, but already she could recognise the desire which was making his face grow tense. She knew what he wanted. What *she* wanted too. Because she hadn't really enjoyed their night apart, last night. And even though the bed had been amazingly comfortable, she kept thinking about Salvio lying next door. Wondering why he hadn't tried a bit harder to sleep with her. Wondering if he'd gone off her and didn't fancy her any more. And—desire aside—wasn't the truth that she felt *safe* in his arms—even if that feeling passed as quickly as a summer storm? She stared into his molten black eyes and, for once, said exactly what was in her heart.

'Yes, I can think of a few things I'd like to do,' she agreed shyly. 'As long as they involve us being horizontal.'

She was unprepared for the curve of his smile as he walked towards her or for the way he lifted her hand to his, kissing each finger in turn before leading her over to the huge bed which overlooked the famous bay. She was eager to feel his naked skin against hers but this time there was no urgency as he began to undress her. This time his fingers were leisurely as they unclipped her bra and her swollen breasts came spilling out, his moan appreciative as he caught one taut nipple between his teeth. Molly squirmed beneath the teasing flick of his tongue but her frustration didn't seem to have any effect on his lazy pace. And didn't her heart pound with joy when he bent his head to drop a series of tender kisses on her belly as if he was silently acknowledging the tiny life which grew inside her?

'S-Salvio?' she stumbled tentatively as she felt the brush of his lips against her navel.

'It's going to be okay,' he said, his voice growing husky.

What was he talking about—their future, or meeting his parents? Or both?

But suddenly Molly was beyond caring as his movements became more urgent.

She cried out when he entered her and clung to him fiercely as he made each hard thrust. It felt so deep—he seemed to be filling her body completely, as if he couldn't get enough of her. And it felt different, more *intimate* than it had ever been before. Was that because he'd trusted her enough to tell her things she suspected he usually kept locked away— or was this sudden closeness all in her imagination? But the pleasure she was experiencing wasn't imaginary. Her senses felt exquisitely raw and heightened so that when her orgasm came, Molly felt as if rocked by a giant and powerful wave—her satisfaction only intensified by the moan he gave as he spilled his seed inside her. Afterwards she felt as if she were floating on a cloud. His breath was warm and comforting against her neck and she missed his presence when he withdrew from her and rolled to the other side of the mattress.

'That was just…perfect,' she said dreamily, the words out of her mouth before she could prevent them.

But Salvio didn't answer and, although the sound

of his breathing was strong and steady, Molly wasn't sure whether or not he was asleep. Was he just lying there ignoring her? she wondered, with a sudden streak of paranoia. Lying there and *pretending*?

But she decided it was pointless to get freaked out by his sudden detachment, even if she'd had the energy to do so. Nestling herself down into the big mound of feathery pillows, Molly gave a little sigh and fell asleep.

CHAPTER NINE

PERHAPS INEVITABLY, THEY slept for longer than they'd intended and Molly woke with a start, looking round in mild confusion as she tried to get her bearings. Maybe they'd been catching up on too many restless nights, or maybe the amazing sex they'd just enjoyed had taken it out of them. Either way, the Neapolitan sky outside their hotel suite was ebony-dark and sprinkled with stars and when she glanced at her watch, she saw to her horror that it was almost seven—and they were due at Salvio's parents for Christmas Eve dinner in just over an hour.

'Wake up,' she urged, giving her sleeping fiancé's shoulder a rough shake. 'Or we're going to be late!'

Hurrying into the bathroom, she had the fastest shower on record before addressing the thorny issue of what to wear when meeting Salvio's parents for the first time. She still wasn't used to having quite so many clothes at her disposal and was more than a little dazzled by the choice. After much consideration, she opted for a soft knee-length skirt worn with a winter-white sweater and long black boots. Taking a deep breath, she did a little pirouette.

'Do you think your mother will approve of what I'm wearing?' she asked anxiously.

Salvio's black gaze roved over her in leisurely appraisal, before he gave a nod of approval. 'Most certainly,' he affirmed. 'You look demure and decent.'

Molly's fixed smile didn't waver as they stepped into the penthouse elevator, but really...*demure* and *decent* didn't exactly set the world on fire, did they?

They reached the lobby and as the doorman sprang forward to welcome them, Molly became aware of the buzz of interest their appearance was creating. Or rather, Salvio's appearance. She could see older men staring at him wistfully while women of all ages seemed intent on devouring him with hungry eyes. Yet despite the glamour of the female guests who were milling around the lobby, Molly felt a sudden shy pride as he took her arm and began guiding her towards the waiting car. Because *she* was the one he'd just been making love to, wasn't she? And *she* was the one who was carrying his child.

The luxury car was soon swallowed up in heavy traffic and before long they drew up outside an elegant house not too far from their hotel. Molly's nerves—

which had been growing during the journey—were quickly dissolved when they were met by a tiny middle-aged woman dressed in Christmas red, her eyes dark and smiling as she opened the door to them. She hugged Molly fiercely before drawing back to look at her properly.

'At last! I have a daughter!' she exclaimed, in fluent though heavily accented English, before turning to her son and rising up on tiptoe to kiss him on each cheek, a faint note of reproof in her voice. 'And what I would like to know is why you are staying in a hotel tonight instead of here at home with your parents, Salvatore De Gennaro?'

'Because you would have insisted on us having separate rooms and this is the twenty-first century, in case you hadn't noticed,' answered her son drily. 'But don't worry, Mamma. We will be back again tomorrow.'

Slightly mollified, Rosa De Gennaro ushered them towards a beautiful high-ceilinged sitting room, where her husband was waiting and Molly stepped forward to greet him. Tall and silver-haired, Paolo De Gennaro had handsomely-rugged features which echoed those of his son and Molly got a poignant glimpse of what Salvio might look like when he was sixty. *Will I still know him when he's sixty?* she wondered, unprepared for the dark fear which shafted through her and the sudden shifting sense of uncertainty. But she shelved the useless thought and concentrated on getting to know the older couple whose joy at their son's engagement was evident. As Rosa examined her glittering ring with murmurs of delight, Molly felt a flash of guilt. What if they knew the truth? That the only reason she was here on Christmas Eve, presenting this false front of togetherness with their son, was because one reckless night had ended up with an unplanned baby.

But guilt was a futile emotion and she tried to make the best of things, the way she always did. The house seemed full of light and festivity—with the incomparable air of expectation which always defined the night before Christmas, no matter how much you tried to pretend it didn't. A beautiful tree, laden with gifts, was glittering in one of the windows and she could detect delicious smells of cooking from elsewhere in the house.

It was a long time since she'd been at the centre of a family and Molly found herself wondering what Robbie was doing tonight. She'd tried to ring him earlier that day but he hadn't picked up. *Please don't let him be gambling*, she prayed silently. *Let him have realised that there's more to life than debt and uncertainty and chasing impossible dreams.* Staring down at the nativity set which stood on a small table next to the tree, she focussed on the helpless infant in the tiny crib and tried to imagine what her own baby would look like. Would he or she resemble Salvio, with those dark stern features and a mouth which rarely smiled, but which when it did was like no other smile she'd ever seen?

She remembered the way he'd kissed her belly just before they'd made love and felt a stir of hope in her heart. He'd certainly never done *that* before—and surely that response hadn't been faked? Because the fleeting tenderness she thought she'd detected had meant just as much as the sexual excitement which had followed. And wasn't tenderness a good place to start building their relationship?

Refusing champagne and sipping from a glass of fruit juice, Molly was laughing as she examined a photo of a fourteen-year-old Salvio holding aloft a shining silver trophy, when she felt a brief pain, low in her belly. Did she flinch? Was that why Salvio's mother guided her towards a high-backed brocade chair and touched her gently on her shoulder?

'*Per piacere.* Sit down, Molly. You must be tired after your travels—but soon we will eat. You are hungry, I hope?'

Obediently, Molly took the chair she'd been offered, wondering why people were always telling her to sit down. Did she look permanently tired? Probably. Actually, she *was* a bit tired. She thought about the reason for her fatigue and her heart gave a little skip as she smiled at Salvio's mother.

'Very hungry,' she said.

'Here in Southern Italy we are proud of our culinary traditions,' Rosa continued before directing a smile at her son. 'For they represent the important times that families spend together.'

Soon they were tucking into a feast of unbelievable proportions. Molly had never *seen* a meal so big, as dish followed dish. There was spaghetti with clams and then fried shellfish, before an eel-like fish was placed in the centre of the elegant dining table with something of a flourish.

'*Capitone!*' announced Rosa. 'You know this fish, Molly? No? It is a Neapolitan tradition to eat it on Christmas Eve. In the old days, my mother used to buy it from the market while it was still alive, and then keep it in the bath until it was time to cook it. Do you remember the year it escaped, Salvio—and hid under your bed? And you were the only one brave enough to catch it?'

As his parents laughed Molly sneaked a glance at Salvio and tried to imagine the billionaire tycoon as a little boy, capturing an elusive fish which had slithered underneath a bed. Just as she tried to imagine him cradling an infant in those powerful arms, but that was too big a stretch of the imagination. At times he was so cool and distant—it was only in bed that he seemed to let his guard down and show any real feeling. She stared at the small piece of *capitone* left on her plate, wondering how it was going to work when she had his baby. She'd already established that his London penthouse wasn't particularly child-friendly—but where else would they live? He'd mentioned other houses in different countries but none of them had sounded like home, with the possible exception of his Cotswolds manor house.

They finished the meal with hard little biscuits called *rococo* and afterwards Molly insisted on helping her hostess clear the table. Efficiently, she dealt with the left-over food and dishes in a way which was second nature to her, washing the crystal glasses by hand and carefully placing them on the draining board to dry, while asking her hostess questions about life in Naples. She was just taking off the apron she'd borrowed when she noticed Rosa standing in the doorway of the kitchen watching her, a soft smile on her face.

'Thank you, Molly.'

'It was my pleasure, Signora De Gennaro. Thank you for a delicious meal. You have a wonderful home and you've been very welcoming.'

'*Prego.*' Rosa gave a small nod of satisfaction. 'I have been waiting many years for a daughter-in-law and I think you will be very good for my son.'

Molly's heart pounded as she hung the apron on a hook beside the door, hoping Rosa didn't want to hear the romantic story of how she and her son had first met. Because there wasn't one. She suspected the truth would shock this kindly woman but Molly couldn't bear to tell her any lies. *So concentrate on the things you* can *say*, she told herself fiercely. *On all the things you wish would happen.*

'Oh, I hope I will be,' she said, her voice a little unsteady as she realised she meant every word. 'I want to be the best wife I can.'

Rosa nodded, her dark eyes intense and watchful. 'You are not like his other girlfriends,' she said slowly.

Was that a good thing or a bad thing? Molly wondered. 'Aren't I?'

'Not at all.' Rosa hesitated. 'Though he only ever brought one other to meet us.'

Molly stilled, telling herself it would be foolish to ask any more questions. But she hadn't factored in curiosity—and curiosity was a dangerous thing. Wasn't it the key which turned the lock in an invisible door—exposing you to things you might be better not knowing? And the crazy thing was even though she *knew* that, it didn't stop her from prying. 'Oh?' she questioned. Just one little word but that was all it took.

'She was no good for him,' said Rosa darkly, after a brief pause. '*Sì*, she was very beautiful but she cared only for his fame. She would never have helped with the dishes like this. She wanted to spend her Christmases in New York, or Monaco.' She touched her fingertips to the small golden cross at her neck. 'I give thanks that he never married her.'

Married her? Molly's heart constricted. Had Salvio been engaged to someone else? The man who had told her he didn't 'do' emotion? The nebulous twist of pain in her stomach which she'd felt earlier now returned with all the ferocity of a hot spear, which Molly bore behind the sunniest smile in her repertoire. But she was relieved when Salvio phoned his driver to take them back to the hotel, and leaned back weakly against the car seat, closing her eyes and willing the pain to leave her.

'Are you okay?' questioned Salvio beside her.

No, I'm not okay. I discovered tonight that you were going to marry someone else and you didn't tell me. That even though I'm carrying your baby you don't trust me enough to confide in me.

But she couldn't face a scene in the car, so she stuck to the positive. 'I'm fine!' she said brightly, still with that rictus smile in place. 'Your parents are lovely,' she added in a rush.

'Yes,' he said, and smiled. 'They liked you.'

But Molly thought he seemed lost in thought as he stared out at the festive lights of his city. Was he thinking about his other fiancée and comparing the two women? She found herself wondering why they had broken up and wondered if she would summon up the courage to ask him.

But the cramps in her stomach were getting worse. Cramps which felt horribly familiar, but which she tried to dismiss as stress. The stress of meeting his parents for the first time, or maybe the stress of discovering that she wasn't the only woman he'd asked to marry. She found herself breathing a sigh of relief when they arrived back in their penthouse suite and she unbuttoned her coat.

'Would you mind if I checked on my emails?' Salvio said as he removed the coat from her shoulders. 'I just want to see if something has come in from Los Angeles, before everything shuts down for the holidays.'

'No, of course I don't mind,' she said weakly, aware that he was already disappearing towards his computer.

She slipped into the bathroom and locked the door behind her, when she felt a warm rush between her legs and the sudden unexpected sight of blood made Molly freeze. She began to tremble.

It couldn't be.

Couldn't be.

But it was. Of course it was. On a deeper level she'd

known all evening that this was about to happen, but the reality was harsher than she ever could have imagined. Her fingers clutched the cold rim of the bathtub as her vision shifted in and out of focus. She found herself wishing she were alone so that she could have given into the inexplicable tears which were welling up in her eyes. But she wasn't alone. She dashed the tears away with the tips of her fingers and tried to compose herself. Out in that fancy hotel room on the night before Christmas was her fiancé…except that the reason he'd slid these diamonds on her finger no longer existed. He would be free now, she thought—as a silent scream of protest welled up inside her.

She found her wash-bag, praying she might find what she needed—but there was no gratitude in her heart when she did, only the dull certainty of what she needed to say to Salvio. But she was loath to go out and face him. To utter the words he would probably be relieved to hear. She didn't think she could face his joy—not when she was experiencing such strange and bitter heartache.

Straightening up, she stared into the mirror, registering the pallor of her face, knowing that she couldn't tell him now. Not tonight. Not when the bells of Naples were peeling out their triumphant Christmas chorus about the impending birth of a baby.

CHAPTER TEN

'So when...?' There was a pause. 'When exactly were you going to tell me, *bedda mia*?'

The words left Salvio's lips like icy bullets but he knew immediately that his aim had been accurate. He could tell by the way Molly froze as she came out of the bathroom, the white towelling robe swathing her curvy body like a soft suit of armour.

'Tell you what?' she questioned.

Maybe if she'd come straight out and admitted it, he might have gone more easily on her but instead he felt the slow seep of anger in his veins as her guile-less expression indicated nothing but a lie. A damned lie. His mouth hardened. 'That you aren't pregnant.'

She didn't deny it. She just stood in front of him, the colour leeching from her face so that her milky skin looked almost transparent. 'How did you...?' He saw the sudden flash of fear in her eyes. 'How did you know?'

Her confirmation only stoked the darkness which was building inside him. 'You think I am devoid of all my senses?' he demanded. 'That I wouldn't wonder why you turned away from me last night, then spent hours clinging to the other side of the mattress...pretending to be *asleep*?' he finished with contempt.

'So it's because we didn't have sex,' she summarised dully.

'No, not just because of that, nor even because of the way you disappeared into the bathroom when we got back from my parents' house and refused to look me in the eye,' he iced back. 'I'm not stupid, Molly. Don't you realise that a man can tell when a woman is menstruating? That she looks different. Smells different.'

'How could I ever be expected to match your encyclopaedic knowledge of women?' she questioned bitterly. 'When you're the first man I've ever slept with.'

Salvio felt the pounding of a pulse at his temple. Was she using her innocence as a shield with which to defend herself? To deflect him from a far more disturbing possibility, but one he couldn't seem to shake off no matter how hard he tried. 'Or maybe you were never even pregnant in the first place,' he accused silkily.

She reacted by swaying and sinking down onto a nearby sofa, as if his accusation had taken away her ability to stand. 'You think *that*?' she breathed, her fingers spreading out over her throat as if she was in danger of choking.

'Why shouldn't I think that?' he demanded. 'I've never actually seen any proof, have I? Is that why you didn't want to tell my parents about the baby— not because it was "too early" but because there *was* no baby?'

'You really believe—' she shook her damp hair in disbelief '—that I would lie to you about something as important as that?'

'How should I know what you'd do if you were desperate enough? We both know you were having trouble paying off your brother's debt and that marriage to me would mean the debt would be wiped out overnight.' His gaze bored into her. 'And I was careful that night, Molly. You know I was.'

She was still staring at him as if he were the devil incarnate. 'You're saying that I…made it up? That the whole pregnancy was nothing but an *invention*?'

'Why not? It's not unheard of.' He shrugged. 'It happens less often these days but I understand in the past it was quite a common device, used by women keen to get a wedding ring on their finger.' His mouth hardened. 'Usually involving a wealthy man.'

Her body tensed and Salvio saw the change in her. Saw the moment when her habitual compliance became rebellion. When outrage filled her soft features with an unfamiliar rage which she was directing solely at him. Her eyes flashing pewter sparks, she sprang to her feet, damp hair flying around her shoulders.

'I *was* pregnant,' she flared, her hands gesturing wildly through the empty air. 'One hundred per cent pregnant. I did two tests, one after the other—and if you don't believe me, then that's your problem! And yes, I was waiting until this morning to tell you, because last night I just couldn't face having the kind of discussion we're having now. So if keeping the news to myself for less than twelve hours is harbouring some dark secret, then yes—I'm guilty of that. But I'm not the only one with secrets, am I, Salvio?'

He heard the allegation in her voice as he met her furious gaze full on and braced himself for what was coming next.

'When were you going to let me know you'd been engaged before?' she continued, her voice still shaking with rage. 'Or weren't you going to bother?'

His eyes narrowed. 'My mother told you?'

'Of course your mother told me—how else would I know?'

'What did she say?'

'Enough.' Her voice wobbled. 'I know the woman you were going to marry was rich and I'm not. I know she was beautiful and I'm not.'

Something about the weariness in her tone made Salvio feel a sharp pang of guilt. He stared at her shadowed eyes. At the milky skin now tinged with the dull flush of fury. At the still-drying shiny hair and the voluptuous curves which had lured him like a siren's call into her arms. And he felt an unexpected wave of contrition wash over him.

'You *are* beautiful,' he stressed.

'Please. Don't,' she said, holding up her hand to silence him. 'Don't make things even worse by telling me lies!'

Her dignified response surprised him. Had he been expecting gratitude for his throwaway compliment about her looks? Was he, in his own way, as guilty as Lady Avery had been of underestimating her? Of treating her like an object, rather than a person—as someone born to serve rather than to participate? Did he think he could behave exactly as he liked towards her and she would just take it?

'You *are* beautiful,' he affirmed, as repentance flowed through him. 'And yes, I was engaged before. I didn't tell you because...'

'Because it's too painful for you to remember, I suppose?'

The pulse at Salvio's temple now flickered. In a way, yes, very painful—though not in the way he suspected she meant. It was more about the betrayal he'd suffered than anything else because, like all Neapolitans, he had an instinctive loathing of treachery. It had come as a shock to realise that Lauren hadn't loved him—only what he represented. He gave a bitter smile. Perhaps he should have had a little more empathy for Molly since he too had been treated like an object in his time. 'It happened a long time ago,' he said slowly. 'And there seemed no reason to rake it up.'

She looked at him in exasperation. 'Don't you know anything about women? On second thought, don't answer that since we've already proved beyond any reasonable doubt that what you don't know about women probably isn't worth knowing. Except maybe you don't know just how far you can push them before they finally snap.' She tugged the towelling belt of her white robe a little tighter. 'Who was she, Salvio?'

Salvio scowled. Did he really have to tell her? Rake up the bitterness all over again? He expelled air from his flared nostrils, recognising from the unusually fierce expression on Molly's face that he had to tell her. 'Her name was Lauren Meyer,' he said reluctantly. 'I met her at an official function on a pre-season tour of America and brought her back here with me to Naples.'

'And she was blonde, I suppose?'

'Yes, she was blonde,' he said, ignoring her sarcastic tone. 'What else do you want to know, Molly? That she was an heiress and that she loved fame and fortune, in that order?'

'Did she?'

'She did. She met me when I had everything.' He gave a short laugh. 'And dumped me the moment I lost it all.'

'So, what…happened?' she said, into the silence which followed.

Salvio's lips tightened, because Lauren had been the catalyst. The reason he had kissed goodbye to emotion and battened up his heart. During his career there had been plenty of women who had lusted after his body and his bank account—but he'd made the mistake of thinking that Lauren was different.

His gaze flicked over to the dark sweep of the bay before returning to the grey watchfulness in Molly's eyes and suddenly he was finding it easy to talk about something he never talked about. 'After the accident, she came to visit me. Every day she sat by my bedside, always in a different outfit, looking picture-perfect. Always ready to smile and pose for the photographers who were camped outside the hospital. She was there when the physiotherapists worked on my leg and she was there when the doctor told me I'd never play professional football again. I'll never forget the look on her face.' His laugh was harsh. 'When I was discharged, she didn't come to meet me, but I thought I knew the reason why. I went home expecting a surprise party because she loved parties, and that's when I discovered she'd flown back to the States and was seeing some all-American boy her parents wanted her to marry all along. And that was that. I never saw her again.'

There was a pause while she seemed to take it all in.

'Oh, Salvio, that's awful,' she said. 'It must have felt like a kick in the teeth when you'd lost everything else.'

'I didn't tell you because I wanted your pity, Molly. I told you because you wanted to know. So now you do.'

'And, did you…did you love her?'

He felt a twist of anger. Why did women always do this? Why did they reduce everything down to those three little words and place so much store by them? He knew what she wanted him to say and that he was going to have to disappoint her. Because he couldn't rewrite the past, could he? He was damned if he was going to tell her something just because it was what he suspected she wanted to hear. And how could he possibly dismiss lies as contemptible if he started using them himself? 'Yes, I loved her,' he said, at last.

Molly hid her pain behind the kind of look she might have presented to Lady Avery if she'd just been asked to produce an extra batch of scones before tea-time, and not for the first time she was grateful for all the training she'd had as a servant. Grateful for the mask-like calm she was able to project while she tried to come to terms with her new situation. Because in less than twelve hours she'd lost everything, too. Not just her baby but her hopes for the future. Hope of being a good wife and mother. Hope that a baby might help Salvio loosen up and become more human. And now it was all gone—whipped away like a rug being pulled from beneath her feet. There was no illusion left for her to cling to. No rosy dreams. Just a man who had once loved another woman and didn't love her. A man who had accused her of lying about her baby.

A baby which was now no more.

She wanted to bury her face in her hands and sob out her heartbreak but somehow she resisted the compelling urge. Instead she chose her words as carefully as a resigning politician. 'I don't want to upset your parents but obviously I can't face going for lunch today. I mean, there's no point now, is there? I don't think I'm capable of pretending everything's the same as it was—especially on Christmas Day. I think your mother might see right through me and there's no way I want to deceive her. So maybe it's best if I just disappear and leave you to say whatever you think is best.' She swallowed. 'Perhaps you could arrange for your plane to take me back to England as soon as possible?'

Salvio stared at her, unprepared for the powerful feeling which arrowed through his gut. Was it *disappointment*? Yet that seemed much too bland a description. Disappointment was what you felt if there was no snow on the slopes during a skiing holiday, or if it rained on your Mediterranean break.

He furrowed his brow. After Lauren he'd never wanted marriage. He'd never wanted a baby either but, having been presented with a *fait accompli*, had done what he considered to be the right thing by Molly. And of *course* it had affected him, because, although his heart might be unfeeling, he was discovering he wasn't made of stone. Hadn't he allowed himself the brief fantasy of imagining himself with a son? A son he could teach to kick a ball around and to perfect the *elastico* move for which he'd been so famous?

Only now Molly wanted to leave him. Her womb was empty and her spirit deflated by his cruel accusations and she was still staring at him as if he were some kind of monster. Maybe he deserved that because hadn't she only ever been kind and giving? Rare attributes which only a fool would squander—and he was that fool.

'No. Don't go,' he said suddenly.

She screwed up her eyes. 'You mean you won't let me use your plane?'

'My plane is at your disposal any time you want it,' he said impatiently. 'That's not what I mean.' His mouth hardened. 'I don't want you to go, Molly.'

'Well, I've got to go. I can't hang around pretending nothing's happened, just because you don't want to lose face with your parents.'

'It has nothing to do with losing face,' he argued. 'It has more to do with wanting to make amends for all the accusations I threw at you. About realising that maybe—somehow—we could make this work.'

'Make *what* work?'

'This relationship.'

She shook her head. 'We don't have a relationship, Salvio.'

'But we could.'

She narrowed her eyes. 'You're not making any sense.'

'Aren't I?' He lowered his voice. 'I get the feeling you weren't too unhappy about having my baby.'

She stared down at her feet and as he followed the direction of her gaze, he noticed her toenails were unvarnished. It occurred to him that he'd never been intimate with a woman whose life hadn't been governed by beauty regimes and his eyes narrowed in sudden comprehension. Was that shallow of him? She looked up again and he could see the pride and dignity written all over her face and he felt the twist of something he didn't recognise deep inside him.

'If this is a soul-baring exercise then it seems only fair I should bear mine. And I couldn't help the way I felt about being pregnant,' she admitted. 'I knew it wasn't an ideal situation and should never have happened but, no, I wasn't unhappy about having your baby, Salvio. It would have been…'

'Would have been what?' he prompted as her words tailed off.

Somebody to love, Molly wanted to say—but even in this new spirit of honesty, she knew that was a declaration too far. Because that sounded needy and vulnerable and she was through with being vulnerable. She wished Salvio would stop asking her all this stuff, especially when it was so out of character. Why didn't he just let her fly back to England and let her get on with the rest of her life and begin the complicated process of getting over him, instead of directing that soft look of compassion at her which was making her feel most…peculiar? She struggled to remove some of the emotion from her words.

'It would have been a role which I would have happily taken on and done to the best of my ability,' she said. 'And I'm not going to deny that on one level I'm deeply disappointed, but I'll… I'll get over it.'

Her words faded into silence. One of those silences which seemed to last for an eternity when you just knew that everything hinged on what was said next, but Salvio's words were the very last Molly was expecting.

'Unless we try again, of course,' he said.

'What are you talking about?' she breathed.

'What if I told you that fatherhood was something which I had also grown to accept? Which I would have happily taken on, despite my initial reservations? What if I told you that I was disappointed, too? *Am* disappointed,' he amended. 'That I've realised I *do* want a child.'

'Then I suggest you do something about it,' she said, her words brittle as rock candy and she wondered if he had any idea how much it hurt to say them. Or how hard it was to stem the tide of tears which was pricking at her eyes. Tears not just for the little life which was no more, but for the man who had created that life. Because that was the crazy thing. That she was going to miss Salvio De Gennaro. How was it that in such a short while he seemed to have become as integral to her life as her own heartbeat? 'Find a woman. Get married. Start a family. That's the way it usually works.'

'That's exactly what I intend to do. Only I don't need to find a woman. Why would I, when there's one standing in front of me?'

'You don't mean that.'

'Don't tell me what I mean, Molly. I mean every word and I'm asking you to be my wife.'

Molly blinked in confusion. He was asking her to *marry* him—despite the fact she was no longer carrying his baby? She thought about the first time she'd ever seen him and how completely blown away she'd been. But this time she was no longer staring at him as if he were some demigod who had just tumbled from the stars. The scales had fallen from her eyes and now she saw him for what he was. A flawed individual—just like her. He had introduced her to amazing sex and fancy clothes. They'd made love on a giant bed overlooking the Bay of Naples and he had kissed her belly when a tiny child had been growing there. She had met his parents and they had liked her—treating her as if she were already part of the family. And somehow the culmination of all those experiences had changed her. She was no longer the same humble person who would accept whatever was thrown at her. The things which had happened had allowed her to remove the shackles which had always defined her. She no longer felt like a servant, but a woman. A real woman.

Yet even as that realisation filled her with a rush of liberation, she was at pains to understand why Salvio was making his extraordinary proposition. He was off the hook now. He was free again. Surely he should be celebrating her imminent departure from his life instead of trying to postpone it?

'Why do you want to marry me?' she demanded.

His gaze raked over her but this time it was not his usual sensual appraisal—more an impartial assessment of her worth. 'I like your softness and kindness,' he said slowly. 'Your approach to life and your work ethic. I think you will make a good mother.'

'And that's all?' she found herself asking.

He narrowed his eyes. 'Surely that is enough?'

She wasn't certain. If you wrote down all those things they would make a flattering list but the glaring omission was love. But Salvio had loved once before and his heart had been broken and damaged as a result. Could she accept his inability to love her as a condition of their marriage, and could they make it work in spite of that?

Behind him, Naples was framed like a picture-postcard as he began to walk towards her and for once his limp seemed more pronounced than usual. And although the thrust of his thighs was stark evidence enough of his powerful sensuality, it was that tiny glimpse of frailty which plucked at her heart-strings.

'I wanted this baby,' he said simply.

Her heart pounded—not wanting to be affected by that powerful declaration. But of course she *was* affected—for it was the most human she had ever seen him. 'You had a funny way of showing it.'

He lifted his shoulders as if to concede the point. 'I'm not going to deny that at first I felt trapped. Who wouldn't in that kind of situation? But once I'd got my head around it, my feelings began to change.'

Molly felt the lurch of hope. Could she believe him? Did she dare to? She remembered the way he'd kissed her belly yesterday—and how loving she'd felt towards him as a result. And that was dangerous. When she stopped to think about it, everything about this situation was dangerous. 'So this time you're not asking me to marry you because you have to?' she continued doggedly. 'You're saying you actually *want* to?'

'Yes.' His shadowed jaw tightened. 'I do. For old-fashioned reasons rather than the unrealistic expectations of romantic love. I want a family, Molly. I didn't realise how much until the possibility was taken away from me. I want someone to leave my fortune to—because otherwise what's the point of making all this money? Someone to take my name and my genes forward. Someone who will be my future.'

Molly's heart clenched as she listened to his heart-felt words. She thought of his pain when he'd lost his career and fortune in quick succession. She thought about the woman who had betrayed him at the worst possible time. The woman he had loved. No won-der he had built a wall around his heart and vowed never to let anyone touch that heart again. She drank in the hardness of his beautiful face. Could she dis-mantle that wall, little by little, and would he allow her close enough to try? She knew it was a gamble—and, despite all the stern lectures she'd given her little brother, a gamble she intended to take, because by now she couldn't imagine a life without him.

But if she was to be his wife then she must learn to be his equal. There had been times in the past when she'd told Salvio what she thought he wanted to hear because that was all part of her training as a servant. But it wasn't going to be like that from now on. From now on they were going to operate on a level playing field.

'Yes, I will be your wife,' she said, in a low and unemotional voice.

He laughed, softly. 'You drive me crazy, Molly Miller,' he said. 'Do you realise that?'

The look she gave him was genuine. 'I don't know how.'

'I think,' he observed drily, 'that's the whole point. Now come here.'

He was pulling her into his arms and for a moment Molly felt uncertain, because she had her period and surely… But the touch of his fingertips against her cheek was comforting rather than seeking and the warmth of his arms consoling rather than sexual.

'I'm sorry about the baby,' he whispered against her hair, so softly that she might have imagined it.

It was the first time he had ever held her without wanting sex and Molly pressed her eyelids tightly shut, her face resting against his silky shoulder, terrified to move or to speak because she was afraid she might cry.

CHAPTER ELEVEN

THEY WERE MARRIED in Naples in a beautiful church not far from the home of Salvio's parents. The ancient building was packed with people Molly barely knew—friends of the family, she guessed, and high-powered friends of Salvio's who had flown in from all around the world. Most of them she'd met the previous evening during a lavish pre-wedding dinner, but their names had flown in one ear and out of the other, no matter how hard she'd tried to remember them. Her mind had been too full of niggling concerns to concentrate on anything very much, but her main anxiety had been about Robbie.

Because Salvio had quietly arranged for her brother to fly from Australia to Naples as a pre-wedding surprise and Molly's heart had contracted with joy as Robbie had strolled into the restaurant where everyone was eating, flashing his careless smile, which had made many of the younger women swoon.

She had jumped to her feet to hug him, touched by Salvio's unexpected thoughtfulness, as she'd run her gaze over her brother in candid assessment. From the outside Robbie looked good—better than he'd looked in a long time. He was tanned and fit, his golden curls longer than she remembered, and his clothes were surprisingly well chosen. But she'd seen his faintly avaricious expression as he'd taken in the giant ring on her finger and the expensive venue of the sea-view wedding reception.

'Well, what do you know? You did good, sis. Real good,' he'd said slowly, a gleam entering his grey eyes. 'Salvio De Gennaro is *minted.*'

She'd found herself wanting to protest that she wasn't marrying Salvio for his money but Robbie probably wouldn't have believed her, since his teen-age years had been dedicated to the pursuit of instant wealth. She'd wondered if his reluctance to maintain eye contact meant that his gambling addiction had returned. And had then wondered if she was simply transferring her own fears onto her brother.

But she wasn't going to be afraid because she was walking into this with her eyes open. She'd made the decision to be Salvio's wife because deep down she wanted to, and she was going to give the marriage everything she could. Who said that such a strangely conceived union couldn't work? She was used to fighting against the odds, wasn't she?

Holding herself tall, she had walked slowly down the aisle wearing the dress which had been created especially for her by one of London's top wedding-dress designers. The whole couture process had been a bit of an ordeal, mainly because a pale, shiny fabric wasn't terribly forgiving when you were over-endowed with curves, but Molly had known Salvio wanted her to look like a traditional bride. And in her heart she had wanted that, too.

'Your breasts are very…generous.' The dress-maker had grunted. 'We're going to have to use a minimising bra, I think.'

Molly had opened her mouth to agree until she'd remembered what she'd vowed on the day of Salvio's proposal. That she was going to be true to herself and behave like his equal because the strain of doing otherwise would quickly wear her down. And if she tried to be someone she wasn't, then surely this whole crazy set-up would be doomed.

'I think Salvio likes my breasts the way they are,' she'd offered shyly and the dressmaker had taken the pins out of her mouth, and smiled.

The look on his face when she reached the altar seemed to endorse Molly's theory—and when they left the church as man and wife, the strangest thing happened. Outside, a sea of people wearing pale blue and white ribbons were cheering and clapping and Molly looked up at Salvio in confusion as their joyful shouts filled the air.

'Some of the supporters of my old football club,' he explained, looking slightly taken aback himself. 'Come to wish me *in bocca al lupo*.'

'Good luck?' she hazarded, blinking as a battery of mobile-phone cameras flashed in her face.

'*Esattamente.* Your Italian lessons are clearly paying dividends,' he murmured into her ear, his mouth brushing against one pearl-indented lobe.

Just that brief touch was enough to make her breasts spring into delicious life beneath the delicate material of her wedding dress and Salvio's perceptive smile made Molly blush. Lifting up her bouquet of roses to disguise the evidence of physical desire, she thought how perfectly attuned he was to her body and its needs. Their sexual compatibility had been there from the start—now all she needed to concentrate on was getting pregnant.

After the wedding they flew to their honeymoon destination of Barbados, where they were shown to a large, private villa in the vast grounds of a luxury hotel. It was the closest thing to paradise that Molly could imagine and as soon as they arrived, Salvio went for a swim while she insisted on unpacking her clothes—because she didn't quite trust anyone else to do it so neatly. *Old habits die hard*, she thought ruefully.

Knotting a sarong around her waist, she went outside where her brand-new husband was lying on a sun lounger the size of a double bed, wearing a battered straw hat angled over his eyes and nothing else. A lump rose in her throat as she watched him lying in the bright sunshine—completely at ease with his bare body which was gleaming with droplets of water drying in the sun. For a moment she couldn't actually believe she was here, with him. His wife. She swallowed. Even her title took some getting used to. Signora Molly De Gennaro.

He turned to look at her, his gaze lazy as it ran a slow and comprehensive journey from her head to the tips of her toes.

'How are you feeling?' he questioned solicitously.

Trying not to be distracted by the very obvious stirring at his groin, she nodded. 'Fine, thank you,' she said politely. 'That sleep I had on the plane was wonderful.'

'Then stop standing there looking so uncertain.' Pushing aside a tumble of cushions, he patted the space beside him on the giant sunbed. 'Come over here.'

It occurred to Molly that if she wasn't careful she

would end up taking orders from him just like before, but it was probably going to take a little time to acclimatise herself to this new life. To feel as if she had the right to enjoy these lavish surroundings, instead of constantly looking around feeling as if she ought to be cleaning them.

Aware of the sensual glitter of his eyes, she walked across the patio and sank down next to him. Straight ahead glimmered a sea of transparent turquoise, edged with sand so fine it looked like caster sugar. To her left was their own private swimming pool and any time they wanted anything—*anything at all*, as they had been assured on their arrival—all they had to do was to ring one of the bells which were littered around the place and some obliging servant would appear.

She stuck out her feet in front of her, still getting used to toenails which were glinting a fetching shade of coral in the bright sunshine.

'You've had a pedicure,' Salvio observed.

She blinked and looked up. 'Fancy you noticing something like that.'

'You'd be amazed what I notice about you, Molly,' he murmured. 'Is that the first one you've ever had?'

'I'm afraid it is.' She lifted her chin a little defensively. 'I suppose that shocks you?'

'Not really, no. And anyway—' he smiled '—I like being shocked by you.'

His hand was now on her leg and she felt his fingertips travelling slowly over her thigh. Little by little they inched upwards and her mouth grew increasingly dry as they approached the skimpy triangle of her bikini bottoms. She swallowed as his hand came to a tantalising halt just before they reached the red and white gingham. 'Salvio,' she breathed.

'*Sì*, Molly?' he murmured.

'We're outside. Anyone can see us.'

'But the whole point of having a *private* villa,' he emphasised, 'is that we *can't* be seen. Haven't you ever wondered what it might be like to make love in the open air?'

She hesitated. 'Maybe,' she said cautiously.

'So why don't we do it?'

'What, now?'

'Right now.'

She swallowed. 'If you're *sure* we really can't be seen.'

'I may be adventurous,' he drawled, 'but I draw the line at rampant voyeurism.'

'Go on, then,' she whispered encouragingly.

Salvio smiled as he trailed his lips down over Molly's generous cleavage which smelt faintly of coconut oil and was already warm from the sun.

Through her bikini top a pert nipple sprang into life against his lips and he thought how utterly entrancing she could be with that potent combination of shyness and eagerness, despite her lack of experience. 'You are for my eyes only,' he added gravely, hearing her sharp intake of breath as he began to undo the sarong which was knotted around her hips. 'Except you are wearing far too much for me to be able to see you properly.'

The sarong discarded, his finger crept beneath her bikini bottoms to find her most treasured spot, where she was slick and wet. Always wet, he thought achingly. Her enjoyment of sex was so delightfully fervent that it made him instantly hard. He expelled a shuddering breath of air as she responded to his caress by reaching down to touch him intimately, and he moaned his soft pleasure. He liked the way she encircled him within those dextrous fingers and the way she slid them up and down to lightly stroke the pulsing and erect flesh. He liked the way she teased him as he had taught her to tease him and to make him wait, until he felt like her captive slave. But today his hunger would not be tempered and he could not wait, his desire for her off the scale. He had let her sleep on the plane because she had looked exhausted after the wedding, but now his appetite knew no bounds. The bikini was discarded to join the sarong as he wriggled his fingers between her legs. She jerked distractedly as he found her tight bud, her nails digging into his bare shoulders as he increased his rhythmical stroke.

'You like that,' he observed, with a satisfied purr.

'Don't…don't stop, will you?' she gasped.

He gave a low laugh. 'I have no intention of stopping, *bedda mia*. I couldn't stop, even if I wanted to.' But suddenly he no longer wanted to pleasure her with his finger and, positioning himself over her, he parted her thighs and drove into her. He groaned as she matched each urgent thrust with the accommodating jerk of her hips. He revelled in the feel of her, the taste of her and the smell of her. Was it because there was no need for a condom that sex with Molly felt even more incredible than it had done before? Or because he was the one who had taught her everything? She'd never taken a man into her mouth before him, nor sucked him until he was empty and gasping. Just as she'd never had anyone's head between her thighs other than his. He closed his eyes as excitement built at a speed which almost outpaced him. Was he really so primitive that he got some kind of thrill from having bareback sex with his one-time virgin? He drove into her again. Maybe he was.

She began to come, her moans of pleasure spiralling up from the back of her throat and hovering on the edge of a scream, so that he clamped his mouth over hers in an urgent kiss. He felt the rush of her breath in his mouth and the helpless judder of her body clenching around him—and his own response was like a powerful wave which crashed over him and pulled him under. With a groan, he ejaculated, one hand splayed underneath her bottom while the other tangled in her silken hair. Beneath the Barbadian sun he felt the exquisite pulsing of his body as passion seeped away.

For a while he just lay on top of her, dazed and contented, his head cushioned on her shoulder as he dipped in and out of sleep. But eventually he stirred, his fingertips tilting her jaw, enjoying the beatific smile which curved her lips as she opened her eyes to look at him.

'So. We have a choice,' he said slowly. 'We can get dressed again and ring for drinks, or I can go inside and fix us something and you can stay exactly as you are, which would be my preference.'

She hesitated for a moment. 'I wouldn't mind you waiting on me for a change,' she said. 'Unless you're going to do that helpless man thing of making a mess of it because it's *domestic*, so that you'll never have to do it again.'

His mouth twitched into a smile as he rose from the lounger. 'Is that what men do?'

'In my experience—well, only my working experience, of course. Every time.'

'Not this one.' He picked up the battered straw hat which had fallen off, jamming it down so that the shadow of the brim darkened his face. 'I don't like to fail at anything, Molly.'

She watched him go. Was it that which had hurt the hardest when his life had imploded around him—the fact that he would be perceived as a failure? Had that been at the root of his reluctance to return to Naples very often? Yet he had picked himself up and started all over again. He had made a success of his life in every way, except for one. Just before they'd boarded his private jet to fly here, he'd told her how delighted his parents were that he had chosen her as his bride and she found herself thinking how skewed life could be sometimes. His mother hadn't liked Lauren Meyer, but Salvio had loved her. He'd told her that himself. And if this marriage was to continue, she must resign herself to the fact that she would only ever be second-best.

But that had been her life, hadn't it? It wasn't as if she wasn't used to it. When you worked in other people's houses you had to put yourself second, because you were only there to help their lives function smoothly. You had to be both efficient yet invisible, because people didn't really see *you*—only the service you provided.

Did Salvio see *her*? she wondered. Or was she simply a vessel to bear his child? The woman he had transformed with his vast fortune, so that she could lie in a Barbadian paradise, looking out over an azure sea as if she'd been born to this life?

The chink of ice made her glance towards the entrance to their villa, where Salvio was standing holding two tall, frosted glasses. As he began to walk towards her she wondered how a man could look so utterly at ease, completely naked save for his sunhat.

Handing her a glass, he joined her on the lounger and for a while they sipped their drinks in silence.

'Salvio,' she said eventually, watching the ice melt in the fruity cocktail.

He turned his face towards her. 'Mmm...?'

'What am I actually going to *do*? I mean, once we get back to England and you go back to work.'

He swirled the ice around in his glass, his fingers dark against the sunlit condensation. 'Weren't we planning to have a baby?'

'Yes, we were. Are,' she corrected. 'But that might not happen straight away, might it? And I can't just sit around all the time just...*waiting.*'

There was a pause. 'You want me to find you something to do?' He studied her carefully. 'There's a charitable arm belonging to my company. Do you think you'd like to get involved in that?'

She hesitated, genuine surprise tearing through her at the realisation he must think her good enough to be a part of his organisation. But it wasn't his validation which pleased her as much as the thought that this would make her a more integral part of his life—and wasn't that what marriage was all about? 'I'd like that very much.' She smiled, but his next words killed her pleasure stone dead.

'You know your brother tapped me for a loan at the wedding?'

The glass she was holding almost slipped from her suddenly nerveless fingers and quickly Molly put it down, her cheeks flaming. *'What?'*

'He said he had an idea for a new business venture and asked if I'd like to invest in it.'

'You didn't say yes?'

'You think I'm in the habit of throwing money away? I asked him how much he had already raised, and how—but he seemed reluctant to answer.' Beneath the shadowed brim of his hat, she saw that his eyes were now as hard and as cold as jet. 'Did you know about this, Molly?'

It hurt that he should ask but, when she thought about it afterwards, why *wouldn't* he ask? Salvio had been a target for women during his playing days and had fallen for someone who saw him as nothing but a trophy husband. He made no secret of not trusting women—so why should he feel any differently about her?

'Of course I didn't know he was going to ask you,' she said in a low voice. 'And if he'd sought my opinion I would have told him not to even think about it.'

He nodded as he stared out at the bright blue horizon and the subject was closed. But Molly's determination not to let his silky accusation ruin the rest of the day only went so far, and suddenly she was aware of the aching disappointment which made the sunny day feel as if it had been darkened by a cloud.

CHAPTER TWELVE

'SO HOW LONG will you be away?' Amid the croissant-crumbed debris of their early-morning breakfast, Molly glanced across the glass dining table at Salvio, who was reading one of the Italian newspapers he had couriered to his London apartment each morning.

'Only a few days,' he said, lifting his dark head to look at her. 'I'm just flying into Los Angeles for back-to-back meetings and then out again.'

'It seems an awfully long way to go,' she observed, taking a final sip of the inky black coffee she'd learned to love and which she now drank in preference to cappuccino. 'For such a short visit.'

'It is. So why don't you come with me?' His eyes gleamed as he put the newspaper down. 'We could add on a few extra days and take the highway to San Francisco. Turn it into a holiday. You've never been to the US, have you?'

She'd never actually been further than the Isle of

Wight and that had been years ago. Highly tempted, Molly considered the idea, until she remembered her own responsibilities. 'I can't. I have a lunch with the charity later.'

'You could always cancel it.'

'I can't just *cancel* it, Salvio, or it won't look like I'm committed. Like I'm only playing at being on the board just because I'm your wife.'

A smile played around the edges of his lips as he got up and moved towards her, his dark eyes glittering with an expression she knew so well. 'Which means you'll just have to be patient and wait for me to get back, *mia sposa*, even though it means you'll be without me for four whole nights. In fact, just thinking about it makes me want to kiss you.'

A kiss quickly turned into Molly being carried into their bedroom with a demonstration of that effortless mastery which still dazzled her, no matter how many times it happened. She loved the way he impatiently removed the clothes he'd only just put on and the way he explored her body as if he had just stumbled across a newly discovered treasure. She loved the warm skin-to-skin contact with this man as they tumbled hungrily onto the bed. She loved him, she suddenly realised, as he plunged deep inside her. She just couldn't help herself.

She was still feeling faintly dizzy with pleasure

when Salvio returned from the shower wearing the lazy smile of the satisfied predator, and she watched him as he began to dress. 'You are insatiable,' she observed.

'And don't you just hate it?' he mocked, picking up his tie and walking over to the mirror to knot it.

She hardly ever noticed his almost imperceptible limp but she noticed it today—and something about the contrast of frailty and strength which existed in his powerful body stirred a memory in her which she had unwittingly stored away.

'Salvio?'

He stared at her reflected image in the glass. 'Mmm...?'

She hesitated. 'You remember our wedding day?'

'I'm hardly likely to forget it, am I?' he questioned drily. 'And even if I had, it wouldn't be a diplomatic thing to admit after a mere three months of marriage. What about it?'

'Well.' His response didn't sound very promising but Molly forced herself to continue. 'I was wondering whether your charitable organisation ought to include some kind of football sponsorship, which I notice it doesn't do at the moment.'

'Some kind of football sponsorship?' he repeated slowly.

'Yes. You know—you could offer a financial

scheme for a promising young player from a poor background.' Again, she hesitated. 'To help the type of boy you once were,' she finished, on a rush.

There was a pause while he finished knotting his tie and when he spoke, his voice was cool. 'But I don't have anything to do with football any more, Molly. You know that. I walked away from that life many years ago.'

'Yes, I know you did. But things have moved on now. You saw all those people wearing your old club's colours who came to wish you luck on your wedding day. They…they love you, Salvio. You're a legend to them and I just thought it would be… nice…' Her words faded away. 'To give something back.'

'Oh, did you?' Moving away from the mirror, Salvio swept his gaze over his wife, who looked all pink-cheeked and tousled as she lay amid the rumpled mess they'd just made of the bed. A muscle began to work in his cheek. He'd thought that, given her previous occupation, she would have been a rather more compliant partner than she was turning out to be. He'd thought it a generous gesture to give her a seat on the board of his charity and had expected her to be grateful to him for that. But he'd imagined her turning up regularly at meetings and sitting there quietly—not to suddenly start dishing out advice. Surely she, more than anyone, must have realised it was inappropriate as well as unwanted? 'I really don't think it's your place to start advising me on how I spend my money, Molly,' he drawled.

She went very still. 'Not *my place*?' she echoed, the colour leeching from her face and her dark lashes blinking in disbelief. 'Why not? Do you think the one-time servant should remain mute and just go along with what she's been told, rather than ever showing any initiative of her own? Are you making out like there's still all those inequalities between us, despite the fact that I now wear your ring?'

'There's no need to overreact,' he said coolly, even though that was exactly what he *did* think. 'And I really don't want an argument when I'm just about to fly to the States. We'll talk about it when I get back.' He dipped his head towards her with a smile she always found irresistible. 'Now kiss me.'

Knowing it would be childish to turn her face away, Molly attempted a close approximation of a fond kiss, but inside she was seething as the door of the apartment slammed shut behind her departing husband. She felt as if the pink cloud she'd been floating on since the day they'd wed had suddenly turned black. Was it because, behind all the outward appearances of a relatively blissful new marriage, nothing much had changed? Despite him giving her a seat on the board of his charity, it seemed she wasn't allowed to have any ideas of her own. She might be wearing his shiny gold wedding band but at that precise moment she felt exactly like the servant she'd always been. And there was another pressure, too. One she hadn't dared to acknowledge—not even to herself, let alone to Salvio.

Gloomily, she got out of bed and went to stare out of the window, where there was no sign of new life. They were already into April but spring seemed to have been put on hold by the harsh weather. Even the daffodils in the planters on Salvio's roof terrace had been squashed by the unseasonable dump of snow which had ground the city to a halt for the last few days.

No sign of life in her either.

Her hands floating down to her belly, she prayed that this month she might get the news she was longing for, even though the low ache inside her hinted at an alternative scenario. She linked her manicured fingers together, dreading another month of unspoken disappointment. Of cheerfully convincing herself it would happen eventually. Of wondering how long she could continue walking this precarious tightrope of a marriage which had only taken place because her wealthy husband wanted an heir. Because what if she *couldn't* conceive? She'd been pregnant once, yes, but there was no guarantee it would happen again. Life didn't provide guarantees like that, did it?

Forcing herself to get on with the day, she showered and dressed—slithering into a dress she wouldn't have dared to wear a few months ago, even if she could have afforded to. But her body shape had changed since living with Salvio—and not just because she'd checked out the basement gym in this luxury apartment block and discovered she liked it. She ate proper regular meals now because her Neapolitan husband's love of good food meant that he wasn't a great fan of snacks, and as a consequence she was in the best shape of her adult life.

She took a cab to her charity lunch, which was being held in the ballroom of one of the capital's smartest hotels and was today awarding acts of bravery involving animals as well as humans. She particularly enjoyed hearing about the kitten who had been rescued from the top of a chimney pot by a nineteen-year-old university drop-out who had previously been terrified of heights. She chatted to him afterwards and he told her that he'd decided he was going to train as a vet, and Molly felt a warm glow of pleasure as she listened to his story.

She was just chopping vegetables for a stir-fry when Salvio rang from Los Angeles, telling her he missed her and, although she wanted to believe him, she found herself wondering if he was just reading from a script. It was easy to say those sorts of things when he was thousands of miles away, when the reality was that he'd made her feel she'd stepped out of line this morning just because she'd dared express an opinion of her own.

Well, maybe it was time to stop drifting around in a half-world of pretence and longing. She would sit him down when he returned from his trip and they would talk honestly because, even though the truth could hurt, it was better to know where you stood. And even though her stupid heart was screaming out its objections she couldn't keep putting it off. She would ask him if he really wanted to continue with the marriage and maybe it was better to confront that now, before there *was* a baby.

But then something happened. Something which changed everything.

It started with an email from her brother which arrived on the day Salvio was due to return from America. Robbie was notoriously unreliable at keeping in touch and she hadn't heard from him since the wedding, even though she'd sent several lovely photos of him dancing with one of Salvio's distant cousins at the reception. She hadn't even mentioned the loan he'd asked her husband for—deciding it was an issue best settled between him and Salvio.

So her smile was one of pleasure when she saw new mail from Robbie Miller, which had pinged into her inbox overnight, with the subject line: Have you seen this?

'This' turned out to be an attachment of an article taken from a newspaper website. An American newspaper, as it happened. And there, in sharp Technicolor detail, was a photograph of her husband, sitting outside some flower-decked restaurant with a beautiful blonde, the sapphire glitter of a sunlit sea in the background.

Her fingers clawed at the mouse as she scrolled down the page but somehow Molly knew who Salvio's companion was before she'd read a single word. Was it the woman's poise which forewarned her, or simply the way she leaned towards Salvio's handsome profile with the kind of intimacy which was hard-won? Her heart clenched with pain as she scanned the accompanying prose.

Heartthrob property tycoon Salvio De Gennaro was pictured enjoying the sea air in Malibu today.

Newly wed to former maid Molly Miller, in a lavish ceremony which took place in the groom's native Naples, the Italian billionaire still found time to catch up with ex-fiancée Lauren Meyer.

With the ink barely dry on her divorce papers, perhaps heiress Lauren was advising Salvio on some of the pitfalls of marriage.

Either that, or the Californian wine was just too good to resist...

Hands shaking, Molly stared at the screen, closing her eyes in a futile bid to quell the crippling spear of jealousy which lanced through her like a hot blade, but it was still there when she opened them again, her gaze caught by the glitter of the diamonds at her finger. The diamonds she had once compared to tears, rather than rain. But there were real tears now. Big ones which were splashing onto her trembling fingers. Pushing her chair away from the desk, her vision was blurred as blindly she stumbled into the bedroom. She rubbed her fists into her eyes but the stupid tears just kept on flowing, even though deep down she knew she had no right to feel sorrow. Because it wasn't as if theirs was a *real* relationship, was it? She had no right to be jealous of a husband who had never loved her, did she? Not really. It had only ever been a marriage of convenience—providing each of them with what they wanted.

Or rather, what she'd *thought* she'd wanted… Security and passion with a man she'd begun to care for and, ultimately, a family of her own. Only now the truth hit her with a savage blow as she forced herself to acknowledge what it was she *really* wanted. Not the fancy penthouse or the different homes dotted all around the globe. Not the platinum credit card with its obscene spending limit.

She wanted Salvio's love, she realised—and that was just a wish too far. He didn't do love—at least, not with her. But he *had* loved Lauren. And try as she might, she just couldn't put a positive spin on his reunion with his ex-fiancée in that sunny and glamorous Malibu setting. For the first time in her life she was right out of optimistic options.

There were no tears left to cry as she walked across the bedroom, but she was filled with a strange new sense of calm as she opened up the wardrobe and took out her battered old suitcase, knowing what she intended to do.

She would do the brave thing.

The right thing.

The only thing.

'Molly?' Salvio frowned as he walked into an apartment which instinct told him was empty. Yet he'd texted her to tell her he was on his way home and he'd assumed she would be waiting with that soft smile which always greeted him when he arrived home from work. 'Molly?' he called again, even though the word echoed redundantly through the quiet apartment.

He found the note quickly, as he had obviously been intended to. One of those brief notes which managed to say so little and yet so much, in just a few stark words. And sitting on top of it was her diamond ring.

Salvio.
I've seen the newspaper article about you and Lauren and I want to do the best thing, so I'm staying in a hotel until I can get a job sorted out.
I'll send you my address when I have one, so you can instruct your lawyers.
*It's been an amazing experience, so thank you for everything. And...*in bocca al lupo.

Crushing the note in an angry fist, he strode over to the computer and saw the article immediately, reading it with a growing sense of disbelief before cursing long and loud into the empty air. Why hadn't any of his staff alerted him to this? Because his assistant had been instructed to treat gossip columns with the contempt they deserved, by ignoring them.

He stared at the photo, thinking that whoever said the camera didn't lie must have been delusional. Because it did. Big-time.

He saw Lauren's finely etched profile and the angled bones of her shoulder blades. Her long blonde hair was waving gently in the breeze and she was leaning forward with an earnest expression on her face. It must have been taken just before his response had made her delicate features crumple and her blue eyes darken with disbelief.

Pulling the phone from his pocket, he found Molly's number and hit the call button, unsurprised when it went straight to voicemail over and over again, and his mouth hardened. Did she think she could just walk out on him, leaving nothing but that banal little note?

Scrolling down, he found another number he used only very infrequently. His voice lowered as he began to speak in rapid Neapolitan dialect, biting out a series of terse demands before finally cutting the connection.

CHAPTER THIRTEEN

MOLLY STARED AT the richly embossed walls of the fancy hotel and the dark red lilies which were massed in a silver vase. She'd chosen the five-star Vinoly because she'd heard Salvio mention it, but as from tomorrow she would start searching for somewhere cheaper to stay. No way was she going to try to cling to the high-life she'd enjoyed during her brief tenure as his wife, because that life was over and she needed to get used to it.

The phone rang but she didn't need to look down to see who was calling. Salvio. Again. After yet another brief internal tussle she chose to ignore it, just like she'd avoided reading the texts he'd been sending. Because what was the point in hearing anything he had to say? What if his smooth weasel words tempted her back into his arms and the guarantee of heartbreak? She didn't want to hear excuses or half-truths. She wanted to preserve her sanity, even if her heart had to break in the process.

But first she needed to start looking for a job. A live-in job she could practically do with her eyes closed. She would sign up with an agency in the morning and tell them she wanted a fresh start. Somewhere she'd never been before—like Scotland, or Wales. Somewhere new so she could be completely anonymous while licking her wounds and trying to forget that for one brief shining moment she'd been the wife of a man who...

She bit her lip.

A man she'd fallen in love with, despite all her best efforts to remain immune to him.

But Salvio hadn't wanted her love. Only Lauren's. She swallowed. Was the beautiful heiress willing to give Salvio a second chance? Was that the reason behind their secret liaison when they'd been making eyes at one another in the Californian sunshine?

She didn't feel hungry but she hadn't eaten anything since breakfast and she always used to tell Robbie that your brain couldn't function properly unless you kept it nourished. Ordering a cheese omelette from room service, she thought about her brother. She hadn't replied to his email, mainly because she couldn't think of anything to say. Not yet, anyway. She wondered if he'd acted out of the goodness of his heart. If sending the proof of Salvio's clandestine meeting was a brotherly intervention to protect her from potential hurt. Or had Robbie been motivated by spite—because his wealthy new brother-in-law had refused to give him the loan he'd wanted?

She paced the room, unable to settle. Unable to shift the dark features of her husband from her mind and wondering whether she would ever be able to forget this interlude. Or to—

Her thoughts were interrupted by a loud rap on the door.

'Who is it?' Molly called out sharply.

'Room service!'

She opened the door to the woman's voice, her heart crashing against her ribcage when she saw Salvio standing there, holding a tray dominated by a silver dome. In the distance was the retreating view of a hotel employee, who'd obviously been rewarded for allowing this bizarre role-reversal to take place. Which was exactly what it felt like. Salvio in a sub-servient role holding a tray, and her opening the door of some swanky hotel room. Except he didn't stay subservient for very long.

'Step aside, Molly,' he clipped out.

'You can't come in.'

'Just try stopping me.'

She didn't dare. She'd never seen him look so de-termined as he stormed into her room. There was a clatter as he slammed the tray down and Molly shuddered to think what damage he must have inflicted on her cheese omelette. Not that she wanted it any more. How could she possibly have eaten anything when she could barely breathe?

He turned round and she was taken aback by the fury which was darkening his imposing features into an unrecognisable mask. 'Well, Molly?' he snarled.

'Well, what?' she retorted. 'How did you find me?'

'You booked this room with our joint credit card.'

'And?'

'And therefore you were traceable. I had one of my contacts look into it for me.'

She screwed up her brow. 'Isn't that…illegal?'

He shrugged. 'When a man wishes to find his errant wife then surely he will use whatever means are available to him.'

'Well, you've wasted your time because there's nothing to say!'

'I disagree. There's plenty to say, and we're having this out right now.'

And suddenly Molly knew she couldn't let him take over and dominate this situation by the sheer force of his indomitable character. Yes, he was powerful, rich and successful, but she was his wife. His *equal*, despite the inequality of their assets. That was what she'd vowed to be when she had agreed to marry him, but somewhere along the way her resolve had slipped. Was that because the more she'd started to care for him, the harder she had found it to assert herself?

Well, not any more. She needed to make it plain that, although she might not have anything of material value, she valued *herself*. And she would not allow Salvio De Gennaro to make a fool of her, or for her heart to be slowly broken by a man who was incapable of emotion.

'I saw the article from the American newspaper.'

'I know you did. Your brother sent it to you.'

'Did you find *that* out illegally, too?' she scorned.

'No, Molly. You left your computer open.'

'Well, if you'd looked a little harder you'd have seen that I also did a room search for the Vinoly hotel,' she said triumphantly. 'Which wouldn't have involved getting someone to snoop on me!'

Unexpectedly, he sighed and a sudden weariness touched the corners of his dark eyes as he looked at her. 'What do you think I did in Los Angeles, Molly?' he questioned tiredly. 'Do you think I had sex with Lauren?'

A spear of pain shot through her. 'Did you?'

He winced as he raked his fingers back through his jet-dark hair. 'No, I did not. She heard I was in town and got in touch with me and I agreed to meet her for lunch.'

'Why?'

'Why?' He gave an odd smile. 'I thought it made sense to put away the past for good.'

'Only I suppose she'd suddenly realised the stupid mistake she'd made in letting you go?' accused Molly sarcastically.

He shrugged. 'Something like that. She is recently divorced. She asked for another chance.'

'And you said?'

There was silence for a moment and Molly actually thought that her heartbeat had grown audible—until she realised that the silver clock was thumping out the hour.

'I said I was in love with my wife,' he said simply. 'Only I'd been too stupid to show her how much.'

She shook her head, not believing him. Not believing he would ever admit to love *or* stupidity. 'I don't believe you,' she whispered.

'I know you don't and maybe I deserve that.' He hesitated, like someone who was learning the words of a new language. 'I know that at times I've been cold and difficult.'

'It isn't that, Salvio! It's the fact that you're completely backtracking on everything you said. You told me you didn't *do* love. Not any more. Remember? That you'd loved Lauren and after you broke up, you'd closed off your heart. And if that *was* true—

if you really *did* love her like you claim—then how come it has all just died? Is love only a temporary thing, Salvio—which changes like the moon?'

Deeply admiring of her logic at such an intense moment, Salvio took a deep breath. He felt as if he were on a platform in front of a thousand people, about to make the most important speech of his life. And he was. But not to a thousand people. To one. To Molly. The only one who really mattered.

And his whole future hinged on it.

'I thought I loved Lauren because that's how I felt at the time,' he said, in a low voice. 'And surely it is a kind of treachery to deny the feelings we once had? That would be like trying to rewrite history.' There was a pause. 'But I see now it wasn't real love—it was a complex mixture of other stuff which I was too immature to understand.'

'What kind of stuff?' she questioned, as his voice tailed off.

'It was more to do with a young man who wanted to conquer the elusive,' he admitted. 'A man who for a while became someone he wasn't. Someone blinded by an ideal, rather than a real person—and Lauren *was* that ideal. And then I met you, Molly. The most real person in the world. You charmed me. Disarmed me. You crept beneath my defences before I even realised what was happening. You made me feel good—you still do—and not just in the obvious way. It's like I'm the best version of myself whenever you're around. Like I can achieve anything—even if my instinct is to fight against it every inch of the way, because there's a part of me which doesn't really believe that I deserve to be this happy.'

'Salvio—'

'No. Please. Let me finish,' he said and his voice was shaking now. 'You need to understand that all this is true, because there is no way I would say it if it wasn't.' His black eyes raked over her. '*Do* you believe me, Molly? That I would walk to the ends of the earth for you and further, if that's what you wanted? And that I love you in a way I've never loved before?'

Molly stared into the molten darkness of his eyes, but she didn't have to give it a lot of thought, because she did believe him. She could read it in the tender curve of his lips, even if he hadn't uttered those quietly fervent words which had rung so true. But if they were shining a spotlight on their relationship then they couldn't allow any more shadows to lurk in unexplored corners, and she needed the courage to confront what was still troubling her.

'But what about the baby?' she whispered.

'What baby?' he said gently. 'Are you trying to tell me you're pregnant?'

'I don't know. I don't think so. But that's the whole

point. What if…?' She swallowed. 'What if, for some reason, I can't give you the child you long for?'

'Then we will go to the best doctors to find out why, or we will adopt. It's not a deal-breaker, Molly. Not even a deal-maker. Not any more. I want you. *You.* That's all.'

That's all? Molly blinked as for the first time she realised that Salvio De Gennaro was truly captivated by her. Her! A flush of pleasure heated her skin and maybe someone else in her position might have briefly revelled in her newly discovered power. But this wasn't about power. It was about love and equality. About consideration and respect. About loyalty and truth.

It was about them.

She smiled, the happiness swelling up in her heart making it feel as if it were about to burst open. 'I believe you,' she said softly. 'And I love you. So much. I think I've always loved you, Salvio De Gennaro, and I know I always will.'

'Then you'd better come here and kiss me,' he said, in a voice which sounded pretty close to breaking. 'And convince me that this is for real.'

EPILOGUE

SALVIO STARED AT the lights as he lay back content-edly. Rainbow-coloured lights which jostled for space among all the glittering baubles which hung from the Christmas tree. Behind the tree glittered the Bay of Naples and, inside the main reception room of their newly purchased home, he lay naked next to his beautiful Molly on a vast velvet sofa which had been chosen for precisely this kind of activity.

'Happy?' he murmured, one hand idly teasing her bare nipple while his lips lazily caressed the soft silk of her hair.

'Happy?' She nuzzled into his neck. 'So happy I can't even put it into words.'

'Well, try.'

Molly traced her finger over the loud rhythm of her husband's heart. Next door their ten-month-old son Marco lay sleeping—getting as much rest as possible in preparation for the excitement of his first

Christmas. And this year, everyone was coming to *them*. Salvio's parents would be arriving later for the traditional Eve of Christmas feast. And so would Robbie, who was currently meeting the parents of Salvio's cousin, who he had recently started dating. Molly prayed he wouldn't let anyone down—most of all himself—but she was hopeful that her brother had finally sorted himself out. Much of it was down to Salvio and the well-intentioned but stern advice he had delivered. He'd told Robbie he would support him through college, but only if he kicked his gambling habit for good.

And he seemed to have done just that. Molly had never seen her brother looking so bright-eyed or *hopeful*. It was as if a heavy burden had been lifted from his strong, young shoulders. Was it the presence of a powerful male role model which had been the making of him?

In the very early days of her pregnancy, she'd persuaded Salvio that his London penthouse apartment was no place for a baby and he had surprised her by agreeing. So they'd moved into his sprawling Cotswold manor house where she had fun envisaging Marco and his siblings playing in those vast and beautiful gardens. Salvio had also bought this seaview home in Naples where they tried to spend as much time as possible.

She sighed against the warmth of his skin. 'You make me so happy,' she whispered. 'I never thought I could feel this way.'

He stroked his fingers through her hair. 'It's because I love you, Molly. You're so easy to love.'

'And so are you. At least, you are *now*,' she added darkly.

He laughed. 'Was I such a terrible man before?'

'Terrible,' she agreed, mock-seriously. 'But terribly sexy too.'

'Are you angling for more sex, Signora De Gennaro?'

'There isn't time, darling. I've got to oversee last-minute preparations for tonight's dinner because there's a lot of pressure when you're cooking for your in-laws for the first time.' She frowned. 'And I'm worried I'm going to ruin the *capitone*.'

His fingertips tiptoed over her belly. 'You're not going anywhere until you tell me you love me.'

'I love you. I love you more than I ever thought possible. I love that you're a brilliant father and husband and brother-in-law and son. I love the fact that you've opened a football academy here in Naples and are giving a chance to poor boys with a dream in their hearts. How's that? Is that enough?'

'Curiously, it leaves me wanting more,' he growled. 'But then you always do.'

'More of wh-what?' she questioned unsteadily, as his hand moved towards her quivering thigh.

'More of this.' He smiled as he found her wet heat and stroked, enjoying her soft moan of pleasure.

'But, Salvio, there isn't time,' she said, her eyes growing smoky as he continued his feather-light teasing. 'What about the *capitone*?'

And then Salvio said something which, as a good Neapolitan, he had never imagined himself saying—but in the circumstances, perhaps was understandable. He pulled her on top of him and touched her parted lips with his own. 'Stuff the *capitone*,' he growled.

* * * * *

If you enjoyed
The Italian's Christmas Housekeeper
you're sure to love these other stories
by Sharon Kendrick!

The Italian's Christmas Secret
Bound to the Sicilian's Bride
Crowned for the Sheikh's Baby
The Greek's Bought Bride

Available now!

#3673 THE ITALIAN'S INHERITED MISTRESS
by Lynne Graham

Isla has escaped to her recently inherited Sicilian villa, and the last person she expects to see is the billionaire who changed her life irrevocably. Alissandru wants what's rightfully his—Isla's inheritance. But what he wants more is Isla...back in his bed!

#3674 MARRIED FOR HIS ONE-NIGHT HEIR
Secret Heirs of Billionaires
by Jennifer Hayward

Santo's stunned to see Giovanna again. Why, after that one forbidden night, did she leave? But when Gia reveals their secret consequence, the Italian will claim his son—and Gia as his wife!

#3675 CLAIMING HIS CHRISTMAS WIFE
Conveniently Wed!
by Dani Collins

After their marriage ended in heartbreak, Travis never wanted to see Imogen again. But to avoid a scandal, they must agree to a temporary reconciliation—leaving Travis tempted to reclaim his wife...for good!

#3676 BOUND BY THEIR CHRISTMAS BABY
Christmas Seductions
by Clare Connelly

To legitimize his son, Gabe knows he must marry Abby—the innocent beauty he shared a steamy festive night with! But can their marriage be in name only, or will red-hot chemistry take over?

HPCNM1118RA

#3677 AN INNOCENT, A SEDUCTION, A SECRET
One Night With Consequences
by Abby Green
When Seb spies Edie's talent for lavish interior decoration, he makes an irresistible job offer—spend the festive season decorating his opulent home! But soon, Edie becomes the sensual gift Seb wishes to unwrap...

#3678 THE BILLIONAIRE'S CHRISTMAS CINDERELLA
by Carol Marinelli
Abe Devereux is famed for his cold heart. So meeting Naomi, who's determined to see the good in him, is a novelty. But will seducing her be his biggest risk, or his greatest chance of redemption?

#3679 PREGNANT BY THE DESERT KING
by Susan Stephens
Lucy is shocked by Tadj's royal revelation: Lucy is carrying the baby of a desert king! Tadj will secure his heir, but can Lucy accept his scandalous solution—that she share his royal bed?

#3680 THE VIRGIN'S SICILIAN PROTECTOR
by Chantelle Shaw
Hired to keep heiress Ariana safe, wealthy bodyguard Santino is intrigued by her hidden vulnerability. Their sexual tension is electric! And when Santino discovers just how innocent Ariana is, resisting her temptation becomes an impossible challenge...

Get 4 FREE REWARDS!

We'll send you 2 FREE Books plus 2 FREE Mystery Gifts.

Harlequin Presents® books feature a sensational and sophisticated world of international romance where sinfully tempting heroes ignite passion.

FREE Value Over **$20**

He set his glass down with a clatter. "I am his *father*. I
have missed three years of his life. You think a *weekend
pass* is going to suffice? A few dips in the Caribbean as he
learns to swim?" He fixed his gaze on hers. "I want *every
day* with him. I want it *all*."

"What else can we do?" she queried helplessly. "You
live in New York and I live here. Leo is settled and
happy. A limited custody arrangement is the only realistic
proposition."

"It is *not* a viable proposition." His low growl made
her jump. "That's not going to work, Gia."

She eyed him warily. "Which part?"

"All of it." He waved a Rolex-clad wrist at her. "I
have a proposal for you. It's the only one on the table,
nonnegotiable on all points. Take it or leave it."

The wariness written across her face intensified. "Which is?"

"We do what's in the best interests of our child. You marry me, we create a life together in New York and give Leo the family he deserves."

Don't miss
Married for a One-Night Consequence,
available December 2018 wherever
Harlequin Presents® books and ebooks are sold.

www.Harlequin.com

The Team-Building Tool Kit

Second Edition

The Team-Building Tool Kit

Tips and Tactics for Effective Workplace Teams

Second Edition

Deborah Mackin

AMERICAN MANAGEMENT ASSOCIATION

New York • Atlanta • Brussels • Chicago • Mexico City • San Francisco
Shanghai • Tokyo • Toronto • Washington, D.C.

This publication is designed to provide accurate and authoritative
information in regard to the subject matter covered. It is sold with the
understanding that the publisher is not engaged in rendering legal,
accounting, or other professional service. If legal advice or other expert
assistance is required, the services of a competent professional person
should be sought.

Library of Congress Cataloging-in-Publication Data

Mackin, Deborah.
    The team building tool kit : tips and tactics for effective workplace teams /
Deborah Mackin.—2nd ed.
        p.   cm.
    Includes bibliographical references and index.
    ISBN-13: 978-0-8144-7439-6
    ISBN-10: 0-8144-7439-X
    1. Teams in the workplace.   2. Interpersonal relations.   3. Organizational
effectiveness.   I. Title.
    HD66M332   2007
    658.4'022—dc22   2007020567

Printing number

10   9   8   7   6   5   4   3   2   1

Contents

6   Team Scoreboards and Performance Assessments   151

7   The Teaming Road Map   179

Acknowledgments

HOW DO YOU TAKE almost twenty-five years of teaming and acknowledge all the people, teams, and organizations that have contributed to the information in this book? Even the most difficult, argumentative, and resistant participants in team training sessions are contributors to the book, through the stories shared and the lessons learned.

Throughout this history, there have been some constants. The team at New Directions Consulting, Inc. deserves a special and first note of deep gratitude: to my dear friend and longest employee, Lisa Dunbar, for her support, guidance, and editing; to Susan Bernier for her decision to come back to us after a ten-year hiatus and be the "magic" that makes our materials exceptional; and to Sarah Leonetti, who manages my schedule and keeps me on track.

I have also had the privilege of working with two very special people—Judy Calhoun and Roy Howard—to help convert two antiquated plants into team-based organizations. They have been willing to use all the tools and techniques created by teams over countless years and not waste any time reinventing the wheel. They have been willing to question, challenge, and, most important, trust, and their success is exciting. I also wish to thank Dave Prochaska for all of his help with the teaming roadmap, Celie White for launching one of the first in-house training teams, Robin Harkness and Helene Galet for their friendship and support, and Todd Jacobi for regularly challenging and demanding the best.

The number of organizations that have contributed over the past decade to the information in this book is now too vast to list here. However, there are some that are, and always will be, special: Delta Faucet Company, Sanofi Pasteur, SII Group in Texas, Pfizer/Specialty Minerals, Hemmings Motor News, Capital Region BOCES, Liberty Enterprises, and National Bank of Middlebury.

I also wish to thank my family—my husband, Paul, for his generous spirit, side-by-side support, and willingness to keep the home front functioning during my travels; and my two sons, Michael and Matthew Harrington, an amazing pair of team builders in their own right.

Introduction

IT HAS BEEN more than a decade since the first edition of *The Team-Building Tool Kit* was published as a resource for start-up and existing teams. Over the course of time, I heard from many individuals who used the book as a "bible" to help them launch and grow their teams. They brought the book to their meetings so that questions could be answered right away, distributed copies to team members as a "read and discuss" training opportunity, and shared the book with reluctant managers or coaches who needed to know the practical "how tos" to embrace the teaming concept.

On occasion, when someone asked a question or referenced something in the book, I would realize how far we have come with teaming since the original book was written. Over the years, each team we worked with had added improvements to agenda formats, star point role descriptions, team decision making, and conflict resolution strategies, to name a few. And, with the advent of the Internet, cell phones, e-mail, e-rooms, and the global workplace, there was information that no longer seemed relevant or applicable. Since the first book was still in print, it made sense to do a second edition. The goal of *The Team-Building Tool Kit 2* is to provide you with the most current information that teams work with and that makes them successful.

The Team-Building Tool Kit 2 is written for all types of teams in both for-profit and nonprofit organizations, especially those trying to transform into flexible, lean enterprises with empowered employees capable of high performance. In addition, trainers and college faculty will find it a valuable reference for teaching team building skills to others. Like the first book, *The Team-Building Tool Kit 2* can be used in a variety of ways. It can be used as a quick reference when setting up a team or as a cover-to-cover read to check for new teaming ideas. Certain parts of the book, such as Chapter 3, which discusses team behavior and conflict resolution, can be read by team members to help them achieve a common level of understanding before discussing these issues as an entire team.

Every chapter in *The Team-Building Tool Kit 2* has been rewritten and updated with additional information that is relevant for teams today. New chapters have also been added: Chapter 4, "Team Accountability and Decision Making," provides specific strategies to improve the level of responsibility teams are willing to assume based on each stage of the team's development, and we have included a step-by-step consensus decision-making guide to help meeting facilitators. Chapter 5, "Team Problem-Solving Process and Tools," provides a simple problem-solving approach that teams love, plus the most popular group process tools to make problem solving easy. Chapter 7, "The Teaming Road Map," puts all the pieces together into a clearly laid-out process for building your teams. Also included are many new charts, diagrams, and other graphics to help in your team building efforts.

To complement what is available in the book, we are also offering supplemental materials online through www.NewDirectionsConsulting .com/samples. Sample team charters, role descriptions, team protocols, and measuring tools will provide additional examples and supports.

In 1994, we probably had a somewhat altruistic view of teams: They would improve morale, increase empowerment, and engage employees in the workplace. Although teams do achieve these goals, today teams are an economic necessity, because organizations can no longer carry six or seven layers of supervision and management and be competitive. The pressure to be a "low-cost producer" in all types of organizations is growing; the necessity to work in teams across global boundaries is a daily reality. The new generation of employees has an even greater tendency toward collaborative workplace models than previous generations. Yet, few organizations derive the full benefits of teaming because they fail to "grow" them correctly. That's where *The Team-Building Tool Kit 2* comes in!

The Team-Building Tool Kit

Second Edition

CHAPTER 1

Getting Started

❖

THE USE OF TEAMS as an organizational strategy to engage employees and improve productivity is now more than three decades old. In the early 1970s, the leadership of Gaines, a Topeka pet food plant, launched a novel experiment to transform its workplace into self-directed and cross-functional work teams when no one else was doing it.[1] The increases in productivity at Gaines caught the eye of other organizations and the rest, as they say, is history. Today, although many organizations have implemented components of teaming, they have yet to realize the full range of possible benefits. Some have simply changed the language they use, calling supervisors "coaches" and group leaders "team leaders," with no real change in structure or empowerment. Others do teaming when everything is okay and then revert to a traditional, top-down model when demands increase, or they don't get the quick results they need. These are only superficial attempts at teaming. In this book, we show you how to develop "real" teams—teams that look different from what you might have seen before.

1

Developing teams begins with leadership systematically providing the following:

- Assurance of job stability (not security) for people who actively participate in the transition, especially as their old jobs "go away"

- Time for teams to meet regularly

- Rewards for both team and individual achievement of goals

- Clear statements of dissatisfaction with status quo—"the way we've always done it"

- A compelling vision that grabs people's imagination

- Carefully delegated authority and responsibility in a way that makes people believe they will be successful

- Movement from individual to team decision making

- Feedback and performance measures on an ongoing basis

- Opportunities to benchmark with others who have been successful in their teaming efforts

- A strong commitment to stick with teaming through the "muck in the middle"

Team building begins with a clear decision by leadership to encourage, and even to require, employees to operate in teams. Leadership must recognize that teaming is a cultural change that will include:

1. Developing awareness of teams as both a tool and a culture shift
2. Acquiring knowledge and understanding about how teams function
3. Learning skills to perform new teaming behaviors
4. Internalizing attitudes and beliefs so that teaming becomes a way of life

The role of leadership is critical through each of these steps. Lack of leadership support remains the number one cause of team failure.

Leadership Commitment

Leadership at all levels must support team efforts openly and without reservation if it expects teams to succeed. Yet managers and supervisors sometimes feel threatened and may even take credit away from their teams when improvements are made. They often fail to realize that their own involvement in team activities will promote trust and cooperation between them and their subordinates and will enhance their own reputation as effective managers.[2]

Typically, we have seen newly formed teams repeatedly look to upper management to test the organization's commitment to the new team structure. Leaders must take special care to reiterate their belief in the team's future and to check critical offhand remarks or statements of frustration. Leadership must also avoid the "on-again/off-again" syndrome, in which they value teams when everything is going well but take time away from team meetings and team decision making when pressures rise.

Leadership must also see teams not only as a "tool" but also as a way of thinking and being. When teaming is marginalized to being "just a tool," it becomes optional whether to pick up the tool or not. In actuality, teaming is a cultural change in addition to being a tool; in a team environment, we must change the way we think and approach tasks. It is no longer "people watching people watching people." There is a firm belief that every person at work is a responsible adult, capable of thinking for himself or herself and making effective decisions about his or her own work. When adults are encouraged to use their knowledge, experience, and skill, a shift in attitude occurs and something magical takes place.

Let's look at the key benefits and drawbacks of teams:

Key Benefits

- Improve productivity by 15 to 20 percent in six months, and up to 30 percent in eighteen months.[3]

- Drive accountability and responsibility to all areas within the organization.

- Create a highly motivated environment and better work climate.
- Share in the ownership and responsibility for tasks.
- Prompt a faster response to technological change.
- Result in fewer, simpler job classifications.
- Elicit a better response to the less formal values of a younger generation of employees.
- Result in effective delegation of workload and increased flexibility in task assignments.
- Improve buy-in and common commitment to goals and values.
- Encourage proactive and often innovative approaches to problem solving.
- Improve the self-worth of the workforce, resulting in improved interpersonal relationships.
- Increase four-way communication.
- Allow for greater skill development of staff; cross-training in roles and responsibilities.
- Promote an earlier warning system for potential problems.
- Excite greater and faster interdepartmental interaction; reduced "silo" thinking.
- Result in more time for management to work on strategic issues rather than day-to-day firefighting.
- Reduce absenteeism as well as the number of accidents and defects.
- Improve housekeeping and efficiency.

Key Drawbacks
- Require long-term investment of people, time, and energy.
- Appear confused, disorderly, and out of control at times.

- Can cause role confusion; members have difficulty leaving "hats" at the door.

- Are viewed negatively by "old school" people who like order and control.

- Require one to three years to be fully implemented.

- Require people to change, especially managers, who must learn to trust and let go.

Researchers have found that the effectiveness of teams is greatly influenced by members' attitudes about the organization. If team members feel support and commitment from management, they will exhibit high productivity. If team members are angry because of a lack of organizational support, they will limit their efforts.[4]

Types of Teams

As an organization begins its team building efforts, one of the first concerns it must resolve is what types of teams to create. The green light for team building is typically a top-management decision. Some organizations begin with high-level policy-making teams charged with identifying broad concerns and setting goals, whereas others begin with small departmental teams. Whether the impetus comes from a company-wide policy review or from a departmental task force, teams should be formed only when an achievable common goal can be identified. The various types of teams are somewhat like the flowers in a garden: All serve a particular purpose and have their own characteristics and set of benefits.

Multifunctional Teams

- Identify major areas of organizational concern/opportunity; articulate organizational needs.

- Develop philosophy, strategy, policies, and direction.

- Include members from various levels of the organization and across functional areas.

- Require regular meetings and meet over extended periods of time.

- Are sometimes called design teams or quality councils.

Task-Force or Cross-Functional Teams

- Include between eight and twelve members; membership based on common purpose.

- Bring together individuals from multiple work areas at a similar level.

- Necessitate regular meetings over either a short or an extended period of time.

- Implement a strategic plan for addressing problems/concerns/opportunities; others may complete the implementation of the plan.

- Assume investigative, corrective, interactive function.

- Are sometimes called steering teams, process improvement teams, product launch teams, or Kaizen teams.

Improvement Teams (Functional or Value Stream)

- Include members of one department or one value stream.

- Focus on problem solving; identifying solutions.

- Restrict scope of activity to within departmental or value stream boundaries.

- Hold regular meetings over a short period of time.

- Have a short life span.

Self-Directed Work Teams (Functional or Value Stream)

- Comprise an intact team of employees who work together on an ongoing, day-to-day basis without direct supervision, and who are responsible for a "whole" work process or segment.

- Assume "ownership" of product or service and are empowered to share various supervisory and leadership functions.

- Are limited to a particular work unit, or in the case of value stream teams, may cross over multiple functions within the value stream.

- Function semiautonomously; are responsible for controlling the physical and functional boundaries of their work and for delivering a specified quantity and quality of a product or service within a specified time and at a defined cost.

- Are all cross-trained in a variety of work skills.

- Share and rotate leadership responsibilities; team members have equal input in decisions.

- Accept the concept of multiskills and job rotation (except for jobs requiring years of training and technical expertise).

- Work together to improve operations, handle day-to-day problems, and plan and control work.

- Set own goals and inspect own work; often create own work and vacation schedules and review performance as a team.

- May prepare own budgets and coordinate work with other departments.

- Usually order materials, keep inventories, and deal with suppliers.

- Are frequently responsible for acquiring new training and maintaining on-the-job training.

- May hire own replacements and assume responsibility for disciplining own members.

- Monitor and review overall process performance.

Most self-directed work teams gradually take on responsibility for these tasks as they gain confidence in their own skills and are able to redefine the role of the supervisor. The shift to self-direction represents increasing accountability and responsibility for employees.

The Basics of Team Functioning

Forming a Team

The first step in forming a team is to define the team's goal on the basis of the purpose or problem to be examined. The founding person or body drafts the team's preliminary charter including the mission, team goals, expected outcomes, time requirements, and authority level. In addition, the founding person or body is responsible for defining, communicating, and negotiating the "what" (direction), "why," and "when" to the team. The team may question aspects of the direction or seek clarification; leadership teams often jointly define direction with management. The team is then responsible for determining the "how" (the approach). Management must resist the temptation to draft a charter that spells out every step so clearly that the team has no latitude to create on its own.

In some cases, the team may have to write its own charter. Although there is nothing wrong with this approach, it will take the team longer to get started on specific tasks than if a manager or design team defines the initial charter for the team.

Getting Started on the Team Charter
(sample charters are available at
www.NewDirectionsConsulting.com/samples)

- Define the mission of the team—its primary purpose for existing—in a sentence or two.

- Identify the time requirements expected of team members when they join the team. This information should be given to prospective team members' managers/coaches to determine availability for the team. The charter should include a statement that time requirements exceeding those stated in the charter must be approved by the coach/sponsor.

- Identify the SMART goals for the team: specific, measurable, achievable, results-oriented, and time bound. We find it helpful to encourage the team to draft work breakdown plans for each goal that identify major milestones and key activities under each milestone.

- Describe the major activities that the team is expected to undertake, including specific objectives to be achieved or strategies, recommendations, or analyses to be performed.

- Spell out the expected outcomes or deliverables once the team's work is complete.

- Identify the resources available to the team, including the team sponsor and subject matter experts (SMEs).

- Identify the type and frequency of reporting and the communication expected of the team, including who should receive copies of the team scribe notes and any interim reports.

- Identify any nonnegotiable requirements or rules that the team is expected to adhere to or that it needs to be aware of.

- Identify the skills and abilities that team members must possess for the team to accomplish its task.

- Identify the team members, and in the case of cross-functional teams, how membership will be rotated.

- Identify the roles and responsibilities of the team sponsor or coach, team members, and star point roles.

- Identify the authority level that the team will have—what decisions it may or may not make—and any spending limitations.

- Identify the key relationships that the team must maintain and/or foster.

- List the key measures to be used to track the team's success.

Determining Level of Authority and Responsibility

When a team is created, the coach or team sponsor must clearly define its level of responsibility and authority, setting the limits within which the team may act autonomously. Although it may be cumbersome, the most effective way to detail authority is to create a RACI chart (see Figure 1-1) for the team. In the beginning, it is important that the coach or sponsor, star point leaders (SPLs), and coaching facilitators be available to give instruction and direction. Over time, as the team matures, these supports will become less and less involved, and the team's authority level will expand.

Authority Options for Task Force or Improvement Teams

When a task force or improvement team begins, the sponsor needs to make clear the authority level the team will have. Below is a progressive list of authority options for a task force or improvement team.

- Look into the problem and provide all the details; others will decide what to do.

- Identify the alternatives available and the pros and cons of each; others will decide which to select.

- Recommend a course of action for others' approval.

- Report what the team intends to do; delay action until approval is received.

- Report what the team intends to do; do it unless told not to.

- Take action; report action; report results.

- Take action; communicate only if the action is unsuccessful.

- Take action; no further communication is necessary.

Authority Options for Self-Directed Teams

The team coach is responsible for defining the level of authority for the self-directed team. The authority is handed to the team gradually, to ensure the team's success; coaches are not to "dump and run." We use six levels of authority for self-directed teams, in addition to requiring the RACI chart:

> **Level 1:** The coach's involvement is a must; the team does not make decisions on its own, and the coach reviews all decisions made by the team.

> **Level 2:** The coach's involvement is necessary—the coach still makes many of the decisions; the team has input into the decision-making process and it makes minor decisions related to team functioning.

> **Level 3:** The coach's involvement is still needed; the team has more participation in the decision-making process, but the coach retains final review of decisions.

FIGURE 1-1 Sample RACI Chart with the Headers at the Top for the People/ Groups Involved and the Tasks along the Side.

Task/Decision	Site VP	Global Functional Head	Steering Committee	Project Leader	Project Team
Establishment of program strategy	R	A	C	C, I	I
Alignment of strategic goals to project goals	C, I	C, I	A	R	R
Communication of plan to internal groups	I	I	A	R	R
Approval of project timelines	R	C, I	A	R	R, C
Addressing problems and bottlenecks	C, I	C, I	C, I	R, A	R

R = Responsible to do or complete the task; responsibility can be shared.

A = Accountable or liable for the results with sign off and/or veto power; typically only one person is accountable

C = Consulted or invited to give advice and/or feedback before the decision is made

I = Informed after a decision or action has been taken

Level 4: The coach's involvement is minimized; the team begins to make its own decisions and consults with the coach prior to implementing the decision.

Level 5: The team makes decisions on its own, implements the decisions, and informs the coach about the decision.

Level 6: The team makes all decisions (within guidelines and procedures); no further action is required.

This process of increasing authority begins when the coach creates the team hand-off plan (Figure 1-2), which details the tasks that will be handed to the self-directed team over the coming months. The hand-off plan and RACI chart are attached to the team's charter to ensure that the team understands how the teaming process will proceed.

The Hand-Off Plan

The team hand-off plan details the tasks to be performed by the team, whether the tasks affect safety (requiring a slower hand-off), the skill level required and existing skill level, and the training required. A typical hand-off plan lists twenty to thirty tasks for the self-directed team to assume over time. The coach shares the hand-off plan with the team during an early meeting to illustrate to the team how the transfer will occur.

The RACI Chart

The RACI chart (Figure 1-1) is a valuable tool to use with self-directed teams and project teams when you wish to be very clear about levels of responsibility and authority. For example, a research project team in a pharmaceutical company found the RACI chart very insightful when defining the responsibility and accountability for three interrelated teams: the project team itself, the steering team, and a high-level strategic council. As the RACI was developed, many questions surfaced about who actually did have accountability. Seeing the "holes" so clearly allowed each team to clarify its role.

When developing the RACI, remember these definitions:

"R" Responsible: the "doer" of the task, responsible for completing the task or making the decision. Multiple people/teams may have responsibility for completing a task or making a decision.

"A" Accountable: the person or team held accountable for ensuring that the task/decision is completed on time and meets expectations. This person does not have to do the task. However, in a team-based environment, the accountability should focus on the "doer" whenever possible. Note that not more than one person or team should be accountable for any task or decision; being accountable to more than one person or team can create not only confusion about expectations but numerous other problems for the team as well.

"C" Consulted: the person/team who will be consulted with by the responsible ("R") person/team before performing a task or making a decision.

"I" Informed: the person/team who will be informed that a task or decision has been completed or made.

Even in traditional management structures, decision-making authority is often not clear. In the excitement of getting started, teams often give themselves much more authority than they truly have or should have based on their development. When the presumed authority is clarified later on, the team often experiences considerable disappointment. It is wise to place clear limits on the team at the beginning and grow the level of authority as the team demonstrates maturity and focus.

Establishing and Rotating Team Membership

Selection of team members begins by referring to the list of skills, abilities, and experiences needed for team members in the charter. The sponsor or team develops a membership matrix (Figure 1-3) list-

FIGURE 1-2   Sample Self-Directed Team Hand-Off Plan.

Name of Task	Affect	When
Work assignments	Y	NOW
Checking safety supply inventory	Y	NOW
Order safety supplies	Y	NOW
Communicate shift-shift transition	Y	NOW
Access to safety equipment	Y	NOW
Access to tools	Y	NOW
Call engineering when needed	Y	NOW
Monitor safety	Y	NOW
Conduct incident investigations	Y	NOW
Staff scheduling	N	NOW
Handle outside contacts	N	3 months
E-mail shift change log	N	NOW
Schedule vacations	N	NOW
JDE completions	N	6 months
JDE issues	N	6 months
Prioritize work from open orders	N	3 months
Schedule team meetings; complete agendas	N	NOW

Level of Skill (H/M/L)		Training Required	Notes
Required	**Existing**		
M	M	Training for Production SPC	
L	L	Show Safety SPC location of form	
M	M	Train Safety SPC on standard order form	
H	H	Set up shift communication log	
L	L	Safety SPC needs keys and plan	
L	L	Team needs keys to tool shed	
L	L	Team needs phone numbers	
H	M	Train on safety audit and interpersonal skills needed to communicate problems	
H	M	Incident investigation training	
L	L	Review scheduling process with Production SPC	
H	M	Introduce team to key contacts list	
M	L	Show log entries	
M	M	Teach policy guidelines	
M	L	Teach JDE system	
M	L	Teach JDE system	
M	L	Shadow as prioritization is completed now	
M	M	Train first facilitators	

FIGURE 1-3   Sample Membership Matrix Used During the Selection of Team Members for a Multifunctional Design Team in a Manufacturing Facility.

	Design Team Candidates			
Required Attributes of Design Team Members	John Jones	Sue Wilson	Terry Smith	Bill Anderson
Interpersonal skills	4	4	3	4
Desire to achieve excellence	4	4	3	3
Ability to support and promote change	4	4	3	3
Able to see opportunities and move quickly	4	4	4	3
Creative thinking	4	4	3	3
High energy	4	4	3	3
Comfort with a high level of empowerment	3	4	3	3
Conflict resolution skills; diplomacy	4	4	3	2
Positive attitude	4	4	3	3
Bias for action	4	3	3	3
Presentation skills	4	4	3	2
Sense of urgency	4	4	4	3
Ability to coach and be coached	4	4	4	3
Abstract thinking and problem solving skills	3	3	3	3
Skill at planning, budgeting, and setting priorities	3	3	4	3
Knowledge of company policies and procedures and compliance regulations	4	4	4	3
High commitment to customer service and quality	4	4	3	3
Analytical skills	3	3	3	3
Persuasive ability	3	3	2	2
Computer skills	3	4	4	3
Ability to delegate and relinquish at appropriate time	3	4	3	2
Data tracking and measuring experience	3	4	3	2
Ability to lead groups	3	4	4	2
Be a change agent	4	4	3	2
Understanding of production requirements	3	4	4	3
Understanding of hourly personnel	4	4	3	3
Teaming experience or understanding	4	4	3	2
Not stretched too thin; has time available	4	3	3	3
Trustworthy; able to maintain confidentiality	4	4	3	3
Dedicated and motivated	4	4	3	3
Understand how teaming fits into the organization and our future outlook	4	4	3	2
Total Average Score	3.67	3.80	3.23	2.74

Rating Scale: 5 = The person displays this all the time. 4 = The person displays this most of the time. 3 = The person displays this sometimes. 2 = The Person rarely displays this. 1 = The person never displays this, Blank = I do not know this person well enough to say.

ing the attributes of team members on the left-hand side of the chart and potential members across the top. Then the sponsor (in the beginning) or each team member (when the team begins rotation) ranks prospective members on the attributes required for membership. Individuals with the highest score are the primary candidates. This system provides a fair and rational way of selecting members; later, team members can illustrate to others the criteria used as a way of explaining why some were selected and others were not.

There are favorable and unfavorable times to introduce new members on a team. Generally, a team that is experiencing problems or has suddenly entered into a new phase of development will not readily welcome a new member; if problems exist, members may use the new member to avoid confronting these problems.[5] We encourage the original team to stay intact for the first year to establish a strong performance culture. However, after the first year, membership should be regularly rotated to keep the team fresh and energized. Although we suggest that two members rotate off every six months, it is important to modify this plan if any of the following exist:

- Too many strong, capable members are rotated at the same time, leaving the team significantly weaker as a result.

- Membership is rotated during the middle of a major project, requiring the team to bring new members up to speed in the middle of their work.

- The sponsor is rotated simultaneously with strong team members.

It is wise for the team to create a rotation protocol spelling out in detail the following components: the term of service for members with extensions under what conditions, the term of service for the sponsor, the team's authority to recommend new members, the team's procedure for recommending new members, inclusion of an immediate supervisor or a manager in discussion about a person's membership, the bridging time between the old member and the new member, and rules for early rotation from a team. (A sample team rotation protocol is available at www.NewDirectionsConsulting.com/samples.)

One of the critical issues that surfaces with team membership is inclusion and exclusion: who is and is not on a team. Members on a team may begin to flaunt their special status; employees not on teams are often left behind to "do the real work," and resentment grows. Membership rotation helps to address this issue. In a team-based organization, it's important to help those who aren't selected for initial teams to understand what they need to do to develop their competencies in order to be selected in the future. This mentoring work can be a turning point for those who have negative feelings toward teams.

For best team functioning, a minimal amount of training should be required of all team members in areas such as how teams work, meeting skills, conflict resolution skills, and problem solving (see Chapter 7, which discusses team training).

Of course, self-directed teams do not participate in member selection or rotation, because all individuals who work in the area are included on the team. It is important, however, to inform the team that it has the right to recommend that a member be removed if the member's performance or behavior is detrimental to the team's functioning. Removal of a team member is a lengthy process that is done only after numerous steps to change the member's behavior have proved ineffective (see "Removing a Member from the Team" at the end of Chapter 6).

Determining Optimal Team Size

If the team's goals and tasks are complex and demand considerable skill, small teams (from six to twelve members) are most effective. If tasks are relatively simple and redundant, teams can be sufficiently larger to encompass the workload. We have seen effective teams with as many as fifteen or sixteen members. If the team is responsible for a task requiring a lot of technological know-how, the team should include enough people who can perform the job, as well as those who can manage—and even design—the product (a cross-functional team).

The decision about team size must be based, in part, on how willing members are to help the team function smoothly. Members of a large team (between fifteen and twenty-five members) have to be mature enough not to speak on every issue and be willing to delegate certain tasks and decisions to subgroups.

It may also be useful to consider the formation of a "core" team composed of full-time members and an "extended" team composed of SMEs or part-time members who participate on an as-needed basis.

Orienting New Members

Orientation of new members is the responsibility of the team, not the new members or the coach/sponsor.

To shorten the start-up time for a new member, make sure he or she is properly oriented to the team, its members, and its work to date. Orientation should occur within thirty days of placement on a team and should include the following:

- An overview of training specific to the team

- A review of the team's history and its purpose in forming, the team charter, the RACI chart, the hand-off plan, and the team's protocols

- A review of team scribe notes, with an emphasis on decisions made to date

- The sharing of all pertinent information and data

- A discussion of roles and responsibilities agreed to by the team

The team's training star point coordinator (SPC) typically has responsibility for training and orienting new members. In lieu of a training SPC, a new member may interview three or four people on the team for specific information. Another option for the new member is either to work one-on-one with a senior team member or participate on the team at the same time as the existing member to create a "bridge" between the old and the new member.

The "Buddy" System

Implementing a "buddy" system helps to address problems when members must be absent. Each team member selects a buddy from the team who takes responsibility for the following:

- Performing the assigned meeting role when the member is absent

- Collecting meeting materials for the member when he or she is absent

- Informing the member of any decisions made in his or her absence and bringing the member up-to-date on the team's work

Handling Resignation Requests

In the normal course of events, teams can expect to lose up to 30 percent of their members in the first year. Resignation requests should be presented to the team in writing.

Whenever a resignation occurs, the team should make every effort to conduct an exit interview to determine why the member has resigned.

Conducting an Exit Interview

If the resignation is accepted, an exit interview conducted by several members of the team is suggested, and a summary report of the interview must be given to the full team.

Questions Included in the Exit Interview

- Why did you decide to leave the team?

- How did the teaming process work for you?

- What needs improvement (structure, communication, conflict resolution)?

- What should stay the same?

- Did you feel you had adequate training while on the team?

- Did you feel you had support from the team?

- What would you change about the way the team approaches tasks?

- What would you change in the team's approach to relationships?

- Are there concerns that you were uncomfortable discussing in the team that you are willing to discuss now?

- Are there any loose ends still to be resolved at this time?

- If circumstances change, would you consider returning to the team? Why or why not?

Most team members disguise the reasons that they are leaving the team in order to preserve their relationships. Even so, it is important for team members to try to surface problems and hidden conflicts. Sometimes a close friend or two can get the individual to discuss the real issues.

Assigning Team Roles

There are numerous roles on a team, including the coach (self-directed) or sponsor (cross-functional), business unit manager (BUM), meeting roles, star points, and SMEs. It is important that team members rotate their roles on a regular basis to ensure that the team builds strength among all team members, not just among the few who are already capable.

Assignment of roles should be based on skill, experience, and commitment, not solely on seniority. The selection of new coaches and sponsors is often done by the Design Team (see Chapter 7) as the transition is made to a team-based structure.

Responsibilities of Team Coach or Sponsor

The role of coach or sponsor is very important to the team's success. A high-performance team recognizes the value of a coach or sponsor and readily includes him or her in the team's activities/meetings. Teams do not have the authority to remove their coach or sponsor, nor to suggest that the coach or sponsor not attend team meetings.

The coach or sponsor performs the following duties:

- Draft the preliminary team charter, including initial team goals.

- Complete the hand-off plan (for self-directed) and RACI chart for the team; delegate authority and responsibility carefully and systematically.

- Facilitate preliminary team meetings until role rotation begins.

- Guide the team in the development of work breakdown plans for each goal; review the team's action plans to provide ideas and resources and to clarify boundaries.

- Help the team clarify and maintain focus on its mission, goals, and measurements.

- Transmit information, knowledge, and skills in a timely fashion to team members.

- Interpret and explain policies, work specifications, and job orders for the team.

- Identify resources needed (people, time, money, materials, facilities) and ensure that they are available.

- Teach team members how to manage work processes effectively and to evaluate results.

- Help the team establish and hold the team accountable for tracking metrics for all deliverables.

- Help eliminate cross-functional barriers and excessive procedures; interact regularly with BUMs and SPLs.

- Monitor team progress and encourage delivery of reward and recognition.

- Model proper team behavior in all areas; help establish team climate and shape attitudes.

- Promote empowerment and self-discipline in team members.

- Encourage effective problem solving and responsible risk taking among team members.

- Reinforce and reward proper team behavior.

- Troubleshoot for the team in areas of expertise.

- Act as a team liaison to the external environment; network the team's results as appropriate.

- Assist team members and the team as a whole with resolving conflicts.

- Address all disciplinary issues during the early stages of team development.

- Provide gentle reminders to stay within protocol guidelines.

- Serve as a sounding board when the team is confronted with tough decisions.

- Promote shared information and collaborative problem solving.

- Foster a learning environment by helping team members learn, grow, and develop.

- Champion the shift to a teaming environment.

Former supervisors and managers who become coaches and sponsors have the greatest role change during the transition to teams, and most need training and support to gain confidence in the new role. Many of the behaviors that proved successful for them in the past will work against them in their new role of coach or sponsor. I often suggest that if a manager is comfortable, he is probably performing his job wrong, and if he is uncomfortable, he is probably doing it right. Much of the anxiety that these former supervisors and managers feel in their new role stems from the fact that even though they are the ones delegating all kinds of tasks, they are still held responsible for the end results. The idea of empowered teams poses a threat to their span of control and ability to trust. Special steps must be taken to help managers and supervisors as they transition to coaches and sponsors, including training, mentoring, and regular feedback on progress. It is helpful if management explains to team members that not only are they going through a tough transition, but the coach/sponsor is as well.

Responsibilities of Executive Sponsor/Champion

On occasion it is helpful to select an executive sponsor for the team, especially if the focus is on changing the status quo. The executive sponsor serves as a liaison between what the team is trying to change and the existing structure that may resist the change. Following are the executive sponsor's duties:

- Function as a liaison between senior-level leadership and the team, regularly communicating about the team's progress.
- Identify issues or concerns at a strategic level that could impact the team's achievement of goals and milestones.
- Help the team to negotiate critical completion dates.
- Provide guidance and direction on issues that the team is unable or not authorized to resolve.
- Meet periodically (monthly/quarterly) with the team to provide support and encourage progress.

Responsibilities of BUM or Value Stream Manager

The BUM or value stream manager oversees the work of numerous teams within a specific unit of operation (assembly, finishing, shipping/receiving) or value stream. The BUM or value stream manager works collaboratively with numerous coaches, paying particular attention to the business needs as well as to the teaming needs. These are the tasks that this individual performs:

- Oversee the smooth functioning of the entire value stream or business unit to achieve business objectives.

- Identify and implement efficiencies within process flow and staff utilization.

- Implement lean process development.

- Grow the business of the value stream.

- Assess and maintain adequate and competent resources.

- Develop and oversee the budgetary process of the value stream.

- Coordinate with other value stream BUMs to maintain and achieve overall organizational goals.

- Work collaboratively with team coaches and SPLs to encourage high performance of all resources within the value stream.

Responsibilities of Coaching Facilitator

Many organizations utilize coaching facilitators who work closely with the team to teach meeting and problem-solving skills. These individuals may have been group leaders or supervisors in the previous structure and have an ability to build bridges and work effectively with the teams. Typically, a value stream has one or two coaching facilitators. The coaching facilitator does the following:

- Regularly work with the team members in the value stream to teach teaming behavior.

- Help guide team members to perform meeting roles effectively.

- Help the team build and maintain its metrics board.

- Supply teaming tools (team surveys, protocols, activities) to enhance team functioning.

- Guide the team goal-setting process; help the team to build work breakdown plans to achieve consensus on the approach to achieving the goals.

- Help acquire resources to support the team's efforts.

- Interact regularly with the team coach and BUM to discuss progress and identify critical developmental needs of the team.

Responsibilities of Subject Matter Expert[6]

The Subject Matter Expert brings specialized skill and experience to the team. These are usually technical skills like engineering, process design, maintenance, and tooling or project management, scientific expertise, and IT. The SME may participate on the team for a period of time and then move on to another task. They do not usually participate in star point role or meeting role rotation.

- Provide expertise in a particular area, such as manufacturing software, technical training, process excellence, scheduling/ planning, sales, shipping/receiving, project management, risk management.

- Participate on the team in area of expertise.

- Collect and gather data for the team; identify causes of variance.

- Gather information from other experts or other teams.

- Lead discussion regarding improvement.

Responsibilities of Star Point Leaders or Business Process Leaders

About thirty years ago, Charles Krone developed the concept of star points, most likely in the Procter & Gamble, Lima, Ohio, plant,[7] to address the need to distribute role responsibilities evenly among team members. As supervisors and managers shifted responsibilities to the teams, the tendency was to give all the tasks, from scheduling and vacation planning to safety audits, to the team leader. It wasn't long before the team leader was completely overwhelmed, doing both the *regular* job and all the team tasks. The development of star points solved this problem.

The tasks are divided like points of a star and assigned to team members, who maintain responsibility for them typically for six to twelve months. In our teams, we use one set of star points for self-directed teams and another set for cross-functional teams. Typical manufacturing star point areas are safety and ergonomics (commonly referred to as "ergo"), communication, human resources (HR), production, continuous improvement, inventory and material services, quality and customer service, and training. To oversee each of these areas, an SPL or business process leader (BPL) is selected; this person coaches and guides the work of all SPCs on the various teams. In the case of self-directed teams, the SPLs are often former supervisors or group leaders, who have considerable knowledge in particular subject areas. For example, a supervisor who demonstrated a strong commitment to safety could become the safety SPL or BPL, overseeing all the safety SPCs on the teams.

The SPL in each focus area is expected to perform the following:

- Actively coordinate the development of team members into the specific star point role.

- Establish goals and desired results for a particular star point area.

- Provide training/guidance for the SPCs in the specific area.

- Meet with SPCs on a regular basis to discuss issues and concerns, and to encourage development.

- Ensure that the star point area is being adequately performed on all teams; monitor effectiveness and apply corrective action when necessary.

- Link SPCs together to problem solve and plan.

- Engage with the coach and BUM on critical issues that need additional discussion/decisions.

- Transfer supervisory functions to the SPCs.

SPLs benefit from the strong support of coaches, BUMs, and plant management. Meeting regularly as their own team to discuss how things are going with their SPCs is often helpful. At any point, an SPL may have thirty to fifty SPCs (one from each team in the organization) reporting to them. Some of the difficult issues SPLs face include getting important information from the coaches to share with the teams, turnover of SPCs on the teams, ineffective backups for SPCs, resistance from team members in performing their star point roles, the amount of training needed for themselves and the SPCs to perform their jobs well, and clarity about what can be resolved at each level.

Responsibilities of Star Point Coordinators

SPCs are team members who volunteer to perform the roles identified in the following lists. Typically, they hold the role for six months to a year; other team members serve as backup star points in each of the roles. Roles should be designed so that they entail roughly the same amount of work, although more often the production star point role is the most difficult. There is no pay differential for the various star point roles because the whole team is responsible for making sure the work gets done. Team members may select roles that more readily suit their skills; they should expect to receive training from the SPL appropriate to their role.

Now let's examine the various roles and responsibilities of the SPC:

Communication SPC

- Keep the team informed about plant and team activities.

- Maintain communication guidelines.

- Teach the team effective communication from materials provided by the communication SPL.

- Coordinate team articles for organization or team newsletter.

- Maintain the team's meeting binder/electronic files.

- Attend plantwide star point communication meetings.

- Perform head count during emergency evacuations.

- Update the team charter.

- Attend regular meetings with the communication SPL.

Continuous Improvement SPC

- Follow up on Kaizen events.

- Assist with CARs/PARs (corrective action reports and preventive action reports).

- Implement process improvement for identified problems.

- Implement improvement ideas and suggestions from the team.

- Provide ongoing Lean education and 5-S compliance.

- Support value engineering, Kaizen, and Six-Sigma.

- Ensure that a visual management scoreboard is being utilized by the team.

- Attend regular meetings with the continuous improvement SPL.

Human Resources SPC

- Distribute HR information to the team (benefits information, policies).

- Coordinate the performance management plan for the team including reinforcements.

- Turn in absent-hour and missed or corrected punch forms.

- Collect and submit time sheets.

- Track the team members' attendance and give the results.

- Assist in planning and coordinating team celebrations.

- Submit members' requests for vacation and time off.

- Help to orient and welcome new members.

- Coordinate labor resources for overtime.

- Communicate with members on extended leave by mail (send a newsletter or cards).

- Schedule members to meet with human resources.

- Attend regular meetings with the human resource SPL.

Inventory and Materials Services SPC

- Ensure that work-in-process (WIP) is moved to the inventory location after production is reported.

- Perform departmental cycle counts.

- Order parts.

- Stage parts for changeovers.

- Stock and stage incoming and outgoing parts.

- Handle "special" shipping requests and transfer orders.

- Maintain inventory accuracy measures; update the performance board.

- Attend regular meetings with the inventory and materials services SPL.

Production SPC

- Run reports on the factory planner.

- Communicate production goals to the team.

- Communicate with production control about "hot" parts or parts issues.

- Organize the daily schedule of changeovers and communicate it to the team.

- Report on compliance misses.

- Schedule and coordinate labor distribution on a daily basis.

- Help maintenance to prioritize work orders and scheduled and unscheduled downtime.

- Maintain production performance measures; update the performance board.

- Schedule overtime.

- Keys in daily production to the system.

- Attend regular meetings with the production SPL.

Quality and Customer Service SPC

- Oversee the team's reject and rework areas as well as key in the inventory.

- Ensure that the team adheres to quality and process control plans, policies, processes, and procedures (including all International Standards Organization documentation).

- Represent the team by reviewing data and reporting problems to suppliers. Report on team improvements and quality measures.

- Handle customer complaints and report the results to the team.

- Assist with customer visits.

- Ensure that all team members are informed of the CAR/PAR correction action system.

- Assist the continuous improvement SPC with identifying the need for CARs/PARs.

- Interface with quality assurance and support staff to improve quality.

- Maintain quality records; update performance boards.

- Attend regular meetings with the quality and customer service SPL.

Safety/Ergo SPC

- Conduct safety orientation with new hires or associates who have transferred into the department.

- Manage scheduled departmental safety compliance or behavior-related audits.

- Ensure that any safety/ergo-related issues that are reported to the SPC are relayed to the safety or ergonomics team.

- Attend regular safety team meetings with the safety/ergo SPL.

- Communicate the department's safety goals, objectives, and issues.

- Ensure that there are monthly safety talks and that they are properly documented.

- Maintain team's safety performance metrics; update performance boards.

- Perform 5-S audits.

- Instruct and lead ergo stretching exercises.

- Assist the coach in accident investigations.

- Attend regular meetings with the safety/ergo SPL.

Training SPC

- Assess the team's training needs; share information with the in-house training team.

- Coordinate the training plan for the team.

- Maintain team training records.

- Conduct new member orientation and training.

- Maintain/conduct on-the-job training for all members as needed by the department.

- Attend training workshops and other skills development training and teach skills to the team.

- Attend regular meetings with the training SPL.

- Post memory aids and other training tools on bulletin boards and/or in team files.

Responsibilities of Cross-Functional SPCs

Cross-functional teams also benefit from the use of SPCs, although the roles are much simpler and there are no SPLs. Members usually hold these roles for three to six months, again with a backup team member in place. Here are the various roles and responsibilities of these SPCs:

Team Leader

- Act as a contact person for the team.

- Oversee the completion of regular reports to management.

- Set up routine review of the team's progress.

- Help the team manage its relationship with outsiders.

- Challenge the team to perform at its best.

Customer Focus

- Represent or look out for the customer's well-being.

- Provide the team with ongoing feedback from customers throughout the process.

- Identify and report on any customer complaints.

- Keep the team energized about customers (handouts, reading material).

Meetings/Administration

- Ensure that regular team meetings are held; determine the location for the meetings.

- Distribute mail and other information to the team.

- Prepare drafts of team memos.

- Maintain all team files; regularly update and clean out the files.

- Serve as a team historian; maintain a record of all of the team's accomplishments.

Quality/Measurements

- Monitor the quality of the team's output.

- Track and maintain a scoreboard on the team's measurements.

- Keep quality measurements up-to-date on all bulletin boards.

- Provide the team with statistics on its accomplishments.

Communication

- Identify and report communication needs to the team throughout the project.

- Communicate with other teams; keep others informed about the team.

- Identify communication barriers; suggest to the team ways to improve communication.

- Maintain the bulletin board and intranet communication.

Training

- Help the team identify training needs.

- Maintain a master of all team training that has been conducted and who has received what training.

- Provide feedback to trainers on request.

- Train any new members of the team.

Technical Adviser/Assistant

- Assist team members with technical (computer use) questions.

- Assist team members with posting to public folders.

- Create subfolders for the team on an intranet.

- Assist team members with other technical matters as needed.

For more information on all star point roles visit www.New DirectionsConsulting.com/samples.

Responsibilities of Team Members

Teams also find it helpful to identify general responsibilities of all team members. These responsibilities are as follows:

- Prepare prior to the meeting by completing assignments and doing any necessary pre-reading in advance of the meeting.

- Attend regularly scheduled team meetings on time, participate in team discussions, and offer suggestions.

- Perform tasks for the team as assigned; try to improve the quality of the work performed by the team.

- Remain proactive when things are not going well for the team.

- Take on extra work when necessary to ensure that the team meets or exceeds its goals.

- Help monitor results and track data for team metrics.

- Offer ideas and options to solve team problems.

- Rotate team meeting roles; perform roles effectively.

- Act as a "buddy" when someone is absent.

- Communicate with team members about problems that might affect team performance.

- Participate in training and practice what is learned.

- Follow operational procedures and team protocols.

- Accept and support consensus decisions of the team.

— Key Components in High-Performance Teams —

High-performance teams display the following characteristics:

- Team goals are considered to be as important as individual goals; members are able to recognize when a personal agenda is interfering with the team's direction.

- The team is able to focus on both task completion and process maintenance.

- The team understands the goals and is committed to achieving them; everyone is willing to shift responsibilities to meet demands.

- Members are accountable to the team and individual members; feedback on performance is welcome.

- The team climate is comfortable and informal; members feel empowered and understand that individual competitiveness is inappropriate.

- Communication is spontaneous and shared among all members; diversity of opinions and ideas is encouraged.

- Respect, open-mindedness, and collaboration are high; members seek win/win solutions and build on each other's ideas.

- Trust replaces fear, and members feel comfortable taking risks; direct eye contact and spontaneous expression are present.

- Conflicts and differences of opinion are considered opportunities to explore new ideas; the emphasis is on finding common ground.

- The team continually works on improving itself by examining its charter, protocols, procedures, and practices, and experimenting with change.

- Leadership is rotated; no one member dominates.

- Cross-training occurs on all key responsibilities owned by the team.

- Decisions are made by consensus and are accepted and supported by the team's members.

- Authority increases as the team demonstrates competence and maturity.

- Team responsibilities become integrated with job responsibilities.

- Members are bound closely together by a shared set of values that in turn reinforce personal commitment and a collective accountability for the results.

Causes of Team Failure

Some organizations believe they can implement teams without changing the traditional hierarchical structure. Within months, the two structures inevitably clash. Typically, the more entrenched structure survives, and teamwork is reduced to a thing of the past.

The most common reasons for a team's failure include the following:

- The team lacks visible support and commitment from top management.

- No real change in structure occurs; the hierarchical structure continues despite name changes.

- The team focuses on task activities to the exclusion of work on process and team member relationships.

- The team has too many members and lacks the strong structure necessary to deal with a large team.

- Management expects immediate return on investment and the team is unable to provide it as quickly as demanded.

- The team experiences poor leadership within and/or outside the team; there is resistance from first-line supervisors.

- The organization fails to use team efforts in any meaningful way.

- Members receive insufficient training to be successful in new roles.

- Conflicting priorities lead to mixed messages about teaming; teaming becomes a "good day" activity.

- Teaming is limited to a "tool" and not seen as a culture change as well.

- Pilot teams are launched before building dissatisfaction with the status quo and a compelling vision, resulting in increased resistance.

- The environment is unionized and will not tolerate role expansion and increased accountability.

Teams in a Unionized Facility

Trying to transform a unionized facility into a team-based organization is difficult, but not impossible. If employee teams are truly empowered to implement their decisions about productivity, quality, performance improvement, safety, and work place organization, they are legal in the United States. However, there are some cautions:

- Teams cannot act or purport to act as a representative of employees and should not be dominated by management members.

- Care must be taken in establishing teams to present formal proposals or ideas to management that management will then respond to. These teams cannot appear to be taking the place of the existing union structure and its dealings with management.

- Employees can be on teams, but they cannot represent other employees.

- Employees cannot make decisions or recommendations about any factors that affect working conditions or employment conditions, issues that would generally be negotiated by the union.

- Workplace decision making should take place within the teams with management providing consultation and assistance.

- A design team cannot act as a representative of employees but, rather, as people who have been selected to explore alternative plant structures. The design team must never have the appearance of being management attempting to create a company-sponsored union.

It is important to bring union officials in on the design and planning of a team culture. Many companies find that a union that formally opposes the use of teams will not object to the company's members (employees) being part of teams if they are working on specific problems. This approach is often a way of starting teaming slowly and building trust over time.

Following are recommended principles for teams in union facilities:

> All teams formed at (*name of company*) will respect the Employee Agreement and will not take actions that directly conflict with any statement in this agreement.

> On all (*name of company*) teams that have Union members, Union members will have as much voice in decision making as non–Union members.

> All teams at (*name of company*) will operate in such a way that they do not represent the Union, including not representing Union employees in place of the Union.

More guidelines on unions and teams are available at www.New Directions Consulting.com/samples.

Closing Out a Team

When a team has completed its purpose, it is important to provide closure for the members. This is a time to reflect on progress and to celebrate the team's accomplishments. However, teams tend to construe closure with failure. Many are concerned that closure will bring about the end to comfortable relationships with team members, and they fear that their accomplishments will get lost. Here is a sample process for making the closure effective:

1. Empower the team by asking its members how they would like to bring closure to the project or merger with another team.

2. Schedule a meeting to present the team's findings and recommendations; invite anyone affected by the team's recommendations.
3. Decide on a review procedure and a completion date for assessing the team's recommendations.
4. Recognize and reward the team's accomplishments in some formal manner (see Chapter 6 for a discussion on how to reward a team's accomplishments).
5. Identify any other areas of the organization that could benefit from the team's ideas or skills.
6. Encourage the team's members to develop "lessons learned" both as individuals and as a team that they are willing to share with other teams.
7. Discuss any transition issues for the team such as team files/records and transfer of information to a follow-up team.

Here are some additional points on closure:

- Share stories about what it was like working on the team.

- Identify key skills learned.

- Develop tips for other teams.

- Determine how improvements will be maintained.

- Complete all documentation and final reports.

- Decide on a way to say good-bye.

Recently we had to shut down a design team when it was announced that the entire plant was going to close. For more than fifteen months, the team had raced to implement a team-based structure, in the hopes of keeping the plant alive. When it didn't work out, the team was devastated and felt that its work had been a waste of time. We suggested that the team pull all of its "lessons learned" into a document that it could send to other plants in the company in the event that they went to teams. This final act of closure helped the team feel that its work had indeed been worthwhile.

Let's Meet: Team Meetings

AFTER A TEAM is formed, its first step is to meet. The team meeting is the team's "playing field," where the processes of initiating, planning, executing, following through, and controlling all take place. Some people feel they can cancel team meetings and still have the team evolve. Such miracles just don't happen. In fact, we've seen situations in which teams that met only once per month stayed stuck in the forming stage of development. Meetings are an important strategy for advancing teams through the development phases. However, a meeting whose only purpose is information sharing will never be effective for a team. The team's meeting must focus on important team activities such as planning, problem solving, and decision making, with as little time spent on information sharing as possible. With e-mail, voice mail, and memos, all the information the team needs can be shared outside the meeting. Then, at the meeting, the team members can bring their questions, concerns, and actions required based on the information shared earlier. There's no more coming to meetings without knowing what's going to happen, because team members have completed their pre-reads and expect to participate and work hard together.

The meeting model described here will seem rigid to new teams, especially those comfortable with ineffective meetings and dominate team members. We encourage you to use the process for five or six meetings and not loosen the reins on the meeting structure until the team has reached a more advanced state and members have their counterproductive behaviors under control.

In addition to the regular, sixty- to ninety-minute weekly team meeting, the team should hold daily ten-minute "huddles" if appropriate. These are informal, touch-base sessions at the beginning of a shift to update each other on any critical issues and to build unity toward the goal. While they may use a facilitator, the members are standing and sharing spontaneously, often around a team scoreboard that records daily metrics. Items requiring more discussion are moved to the team's weekly meeting.

Typical Meeting Problems

Although meetings are vital for the team's health, they also can be a source of considerable wasted time. Here are some of the problems often encountered in poorly run meetings:

- Meeting roles are poorly performed by team members, resulting in other team members taking over. This is especially true for the facilitator's role.

- The team jumps into discussing agenda topics before planning the work: agreeing on the goal of the discussion and structuring the approach the team will use.

- Members' silence is treated as if it means agreement, when often it doesn't.

- The team relies on the coach or sponsor to generate ideas.

- Meetings are allowed to start later and later each time.

- No outcomes are identified for agenda items, and the meeting goal is not clear.

- No agenda exists, the agenda is not distributed in advance, or the agenda is too "lightweight" in terms of topics.

- The facilitator is not prepared or monopolizes the discussion.

- Only a few members speak; others withdraw nonverbally.

- The meeting focuses on informational "show and tell" rather than on planning or problem solving.

- Members interrupt each other or "cross-talk," excluding others.

- The real meeting discussion occurs after the meeting in small-group "triangles."

- The team reaches no decisions or it continually revisits previous decisions.

- Few actions are identified and assigned; all actions are assigned to just a few people.

- No plan for follow-through is developed.

- Assignments are not completed on time.

The best way to avoid these problem behaviors is to have the team establish a Help/Hinder list at the very first meeting. The Help/Hinder list is created by the team members, not management, with them identifying what behaviors have historically helped them function effectively and what behaviors have historically hindered their performance (see Figure 2-1). The team then agrees to be held accountable for the behaviors and to allow the process observer to interrupt if a team member is doing a behavior on the hinder list. No longer is management responsible for meeting behavior as now a member of the team assumes that responsibility on a rotating basis.

FIGURE 2-1   Sample Help/Hinder List for a New Team.

Behaviors in the Team that HELP	Behaviors in the Team that HINDER
Be on time, prepared and ready to go	Negative body language (falling asleep,
Participate, volunteer to do tasks	sighing, eye rolling, folded arms, shaking
Engage in open, honest communication	head no, looking down, and not involved)
Listen to understand; speak to	Show little or no enthusiasm for the
be understood	team's work
Ask questions and value others' opinions	Attack team members personally
Have an agenda and stick to the agenda	Dominate discussion
Build on others' ideas	Engage in name calling/stereotyping
Be optimistic/positive about team	Make manipulative, guilt-throwing
Critique ideas, not members	statements
Perform promised follow-up	Jump from one topic to another
Pay attention, stay open-minded	Mask statements as questions
Take problems seriously	Agee with everything
Be courteous, honest, trusting	Avoid decision making or closure
Say what you feel/think	Interrupt others
Take responsible risks	Say "no" before thinking "yes"
Use "we" expressions and thought more	Express futility, resignation, or helplessness
than "I" expressions	Opinions without facts
Support each other in and outside	Taking phone calls within the meeting room
team meetings	Checking emails during the meeting
Show commitment toward making it work	Reflect boredom/don't pay attention
Display a sense of humor	Side conversations
Set realistic goals/time frame on goals	Everyone talking at once
Appreciate members, skills, abilities,	Not listening
and personality differences	Closed-mindedness
Establish clearly defined roles	Using "you" statements
Distribute tasks equally	Judging ideas/others
Leave titles behind	Do other distracting work
Demonstrate positive body language	"Triangling" outside the meeting
Facilitator sits at head of the table	Cross talk (between two people that leaves
Demonstrate consensus signal quickly	other members outside the discussion)
	Sarcastic or caustic remarks
	Drill down into minutiae
	Going off the agenda—"chasing rabbits"

Setting the Agenda

An agenda should always be prepared and distributed before each team meeting, typically by the facilitator. We encourage teams to use an agenda preparation form (Figure 2-2). On this form, any team member can enter meeting topics, presenters, time required, and topic priority in advance. The agenda is distributed to team members twenty-four to forty-eight hours in advance. Every meeting must have an agenda, even if it is developed as the first activity of the meeting on a flipchart sheet. All agendas are tentative until agreed to by the team.

There are four components to the meeting agenda:

1. *Meeting opening and housekeeping.* This is when meeting role assignments and agreement on agenda are verified and due or delinquent action items from previous meetings are reviewed.
2. *Standing agenda sections.* Teams may need to hear from their coach and star point coordinators (SPCs) on a regular basis. This section provides time for them to report to the team.

FIGURE 2-2   Sample Agenda Preparation Form.

Meeting Date: ___September 6, 2XXX___

Facilitator: ___Jim Smith___

Agenda Item	Presenter	Priority (1–3; 1=high)	Time Needed	Special Notes
Winter retreat	Sue	2	30 min.	Members please bring ideas to brainstorm
Equipment upgrades	Joe	3	30 min.	
Financial update	Lisa	1	15 min.	Managers please bring next quarter's budgets to meeting

To not use up too much of the meeting time, the SPCs are rotated through a month's worth of meetings, rather than have each one report out at every meeting. Remember, the focus of the content is on planning and problem solving, not information sharing.

3. *The body of the agenda.* Agenda topics are listed in priority order so that difficult tasks are done first, when the team is freshest, with a desired outcome identified for each item. If the desired outcome is information sharing, the facilitator must try to remove it from the agenda.

4. *Meeting closure.* This is when action items from the scribe, team behavior from the process observer, feedback from the coach, and agenda preparation for the next meeting are reported.

The teams we work with are always improving their meeting agendas. For example, a research management team redesigned the agenda format so that scribe notes and action items are recorded on the agenda directly below the agenda topic, rather than on separate sheets of paper. Visit www.NewDirectionsConsulting.com/samples for a sample of this type of agenda.

Meeting Roles

During team meetings, the goal of the team is to try to complete tasks and manage the process for how that is achieved. The facilitator, scribe, and timekeeper focus on moving the tasks along; the process observer pays attention to the process—how the team is managing itself. A brief description of each role follows.

Responsibilities of Facilitator

It is very important for the team meeting facilitator to be a member of the team and not an outsider. The team must learn to manage itself and to respect and listen to its own members who are performing new roles. It is also important to rotate all of the meeting roles among all of the members, rather than allow just the "good ones" to do the job. When the team realizes that everyone will have to participate and perform key functions, it begins to accept responsibility for meeting outcomes. For any team member who is particularly shy or lacks experience, it is perfectly acceptable to have another team member or the coaching facilitator help that individual until he or she feels comfortable in the role.

The responsibilities of the facilitator are as follows:

- Make it easy for members to participate; "scoop" them into the discussion.

- Remain neutral during discussion, speak last on any topic and only if necessary, and "pass the baton" if presenting an agenda topic so that facilitation will continue.

- Schedule, arrange, and conduct the meeting; get the meeting started on time.

- Prepare and distribute the agenda before the meeting and ensure that the agenda is followed during the meeting; check for agreement on the agenda at the beginning of the meeting.

- Ensure that all other meeting roles are in place prior to the meeting (scribe, timekeeper, and process observer).

- Check that the desired outcome and presenter are identified for each agenda item; remove "information only" items from the agenda so that the focus is on planning, problem solving, and decision making.

- Ensure that all team action items are assigned to various team members.

- Summarize and organize the ideas discussed to gain commitment.

- Identify common topics or subjects in the discussion to maintain the direction of the discussion.

- Ask questions to clarify comments and restate if members are confused.

- Test for consensus by stating the position that appears to be the team's conclusion.

- Join the process observer in pointing out feelings that are interfering with the team's work.

- Help the team sort out areas of agreement from areas of disagreement.

- Model performance standards, active listening, and trust-building behaviors.

- Protect the right of team members to have and express different points of view.

- Encourage the team to finish each agenda item before moving on to the next.

- Encourage critical thinking by challenging the team's assumptions.

- Encourage the integration of new members into the team's activities.

Responsibilities of Scribe

Today's scribe becomes tomorrow's facilitator in the team meeting role rotation. The scribe is a team member who writes down very specific information: the topic of discussion, key discussion points, decisions made, actions, who is responsible for completing the actions, and deadlines for the actions. The scribe does not take copious minutes of the meeting, nor records of who said what. The scribe is responsible for doing the following:

- Record what is discussed, actions, owners, and deadlines during the meeting.

- Distribute the scribe notes (Figure 2-3) and place them in the team file (electronic) folder twenty-four to forty-eight hours after the team meeting.

- Record actions from the meeting on an open action items list (Figure 2-4).

- Highlight delinquent action items during the "update" section of the team meeting.

- Help the facilitator by pointing out the need for a deadline/ person responsible for completing an action item.

- Ensure that an owner and a deadline are assigned for every action item.

- Restate all action items at the end of the meeting.

- Gather copies of materials distributed during the meeting to keep in the team binder.

Team members often use many different excuses to avoid scribing. It is helpful to point out to them that although it's not a pleasant job, everybody has to do it.

Responsibilities of Timekeeper

The role of timekeeper is an easy role for a team member, as it simply requires notifying the facilitator of the amount of time left (at various intervals) for every agenda topic. For example, if the agenda item is slotted for fifteen minutes, the timekeeper will notify the facilitator at 10 minutes, Half Way, 5 minutes, 2 minutes, and Out of Time. This allows the facilitator to say to the team, "We're about half-way through our allotted time, and we may want to speed up our discussion in order to end on time." If an agenda item runs over the allotted time, the timekeeper is responsible for helping the team to re-allocate the remaining agenda items within the time frame of the meeting.

FIGURE 2-3   Scribe Form.

Scribe Form

Attendees: _____   Date: _____

_____   Facilitator: _____

_____   Process Observer: _____

_____   Scribe: _____

Absent: _____   Timekeeper: _____

Topic Discussed	Summary of Topic Discussed	Decision/Action to Be Taken	Deadline/Person Responsible	Action Item Completed

FIGURE 2-4   Open Action Items List.

Open Action Items List

Topic	Summary	Action to be Taken	Assigned To	Deadline	% Completed

- Assist in setting time limits for agenda items and breaks.

- Monitor discussion time and alert the facilitator throughout the meeting using time cards to note the amount of time remaining for each agenda item.

- Reorganize time if changes are made to the agenda during the meeting.

- Point out chronic time management problems to the team.

Responsibilities of Process Observer

All of the previous meeting roles focus on getting the tasks completed. Without the process observer, no one really speaks to "how" the team is functioning. The process observer starts from the very first meeting of the team to provide feedback at the end of each meeting about how the team is functioning. High-performance teams often record the process observer's feedback in their scribe notes and regularly check to see that problem behaviors are addressed. The process observer can interrupt at any point during a meeting if a member is doing a "hinder" behavior; sometimes just tapping on the help/hinder list is all that is needed to bring the member back in line. Here are the duties of the process observer:

- Make certain the team adheres to its help/hinder list.

- Observe and report on relationship and process issues for the team.

- Assist the facilitator with identifying members who wish to speak.

- Point out when team participation is breaking down.

- Interrupt the meeting and surface individual/team problem behaviors or hidden agendas that are interfering with the meeting (e.g., using cell phones, interrupting, engaging in side conversations).

- Observe and report on the team's support of agreed-upon rules and protocols.
- Surface team conflicts and aid in their resolution.
- Report on the team's effectiveness at the close of every meeting.

It's often difficult to get new team members to accurately assess their team's performance at the end of meetings. They have a tendency to sugarcoat and qualify problem behavior. To improve the quality of the feedback, we have developed a process observer log (Figure 2-5) that is scored during the meeting and presented by the process observer at the end.

Responsibilities of Coach or Sponsor

Coaches and sponsors often question what their role should be during team meetings. We suggest that they function very much like a sports coach, running along the sidelines, encouraging and guiding, but not playing on the field. The coach or sponsor does not participate in the consensus process. The coach or sponsor has these responsibilities during team meetings:

- Provide direction and coaching.
- Offer information and advice.
- Update the team on appropriate issues (e.g., data, reports).
- Bring in outside perspectives.
- Encourage team accomplishments.
- Reflect on process improvements either performed or needed.

Structuring the Team Meeting

The meeting should start on time with a review of meeting roles and consensus on the agenda. Throughout the meeting, the facilitator and

FIGURE 2-5 Process Observer Log.

Team Meeting Process Observer Log

Item #	Question	Yes 5 pts.	No 0 pts.	Score
1	Did the meeting start on time?			
2	Was an agenda prepared and followed?			
3	Was attendance satisfactory?			
4	Did all discussions pertain to the agenda topics?			
5	Was there an expected outcome for each item on the agenda?			
6	Was the outcome achieved for each item?			
7	Did the facilitator remain neutral?			
8	Was the meeting orderly?			
9	Did we agree on our goal and approach for each item discussed?			
10	Did we make important decisions by consensus?			
11	Did we control negative or counter-productive behaviors?			
12	Did members actively participate?			
13	Did the scribe look for and record action items, deadlines, people responsible?			
14	Did the timekeeper alert the facilitator to time limitations?			
15	Did the coach provide coaching guidance as needed by the team and not "take over?"			
16	Did the facilitator control interruptions?			
17	Were all members engaged & contributing? (circle one) 1 2 3 4 5 6 7 8 9 10			
18	Was the meeting productive? (circle one) 1 2 3 4 5 6 7 8 9 10			

Total Score

Process Observer _____ Date _____

How to use this form:

1) Follow general process observer role requirements.

2) Make sure to note any situations that violate the Help/Hinder list of the team that is under observation. These should be listed in the "Comments" section below.

3) At the end of the meeting, take time to review your notes and answer the questions for items 1–18.

4) If an item is answered with a "yes" then that item is scored as 5 points. If an item is answered as a "no" then that item is scored as 0 points.

5) Add and total the scores. If your score is 100, you had a perfect meeting.

6) Return this form to the _____ after you have completed it. This form will remain in the team's binder and be used to check your team's meeting progress.

7) Based on the individual items, your team can see where their meetings can be improved.

Comments:

_____

_____

_____

the team manage their agenda. Often topics will take more time than expected, and the team will need to decide whether to "borrow" time from another agenda item. Such decisions may seem minor, but they help the team begin to take ownership of their own actions. New, non-critical items that come up are placed on a "parking lot list," which the team reviews at the end of the meeting to determine whether to place them on upcoming agendas. The team must learn to function within the time frame of the meeting and not develop the habit of extending meeting times.

The role of the facilitator is to make it easy for others to participate; a good facilitator "scoops up" quiet people on the team and encourages them by name to participate in the discussion. For each agenda item, the facilitator begins by reminding the team of the desired outcome for the topic, or goal of the discussion, and then discussing with the team how to approach the agenda item. Without clearly defined outcomes, teams tend to allow discussion to wander in many different directions, losing valuable meeting time and frustrating result-oriented team members, who either try to get the team back on track by taking over for the facilitator or withdrawing altogether.

The facilitator works in a "V" design (see Figure 2-6). At the top of the "V," there is wide-open discussion and brainstorming on the topic. As the facilitator gets the halfway reminder from the timekeeper, the facilitator helps the team narrow the discussion to the key points being made. At the bottom of the "V," when the facilitator gets the two-minute warning from the timekeeper, the facilitator starts asking the team members how they wish to bring closure to the topic. If the facilitator senses that the team is ready to make a decision, the facilitator asks if someone would put forth a proposal for consideration. This process of asking for proposals is also critical to the team's development. Team members must learn to move ideas from concept to working proposals. A significant boost to self-esteem occurs when a team member takes ownership and says, "Yes, I'd like to propose that we . . .".

As you can see, the timekeeper actively cues the facilitator (and the team) throughout the meeting. Time is an important commodity and the team must learn to manage its time effectively. Teams are required

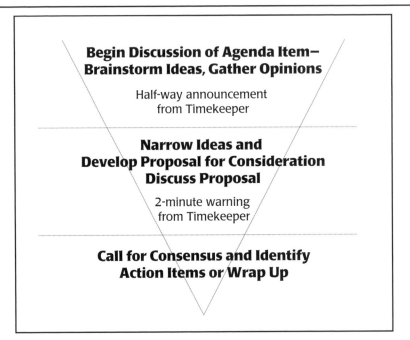

to work within the allotted time frame for their meetings. Learning to manage such a simple task lays the foundation for being able to manage more complex issues later on.

Team meetings should demonstrate a "bias for action." The meeting scribe, therefore, is always on the lookout for actions resulting from the team's decisions. Frequently, scribes will interrupt a meeting to say, "Do we have any actions coming out of that decision?" The scribe ensures that an owner and a deadline are identified for each action item. Whereas teaming is a "we" event, accountability is an "I" event, and every action must have an owner. The scribe role is rotated among the team members, even if the scribe's notes are later handed off to someone else to type up. These days most teams bring a laptop to meetings and type in their scribe notes during the meeting. The team scribe notes identify discussion points, decisions reached, actions committed to, individuals responsible, and deadlines set. It's very easy for the coach or sponsor to review the scribe notes and open action items list quickly to determine whether the "bias for action" exists.

Throughout the meeting the process observer monitors both the positive behaviors of team members and those that need improvement. The process observer summarizes the team's behavior at the end of the meeting, either by referencing the help/hinder list or by completing the process observer log. This team assessment process begins at the first meeting. The team rotates the process observer role among all members and must agree by consensus that the process observer has the authority to interrupt and correct members on their behavior.

The following are the critical process steps in a typical team meeting:

1. Select a facilitator, scribe, timekeeper, and process observer.
2. Review the tentative agenda and gain agreement.
3. Review delinquent or due action items for updates.
4. Discuss agenda topics in priority order.
5. For each topic, agree on the process the team will use to discuss/resolve the topic.
6. Encourage broad participation in the discussion of the topic.
7. Explore alternatives.
8. Summarize the discussion and invite proposals for consideration.
9. Agree by consensus on the best proposal.
10. Decide on actions to be taken; assign tasks, owners, and deadlines.
11. Provide a summary of all action items at the end of the meeting (scribe).
12. Address "parking lot" items to determine whether they warrant inclusion in the next meeting agenda.
13. Summarize feedback on team process/behavior at the end of the meeting (process observer).
14. Schedule the next meeting time, date, and roles (unless done so already).

Facilitating Team Meetings

The role of facilitator is critical to the success of a meeting. A skilled facilitator has the ability to ask just the right question to open discussion and keep the team moving. It is critical for the balance of power that the role of facilitator be rotated among team members.

Here are some general pointers to keep in mind when you facilitate team meetings:

- Remember that every agenda item must have a desired outcome identified, and these outcomes must focus on planning, problem solving, and decision making. Information-sharing items should be moved off the agenda whenever possible.

- Remember that the tentative agenda requires the consensus of the team before proceeding. Change the agenda only when the entire team agrees, not when only one person suggests a revision. If an agenda item does not have consensus, then it must come off the agenda.

- Follow our suggestion that if members volunteer other members for roles or tasks ("Hey, Harry would make a good scribe, don't you think?"), then they get the job themselves.

- Be suspicious of agreements reached too easily.

- Hold people to speaking only for themselves (e.g., discourage generalizations such as "Some people say . . ." and "We all know . . .").

- In tense situations or when solutions are difficult to reach, remember the value of small-team discussion, humor, quick games for energy, affirmation, and silence.

- End the meeting with a sense of gathering together and a summary.

The following phrases provide the facilitator with some useful tools for managing the team meeting:

1. *Get the meeting started.* "Let's review the agenda, confirm the meeting role assignments, and add or delete any items we need to . . ." "Our desired outcome for the meeting today is . . . Does anyone see it differently?"

2. *Encourage communication and involvement of all members.* "Let's go around the room and get everyone's opinion about . . ." "How do you feel about this?" "How would you answer that question?" "We haven't heard from you yet. How do you feel about this?"

3. *Ask team members for opinions and feelings to encourage discussion.* "Do you agree with . . . ?" "What is your reaction to . . . ?" "How do you feel about . . . ?" "Would you say that . . . ?" "We've heard from you already on this topic. Sherri hasn't spoken yet and may want to add something."

4. *Ask for a summary of the discussion.* "A lot of good ideas have been presented in the last half hour. Will someone summarize the major points before we go on?" "I have heard a number of suggestions. Will someone summarize what has been agreed to?" "I think we have gotten off course. Will someone summarize what has been said so far?"

5. *Paraphrase what someone has said to help members understand each other.* "I'm not sure I understand. Are you saying that . . . ?" "What I'm hearing is . . . Is that right?" "It sounds as if you're asking me to . . ."

6. *Ask for specific examples to improve understanding.* "Will you give some examples of what you mean?" "Can you expand on that? I'm not sure everyone understands."

7. *Clarify assumptions.* "Your idea assumes that everyone wants to participate." "Your proposal assumes that unless we use threats, they won't cooperate. Is that right?" "Your suggestion assumes that we cannot meet the deadline. Is that right?"

8. *Ask for explanation in order to eliminate confusion and repetition.* "We have been everywhere with this issue. Can

someone suggest how we might proceed?" "I didn't understand what you were saying. What would you do if . . . ?" "The examples you gave apply to . . . Do they also apply to . . . ?" "It's still not clear to me. What do I do when . . . ?"

9. *Probe an idea in greater depth.* "How about someone offering a totally different opinion?" "What are some other ways to approach this problem?" "Are there other things we should consider?" "What would you add to what has already been said?"

10. *Suggest a break or rest.* "We have been working on this problem for about an hour. I suggest we take a ten-minute break."

11. *Solicit a proposal for consensus.* "We have several ideas here. Would someone like to make a proposal for the team to consider?"

12. *Manage multiple proposals at once.* "We already have a proposal we are considering. Is this an addition to the original proposal or something new? If it's new, let's wait to consider it until after we've dealt with the proposal we're working on now." "Do we need to capture the other proposals on the flipchart in case we need them?"

13. *Move the team toward action.* "What actions should we take to move this forward? What would you do first?" "How would you suggest that we proceed on this?" "I'd like some suggestions on possible ways to get started." "How would you propose we get started?"

14. *Informally poll members.* "How does everybody feel about this?" "How many believe this is an idea worth pursuing?" "Let's ask each member how he or she feels about the proposal."

15. *Encourage open-mindedness.* "I don't think you heard what he was trying to say. It might help if you tell us what you heard him say before you state your objections." "Let's go around the table so everyone gets a chance to comment on this."

16. *Recommend a process.* "I suggest we go around the table to see how everyone feels about this issue." "Would it help

if we put the agenda items in priority order before we start?" "Let's try brainstorming to get some new ideas on the table."

17. *Step out of the facilitator role.* "I feel strongly about this issue and would like to make some comments. Would someone serve as facilitator for a few minutes so I can state my opinion?" "I am the presenter on this topic and would like to have someone else facilitate."

18. *Stop discussion to focus on team feelings.* "Let's take a break from the tasks for a few minutes and have each of us talk about what he or she is feeling right now." "I'm frustrated. I think we should take this problem up next week when we have more facts. How do the rest of you feel?"

19. *Reflect for the team what someone else is feeling.* "I get the impression that you are not satisfied with the answer. Is that right?" "Her comments tell me that she needs to ask some questions on this. Is that right?" "It sounds to me as if . . ."

20. *Get back on track.* "I think we've lost our focus." "How does what we're talking about relate to our agenda item?" "I need help finding a common thread here."

21. *Surface differences of opinion.* "You haven't said so, but it's clear to me that you don't agree. Is that right?" "I'm afraid people are saying what they think others want to hear. What do you think about this?" "You seem to be holding back on this. Is there something here you disagree with?" "I think we're trying to avoid disagreeing with each other. Who would be willing to voice a different opinion?"

22. *Check team progress.* "Are we asking the right question?" "Are these the most important goals?" "Is this the best way to get your support?"

23. *Encourage new thinking.* "Why don't you take the role of a customer for a few minutes? Now, as a customer, how would you react to this proposal?" "Pretend you are the department head for a moment. Would the issues be the same?"

24. *Explore potential results.* "If we did it this way, what is the worst thing that could happen?" "If it doesn't work, what will we have lost?" "If it works, how will it affect our goal?"

25. *Test for consensus of the team.* "Can we identify any areas we still disagree on?" "It seems that we have come to agreement on this issue. Does everyone accept the idea that . . . ?" "Do we have consensus that the best approach is . . . ?" "I sense that we are in agreement. Does anyone see it differently?" "Is this something we can all live with?"

26. *Handle consensus blockers.* "We don't have consensus on this issue. It's an appropriate time for those blocking consensus to share their reasoning and try to offer something they could live with." "Is there a compromise you would like to offer?" "Would you be willing to stand aside if we did this for a trial period?"

—— Handling Specific Team Meeting Issues ——

Absences

Irregular attendance at meetings by team members is very destructive to the team process. The team's efforts and energies are diverted from working on the goals to figuring out how to move forward when members aren't present. Poor attendance is often an indicator of problems with the lack of progress on the team, team conflicts, or lack of management support to release a member to attend meetings.

Absences occur most often when there is questionable commitment from top management for the team process. Dramatic improvements are seen when team members express their feelings of anger and frustration directly to late or absent members.

A team member who must miss a meeting or arrive late should, if possible, contact his or her buddy and ask the buddy to perform any roles assigned to the individual, pick up meeting materials, and schedule a time to connect to review the scribe notes.

If a member arrives late, the facilitator should stop the meeting and ask a member to update the late arriver on what has happened or been decided so far. When this doesn't occur, the member is left in the dark and cannot be an effective contributor. This is a small and subtle courtesy that helps to shape the team's process of caring for and supporting each of its members. However, when many members arrive late, it can be disruptive to those team members who arrived on time and may require team discussion.

Cell Phones, Laptops

It's startling how many times people in meetings answer their cell phones and talk to the caller right in the meeting room. Likewise, there are people who periodically check their e-mails on their laptops or Blackberries while others are talking. These behaviors are rude and should not be tolerated. One time when I was working with a global project team, it took more than an hour to bring this type of behavior under control. When the cell phones started ringing, I asked, "Do we have consensus of the team to take cell phone calls in the room during the meeting?" Of course, the answer was no. Then people started checking e-mails. Again, "Do we have consensus for all of us to check e-mails whenever we desire?" Then team members started walking in and out of the meeting without checking to see if it was an okay time to leave, so I asked, "Do we have consensus for all of us to jump up and leave whenever we want to without checking with the team?" By asking if consensus existed and suggesting that what was good for one must apply to all, the team was able to bring these behaviors under control. It brought to light, though, how difficult it is for some people to submit to the team's authority and not just do their own thing.

Confidentiality

One of the early decisions a team must make concerns the level of confidentiality it wants to maintain. The following guidelines have proven effective:

In Team Meetings

- Topics are designated confidential when discussion of the topic is completed.

- Members will honor any individual's request for confidentiality.

Outside Team Meetings

- Members may share general information about what was discussed but may not make specific references to what any individual said.

- Members will not share specifics about individuals or individual statements.

- Issues and discussions of the team must be reported to the company except when designated confidential.

- Video- or audiotapes of meetings may not be shared outside the team unless permission is granted by the team.

- A breach of confidentiality is a serious offense and will result in team disciplinary action.

- The team will review these rules whenever they become a problem.

Pressure to Fit In

As the team becomes effective and members begin to bond with each other, it's easy for the team to get into a pattern of "groupthink," a term coined by psychologist Irving Janis in 1971.[1] Groupthink emerges as the pressure for team cohesiveness increases. Under pressure to fit in, no one wants to be different from the others. To avoid this weak spot in decision making, it's helpful to build the role of "devil's advocate" or "challenger" into the meeting discussions early on. The facilitator can simply say, "Would someone play devil's advocate and argue the opposite point of view for us?" As the team becomes accustomed to this process, members often enjoy the challenge of having to argue a different point of view.

Guests

Guests are welcome at team meetings as long as the team receives prior notification from the individual who is inviting the guest. The team should have the option of agreeing or disagreeing to the guest's presence at the meeting. At the start of the meeting, the facilitator should introduce guests, present them with a brief summary of the team's tasks, and brief them on confidentiality rules. Guests who are not familiar with the meeting process of the team should be given a brief summary of the roles and what to expect.

Leftover Agenda Items

Especially in the beginning, teams often have more items on their agendas than they can possibly handle in a single meeting. To prevent this from being a frustrating and demoralizing problem, the team may choose to use one of the following strategies:

- Assign each member a leftover agenda item, and ask each one to collect materials and prepare handouts before the next meeting.

- Identify the first step to be taken on an item, and assign an owner and a deadline.

- Have each person complete written comments on the agenda item and copy and distribute them to all members before the next meeting. Have the facilitator organize ideas.

- Keep a running flip-chart list of "other agenda items" to avoid losing track of any of them.

- Limit the agenda to one or two topics, and break down those topics into smaller agenda items.

Icebreakers

Icebreakers are a terrific way to help break down social barriers and show members the things they have in common with each other. They are especially helpful with a large team that meets irregularly. Icebreakers can also be training tools to teach open-mindedness, listening skills, and trust-building behaviors. One reminder here: The ice-breaker should only take about five minutes. Some teams extend this time to the point where it cuts into the working time of the team. Here are some examples of icebreakers:[2]

- *Position in the Family.* Divide the team members by those who were firstborn, middle child, and baby or only child, and ask them to discuss what they liked best and least about their position in the family.

- *Snag Tag.* Have team members walk about the room with one hand on their hip and the other free at their side. At the cue of the facilitator, members "snag" the elbow of a partner until groups of four or five are formed. Members then sit with their new snag partners. This icebreaker is ideal for breaking up established cliques.

- *Getting to Know You.* Ask team members to pair up with another member and have one partner describe to the other partner two physical attributes, two personality qualities, and one talent or skill he or she likes about himself or herself. Then have the other partner do the same.

- *Scavenger Hunt.* The facilitator or meeting SPC can make up a list of ten questions about little-known facts (e.g., "How many red stripes are on the American flag?"), and then work in small groups for ten minutes to find the answers.

- *Bingo Card.* Write something about each member on a bingo-style card. Next have members match the written statement to the person, who then signs the card in the square about himself or herself. The person who gets squares signed in a diagonal, vertical, or horizontal row is the winner.

- *Circle Within a Circle.* Ask each member to develop a list of eight to ten incomplete statements prepared by the facilitator or meeting SPC (e.g., "The thing I like best about this team is . . ."). Then divide the team into two concentric circles that face each other. Ask team members to greet each other nonverbally, and have the facilitator read a statement. Ask a person on the outside circle to answer the statement, with his or her partner closing nonverbally. Then have the outside circle move one person counterclockwise. Continue the process until everyone has had a chance to participate. Debrief the process by having members talk about such things as how they felt or what was the easiest or hardest statement to answer.

Individual Participation

Participation in discussion at team meetings is a requirement for all team members, although the team must be patient in the beginning with individuals who are shy or have difficulty speaking in groups.

If a member has not participated in discussions by the fifth or sixth meeting, the facilitator and process observer (or the coach) may meet with the individual to determine whether something is wrong. The message must be clear: Nonparticipation in meetings is not acceptable. Participation may be encouraged by using any of the following techniques:

- Rotating all team roles

- Sitting in a "huddle" design with everyone around the circle

- Giving members a limited number of an item (paper clips, toothpicks) and requiring "payment" when the person speaks, thereby restricting a few members' tendency to dominate the group

- Passing a baton from person to person

- Brainstorming ideas

- Going person by person around the room soliciting input

- Having small-group discussion prior to all-group discussion

- Asking open-ended questions

- Calling on people directly

- Giving out tasks between meeting assignments

- Using icebreakers

- Using Post-it notes for affinity diagramming and then having members summarize what has been written by others

Interruptions

I was once asked to facilitate the first strategic planning meeting of a nonprofit agency, composed of ten or so very polite people. We opened the meeting by getting volunteers for the other roles and agreeing on the agenda. Everything was going very smoothly until we started on the first agenda topic. Within five minutes, these very polite people were interrupting each other, cutting each other off in midsentence, and talking at the same time. Despite my attempts to regain control, it was hopeless. I finally banged a spoon on a glass to get everyone's attention and said, "Stop! From now on it's the queue for you." They looked at me strangely. I explained that they were to raise their hands (actually just a finger), and I would put them in the "queue" to speak. They reacted with disgust; they didn't need that type of structure and, besides, it would take away their creativity. I relented and let them begin again. Within five minutes it had deteriorated again. This time a team member said, "Maybe we should try the queue." For the rest of the meeting we used the queue—with each member signaling (raised finger or nod of the head) when he or she wished to speak. Afterward, the process observer commented, "We've never had a meeting like this where we actually listened to each other."

The queuing process brings out strong reactions from members who have enjoyed the freedom of jumping in whenever they choose. If they suggest that they'll forget what they wish to say while waiting their turn, just encourage them to jot down a reminder. Then, when their turn comes, they will know what to say.

Premium Pay

On occasion, hourly (nonexempt) employees may question whether they will be paid for time spent at team meetings or team training outside the regular workday. In all cases, nonexempt employees participating on teams should be paid their regular wages for time spent on team activities, including overtime pay, when appropriate.

Physical Setting

Poor physical surroundings deter team effectiveness. Traditional classroom seating, cramped seating that creates two or three pockets of seating, and standing in an informal group for a long time are three formats that don't work. In addition, poor lighting and ventilation, noisy distractions, and a lack of writing space (flipchart, blackboard) can all affect team productivity.

Basically, the meeting space should give the impression of a "huddle," with team members able to see everyone and with the facilitator seated at the head of the table. Many in-house training teams supply meeting rooms with markers, tape, Post-it notes, and flipchart sheets. In addition, they allow teams to hang lists of meeting dos and don'ts and the team's help/hinder list on the walls. A meeting assessment and several meeting tools are available online at www.NewDirections Consulting.com/products.

Time Constraints

In a team structure, the timekeeper reminds the facilitator how much time remains for discussion. When the time remaining is not sufficient to end discussion on an item, the facilitator should ask the team how it wishes to proceed. The team may choose either to continue discussion by apportioning time from another agenda item or to table the item and put it on the next meeting's agenda.

Subteaming

Subteaming (team members meeting informally without the rest of the team) is perfectly acceptable if the purpose is to divide and conquer the tasks to be done. In fact, the team must learn to expedite tasks as efficiently as possible, and assigning work to subteams is the most popular way. A representative subteam can work between scheduled meetings and bring drafts and proposals back to the entire team for consideration.

When a team is experiencing personality conflicts, subteams should never be formed as a means to vent individual frustrations and divide members into cliques.

Tardiness

Tardiness should not be permitted without prior notice to the facilitator. Tardiness, like irregular attendance, usually signifies a problem. When several members are often late or absent, the team may want to search for the source of the problem.

Tardiness is perhaps the most common problem that teams have to confront during their first month or two. Team members may need to be reminded that they demonstrate their commitment to the team, in part, by arriving on time, prepared to participate. Chronic tardiness may be a passive/aggressive response to a deeper problem that the team member has with being controlled or believing he is "in control" by being late.

Team Files

The team is expected to maintain its team electronic folders, whether on a common drive or in an e-room. Team files may contain minutes, memos, reports, proposals, and works in progress. Rules regarding confidentiality and access to team files should be determined by each team at the start of its work.

CHAPTER 3

Team Behavior

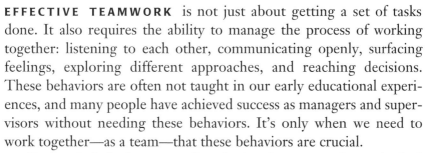

EFFECTIVE TEAMWORK is not just about getting a set of tasks done. It also requires the ability to manage the process of working together: listening to each other, communicating openly, surfacing feelings, exploring different approaches, and reaching decisions. These behaviors are often not taught in our early educational experiences, and many people have achieved success as managers and supervisors without needing these behaviors. It's only when we need to work together—as a team—that these behaviors are crucial.

I'm reminded of a group of professional team members who had come together to work on their data management problems. They sat at the table with their laptops open answering e-mails. Cell phone calls were taken in the room while the meeting was going on; side conversations were commonplace; interruptions were the norm. These people were accustomed to having no boundaries placed on their behavior. It was a "do your own thing" atmosphere, with no one accountable to anyone else.

Teamwork recognizes that we are accountable to each other for our behavior. It's not uncommon for about 20 or 30 percent of the employees involved on teams to struggle and resist the requirement to change their behaviors.[1] Very early in the team process, members must define what will be acceptable behavior and what won't. Inattention to the relationship functions in the team is a primary cause of problems later on and often prevents a team from maturing properly.

Over the course of two decades, we have identified the sixteen behaviors given in Figure 3-1 as critical to team success.

Team Rules of Behavior

Each team begins by developing a help/hinder list (see Figure 2-1), a set of acceptable and unacceptable behaviors that the team agrees to perform. The help/hinder list is designed to:

- Create common expectations of behavior among team members.

- Encourage desirable behavior.

FIGURE 3-1   Critical Team Behaviors.

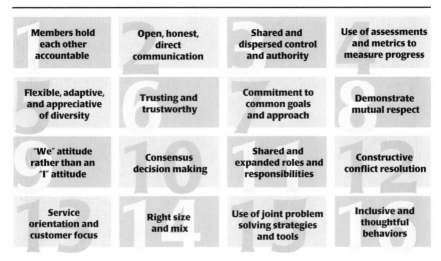

Members hold each other accountable	Open, honest, direct communication	Shared and dispersed control and authority	Use of assessments and metrics to measure progress
Flexible, adaptive, and appreciative of diversity	Trusting and trustworthy	Commitment to common goals and approach	Demonstrate mutual respect
"We" attitude rather than an "I" attitude	Consensus decision making	Shared and expanded roles and responsibilities	Constructive conflict resolution
Service orientation and customer focus	Right size and mix	Use of joint problem solving strategies and tools	Inclusive and thoughtful behaviors

- Enhance the self-management of the team.

- Help new members know what's expected.

- Bring problem behavior back into line.

The process observer role rotates among team members, and the person performing this role is responsible for ensuring that the team adheres to the help/hinder list. The team gives the process observer authority to surface counterproductive behaviors during team meetings and even outside the meetings as the team works. In the early stages of the team's development, the team should review the help/hinder list regularly (every eight weeks). Later on the team should develop an advanced help/hinder list (see Figure 3-2) that builds expectations of even more mature problem-solving and decision-making behavior. The help/hinder list is often laminated and available on the table in front of the process observer at every team meeting. A process observer cannot correct team members on behavior that is not on the help/hinder list. However, a process observer can bring up problem behaviors and ask that they be added to the list.

Behavior Changes

Teamwork becomes particularly difficult when members recognize that they will each have to change some parts of their behavior. The strongest resistance will occur as the day for changing draws closer. Making excuses, procrastinating, blaming, and feigning ignorance are just a few of the stall tactics members will use.

Here are important behavior changes for employees, supervisors, and managers:

Critical Behavior Changes for Employees

- Learning to speak up in groups

- Taking responsibility for one's own thoughts/actions

- Learning to state an opinion and offer a proposal

FIGURE 3-2   Advanced Team Help/Hinder List.

HELP	HINDER
Preparing in advance for team meetings through pre-reads	Assuming a position on a topic before topic is fully explored
Careful allocation of meeting time to maximize actions; focus on planning, problem solving, and decision making	Treating assumptions as if they were facts
	Promoting mental models that are based on assumptions
Demonstrating a "bias for action" in all tasks and processes	Failure to help assist with dialogue and discussion
Successful communication: —listening —asking questions —paraphrasing —inquiry more than advocacy	Saying "no" before thinking "yes"
	Allowing sarcastic or caustic remarks
	Getting too competitive
Open dialogue on issues with active agreement and disagreement as needed	Losing sight of the big picture; focusing too much on "small potatoes"
Contributions to discussion outside of one's own functional area	Drilling down into minutiae
	Giving opinions without facts
Sharing of responsibilities for tasks within and outside the team	Expecting others to over-function
Active intervention if the team is not working effectively; team responds well to feedback	Deferring to "positional power" when truly opposed to an idea (going to Abilene)
Careful prioritization of tasks and responsibilities to manage workload	Failure to deliver on promises and not personally notifying the team if deadlines will be missed
Constant review of goals and approach to make sure team is in agreement —leave meeting at breaks only —call for break if needed	Doing any behavior that would purposefully divide the team
	Giving greater support and interest to one's own functional area over the team and/or the organization
Challenging of group think and "sacred cows"	Any withholding of information that is needed by the team
Excellent facilitation of discussions; team utilizes facilitator to guide meeting progress	

- Receiving and expressing positive and negative feelings
- Saying no
- Responding to criticism
- Making requests of authorities
- Negotiating for something desired

Critical Behavior Changes for Supervisors

- Being willing to share power and responsibility
- Proposing ideas for discussion
- Asking questions instead of making statements
- Listening to others
- Remaining open-minded

Critical Behavior Changes for Managers

- Having the courage to resist recommendations that are not beneficial
- Accepting decentralized decision making
- Believing that everyone has good ideas
- Being willing to implement team suggestions whenever possible
- Recognizing team accomplishments
- Seeing teams as a long-term effort
- Thinking "yes" before saying "no"

A push-pull phenomenon exists as people experiment with new behavior. As much as we might desire a change in behavior from someone else (the push), we resist it (the pull) because the dynamics of the relationship will also have to change if the behavior of a participant changes. For example, if an autocratic, demanding boss gradually learns to be participatory and inclusive, the team members will have to change all their previous assumptions and conclusions about the boss. For whatever reason, most people will hold back, waiting for the manager to revert to the old behavior, and may even try to lure the manager back to the old behavior just to be able to say, "I told you so!"

Expectations of Team Members

In the beginning, team members often develop unrealistic expectations about the team process. They often believe they should be involved in all decisions or have authority to remove their coach. These false expectations and assumptions should be surfaced, discussed, and evaluated on a regular basis to avoid trust issues.

Following are examples of realistic and unrealistic expectations:

Realistic Expectations

- Team members will pitch in and help if asked.

- This teaming process, once started, will never end.

- Everyone in the organization will be affected by the change to a team culture.

- Things will be difficult in the early months of transforming to a team culture.

- Management will have as much difficulty transforming as staff will.

- The new teaming skills will cause feelings of stress, inadequacy, and frustration.

Unrealistic Expectations

- Team members will pitch in and help out without being asked.

- Everything will be great.

- People who were difficult before will transform into effective team members.

- Team members will support each other on every issue.

- Nobody will ever get fired again.

- The team will be able to tell the coach and/or management what to do and whether to attend the team's meetings.

Sometimes the level of misapprehension can be surprising. For example, a financial organization discharged a poorly performing team member and did not anticipate the staff reaction. Apparently, team members had assumed that no one would get fired in a team environment. Although team members had complained about the individual's performance on numerous occasions, they did not expect management to take action. The organization diffused the concern by noting that all team members are accountable for their performance both as individuals and as a team.

Team Member Behavior

Team members are not expected to exhibit perfect team behavior in the beginning. Rather, team members need to show a willingness to explore new approaches. Following are examples of helpful behaviors:

Helpful Member Behaviors

- Participating, contributing ideas, and setting goals

- Relying on and learning to trust other team members

- Communicating effectively

- Sharing and valuing different ideas

- Considering other viewpoints

- Delaying judgment

- Tolerating confusion

- Seeking alternatives that all can agree to

- Supporting and implementing the team's decisions

There are a number of behaviors that are considered counterproductive to any team effort, and these should not be tolerated by either the facilitator or the team. Following is a list of these behaviors and measures a facilitator might use to correct them:

Destructive Member Behaviors

- *Agreeing with everything.* Ask the member to play devil's advocate and express the opposite point of view.

- *Attacking personality.* Redirect the member's focus to a performance issue or problem and away from personal attributes.

- *Being inconsistent.* Seek to clarify all apparent inconsistencies by simply stating, "I'm confused."

- *Binding others' behavior.* Remind a member who says, "You're going to love this idea" to speak for himself or herself; consider trying to surface the "bind."

- *Changing the subject without explanation.* Point out the need to return to the agenda; suggest putting the new topic on the agenda for a later time.

- *Chatting.* Stop noncontributive talking by team members. Consider asking, "Did you have something you wanted to contribute?"

- *Complaining.* Ask the member to express his or her concerns; say that negativity is hindering the whole team and ask, "Do you have an idea?" Give a response and support.

- *Criticizing.* When team members criticize the team or each other behind their backs, they should bring the criticism to the team meeting and discuss whether the criticism is valid, vague, or manipulative. If it is valid, the team can suggest making changes in the way the job is done or the member's behavior. If the criticism is not valid, remind the member(s) that general criticism hinders team progress.

- *Displaying anger.* Stop the process, acknowledge the anger, and ask its source.

- *Displaying superiority/dominating.* Recognize the value of the member's input, and move the process toward involving the rest of the team.

- *Engaging in distractions (doodling, writing memos, doing other work, and making other displays of lack of interest).* Ask the team member for input in order to bring him or her back into the process.

- *Escaping (taking calls).* Ask the member if there is a better time to meet when he or she could give the team his or her full attention.

- *Explaining another's behavior.* Encourage the member to speak only to his or her own behavior or opinions.

- *Frequent head shaking.* Surface the head shaking and ask why the person is disagreeing.

- *Glossing over problems.* Encourage the team to explore difficulties and their causes.

- *Goofing off.* Redirect the member's attention back to the process.

- *Hairsplitting.* Acknowledge that a consensus has been reached, and move the process forward.

- *Interrupting.* State the ground rules, and reinforce members' speaking one at a time.

- *Making decisions without the team's knowledge.* State disapproval of that method; remind the member (or members) about the importance of team involvement in the decision-making process.

- *Misinterpreting (misstatement of ideas or suggestions made by the process observer or facilitator)*. Be assertive about your own viewpoint.

- *Missing many meetings.* Ask the member if there is a problem (too busy or loss of interest) with attending meetings; point out the assets of having the person attend as well as some of the positives he or she has done for the team.

- *Not completing tasks on time.* Ask if other team members can help; give the member a second chance to do the task or allow him or her to back out; talk about accountability.

- *Not doing a job in a responsible way.* Talk to the member and clarify expectations; set quality standards for how the job is to be done by everyone, every time.

- *Not participating in team decisions.* Ask the member if there is a problem and seek the member's involvement in the decision-making process.

- *Not taking the process seriously.* State that each member is expected to value the process enough to spend time discussing the issues.

- *Offering putdowns.* Explore why the member has that point of view; ask the member to contribute information and options, rather than judgment.

- *Prejudging.* Note that a conclusion is being reached before the data are in; acknowledge feelings; seek the member's involvement and input.

- *Pretending not to understand in order to avoid being part of the decision.* Ask the member what he or she needs in order to be able to participate in the decision. Do not allow the member to abdicate.

- *Seeing only one way ahead.* Ask the member to explore other options.

- *Seeking sympathy.* Surface the behavior by asking the member what he or she needs from the team.

- *Solving others' problems.* Encourage the member to let others suggest their own solutions.

- *Speaking in "shoulds."* Redirect the focus to what to do next, given the realities.

- *Talking too much.* Ask the member to state points one at a time. Encourage the involvement of other team members.

- *Volunteering other team members to do tasks.* Ask members to take responsibility for volunteering themselves.

- *Withdrawal.* Ask to hear from members who haven't shared their ideas yet.

One of the classic ways for a team member to resist change or delay a difficult decision is to employ various disruptive behaviors. New teams are particularly vulnerable to this kind of behavior and may need help from experienced teams in managing members' behavior.

Facilitator Behavior

Facilitation skills develop through experience and training. Typically, team members in the facilitator role find the first couple of meetings difficult. One of the benefits of rotating this role is that team members tend to be less critical when they know that their turn to facilitate will come up quite soon. Let's look at some behaviors that facilitators can use:

Helpful Facilitator Behaviors

- *Appearing interested.* Assume an alert body position, demonstrating facial expressions and body gestures that convey an active interest in the team and in the progress being made. Openly listen and pay attention to participants. Be alert to verbal and nonverbal clues in others, such as tone of voice, pauses, gestures, facial expressions, and posture.

- *Confronting.* Confront inappropriate behavior such as interrupting, labeling, or making judgmental statements and responses, especially if an individual's personality is being attacked.

- *Correcting.* Check inappropriate behavior of group members, and reinforce productive behavior whenever possible.

- *Evaluating.* Summarize what has happened in the team so far; evaluate the team's progress.

- *Modeling.* Set the behavior standard for the team; demonstrate trust, openness, and cohesiveness, as well as a goal-oriented focus.

- *Observing the team's needs.* Provide short silences or special activities so that members have time to process information.

- *Offering support.* Reinforce the statements of others by asking open-ended questions and encouraging the tolerance of new ideas.

- *Prompting.* Use questions and comments as a way of stimulating discussion and deeper thought.

- *Refocusing.* Redirect comments to the whole team, especially when a team member's comments are directed at you.

An untrained or inexperienced facilitator may exhibit many unproductive behaviors. Teams typically have considerable difficulty surfacing these behaviors in a group setting; it is better to have the process observer talk to the facilitator in private. If the facilitator happens to have considerable positional power, it is especially difficult to get team members to discuss the behavior problems openly. Here are some behaviors that facilitators should avoid:

Destructive Facilitator Behaviors

- *Arguing with team members.* Engaging in continued conflicts with a team member; repeatedly turning to one team member for support; ignoring suggestions of certain team members.

- *Being too easygoing about the facilitator role.* Being unprepared to facilitate; being late to or missing meetings; being uninvolved with the team, as shown by overly relaxed body language and little or no eye contact.

- *Giving priority to one's own agenda items.* Interpreting others' comments to support one's own agenda; continually changing the topic; suggesting similarities between the team discussion and one's own agenda.

- *Lacking good team manners.* Not updating a late-arriving team member; taking calls or doing other work while trying to facilitate.

- *Letting the team wander for long periods.* Providing no direction or help with closure; not defining the role up front; offering pointless comments, humor, or rambling stories; allowing cross-talk between team members.

- *Manipulating and controlling the discussion.* Making statements such as, "Some teams are . . ." or "Some teams have . . ."; making suggestions without clearly identifying them as such; making "You should" statements.

- *Minimizing the roles of others.* Neglecting others, including the process observer; putting down members; criticizing a member's comments; trying to "one-up" a team member.

- *Neglecting the needs of team members.* Not protecting a team member when he or she is under attack; letting one member monopolize the discussion; not checking that all members have handouts.

- *Putting team members into categories.* Dealing with the member rather than the attitude; always calling on the same members to do certain tasks.

- *Telling the team what to do.* Deciding on the agenda; monopolizing the discussion; offering long-winded explanations and making reference to prior teams; imposing specific solutions on the team.

- *Violating team rules.* Giving a double message of "We're not supposed to but . . ."; selectively forgetting rules.

People typically hesitate to intervene when a facilitator is doing a poor job. However, it is well worth trying to get on track by doing one of the following:

- Have the process observer interrupt and state the needs of the team.

- Call for a break and have several members talk to the facilitator.

- Ask the team to evaluate its progress and provide feedback to all members.

- Have an outside consultant say what team members are not yet able to surface.

Managing Team Conflict

Most people have considerable difficulty surfacing and working through problems and conflicts. They "collect stamps," or little injustices, for long periods of time and use passive-aggressive tactics (triangling, procrastination, perfectionism, stubbornness, sniping) to surface their difficulty. In teams, group conflict cannot be shoved under the rug. Process observers must be empowered by the team to surface conflicts and problems while they are still minor. A simple wave of the help/hinder list has been known to bring problem behavior back in line.

On occasion, members may experience serious difficulty with each other. Personality conflicts or irritable behaviors can undermine the team's efforts unless they are dealt with openly and directly.

Triangling

Triangling (or talking behind someone's back) is when we talk with a third party about something that is bothering us about another person. Triangling is so prevalent in organizations that I often tease that if we had infrared lights on all the triangles going on, the entire organization would light up. We may think that we're talking to the third party for support for our position, but I contend that what we really want is for that person to talk with the person who is upsetting us. Then, when the person says, "I understand that you're upset with me," we can say, "Who told you that?" as a way to keep the focus off of what we have done. People who triangle like to come across as squeaky clean and let others do their dirty work. Triangling is extremely detrimental to the team and must be stopped.

Stamp Collecting

Many team conflicts have been brewing for some time and simply come to a head when there is no longer a supervisor to intervene. I call these old resentments "collecting stamps." A team member experiences a resentment and rather than deal with it directly, she opens her imaginary book of stamps to the page with the individual's name, licks a stamp, and puts it in the book. Then, each time the individual does something wrong, the team member uses the behavior to validate the original stamp. Meanwhile, the other person doesn't have a clue that his colleague has been upset with him for years. After a while, some people develop bulging books of stamps containing all the "bad" things that other people have done to them over an entire work history. These stamps are the seedbed for much of the conflict on teams. Obviously, teams can't function effectively with bulging books of stamps, so they must commit to surfacing old stamps and not collecting any new ones.

One of the advantages of using terms such as *triangling* and *stamp collecting* is that they give the team a common language to use when discussing things that are difficult for them. For example, a team member may approach an individual he is having a problem with and say, "I'm starting to collect a stamp on this and I'd like to talk with you about it."

————— Learning to Give and Receive Feedback —————

When team members are learning how to handle conflict with each other, they need to understand that sharing feedback about how they feel is actually a "gift" to the other team member. We teach them three rules about receiving feedback:

1. *Don't kill the messenger.* There are several ways we "kill" people who are trying to give us feedback: being defensive, blaming them instead, or even ignoring the person altogether.

2. *See the feedback as a gift.* A team member could choose to triangle or stamp collect, so to be brave enough to share the feedback directly is just like bringing a beautifully wrapped gift to the person. When team members can see that clearly, they respond differently when receiving the feedback. Learning how to say, "Thank you for the feedback" is an important step before suggesting that team members handle their own conflicts.

3. *Separate getting the feedback from deciding what to do with it.* When we receive feedback, it's natural to have a fight/flight response. Rather than respond during this emotional phase, team members learn to say, "Thank you for the feedback. I'd like to think about what you've said and get back to you." This delay allows the team member to sort the feedback into three piles: valid feedback, vague feedback, and manipulative feedback. Once sorted, the feedback becomes more manageable for the team member to address. Although the team member has a responsibility to respond to the feedback, nothing says that that response has to be immediate.

Team members also have to learn how to give feedback in a way that minimizes the fight/flight response in another team member.

Rather than make aggressive "you" and "should" statements, team members apply what we call the RISC and PAUSE model[2] to give and receive the feedback.

The acronym RISC stands for:

R = **Report** the facts. When initiating feedback to another team member, the first sentence should be factual: "Yesterday at the team meeting, I suggested we try a different approach and you responded, 'How dumb is that!'"

I = State the **Impact** and why. Here team members are taught to express the feelings they are having as a result of the action that occurred in the Report statement: "It made me feel really upset because everybody laughed at my expense."

Now at this point, the team member pauses to see how the other team member will respond to the feedback. If the other team member apologizes, then the process stops right there. However, if he or she refuses to accept responsibility, then the team member continues.

S = **Specify** what you prefer. The team member makes a preference statement about what he or she would like to see happening instead: "I prefer that when you disagree with my ideas, you simply say that instead of suggesting that I'm dumb."

C = State the **Consequences.** The team member begins with the positive consequences that will happen if the other team member responds to the request: "We're going to get along much better as team members if you can do this." However, he or she must also be prepared to state the negative consequences that will occur if the other team member ignores the request and behaves the same way again: "If you continue to try to embarrass me in front of the other team members, it's important for you to know that I'm prepared to bring it up at a separate team meeting to have us discuss respect and courtesy as a whole team."

As the one team member uses the RISC model to get the first four sentences out in a constructive manner, the other team member uses

PAUSE to help him or her keep defensiveness to a minimum. PAUSE stands for:

P = Paraphrase what you hear: "Let me make sure I understand what you're saying to me. I said at a meeting last week that you had a dumb idea?"

A = Ask questions: "Did I say it in front of other team members or just to you alone?" "What was my tone like when I said it? Was I jesting?"

USE = Use time: "I don't recall the incident that you're relating, but I'd like to think about what you've just said and get back to you."

Prior to any one-to-one conflict resolution among team members, they must have training in how to give and receive feedback in a professional and constructive manner. The RISC and PAUSE model has proven to be extremely easy to use and helpful when structuring the conflict resolution session.

Conflict Resolution Protocol

During the forming stage of the team's development, when members are friendly and accommodating, the team needs to develop a conflict resolution protocol. The protocol spells out how the team will approach conflicts. It's valuable for the team to have this protocol completed before entering the storming stage, when conflict is commonplace.

The protocol begins with defining general rules that team members must follow when conflict occurs:

- It must be understood that the goal of the protocol is to result in a win/win resolution of conflicts.

- All important decisions in the conflict resolution process must be made by consensus.

- A check must be made early in the process to make certain the conflict is appropriate for the team members to resolve.

- Discussion cannot be closed until every party in the conflict has had a chance to speak.

- Talking about the conflict with others outside the team is not allowed.

- Triangling (talking behind somebody's back, which avoids resolution of the conflict) and stamp collecting (holding grudges) during the conflict resolution are not allowed.

- No swearing or yelling is allowed during discussions.

- A private space must be used for conflict discussions.

- When using a mediator, the team must select someone who is perceived by both parties as neutral and has good facilitation skills.

- A team member has the right to seek coaching from another individual with a caution not to triangle (take sides). The emphasis should be on encouraging the member to talk with the other member with whom they are in conflict.

- Team members are to use RISC and PAUSE to facilitate conflict discussion.

The following is a sample four-step method for resolving conflicts within the team. The team must discuss, and agree by consensus, on the method it chooses to use.

1. *Have a one-on-one discussion with the team member with whom there is a conflict:*

- Set up a time to meet with the member privately.

- Open the discussion by surfacing the problem: "I'd like to talk with you about a problem I'm having with something that happened . . ."

- Use the RISC model to share the details of the problem and to speak assertively.

- Allow the other team member to respond to the conflict using the PAUSE model.

If the individual being spoken to shows no willingness to change his or her behavior, or initially agrees but then doesn't change the behavior, then the individual who initiated the discussion has the responsibility of moving to the second step of conflict resolution.

2. *Go back to the individual and have either a second one-on-one or a two-on-one.* (The team decides by consensus which option to elect.) For the two-on-one option, the new member invited to participate is a team member who joins in simply as a listener who can report back to the team that a conversation between the two parties did occur.

- Ask another team member (preferably someone who is neutral) to join the two-on-one dialogue as a listener.

- Set up the time for the three-party meeting.

- Use RISC to speak assertively; express frustration that no behavior has changed since the first conversation.

- Clearly state what is needed in terms of behavior change.

- Allow the individual responding to use PAUSE.

- Close the conversation with an agreement between the parties for the behavior that needs to change.

On occasion, the conflict continues beyond the two-on-one dialogue and requires the intervention of the entire team.

3. *Bring the conflict to the team for resolution.*

- Select a facilitator within the team; this person will remain neutral until it is time for a decision to be made.

- Invite the coach/sponsor to be present, if desired, to listen and encourage a well-balanced process.

- Place the conflict resolution on the team's meeting agenda.

- Set and agree to team ground rules for the conflict resolution session.

- Hear each side of the problem without interruptions.

- Encourage parties to use RISC to speak assertively.

- Identify what needs to happen to fix the problem.

- Make appropriate amends and apologies.

- Identify the agreements people are willing to make to help eliminate the problem.

- Set up a time to revisit the problem to be certain it is resolved.

If the member with whom there is a conflict does not respond to the team's effort toward conflict resolution, it is necessary to move to the fourth and final step.

4. *Refer the situation to the coach or team sponsor for disciplinary or other corrective action according to the organization's personnel policies.* The coach will use the team's written record of the circumstances with the individual to determine how to proceed. The coach will notify the team of the final decision and the requirements placed on the team member; however, the coach will not share the details of the conversation about disciplinary action with the team.

It's important to recognize that team members must be required to seek resolution of their conflicts and that they cannot simply continue exhibiting annoying or disruptive behaviors because they disagree with the other team members.

In-House Team Conflict Mediators

Conflict resolution is such an important yet difficult component of teaming that we have found it helpful to train in-house team conflict mediators to assist team members. Mediators are often members of the in-house training team who already have become proficient in training on conflict resolution. They are then trained on additional skills of mediation to help with informal problem solving, peer and team conflict resolution, and facilitation of peer review boards. The role of team conflict mediator includes performing the following tasks:

- Facilitate conflict discussion; remain neutral.

- Establish an effective conflict resolution environment and approach that supports all parties.

- Maintain the commitment to ground rules.

- Listen carefully and surface different perspectives.

- Assist individuals in working toward a behavioral commitment among all parties.

- Bring in additional resources if needed.

- Ensure that follow-through occurs at regular intervals.

This approach to conflict resolution utilizes a collaborative model[3] that includes:

- Checking for an attitude of resolution among the parties. Have they come to the session with the intent of resolving the conflict?

- Hearing all sides of the issue. This means listening to individuals speak as long as needed to completely vent their frustrations and upsets and not allowing the other person to interrupt and interject during this process.

- Separating the individual and his or her personality from the problem behavior. The person is fine; it's the behavior that may need to change.

- Focusing on common interests, rather than on the things that divide the parties. For example, if both parties are interested in better communication, more trust, and easier procedures, point out the shared goals between them. Often, you'll need to start with basic, low-level shared interest and work your way up to agreement on the tougher issues.

- Exploring for options that will be beneficial for all parties.

- Evaluating the options and selecting the best option for all.

- Generating a written agreement including specific dates for follow-up discussions that is agreed to and signed by all.

Disciplinary Action

It takes a long time for teams to get comfortable with disciplining team members. In union settings, disciplining is typically not an option, because rules for discipline are governed by union agreements. In a self-directed environment, disciplining is usually a phase-three activity, one developed after at least a year of teaming.

The team therefore needs an agreed-upon process that encourages it to handle the discipline before management becomes involved. Throughout the process, it is essential for all members to be treated fairly, with consideration and courtesy; issues should be discussed openly and frankly. Here is a sample ten-step process:

1. The team checks to be certain that the conflict resolution protocol has been followed and that the team member has not responded to the team's requirements.
2. The team facilitator arranges a meeting of the parties to discuss the problem. No meeting should be held until all parties involved can attend.
3. The facilitator has the option of bringing in the coach or sponsor or seeking advice for the team from the coach or sponsor.
4. A summary of the discussion and any decision(s) reached is written up and given to all involved parties as well as to the coach or sponsor; the summary is signed by all. (The summary may be written as a contract to demonstrate the member's commitment to change his or her behavior.)

5. The team member is given a chance to correct the problem behavior.
6. If the team member feels wrongly accused, he or she can either go to the facilitator and request another team meeting, go to the coach or sponsor, or go to the process observer.
7. The team reviews and follows up after fifteen days to see if the team member has stopped the problem behavior. If so, the team recognizes that the team member has improved his or her behavior.
8. If the problem has not stopped, the team sends a written document to the team member expressing its concern and stating clearly what will occur if the behavior doesn't change.
9. The team has the option of recommending that the team member be removed from the team. If the problem behavior continues, the team reaches consensus on its recommendation and refers it to the coach or sponsor for handling.
10. The coach or sponsor reviews the entire process and documentation and typically supports the team's recommendation. At this point, human resources is brought in to arrange for the team member's removal.

It's very important that team members realize that they do not have to be stuck with a difficult, destructive team member forever. The team has the power to remove a team member if it follows a constructive, mature process. During this process, the coach or sponsor is actively engaged in helping to instruct both the team and the problem team member, working for the best outcome for both.

Common Issues in Group Behavior

Certain characteristics that emerge in teams are important to know and understand. These behaviors must be managed for the team to be effective. Teams struggle with issues of trust, power and control, inclusion and status, the need for approval and structure, competition with each other, and degrees of intimacy. Studies in group behavior provide us with some insights as to why these issues are so powerful.

The Majority Effect

The power of peer pressure is a well-established fact. Faced with a majority of team members who agree with a particular position, the rest of the team is likely to adopt that position whether it is right or wrong (Asch, 1956).[4] If a team member takes a dissenting viewpoint and refuses to budge, she risks rejection from the team. The team will dislike the person and make her feel unwelcome. Although we may think that a majority has to be large, research has shown that a majority of three has maximum influence.[5] Teams are most likely to conform to the majority when the task is difficult or ambiguous and members are uncertain about how to proceed.

Anonymity is an important factor in reducing conformity. Teams that allow members to give anonymous answers have shown substantial reduction in conformity.

Encouraging the presence of a dissenter is important for reducing conformity. If another team member joins in with a "me, too" dissent, conformity is significantly reduced. The paradox here is that teams often value unity and cohesion to the extent that different points of view are no longer surfaced. Yet the stimulation of divergent thinking causes people to identify better solutions and improve consensus decision making. When it is known that team members will have difficulty encouraging dissent on their own, it's important to structure dissention so that team members see it as a role, rather than belonging to any one member. However, studies do show that honest dissent by a member with the courage to speak his mind is more powerful than the "devil's advocate" role.[6]

Minority Viewpoint

Studies have found that minorities exert power in quite different ways than majorities.[7] Because they don't have the sheer numbers, minorities must use other strategies. Studies show that minorities must be consistent in their position over time to be persuasive. If they compromise or show inconsistency, they will have no impact. If the dissenter is confident, consistent, and willing to pay a price, others will consider the dissenter's position or at least reconsider their own. Minorities also have greater success doing their persuading in private or indirectly rather than in public. Team members will privately shift position toward the minority when the individual creates a perception of confidence.

Directive Leadership

If a leader is strong, states his or her position at the outset, and appears to have a strong preference for a particular outcome, the team is less likely to consider differing information or solutions. Directive leadership is linked to less information considered, fewer solutions found, discouragement of dissent, and more self-censorship (Flowers, 1977; Leana, 1985; Moorhead and Montanari, 1986).[8]

The Abilene Paradox

Dr. Jerry Harvey coined the phrase the Abilene Paradox[9] to describe the irony when teams take action that nobody wants just to avoid conflict. Everyone fails to communicate his or her true thoughts and feelings, and as a result, the team experiences anger and frustration. Harvey suggests that the issue is truly about the failure to achieve agreement, rather than about conflict. Members experience action anxiety and fear of being labeled non–team players. Overcoming the Abilene Paradox requires team members to be assertive in a group setting and to calculate the risk of taking action versus the risk of not taking action at all.

Groupthink

In 1971, Irving Janis coined the term *groupthink*[10] to describe the phenomenon where team members succumb to team pressure even when it's in direct contradiction to their values and goals. Janis identified eight factors that influence groupthink: an illusion of invulnerability in which team members believe they can't possibly be wrong if everyone agrees; an illusion of inherent morality in which teams believe they will make the morally correct choice; collective rationalization in which members distort information to fit their rationalization for a certain position; peer pressure; negative stereotyping of people who don't fit the mold; pressure for self-censorship of contrary members; mindguarding in which team members withhold information that doesn't support the team's position; and an illusion of unanimity in which silence is treated as agreement and agreement is more important than correctness.

Polarizing

If a team favors a particular position, it will make riskier decisions about that position than as individuals alone. The same is true if a team believes that a team member has done something wrong. If the team members discuss the situation with each other, they will come to believe that the person is even guiltier than they originally thought.

Sharing of Information

According to research, the information that is likely to be shared on a team is information that people have in common. "Unique" information, held by one or a few team members, is less likely to be shared (Stasser & Titus, 1985).[11] There are several ways to break this sampling bias and get people to express information that they uniquely hold. One way is to make them aware of the fact that they hold unique pieces of information. They then are more likely to share it (Henry, 1995).[12] Another way is to assign expert roles (subject matter experts) to individuals based on the fact that they have unique information. Research also suggests that extending the amount of time for discussion will cause people to eventually share unique information (Larsen, Christensen, Franz and Abbott, 1998).[13]

— Problems Experienced by Teams and Coaches —

It's no surprise that problems on a team are not limited to interactions between members. Many times teams have just as much difficulty with their coach. Here are some typical problems that team members have identified with their coaches:

- Incomplete charters with vague information
- Lack of training for the coach
- Coach engaging in triangling with other coaches or a sub-group of the team
- Untrustworthy behaviors
- No buy-in to the goals and approach
- Lack of team involvement in decisions
- Perceived inconsistency in enforcing policy
- Favoritism shown by the coach
- Conflicting production and teaming goals
- Not feeling appreciated by the coach
- Communication barriers and breakdowns
- Lack of team building effort by the coach
- Short-term versus long-term plans
- Not meeting with the team
- Lack of consistent, open communication
- Role confusion
- Coach not visiting regularly in the team's environment
- Cloudy vision
- Coach having too much to do and not enough time for the team

- Providing little or no positive reinforcement
- Not backing the team up when things get tough

We encourage a regular feedback process between the team and the coach to help eliminate or reduce these problems. Problem behavior left unchecked, especially as the team is being formed, will cause far greater problems as the coach releases more and more authority to the team. The trust between the team and the coach is critical for successful teaming.

CHAPTER 4

Team Accountability and Decision Making

SOME TEAMS think that as soon as they're called a team, they have the right to make all the decisions without any involvement of others, including their coach or sponsor. That is not the case. The transfer of authority and accountability is a gradual process that occurs as the team develops and matures. Similarly, decision making begins with small decisions such as when to have meetings and how to rotate star point roles before the team tackles larger and riskier decisions. The negotiables/nonnegotiables chart (see Figure 4-1) that is attached to the team charter defines the boundaries early on for the team. Items inside the box are the areas within the team's authority; items outside the box are areas outside the team's authority. Following are the tools that are frequently used to help the team understand its authority framework. Some of these tools have been introduced in earlier chapters:

FIGURE 4-1   Sample Negotiables/Non-Negotiables Chart.

Non-Negotiables

Team membership

Human Resource
laws, regulations,
and requirements

Safety and
regulatory
requirements

Whether to hold
team meetings

Hiring and other
job-related decisions

Whether to have
Star Point Roles

Selection and
assignment of
coach or sponsor

Negotiables

Meeting agenda content
and meeting role rotation

How to do
process steps

Selection of new
members to
the team

Communication
with the
organization

Job and process
redesign ideas

Training
and other
resources

Changes to team
job duties

Communication not agreed
to by consensus

Work production
requirements

Attendance of coach/sponsor
at team meetings

- Team charter (defines the goal, roles, and responsibilities of the team)

- Completed work breakdown plans for all of the team's goals (identifies specific milestones and tasks for each goal; identifies team member champions with deadline dates, see p. 149)

- Gantt chart (lists all the goals, milestones, and specific tasks to be done, including team champions and deadline dates)

- RACI chart (identifies specific responsibilities and account-abilities)

- Negotiable/nonnegotiable chart (puts the team's boundaries in a clear, pictorial form)

- Coach's hand-off plan (lists specific responsibilities that are handed to the team, when they will be done, and the training required)

- Team measurement system, including scorecards or dash-boards (tracks achievement of deliverables, see Chapter 6)

- Conflict resolution protocol (defines how the team assumes responsibility for the first three steps of conflict resolution)

- Decision-making protocol (defines the process the team will use when making decisions)

Accountability: An "I" Experience

Even though we think of teaming as a "we" experience, the act of assuming accountability is actually an "I" experience. As a result, we try to identify all the opportunities for individuals to be specifically assigned tasks to build their accountability to the team's results. Here are a few examples:

- The requirement of rotating team meeting roles throughout the entire team.

- The scribe recording action items with specific names of team members who assume responsibility for getting tasks done with definite deadline dates.

- The maintenance of an open action items list with names and deadlines assigned. Teams have found it helpful to cross out missed deadlines but not remove them from the list, to illustrate how many weeks something has not been completed. This action drives accountability in the team member assigned to the task.

- The assignment of "buddy" roles, in which each team member has a buddy who is responsible for performing the meeting role, collecting materials, and updating the member when he or she is absent.

- The assignment of star point roles, for both self-directed and cross-functional teams, to distribute accountability for team support tasks to all members.

- The assignment of subject matter experts (SMEs) within the team who have specialized capabilities in certain skill areas.

- The requirement in the conflict resolution protocol that team members go "one-on-one" first when a conflict occurs before going to a coach.

- The individual assessment by team members of how the team is doing and reporting of the results to the team. We use assessment thermometers for this purpose (see p. 164). Each team member marks on the assessment thermometer his or her rating of the team's progress and ideas that he or she has for how to improve. This feedback system is implemented within the first two months of the team's existence.

If a team is not assuming accountability for its actions, it may be worthwhile to examine whether enough "I" accountability experiences are happening daily that will ultimately accumulate into a "we" accountability.

In a virtual teaming environment, managing accountability is even more difficult because members are so dispersed geographically. Quickly distributed scribe notes, open action items lists, and Gantt charts, as well as the use of project managers, help to build more accountability among the members of a virtual team.

The chart in Figure 4-2 uses the four team developmental stages (forming, storming, norming, and performing[1]) to illustrate how accountability is transferred to the team in incremental steps.

FIGURE 4-2   Accountability in Team Development Stages.

Stage Forming	Team's Development	Accountability is transferred when:
Forming This stage lasts 1-3 months depending on how frequently the team meets	Early stage of teaming; superficial friendliness; trust is on a "wait and see" basis	• Team focuses on mastering meeting skills. • Team holds daily "huddle" meetings (10–15 minutes) and weekly meetings (45–60 minutes). • Members rotate meeting roles. • Team members enter agenda items onto the agenda preparation form prior to each meeting. • Facilitator (team member) drafts and distributes agenda; members agree on agenda. • Scribe records action items at each meeting with members volunteering to take on tasks with deadlines. • Timekeeper tracks and signals time allotments for agenda items during team meetings. • Team uses "parking lot" for non-agenda items and assigns members to the issues identified. • Process observer provides feedback to team at conclusion of every meeting. • Team begins to make consensus decisions on easy items. • Team reviews and agrees to charter including negotiables, RACI chart, and hand-off plan. • Team completes all protocols and help/hinder list. • Team assigns star point roles (with back-ups). • Team agrees on buddies who are responsible for doing the work of the member if the member is absent. • Team members generate proposals as part of the consensus decision making process. **Coach/sponsor role:** transfers accountability slowly with time for training and practice; encourages team to make lots of little decisions and recommendations for bigger decisions; requires members to share roles, despite resistance; does much of the reward and recognition for team accomplishments.

FIGURE 4-2   (continued)

Stage	Team's Development	Accountability is transferred when:
Storming Teams can stay in storming for months if they don't have the accountability pieces in place as outlined in the forming stage	Team members express differences of opinion or style which causes conflict on the team; lots of jockeying for control; cliques and triangling are commonplace.	• Team members must follow their conflict protocol which requires one-on-one as the first step toward resolution. • Members are assigned and assume responsibility for tasks on hand-off plan. • Team begins informal team assessments. • Team sets up sub-teams to distribute work with facilitators assigned for each sub-team from among the team members. • Team addresses action items that are delinquent at the beginning of every meeting. • Team continues to hold daily "huddle" meeting to surface problems and reassign tasks; meeting facilitator guides the process. • Team tracks performance measurements on a daily or weekly basis, reporting results to the team and the coach. • Team members build strength in the consensus process by playing the "challenger" role. **Coach/sponsor role:** Ensures that all are taking accountability, even those who don't want to (tendency is to give accountability to the strong ones and let the weak ones stay weak. This must change). Gradually increases the team's authority to make important decisions; confronts belief systems that are not team-based; encourages team to set up reward and recognition plan.

FIGURE 4-2   (continued)

Stage	Team's Development	Accountability is transferred when:
Norming Norming is often a quick stage, especially as team values increasing accountability	Team members really commit to being a team for the first time; agree to follow protocols and norms; hold members accountable	• Team members require each other to use the conflict resolution protocol; they don't tolerate triangling or stamp-collecting. • Star point role rotation begins to occur with back-up moving into the role. • Team conducts audits of its processes being measured; reports feedback on results to the team. • Process observer feedback is much more directed toward problem behavior, including identifying behavior that individual team members need to change. • Team revises goals and work breakdown plans as needed to meet deadlines. • Team assumes responsibility for intra-team relationships. • Members surface dysfunctional decision making issues such as "groupthink" or false consensus. • Members begin cross-training on job related roles. • Team maintains matrix on training requirements and makes certain that members receive appropriate training. • Team rewards and recognizes performance based on guidelines set by the coach. • Team manages all meeting mechanics on its own. **Coach/sponsor role:** Increases the level of authority significantly; often leaves the team alone to run its own meetings; continues to review scribe notes and process observer feedback.

FIGURE 4-2 (continued)

Stage	Team's Development	Accountability is transferred when:
Performing Teams often don't stay in this stage very long because of membership changes which cause them to return to the performing stage	Team is highly competent and highly committed to its performance	• New members are rotated onto the team and existing star point roles orient and train new members. • Team proposes own goals and milestones as it updates its charter and presents it to the coach. • Team develops own work breakdown plans, training plan, and communication plan. • Team conducts extensive team and individual performance appraisals; incorporates corrections into team goals. • Team identifies how it will recognize and reward members; presents budget to coach for consideration. • Team drives continuous improvement among all members. **Coach/sponsor role:** Increases the amount of information being provided to the team (financials, business, customers); mentors members on leadership skills, facilitation skills, etc.; retains veto power on high risk decisions; provides new challenges to spark new development for team members; distributes high levels of authority to the team; encourages team members to attend meetings the coach previously attended.

Team Decision Making

Team decision making and accountability go hand in hand in the teaming process. This stems from a fundamental belief that "we" are smarter together than any of us alone. The team begins to make simple decisions at the first meeting: How will we assign meeting roles? How will we rotate them? How quickly do we want our scribe notes after a meeting? How shall we maintain our electronic team folder? Who should have access? These are all low-risk decisions for the team to make, yet they give the team the sense that they are in charge of their process from the beginning.

Although most teams use the consensus process for making their decisions, a team truly has a range of decision-making options it can use. For example, the team can decide by consensus to authorize a team member to make an autocratic decision, such as what item to buy when talking with a vendor. The team can authorize minority rule by having a few members make the decision in a subgroup. In an impasse, the team can decide by consensus to use majority rule (voting) to help break the stalemate. However, although all of these options are available to the team, the members must decide by consensus to exercise any of them.

The Decision-Making Process

Teams are encouraged to use these five steps when establishing their decision-making process:

1. *Agree as a team on how to approach reaching agreement:*

   - Determine whether the decision is an important yet routine one, where the process is clearly understood, or if the decision is out of the ordinary and needs special support.

- Clarify "what" decision is being made, "how" the decision will be made, and "who" is appropriate to make the decision.

- Make certain that the people involved in implementing the decision share the same goals and are available to work on its implementation.

- Determine the level of authority the team has to make the decision (provide input, recommend, or decide).

- Determine whether the team has the required information.

- Decide whether support and acceptance from others is critical to effective implementation.

- Determine who needs to be informed of the decision.

- Decide how the team will make a fall-back decision if it can't reach agreement.

2. *Gain agreement on the decision-making process:*

- Make sure the correct people are assembled to make the decision.

- State the decision to be made (the goal).

- Share relevant information, including an explanation for why the decision needs to be made.

- State the impact of not deciding.

- Define the criteria to be used to evaluate the decision options.

- Identify the alternative options to be considered.

- Describe the pro and con effects of each option.

3. *Focus on understanding each other:*

- Question whether everyone understands the alternatives being considered and which need clarification.

- Focus on asking questions more than advocating and arguing positions.

- Practice patience to encourage members to communicate with each other.

- Surface concerns early in the dialogue.

- Utilize the role of challenger to explore implications of each decision option.

4. *Work hard to gain true agreement:*

- Invite team members to make proposals for the team's consideration.

- Encourage team members to surface concerns and questions before calling for consensus.

- Work to mitigate concerns before attempting consensus.

- Agree on ideas, or an approach in general, before working on agreement in specific.

- If multiple options emerge, complete a decision matrix (see Figure 4-3) to identify the best options rather than repeatedly argue specific options.

FIGURE 4-3   Sample Decision Matrix.

list your own criteria here

Decision Options	Easy to Implement	Cost High/Low	Team and Mgmt Support	Total Score
Option A	Yes (3)	High (1)	Some (2)	6
Option B	No (1)	Low (3)	Yes (3)	7
Option C	Yes (3)	Low (3)	Yes (3)	9

Weak = score of 1   Moderate = score of 2   Strong = score of 3

- If no option emerges as a clear winner, work to identify a combined option or new alternative that the team can support.

- Allow modifications of the original proposal if the originator of the proposal agrees.

5. *Take action, monitor, and follow-up:*

- Record the team's decision in the scribe notes.

- Establish the action items, owners, and deadlines.

- Monitor the decision to determine whether it has worked as planned.

- Perform a "lessons learned" session to discuss the decision-making process and whether any improvements are needed for next time.

- Add recommendations for improvements to the decision-making process to the team's decision-making protocol if appropriate.

The decision-making protocol spells out the team's decision-making structure by defining the following:

- The number of team members required to be present for important (strategic) decision making

- The number of team members required to be present for all other decisions

- How an absent member will register an objection to the team's decision and within what time frame

- The possibility of participation in decision making in absentia, provided that the member has been part of the discussion in earlier meetings

- The rules of consensus and the method to be used for showing consensus (discussed in the next section)

- The rules for blocking consensus and introducing stand-asides

- How the team will decide when to use forms of decision making other than consensus

- How the team will break an impasse if one occurs

- Under what conditions the team will reconsider a previous decision

Visit www.NewDirectionsConsulting.com/samples for a sample decision-making protocol.

Consensus Decision Making

Consensus decision making is a fundamental belief that "you see something I can't see." To illustrate this in training, I have participants read a simple sentence and count the number of *F*'s they see:

Feature films are the result of years of scientific study combined with many years of experience.

Invariably, some see only three *F*'s, some see four, and some see six (six is the correct answer, in case you missed a few). Many times in training, only a few people see the correct answer, with the majority seeing the wrong answer. I mention to them that if they had voted, the correct answer would have been lost. That's the important point of consensus: Sometimes others see what we can't see and it's to our advantage to explore what they see—because they might be right. In teams, we try to avoid voting or any decision-making process that divides the team by leaving some members winners and some losers. There are other key points to mention as we begin our discussion about consensus:

- Consensus is about agreement and support. Therefore, it's wise to use consensus when we know we'll need the buy-in and support of team members and others.

- Consensus treats silence as disagreement, not agreement. Most groups have a very laid-back decision process: A member suggests an idea, a couple of people nod their heads, and a decision is made. If you don't say anything, it's assumed you're in agreement. We know from experience that silence rarely means agreement and that ownership and accountability occur when we require every member to express his or her commitment to the decision.

- Consensus works well when the size of the team is reasonable. As the team gets larger, consensus becomes almost impossible. When the team reaches about forty people, it makes sense to use the concept of "supermajority" or two-thirds of the members agreeing by consensus.

Here are some basic rules of consensus:

- Each member must feel he has been heard and understood by the rest of the team. This requires the facilitator to "scoop" people into the discussion before calling for consensus.

- Each member must be able to "live with" the decision or solution. It may not be the member's favorite decision or the one she proposed, but she is willing to accept it for the sake of the team.

- Each member must be willing to commit to his role in carrying out the decision or implementing the solution.

- Each member must agree to support the consensus decision "outside" the team. This eliminates the "meeting after the meeting" when people gather to discuss how they really feel.

- Everyone must use an agreed-upon signal to indicate consensus. The signal may be a thumbs-up, indicating "I'm in consensus"; a thumbs-sideways, indicating "I need more time to discuss"; or a thumbs-down, indicating "I block the consensus." Team members may also raise three fingers, two fingers, or one finger to indicate these positions, respectively, or use pencils at different positions. The key here is that every team member must make a clear signal so that the facilitator can determine whether there is a consensus agreement among all members.

Our culture is not practiced in the art of consensus. Most people become very impatient with the time and energy required to look for answers that are acceptable to everyone. They would rather use majority rule and risk the noninvolvement, and even potential sabotage, of the minority.

The attitude and spirit of a team that has achieved consensus are markedly different from those in groups that vote. A team can "feel" consensus when it occurs, and the energy generated is well worth the struggle of achieving consensus. Not every decision made by a team, however, requires consensus. Use consensus decision making in the following situations:

- The issue being considered is an important one and the unity gained is worth the time.

- A sense of synergy among team members is a priority.

- A number of alternatives and courses of action should be explored and considered.

- It's important to explore as many facets of an issue as possible.

- The solution to a problem creates new problems.

- The process for reaching the decision is as important as the decision itself.

- The delay caused by the process of reaching consensus will prevent the team from jumping to conclusions about a problem.

- The decision is final.

Consensus Guidelines

Figure 4-4 details the step-by-step process of working consensus on the team. It begins with a team member or the facilitator stating a proposal for the team to consider. Before calling for consensus at this point, the facilitator asks for any questions or concerns. It is important to encourage concerns at this time in order to prevent a member from blocking the consensus later on. As concerns are raised, all team members work to mitigate the concerns; often this is done by modifying the original proposal. Modifications are welcome as long as agreed to by the proposal's originator.

When all of the concerns have been addressed, the facilitator is ready to "call for consensus on the proposal." The facilitator does not indicate his or her position, in order to maintain the sense of neutrality in the role. However, if a facilitator has difficulty with a decision, he or she would be expected to present the objections prior to the call for consensus. On occasion, a facilitator may need to "hand off" the role of facilitator to another team member, because of the difficulty in engaging in discussion while remaining neutral.

Developing Stand-Asides

When a team is experiencing difficulty reaching consensus, it's effective to ask the team to develop "stand-asides," or modifications that would help the team reach consensus. These are the most common stand-asides:

- Setting a trial period for testing the decision and its implementation

- Not requiring the team member to work on a given task

- Recording the dissenting viewpoint in the scribe notes

- Stipulating that the decision does not set a precedent and therefore cannot be used as a basis for future decisions

FIGURE 4-4   The Consensus Process.

1. **State the Proposal**	"We have a proposal before the team to do X" or "Would you restate your proposal for the team so we all understand it?"
2. **Surface Concerns**	"Are there any additional concerns or questions that people have before we call for consensus?"
3. **Address Each Concern/Question**	"Let's list each of the concerns/questions and see if we can address each one before proceeding."
4. **Call for Consensus**	"Let me restate the proposal now that we have addressed the concerns. We have a proposal to do X. Is there consensus on this proposal?" (Team members show their consensus signal).
5. **More Discussion (thumb sideways)**	"We do not have consensus. There is a request for more discussion. Let's open up the floor to more discussion."
6. **Block (thumb down)**	"We do not have consensus. We need to either surface other concerns or explore if there is a philosophical or values difference. Who would like to open discussion?" (At this point, the blocker is expected to surface his/her concern without being identified by the facilitator.)
7. **Stand-Aside**	"We are still struggling with some basic philosophical issues. Would someone like to propose a stand-aside? Would it make sense to try the proposal for 30 days and then have more discussion?"
8. **Second Call for Consensus**	"We have incorporated our stand-aside into the proposal. Do we have consensus to proceed with X?"
9. **If Second Block**	"We do not have consensus. We have addressed the concerns and philosophical differences. We may need to explore our personal needs. Let's discuss how personal needs might be interfering with our ability to reach consensus and see if we can resolve any personal issues. (Again, the blocker is expected to surface his/her concern without being identified by the facilitator.)
10. **Third Call for Consensus**	"We have addressed our concerns, philosophical issues, and personal needs and are now ready to consider the proposal. Do we have consensus to do X?"
11. **Consensus**	"We have consensus to proceed with X. Let's get the decision down on our scribe notes. Are there any action items coming out of this decision?" "Who will own them and what are our deadlines?"
12. **If Third Block**	"We still do not have consensus. It is best at this point if we take a break and then explore a different proposal. (Typically, the team would not continue past three blocks of the consensus.)

Blocking Consensus

Every team member has the right to block a decision if he or she can't live with it. If a member blocks the decision, the team cannot go forward. This aspect is one of the critical differences between consensus and voting. Let's say a proposal for "option A" is on the floor for discussion and one member blocks the consensus. The blocking member and the team must try to identify an "option B" that will be agreeable to all team members. This is where the notion of "you see something I can't see" comes in. We accept that the blocking member sees some difficulty with the decision that we just can't see. That's why there are rules for blocking—both for the blocker and for the team. The blocker must:

- Have participated fully in discussion prior to blocking.

- Consider the needs of the whole team in addition to his or her own needs.

- Clearly explain the reasons for blocking the decision without prompting from the facilitator.

- Try to offer an alternative or a compromise; advanced teams require the blocker to offer an alternative.

The team must:

- Not be afraid to challenge the blocker to ensure that the reason for the block is clearly explained.

- View the block as an opportunity to explore other options, rather than as a problem.

- Use stand-asides to make the agreement more acceptable to the blocker.

- Critique the block, not the blocker.

- Avoid taking blocking personally.

- Avoid body language that might appear hostile to the blocker.

Resolving an Impasse

On occasion a team reaches an impasse during the decision-making process. In the team's decision-making protocol, it will have addressed what to do at that point in time. Typically, a team will make several attempts to reach consensus by doing the following:

- Break the proposal into sections; reach agreement on each segment, one at a time.

- Review the criteria and standards; determine whether anything can be changed.

- Let those team members most affected by the decision decide.

- Allow the SME to make the decision.

- Ask the coach to break the impasse.

- Resort to voting.

- Adjourn and "sleep" on it.

Whatever route the team takes, it must decide by consensus to take that action. If the team can't reach consensus on the action, then the proposed decision dies.

Best Team Decision-Making Behaviors

There are six behaviors that the best teams use when making decisions:[2]

1. *Ask many questions and avoid positioning.* Team members must ask positive, provocative questions rather than take sides or defend a position.
2. *Develop multiple alternatives.* Team members need to develop at least three options for the team to explore. That way if the option chosen doesn't work, the team can go back to earlier options to get started again.

3. *Test all assumptive statements.* Team members need to become adept at distinguishing between things people say that are truly facts and things they say as if they were facts but are actually assumptions. Those assumptions should be tested by having a team member say: "How do we know that? Where are the facts?"

4. *Identify well-defined criteria.* Prior to making any decision, the team must develop the criteria it will use to determine whether a choice is a good one. A decision matrix is an effective tool for doing this (see Figure 4-3). This tool allows the team to score each decision option according to the criteria.

5. *Encourage challenge and debate.* Early in the team process, it helps to identify one or two members to play the role of "challenger" so that healthy debate exists for all the options.

6. *Use a fair process.* When people don't feel a process is fair and the decision has already been made, they begin to "vote with their feet" and miss team meetings. Research shows that when members feel the decision process is fair—even if their preferred choice is not selected—they will support it.[3]

What Impairs Team Decision Making?

The biggest problem for teams in decision making is the effect of errors in the way the team processes information, or what is called cognitive biases. Experts identified these biases with the space shuttle *Challenger* accident in 1986 and again with the Mount Everest mountain-climbing tragedy in 1996.[4] Both teams experienced these common biases in their decision making:

- *Sunk Cost Effect.* This is a tendency to increase the level of commitment to a particular course of action based on the amount of time, money, or energy that has already been invested. The more emotionally involved a team is in a particular solution, the less likely it will be to change course, even when warranted.

- *Overconfidence in Their Own Judgment.* People are typically overconfident about their ability to make the correct decision and, as a result, ignore important contrary information.

- *Recency Effect.* The team places too much emphasis on information or evidence that is easily available or recent in its experience.

- *Team Effectiveness.* Failure to discuss previous mistakes, exchange information freely, and challenge viewpoints and assumptions are common problems with ineffective teams. When the team's psychological safety is low, members withhold vital information that will affect the team's decision making.

- *Complex Interactions and Tight Coupling.* When things that are unexpected or difficult to understand happen and there is little slack in the time line or system, the problem in one area will trigger a problem in another area. No team is immune from the actions of other surrounding teams. Team decisions under these conditions can often result in serious errors.

Several counter-strategies can help the team address these biases:

- Break the typical rules of protocol and allow more open-ended discussion.

- Teach team members to listen generously to others.

- Bring in outsiders to avoid the isolation and insularity of the group.

- Use the role of challenger or critical evaluator to bring new information to the team.

- Avoid a too-directive approach that shuts down dissent and debate.

- Craft propositional statements ("what ifs") to generate energy and excitement.

Sometimes people question the value of spending so much time having a team reach consensus. It's clear that they haven't seen the results that emerge from a true consensus decision. People are smiling and talking freely, and their eyes are lit up. No negative talk occurs outside the meeting or in the halls or bathrooms after the decision. Some people look at the speed at which a group votes, and if it's quick, they call it decisive decision making. If only we could measure the lost energy, the decrease in motivation and drive, the bitterness and resentment, and the extra time and energy spent dealing with the resistance. The time spent on consensus would then seem cheap.

CHAPTER 5

Team Problem-Solving Process and Tools

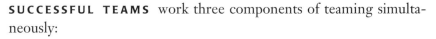

SUCCESSFUL TEAMS work three components of teaming simultaneously:

1. *Task:* getting tasks done and producing results through goals, work plans, and timelines
2. *Process:* managing processes such as meetings, information sharing, problem solving, and decision making
3. *People:* blending the skills and knowledge of members to create something that is better than any individual could create alone.

Effective problem solving tests all three of these capabilities on the team. When the team is clear about the problem to be solved, has process skills to implement an effective approach, and draws on the talents of members, the probability of effective problem solving increases dramatically. With the advent of Six Sigma and Lean, the need for problem-solving capability on teams has significantly increased. Kaizen events, Journey to Excellence teams, and Six Sigma projects all use teaming as a foundational tool.

However, most team members dread the idea of trying to solve problems as a whole team. They anticipate that a few people will dominate and argue, that the problem will never be clearly defined, and that the solution chosen will be the one that's easiest to implement. Let's face it, the skills of effective group problem solving were not taught in school. When asked in training how they learned to solve problems growing up, most team members respond that they cheated, memorized, waited for the smartest person in the class to answer, thought of an answer that sounded good, used an encyclopedia, asked the teacher something else and hoped he or she would forget the question, or asked a smart friend. Yet one of the true benefits of teaming is the synergy created when talented minds create an idea or approach that no one person would have suggested alone.

Here are the most common problems with team problem solving:

- Not knowing how to organize a process to tackle problems effectively

- Attacking problems that are too vague or broad or symptoms of other problems

- Being confused about the goal and never reaching agreement on the goal

- Jumping to conclusions and solutions rather than taking the time to analyze data

- Not gathering enough or the right data or knowing how to evaluate the information

- Not involving the people who will be impacted by process changes in solving the process problems

- Rehashing information and revisiting decisions

- Not considering "out of the box" ideas

- Not adequately planning out the implementation

- Not evaluating whether the solution is working

- Not gaining the support of management early in the process

- Not processing "lessons learned" to improve for next time

——— A Simple Problem-Solving Approach ———

Most teams need to have a common problem-solving approach that they can use over and over to the point that it becomes automatic for them. The approach presented here is a hybrid from numerous quality problem-solving approaches based on what, from our experience, works most effectively with teams:

1. *Find the problem to work on:*

   - Brainstorm a list of problems to work on, select one by using prioritization dots (see page 134), and draft a clear statement about that problem.

   - Identify the impact of the problem in terms of failure costs: How much is this problem costing us in terms of delays, rework, and upset customers? This is used as a check to make sure that the team is working on a problem that has substantial impact on failure costs.

   - Draft a statement of the SMART goal to be achieved when the problem is fixed.

2. *Analyze the problem:*

   - Identify the assumptions being made about the problem. We teach teams about Chris Argyris's Ladder of Inference[1] to surface assumptions (see page 137). It begins with a small piece of data, to which the team adds meaning, expands that meaning to an assumption, forms a conclusion, and develops a belief. Based on that belief, the team takes action that often perpetuates the original problem. Requiring the team to list its assumptions about the problem is a very enlightening experience.

- Identify the data needed to test whether the assumptions are true.

- Identify any other data needed to understand the problem more fully.

- After the data are collected, synthesize the data into a clear understanding of the root causes of the problem. Fishbone diagrams and interrelationship diagramming (see pages 143–144) are helpful tools at this point.

3. *Develop and select a best solution:*

- Identify the criteria to be used for selecting a solution, and weight the criteria and what an acceptable score would be. For example, if the team uses five criteria and a five-point scoring scale, the top score would be 25. The team should identify how low a top idea can score as well. Even though an idea scores a top score of 12, it's not a high enough score overall to proceed.

- Generate at least three solution ideas. Teams benefit from having more than one solution idea considered. If the first idea falls through, they have two or three more they can continue to explore.

- Give voice to both pro and con arguments for each idea to avoid groupthink.

- Score each idea against the team's criteria to surface the top idea.

- Reach consensus to go forward with the top idea.

4. *Execute the solution idea to solve the problem:*

- Define a specific goal for problem resolution including a deadline.

- Create a work breakdown plan (see page 148) that spells out the milestones or "buckets of work" that must be accomplished to solve the problem. Identify an owner/champion for each bucket and specific time frames for completion.

- Capture all deadlines on future team agenda prep forms to discuss progress and difficulties.

- Complete a RACI chart (see Figure 1-1) showing responsibility and accountability for solution implementation.

- Develop a Gantt chart (see Figure 6-1) to track all tasks associated with the solution plan.

- Assign subteams to complete specific buckets of work if needed.

- Develop a method to monitor and measure whether the solution is working.

- Establish a corrective action plan if the solution idea is not effective.

A manufacturing team was experiencing a tremendous problem when the shutdown of one facility meant that all the parts and equipment would be moved to another plant. Instead of five days of inventory on the dock, the number of days of inventory was climbing to seventeen. As they started to work on the problem, everyone immediately offered solutions. I asked if I could facilitate and show them a better way to work on the problem. Using the model presented here, it took approximately forty-five minutes to work through each step and have a plan in place to present to senior management. One continuous improvement engineer commented, "I knew about these tools but I never thought we could use them in forty-five minutes; I always thought it took days."

For each of the problem-solving steps, there are specific tools that speed the process and keep the team unified in its approach. Visit www.NewDirectionsConsulting.com/products for more information on these tools.)

—— Team Skills Required for Problem Solving ——

The skills needed for effective problem solving don't develop overnight. All of the small activities done with the team in the beginning lay the foundation for later problem-solving competencies. The team must be able to demonstrate the following:

- Hold effective meetings and brainstorming sessions.

- Recognize and accept constraints (i.e., time, money, resources).

- Identify available resources prior to determining the plan.

- Separate facts from assumptions.

- Question assumptions openly and effectively.

- Discuss and assess uncertainties and risks.

- Develop SMART goals.

- Identify relevant sub-objectives.

- Discuss constraints and forces working against the objective.

- Generate new ideas and show interest in others' ideas.

- Delay judgment of others' ideas.

- Work a process rather than complain about a problem.

- Recognize and accept solution criteria developed by the team.

- Explore "outside the box" thinking.

- Focus more on the organizational goal than on a personal agenda.

- Seek outside resources if solution ideas are inadequate.

- Use the tools of consensus to come to team agreement.

- Think creatively to modify potential solution options.

- Surface and resolve interpersonal conflicts.

- Understand the influence of personality and learning styles on problem-solving approaches and preferences.

- Use appropriate problem-solving tools to facilitate effective teamwork.

———— **Gathering Ideas to Find the Problem** ————

One of the strongest reasons for putting together a team is to utilize the minds in the room to generate ideas. However, many of us have seen seemingly bright people sit in a team meeting and say nothing. How do we get them to open up and contribute? People often worry that if they offer ideas others will quickly judge their ideas as stupid and worthless. So we have to bypass the worry about judging by creating an atmosphere that doesn't allow critiquing in the early stage of generating ideas.

Round-Robin Brainstorming

Round-robin brainstorming allows the offering of ideas from each team member without others making comments or criticisms until the end of the session. The session has an "anything goes" atmosphere, which helps maintain the tempo. A topic is chosen for discussion, and then team members take turns giving ideas about the topic (only one idea is allowed per turn). Team members are allowed to pass if they have no idea to give during a turn. Each idea is recorded on a flipchart or blackboard list so that everyone can see the ideas. Ideas continue to flow until everyone has said "pass" or until it's time for the brainstorming session to end. At the end of the session, team members are given the opportunity to ask questions and offer comments or criticisms about the ideas generated.

The slip method of brainstorming is particularly effective when team members are hesitant to say their ideas out loud. At the end of round-robin brainstorming, slips of paper are distributed and team members are asked to write down any remaining ideas that they might not have mentioned already. All of the slips of paper are collected, the ideas are written on the flipchart, and the papers are torn up so no one knows who suggested what. The slip method always yields another batch of ideas that people were too shy to say out loud.

Brainwriting

Brainwriting[2] is particularly helpful when members are not comfortable with the speed of brainstorming or when the issue carries some conflict.

Here's an example of how brainwriting works. A team of real estate agents was struggling with the problem of vacation scheduling. The agents had spent several hours listening to each other's point of view but getting no closer to a solution. Brainwriting allowed them to focus on the question: "How can we solve the vacation schedule problem?" They generated more than twenty-five ideas in ten minutes and reached a solution by multivoting (see page 134) to determine which choices everyone liked best. Use the following steps for brainwriting:

1. Distribute a piece of paper with fifteen squares (five rows of squares with three per column) on it to each member.
2. Have each member write down three ideas and put the paper in a center pool.
3. Ask each member to draw a new paper from the pool and add three more ideas that are either new or expansions of ideas a team member has already put on the paper.

4. Have members exchange papers until each member's paper is nearly full.
5. Have members read aloud (in round-robin fashion) the ideas on the papers (members should cross out ideas that are repeated on their own paper).

Affinity Diagram

An affinity diagram is particularly useful when a team wants to generate ideas and group or order them according to some organizing principle. Affinity is very effective with larger groups or when the topic offers a wide variety of choices that require categorizing. For example, a diverse team is discussing improvements in customer service. The discussion grows disjointed, with lots of ideas flying in different directions, many apparently at odds with one another. An affinity diagram can help organize the discussion and keep the team unified.

Follow these steps to create an affinity diagram:

1. Distribute Post-it notes and felt-tip markers to all team members.
2. Write the topic on a flipchart sheet and ask members to generate ideas and write them on their Post-its.
3. All at once, have members go up and put their Post-its on the flipchart sheet. If there is a large group, have the members go to the flipchart in "waves" of five or six people.
4. Have the team sort the Post-its into groups or categories and label each category. Some people recommend that this be done in silence, but it also works when team members talk with each other about the sorting and categorizing.
5. Place those Post-its with similar wording directly on top of each other and those worded differently one after the other to create a group of like things.
6. Look for patterns: Which category has the largest number of Post-its? Which the least?
7. Prioritize the categories (use dots to prioritize if this is deemed important).

Team members "grow into" the idea generation process. They may have stopped sharing ideas because of negative responses from a supervisor or manager and may need to test the water with fairly benign ideas before they feel comfortable taking any significant risk.

Prioritizing Ideas

There are several techniques for narrowing ideas into priorities. They include prioritization dots, multivoting, and nominal group technique (NGT).

Prioritization Dots

Using round, colored "dots" or stickers (available at most office supply stores) with prewritten points on them is a very quick method of prioritizing.

1. Select rows of red, blue, yellow, and green dots. Distribute 10 points on the dots (e.g., red has 4 points, blue has 3, yellow has 2, and green has 1).
2. Give each team member a set of dots with 10 points to distribute.
3. Tell team members they can distribute their points any way they'd like. They can put all 10 points on one idea or they can put each of their points on a different idea.
4. After the team is done "dotting," count the points on the dots. The highest-scoring item has the highest priority.

Multivoting

Multivoting is used to narrow the number of items for consideration:

1. Have each team member vote for as many ideas as he or she likes.

2. Circle the ideas that get the most votes.
3. Consolidate the remaining ideas where possible.
4. Have each member vote again but this time for only half the number of ideas that are circled.
5. Continue with multivoting until the list is down to at least three—but no more than five—ideas.

Nominal Group Technique

The purpose of NGT is to provide a way to give everyone on the team an equal voice in selecting problems. It is called nominal group because of the limited discussion and participation involved in the procedure. The steps in the process are as follows:

1. Have the team generate a list of items that need prioritization.
2. Have the team number the items and ask members to write the numbers on a sheet of paper. For example, if there are five items, members would each write the numbers 1 through 5 on a sheet of paper.
3. Have the members decide the priority of each item and write the priority next to its number on their paper. For example, item number five might be given third priority.
4. Have the facilitator write the list of items on a flipchart and then draw columns to write in each team member's numbers. Then ask the facilitator to total each item horizontally to determine which has the lowest score among all team members; in this case the lowest score wins (see Figure 5-1).

Analyzing Ideas

Ladder of Inference

Chris Argyris first introduced the Ladder of Inference in 1990 as he explored the idea of Mental Models, or patterns we establish that can

FIGURE 5-1   Nominal Group Technique Chart.

Items for Prioritization	Henry	Clara	Sid	Hong	Total
Item 1	5	5	1	4	15
Item 2	3	4	4	3	14
Item 3	2	1	3	3	9
Item 4	1	2	1	1	5*
Item 5	4	3	5	5	17

* lowest scoring item therefore highest priority of the team

keep us locked in our current mode of thinking.[3] Here is how the ladder (see Figure 5-2) is used with teams to help surface assumptions:

1. Have each team member draw a ladder with five rungs on a piece of paper. Each team member will go up his or her own ladder, putting a piece of information on each rung.
2. Have each team member identify a piece of data (real or imagined) that stands out about the problem and write it on the bottom rung.
3. Have team members determine the meaning given to the problem based on the selected data and write this on the second rung. For example, let's say the data selected is that four of the last eight tasks given to the team haven't been completed on time. The meaning team members might give that information is, "People don't want to do the tasks."
4. On the third rung, have team members write the assumption that is made given the meaning that was added. One assumption for our example might be, "People don't want to be on the team and that's why they're not doing the tasks."
5. On the fourth rung, have team members write the conclusion they draw from the assumption. One conclusion for our example might be, "People just don't care what happens around here at all."

FIGURE 5-2   Ladder of Inference.

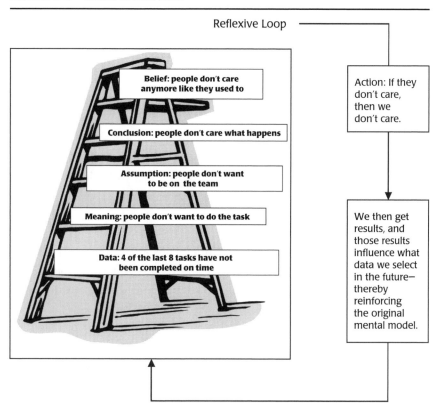

Reflexive Loop

Belief: people don't care anymore like they used to

Conclusion: people don't care what happens

Assumption: people don't want to be on the team

Meaning: people don't want to do the task

Data: 4 of the last 8 tasks have not been completed on time

Action: If they don't care, then we don't care.

We then get results, and those results influence what data we select in the future—thereby reinforcing the original mental model.

6. On the fifth rung, have members write the belief they have formed as a result of the conclusion. One belief for our example might be, "People don't care anymore like they used to." Note how much larger this has grown since the first rung on the ladder. Based on the Argyris ladder, we take action based on our beliefs. One action for our example might be, "Don't invite people to be on teams if they don't even care anymore." This is called the reflexive loop, where our actions actually serve to reinforce the original problem.

I used this exercise with a management group and a union group that were trying to improve their relationship with each other. Each group was complaining about the number of assumptions that the other group had about it. I asked each group to list all of the assumptions it thought the other group had about it. I then unveiled the two lists of assumptions, and to everyone's surprise, the lists were identical. This breakthrough allowed the groups to start truly talking with each other and moving forward.

Process and SIPOC Mapping

Once the assumptions have been identified and explored, data on whether the assumptions are true need to be gathered. What other data are needed to solve the problem also need to be identified. It's helpful for the team to flowchart its current process using either a SIPOC chart (see Figure 5-3) or a process map (see Figure 5-4). A SIPOC chart looks beyond the process flow to include both inputs and outputs of the process identifying issues at each step. A process map is helpful in identifying specific detail within the process and where problems with procedures, communication flow, and decision points exist.

It's often helpful to have team members compare their individual charts. More often than not, valuable information emerges about how each person handles a particular process and how he or she assumes that others handle it.

Process flowcharting can help teams understand where bottlenecks exist in a particular process; where weak links exist as a result of equipment, documentation, or training problems; where steps are poorly defined; and where redundant, unnecessary, or time-consuming steps exist. Most teams get very excited when they uncover problems that affect their immediate work and are clearly able to be fixed.

The "Five Whys"

The "five why" analysis helps the team uncover the real reasons—or root causes—underlying a problem. The process is as follows:

1. Develop a problem statement.
2. Ask why the problem occurs and list the initial reasons given.

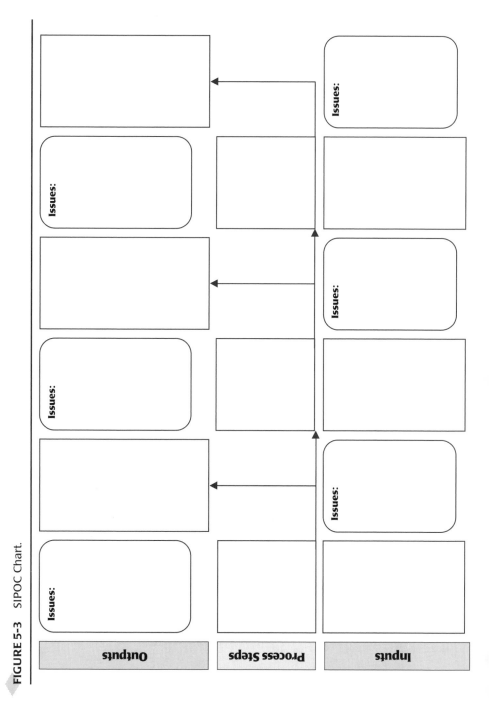

FIGURE 5-3   SIPOC Chart.

FIGURE 5-4   Sample Process Map for Arranging Travel.

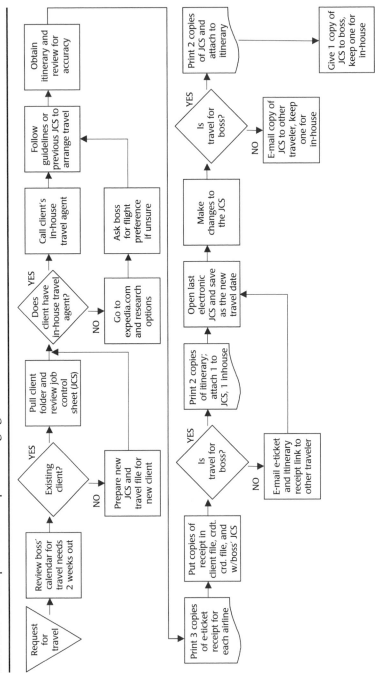

3. Ask why those reasons occur until you have asked five times.
4. Stop the why process at the last point, where the team has control to fix the reason (or cause) being identified.
5. Once the root cause is identified, have the team determine how to gather data on the cause or pilot a small-scale solution to see if the root cause is true.

Collecting Data

Team problem solving and decision making must include collecting and presenting data to the team itself or to other teams. Sometimes simple charts are sufficient, especially charts that identify how many times the problem occurs, what type of problem occurs most often, what times of day the problem occurs, and where the problem occurs. Team members are encouraged to make simple pencil-and-paper charts and to share even preliminary results with other members.

Green, Yellow, and Red Charts

As the team determines what data to collect, the team sets up a chart where members (or the continuous improvement star point) record and color code data on a daily basis. If the results meet or exceed the goal, the data are color-coded in green; if the trend is slipping, the data are color-coded in yellow; if the results are below standard, the data are color-coded in red. To set up this process, the team must decide how to color code its data and how to respond to each type of data. Often teams will bring the chart to their daily huddles and work on solving problems immediately. The team maintains an action log recording the problems identified, the actions to be taken, and who will take the actions and when.

Pareto Chart

A Pareto chart is designed to identify the "vital" few from the many (see Figure 5-5). The chart provides both the frequency of occurrence

FIGURE 5-5   Sample Pareto Chart.

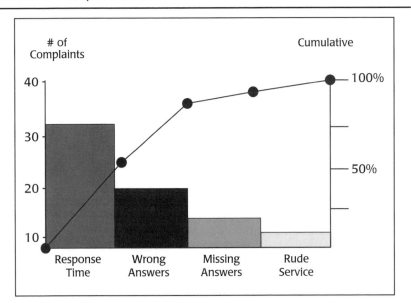

and the percentage that occurrence represents of the whole. As a bar chart, it illustrates problems or causes from highest to lowest. A line shows the cumulative effect as a percentage as you move from left to right.

The Pareto chart is designed to illustrate the 80:20 rule: Eighty percent of our complaints come from 20 percent of our customers; eighty percent of the information we want comes from 20 percent of the newspaper. This awareness helps the team identify the vital few that cause the majority of the problem. Items are listed in descending order, and when the cumulative percentage totals 80 percent, the team has identified the most important components of the problem.

Fishbone Diagram

After the team has identified the "vital few" problems, it's time to push deeper by developing a Fishbone Diagram (see Figure 5-6) to look for root causes. The fishbone helps the team investigate the root causes by grouping and exploring them in detail. First the problem statement is written at the head of the "fish" or diagram. Then the major categories that are potential sources of the problem are identified. Many fishbones use the standard categories of materials, methods, measurements, people, and culture or mother nature. Other category options can include processes, policies, procedures, facilities, technology, structure, staff, systems, and training, to name a few. During the process, the team brainstorms various reasons for problems in each category and places them on the "bones" of the fish. The diagram will visually illustrate the most heavily involved categories.

Interrelationship Diagram

Interrelationship diagramming (see Figure 5-7) is very helpful when there are multiple issues with a problem and the team needs to identify which are the drivers or root causes. The process is as follows:

1. Brainstorm all the issues and write them on a large piece of flipchart paper.
2. Draw an "in" and an "out" box at the bottom of each issue identified.
3. Start anywhere on the flipchart and ask: "Does this issue cause the next issue or does the next issue cause this issue?" Each time the issue causes another issue, draw an "out"

FIGURE 5-6   Sample Fishbone Diagram.

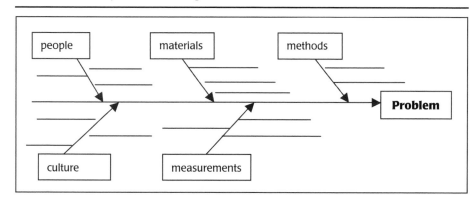

FIGURE 5-7   Interrelationship Diagram.

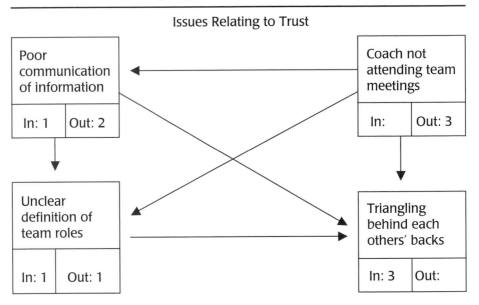

Issues Relating to Trust

Note: In this example, the coach not attending team meetings is the strongest driver of distrust whereas triangling is the symptom rather than the driver.

    arrow. Each time it is affected by the other issue, draw an "in" arrow.
4. Go through each of the issues and determine which ones are the drivers (greatest number of out arrows). These are most probably the key causes of the problem.
5. Once you have identified the drivers, use the five whys to unearth root causes.

Developing Solution Alternatives

Decision Matrix

Once the team has identified its top problem and brainstormed several solution ideas, it needs to identify the criteria to use to select the best decision option. Typical criteria might include ease of implementation, cost, support of management, whether the deadline can be met, and customer satisfaction. Once the criteria are identified, the team needs to determine what an acceptable score would be for a best decision option. This is done by multiplying the number of criteria by the number of points being used and seeing that as a highest score. The team then identifies what would be the lowest acceptable score of any solution. The team completes the matrix by scoring each option. If all the scores are low, the team must generate new ideas; if the top score is low, the team may want to try to combine one or two ideas to create a better solution (see Figure 4-3).

The 2 × 2 Chart

Sometimes a team has so many problems or issues to work on, or items to consider, that the whole process seems overwhelming. By creating a 2 × 2 chart (see Figure 5-8), the team can sort the items on two variables (one on each axis of the chart). Recently, a very contentious

FIGURE 5-8   Team 2 x 2 Chart.

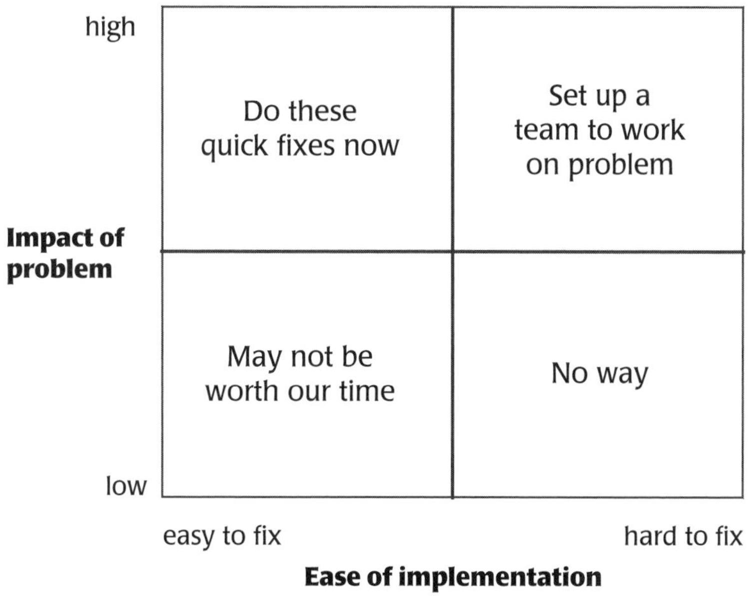

group of team members brainstormed the changes that they wanted to see in the communication with suppliers. Each team member had four or five problems that seemed to need fixing immediately. By placing them on the 2 × 2, using one axis to identify impact on the organization and the other axis to identify the ease of implementation, the team quickly sorted the suggestions and then used dot prioritization to put the suggestions in priority order. All of this happened with no wrangling, positioning, or criticizing; the team stayed together and the members kept their focus.

Planning Tools

Implications Wheel

When trying to determine the implications of a certain solution or problem, it's helpful to create an implications wheel. The wheel begins in the middle of a sheet of paper with a statement of the problem or proposed solution. The team brainstorms the implications of the solution/problem and adds a spoke and wheel for each of the implications. The team can carry out this process to the third or fourth level of implication, color coding those of a more serious nature.

Force Field Analysis: Driving and Restraining Forces

The use of force field analysis in the problem-solving process helps the team identify the driving (positive) forces that will help and sustain the improvements and the restraining (negative) forces that will block successful problem resolution. Here's how it works:

1. Draw a vertical line down the middle of a flipchart sheet. Write "driving forces" on the left side and "restraining forces" on the right side.

2. Brainstorm all the driving forces that will support a certain action. Write them on the left side of the flipchart with arrows pointing right, toward the line.
3. Brainstorm all the restraining forces that will prevent an action from happening. Write them on the right side of the flipchart, with arrows pointing left, toward the line.
4. Discuss ways to diminish or eliminate the restraining forces and strengthen the driving forces.

Tree Diagram

The tree diagram (see Figure 5-9) helps the team identify all the essential steps in the solution or decision. To craft a tree diagram, proceed with the following:

1. In the first box, define the outcome you expect to achieve with the solution identified above.
2. Identify key strategies in the next set of boxes needed to accomplish the outcome.
3. In the third set of boxes, record the specific tasks or actions that need to be done for each strategy.

FIGURE 5-9   Tree Diagram.

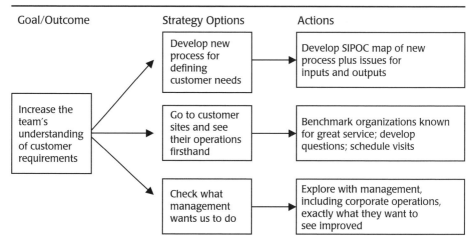

Work Breakdown Plan

The work breakdown plan (see Figure 5-10) creates a clear visual of the goal and milestones (what we call "buckets of work" needing to be done) and the start and end dates for each bucket. We encourage teams to create high-level work breakdown plans for each of their goals and then sub-level work breakdown plans for each activity.

Activity Network Diagram

The activity network diagram (see Figure 5-11) shows the flow of work and the dependencies between each of the tasks. This diagram helps the team establish the most efficient path and realistic schedule for the completion of a project. These are the steps:

1. Brainstorm all the tasks needed for the project. Write them on Post-its.
2. Select the first task and place it on the far left side of the diagram page.
3. Ask: "Do any of these other tasks need to be done at the same time as the first task?" If yes, put the next task underneath the first task. If no, go on to the next task in the sequence.
4. When the entire flow is done, number each of the tasks and the amount of time required for each.
5. To determine the total required time, add the estimated time amounts. The path with the longest cumulative time is called the *critical path*.

Gantt Chart

The Gantt chart lists each process step to be completed and the schedule for when the work will be done (see Figure 6-1). Project management software programs often use Gantt charts to help facilitate the timing of dependencies between steps.

FIGURE 5-10 Sample Work Breakdown Plan.

Goal:
Adequate staff in place for transition plan.

major task/milestone:	
Hire 1 new staff member	
Scheduled Start	Scheduled Finish
1-10-XX	3-30-XX

- Role clarifications
- Job descriptions
- Run ad in local newspapers
- Interview (full-time, salary)

major task/milestone:	
Salary adjustments	
Scheduled Start	Scheduled Finish
1-30-XX	2-30-XX

- Projections

major task/milestone:	
Hire additional trainers	
Scheduled Start	Scheduled Finish
3-30-XX	6-30-XX

- Run ad in training magazines
- Write job descriptions
- Explore other trainers

major task/milestone:	
Manage schedule	
Scheduled Start	Scheduled Finish
1-10-XX	

- Keep calendar "free" on Friday's— at least 2 days/month
- Schedule all appointments through assistant

major task/milestone:	
Staff development	
Scheduled Start	Scheduled Finish
1-10-XX	12-30-XX

- Sue and Lisa to have plan by end of Jan. as to what training and/or classes they want to attend
- Look into online courses/local community colleges
- Register and attend classes

major task/milestone:	
Scheduled Start	Scheduled Finish

FIGURE 5-11 Activity Network Diagram.

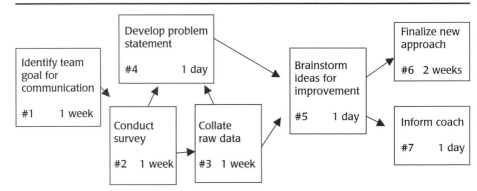

Most people come to a problem-solving session with a solution in mind. Very quickly, people jump into arguing about which solution is best without ever fully defining and analyzing the problem. As a result, the team ends up fixing a symptom only to have the root of the problem reoccur down the road.

A high-performance team plans out the process it will use to work on the problem in addition to the result it is trying to achieve.

Tips for Problem Solving

- Talk about and agree on the process your team will use to work on the problem before jumping into discussion of the problem.

- Beware of problems stated as solutions: "We need more time for team meetings."

- Remember, as Edward Deming suggested, 85 percent of problems are with the system, not the people.[4]

- Avoid the rush to solutions by following an agreed-upon problem-solving process.

- Be sure to check the team's authority before implementing any solution.

Team Scoreboards and Performance Assessments

IN THIS CHAPTER, we examine how to create measures to track team results and assess team performance. The quality saying "what gets measured gets done" applies to a team-based organization as well. The team will need to design two processes: one to track its performance and one to determine how it is functioning as a team.

In the team charter, the team defines the expected measures it will maintain throughout its process. These measures might be achievement of the team goals, progress on the team's performance, or other measures defined by the coach or sponsor.

Team Measurement Systems

As soon as possible, the coach or sponsor will want to help the team determine what results to measure on an ongoing basis. The team might measure the amount of work produced; the number of error-free days, customer complaints, or delinquent action items; and improvements in cycle time, downtime, and safety audits. Usually the team identifies four or five measures that it will track and discuss. In the case of self-directed teams, the measures should be tracked daily and the results discussed at the team's top-of-the-shift daily huddles. For cross-functional teams, the measures might be reviewed at one of the team's monthly meetings. This process of measuring results helps to build a sense of ownership and responsibility among team members.

To prevent a team from becoming too insular, it is helpful to include some measures that require the team to work closely with other teams or to be sensitive to the organization as a whole. However, it's important that the measures represent items that the team can control or influence through its own results. The goal is to get the team to own its measures rather than management. That means the team must determine what it will measure, how it will measure, and how it will analyze the results and discuss when things are going right or need improvement.

The concept of visual management is important to the team's success. At any point in time, the team should be able to see how it is doing and whether it is on target to meet its goals. Most groups and committees do little to track performance visually for all members to see and discuss; management is viewed as the only one responsible for knowing how things are going. Teams—especially Lean and Kaizen teams—use visual management as a core philosophy, and everyone has access to the data he or she needs to see and can challenge the team's results. Information that once was unknown to the team becomes widely known to all members.

Typically, a team maintains two display boards: a whiteboard and a corkboard (bulletin board). On the whiteboard, the team records daily action items, brainstorming ideas, and information to be communicated between shifts. The cork board is used to post the team's metrics, safety issues and concerns, quality issues, work schedule, and assessment tools. The information and data on these boards are very current and relevant to the team's accomplishments.

During the early stage of team development, part of the coach's and/or sponsor's job is to help the team develop a measurement system that is appropriate to the team's tasks. For example, a Gantt chart (see Figure 6-1) could be used by a project team to track completion of team activities; a cross-functional team to post its list of successfully completed tasks each week; and a self-directed team to track machine loading time, machine downtime, cycle time, and scrap. These charts are usually simple pencil–and-paper tracking/counting systems, not elaborate computerized documents. Teams respond very positively to using a color-coding system that alerts the team when results are falling below an acceptable level. For example, the team identifies what measures represent acceptable (color coded green), what measures represent some slippage (color coded amber), and what measures represent a problem (color coded red). When a team member enters the data on the visual scoreboard (see Figure 6-2), the member also color codes the data to alert team members to either a good day or a problem.

The team measures should be visual for all team members, through either an easel, a whiteboard, a bulletin board, or an electronic tracking system where measures are regularly posted. One self-directed, cellular production team had an electronic system that

FIGURE 6-1   Team Gantt Chart.

ID	Priority	Task Name	Duration	Start	Finish	% Complete	Champion	Resources
63	600	New roles for management identified and defined	60 days	10/13/06	12/13/06	35%	Mark	Linda and Franco
64	600	Development of teaming principles for organization	30 days	11/10/06	12/10/06	40%	Liel	George and Mark

FIGURE 6-2   Sample Visual Scoreboard.

Team _____   Week of _____

Items to be scored	Target	11/1	11/2	11/3	11/4	11/5	11/6	11/7	11/8
Lost time accidents	0								
Cycle time average	:26								
Defects	0								
Daily housekeeping	100%								
Open action items completed on time	100%								

posted the seconds required for them to move the production pieces through the team's cell. If the production time was within range, the seconds posted were in green; if the time was outside the range, the seconds posted were in red. All day long the team worked hard to keep itself in the green, encouraging and helping each other continuously. Within six months the team had reduced its production cycle time from 26 seconds to 18 seconds, improving productivity by 33 percent.

In addition to the team performance board (whiteboard and corkboard), a team needs to maintain a notebook where actions taken by the team to correct problems are listed, including who is responsible for taking the action, by when, and the result when completed. Actions that remain open past the expected due date, or those that run into difficulty getting fixed, are addressed at the weekly team meeting.

Sharing Measurement Feedback

In many organizations, the strategy for handling negative feedback is to hide it under the table and hope no one sees it. The opposite is true in a team environment. Negative feedback is considered important information for the team to process and address. It's an opportunity to huddle together and use the team's brainpower to fix the problem. Many teams take great pride in their ability to problem solve once they get good at it. However, it's helpful early on for the team to develop some feedback guidelines, particularly when sharing negative results with team members:

Feedback Guidelines

- Describe what happened in factual, specific terms.

- State the impact the problem has had on the team and on individual members.

- Avoid making assumptions about why something happened without supporting data.

- Be gentle toward the person if an honest mistake was made; avoid a rush to judgment and don't allow members to accuse or point fingers.

- Speak about the problem as a "we" rather than a "you."

- Agree on a statement of the problem before trying to offer solutions.

- Apologize, if appropriate, for any part that the team or members had in causing the problem (incomplete communication about an assignment, inadequate training).

- Focus on what the team can control, not on what others may or may not have done.

- Encourage the person who caused the problem (if that is the case) to offer the first solution for fixing the problem.

- Brainstorm more than one solution, in case the first one ultimately doesn't work.

- Maintain an action log on the team's decision and action taken as a result of the data. Over time, the team can see how many problems it has faced and fixed.

Sharing Performance Information and Feedback Between Shifts

Teams that work on the same tasks but different shifts must establish a plan for communicating information and sharing feedback between the teams. Typical data shared between shifts focus on the following:

- Actual performance results compared to the goal or schedule

- Causes of downtime or interruption and actions taken to resolve them

- Customer problems or complaints

- Maintenance issues or incomplete repairs

- Safety issues

- Quality and housekeeping issues

These data can be shared in a shift log or on a "between teams" section of the bulletin board or whiteboard. The team communication star point is typically responsible for leaving messages and information for the next team arriving. Teams may also leave feedback for the next team, although face-to-face discussions are encouraged if the feedback is corrective in nature. Frequent misunderstandings occur when inter-team communication is only via e-mail or notes.

Maintaining Records of Continuous Improvement Accomplishments

In the daily huddle, the team reviews its performance data and often has immediate suggestions for improvements that can be made. The team describes and records the data on a continuous improvement log that includes the area or process under discussion, the problem description, the actions taken or that need to be taken, the results or expected results, and what the problem looked like before and after correction (Figure 6-3). The team also records any output measures

FIGURE 6-3   Team Continuous Improvement Log.

Date and Time	Area or Process under discussion	Problem Description	Actions to be taken including deadline
The expected results	"Before" picture of problem (output measures)	Expected "after" picture of problem (output measures)	Champion

when the problem existed and after the problem was resolved to determine the impact of the change. These continuous improvement sheets are maintained in the team notebook to track and illustrate how the team is managing its own problems.

— Management's Role in the Feedback Process —

The coach and business unit managers are seen as resources to help the team when its problems exceed its capabilities or the boundaries of its work area. When a team is faced with negative performance data, the expectation is that the team will take ownership of the problem. Often teams try to deflect ownership back to the coach or management or to blame another team or area. It is the coach's or manager's responsibility to set a new boundary here: Will the coach or manager take back authority and tell the team what to do and how to address its data or will he or she say, "What do you think you should do?"? When the coach or manager puts the question to the team and it responds, "We don't know," then he or she must assess whether the team truly doesn't know, or whether it responded this way in order to get out of thinking of a solution. If the team truly doesn't know, the coach or manager should ask, "May I offer an idea or possible solution?" and get the team's agreement before sharing the solution. If the team most likely knows what to do, the coach or manager should suggest that the team work on a solution and come back later with their ideas. This process can be long and tedious, depending on the length of time people have previously been in an authoritative environment. However, once the team knows the coach will be a resource and not a quick fix, the team's collective intelligence will grow by leaps and bounds.

It's very important that the entire process of measuring and assessing be owned by the team; management's role is not to police, audit, criticize, or cajole. One of the best examples of management's role I can think of comes from my experience with a director of manufacturing. This manager walked through the production area of a plant and wrote notes of encouragement and insightful questions on the team performance scoreboards. As he walked away, team members quickly went to their scoreboards to see what he had written and were pumped up by his words of encouragement.

Team Assessments

To mature effectively, a team also must regularly measure its progress as a team. Team growth can typically be divided into three phases: start-up, developing (or growing), and mature (see example of cross-functional team phases in Figure 6-4). The team tasks are very different for each phase, graduating in complexity and responsibility. For example, while a start-up team works on protocols and meeting skills, a developing team will be expanding its planning and decision-making capability.

Most people prior to teaming are not used to being openly assessed on their performance. The first time a team's process observer (another team member) gives feedback on the effectiveness of the team's meeting, including such things as lack of member participation, interruptions, and starting on time, the team is often surprised and

FIGURE 6-4   Cross-Functional Team Growth Phases.

PHASE 1	PHASE 2	PHASE 3
"START UP"	**"GROWING"**	**"MATURE"**
❏ Agree to drafted team charter including goals and measures	❏ Set own team goals (strategic, operational, and tactical) and update charter	❏ Active continuous improvement efforts ongoing
❏ Help/Hinder list	❏ Develop Work Breakdown Plans and agree on approach	❏ Participate in new member recruiting processes
❏ Team meetings (agenda, scribe notes, action items)	❏ Share work assignments	❏ Redesign work processes
❏ Simple, rotating of team meeting roles	❏ Track and complete action items on time	❏ Propose new capital and process improvements
❏ Process observer feedback	❏ Resolve conflicts between members	❏ Interface with all stakeholders
❏ Consensus decision making	❏ Team planning and problem solving	❏ Propose new ideas/ ventures
❏ Meeting protocol	❏ Star Point role implementation	❏ Conduct full team performance management
❏ Decision making protocol	❏ Conduct new member orientation	❏ Deliver rewards and recognition
❏ Conflict resolution protocol	❏ Cross-train on key roles and responsibilities	❏ Negotiate with suppliers, external stakeholders
❏ Communication within/ outside the team	❏ Train new members	❏ Extensive decision making authority
❏ Team training—basic	❏ Offer and receive member performance feedback	❏ Advanced team skill training
❏ Understanding of RACI chart	❏ Conduct team performance feedback	❏ Complete complex problem solving, planning, and decision making
❏ X-functional Star Points selected and trained	❏ Develop and use team performance metrics	❏ Sponsorship of sub-teams
❏ Informal team feedback	❏ Develop performance standards	❏ Challenge team performance to greater limits
❏ Preliminary decision making authority: authority to recommend	❏ Deliver presentations	❏ Benchmark with other successful organizations and incorporate learnings
	❏ Increased decision making authority	❏ Address any team problems without prompting
	❏ Advanced team skill training	

uncomfortable. Although these issues may have always bothered people, they were typically discussed outside the meeting with the "offenders" out of range. Now, the feedback is done with everyone in the room, eye to eye. The results are profound and previous problem behavior begins to change.

Purpose of Assessments

A team assessment system is typically designed to serve a number of different purposes:

- Inform team members about their performance.

- Motivate the team toward improved performance.

- Encourage increased competence and growth among team members.

- Enhance and improve communication.

- Improve problem behavior/performance.

- Develop back-up data for management decisions (promotions, demotions, discharge).

- Encourage ownership and responsibility on the team.

Benefits to Team Assessments

When employees are assessed by management on an annual or semi-annual basis, they often appear to be unclear about what is being measured and rarely engage in improving performance until close to the measuring date. However, with teams, those who will evaluate the team are all around the team every day. They know whether a team member is a good performer or not; they know how long the team member goes on break and whether she carries her own load; they know the mood swings and the fake excuses. A poor performer gets away with nothing in a team environment. This change of approach is not welcomed by team members who have been poor performers for many years. The coach or manager must anticipate some resistance when implementing a full team assessment process.

Special Tips on Team Assessments

Assessing a team's performance is not designed to put the team on the spot and show weaknesses. It is designed to help the team grow and develop, learning from its strengths and weaknesses. Along the way, certain points have proven to be important:

- The assessment system must reinforce and support the beliefs, attitudes, and behaviors required in a team-based organization.

- The team assessment process must begin early in the team's development and not be aligned initially with compensation or tangible rewards. Members should not be looking for a reward for standard performance required of all team members.

- It is best to assess total team performance before having members conduct peer reviews.[1]

- Avoid linking other personnel decisions such as promotions, demotions, and compensation to the feedback process, especially if negative feedback is likely.

- Individual peer reviews are best conducted when a team has reached an advanced stage of team building.[2]

- When team members openly discuss problems they are having with other team members, they may exaggerate and generalize about the problems to gain team support. Members must actively work to avoid the bandwagon effect and maintain a level of open-mindedness.

- Plan to implement the individual team member review system, along with the compensation system, as the last areas in the team sequence.

Advantages and Disadvantages of Team Assessments

There are various benefits and drawbacks of team assessments, including the following:

Benefits

- Team members see each other's work on a regular basis, so their observations are very accurate.

- Peer pressure is a powerful motivator for team members.

- Team reviews solicit numerous opinions within and outside the team and are not dependent on one person's opinion or bias.

- Team assessments support the development of skills among team members.

- When team members recognize that other team members will be evaluating their work, they show increased commitment and productivity.

- Team members become more aware of performance standards and behavior requirements because they are accountable for maintaining and measuring them in others.

- The team conducts the assessments, rather than managers, thus saving managers' time.

Drawbacks

- They are time-consuming.

- It is sometimes difficult to distinguish between the contributions of the team and those of individual members.

- Some members feel uncomfortable evaluating the behavior of other team members.

- Considerable training is required in order to become competent in giving and receiving feedback.

Early Assessments for the Team

Rather than make a team assessment a big deal in the beginning, it helps to start by having the team assess its performance through its process observer reports at the end of each meeting. In the beginning, the process observer reports will sound quite general and bland: "We did a pretty good job today; maybe we were a little bit late getting started." The coach or sponsor can encourage a more honest assessment of the team's functioning as the team develops. In addition, the team meeting process observer log (see Figure 2-5) helps the process observer to be more honest with other team members. Most importantly, a method for regularly reviewing team performance should be implemented at the very beginning of the team's development and carried on throughout its work. As the team matures, a decidedly noticeable change in the feedback members are giving each other will be seen. The feedback becomes more specific and direct: "Jim, I think the team is struggling with the number of times you are interrupting others." It's also appropriate for the coach or sponsor to provide the team with feedback, but only after the process observer has done so first.

If the team is not addressing items that the process observer brings up, encourage the team to write the process observer notes on the scribe form so that the team can see week to week what problems are being repeated.

In the early days of teaming, I would often provide feedback to the team as a consultant or coach. Each time I would start out by pointing out some of the good things the team was doing and then I'd list the improvements I thought it should work on. Team members often responded by getting quite defensive, either making excuses for the behavior or pointing out that I just simply didn't understand their world. I soon learned a very important lesson as a coach: Do not provide feedback to a team until it has performed its own assessment of its behavior. If the team's feedback suggests that it is very comfortable with the way things are going, it will take some finesse to get the team to see things differently. Hitting the nail on the head, in this situation, is not a good idea.

Performance Thermometers

At the three-month mark, it's helpful for teams to complete their performance thermometers (see Figure 6-5). These measuring devices seem to work much better for new teams than written assessments because they are quick and easy to do, create a visual picture for the team, and are done as a team building activity.

The coach and the team determine what to measure for the first round. Often the factors are quality of the team meetings, handling of team conflicts, communication with each other, and performance of team tasks. Each team member completes his own thermometer including suggestions for improvements. Team members then transfer their results onto a larger, similar set of thermometers, with each team member drawing a line indicating his rating for each item being measured and writing suggestions around each thermometer.

Once the data have been transferred to the larger thermometers, the team discusses high- and low-scoring items and items for which there is considerable discrepancy between team members. The team reviews the suggestions for improvement and places the most popular ideas on the team's agenda for further discussion. Teams often keep their early thermometers to refer back to later in order to see how far they've progressed.

Thermometers can be posted on team scoreboards so that the team is constantly reminded about teaming behaviors that need work.

Performance Thermometers and Formal Assessments

To introduce a team slowly to the concept of assessing performance, we combine the thermometer format that the team is used to with specific measures for each of the items on the thermometer. For example, if the team is measuring its effectiveness in sharing information, we identify specific items for the team to examine, such as handling of communication at the beginning of the shift (the huddle), operator-to-operator communication, star point leader–to–star point coordinator information flow, team meeting information flow, and coach's information flow. Each of these is rated on a 10-point scale, added to-

FIGURE 6-5   Completed Team Performance Thermometers.

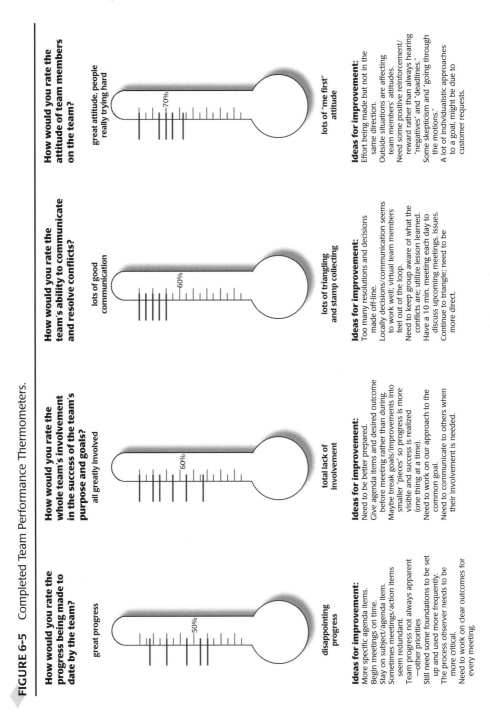

How would you rate the progress being made to date by the team?

great progress

50%

disappointing progress

Ideas for improvement:
More specific agenda items.
Begin meetings on time.
Stay on subject/agenda item.
Sometimes meetings/action items seem redundant.
Team progress not always apparent —other priorities
Still need some foundations to be set up and used more frequently.
The process observer needs to be more critical.
Need to work on clear outcomes for every meeting.

How would you rate the whole team's involvement in the success of the team's purpose and goals?

all greatly involved

60%

total lack of involvement

Ideas for improvement:
Need to be better prepared.
Give agenda items and desired outcome before meeting rather than during.
Maybe break goals/improvements into smaller "pieces" so progress is more visible and success is realized (one thing at a time).
Need to work on our approach to the common goal.
Need to communicate to others when their involvement is needed.

How would you rate the team's ability to communicate and resolve conflicts?

lots of good communication

60%

lots of triangling and stamp collecting

Ideas for improvement:
Too many resolutions and decisions made off-line.
Locally decisions/communication seems to work well; virtual team members feel out of the loop.
Need to keep group aware of what the conflicts are; utilize lesson learned.
Have a 10 min. meeting each day to discuss upcoming meetings, issues.
Continue to triangle; need to be more direct.

How would you rate the attitude of team members on the team?

great attitude, people really trying hard

70%

lots of "me first" attitude

Ideas for improvement:
Effort being made but not in the same direction.
Outside situations are affecting team members' attitudes.
Need some positive reinforcement/ reward rather than always hearing "negatives" and "deadlines."
Some skepticism and "going through the motions."
A lot of individualistic approaches to a goal, might be due to customer requests.

gether, and divided by the number of items to come up with an average score for information sharing. That score is recorded on the individual's thermometer and then on the team's collective thermometer for information sharing.

This process allows the team to gain greater comfort with the idea of measuring itself. By encouraging the team to define its own measures for each item, the team becomes very clear about what is important to address. A sample of the advanced thermometer tool is available at www.NewDirectionsConsulting.com/samples.

Formal Team Assessments

At the end of the first year, a team is typically ready for a full team assessment. We use an online assessment tool that measures twenty-two team competencies (see Figure 6-6). The full-scale assessment process is not introduced earlier than at twelve months because new teams have a tendency to inflate their ratings. Later on, when teams have actually improved, they will score themselves more critically and their ratings will drop as a result.

A formal team assessment should not proceed unless the following criteria are present:

- Trust and respect between management and teams (management has to feel the team is capable of completing accurate reviews)

- Agreement about goals, procedures, and timing of the team review process

- Clear and well-defined performance objectives for the team and for individual members

- Performance measures that have been agreed to by all

- Feedback systems about team performance that provide numerous opportunities for informal assessment, coaching, and review

FIGURE 6-6   22 Competency Team Assessment.

Competencies	Scoring Range: Phase I	Scoring Range: Phase II	Scoring Range: Phase III
Culture and Direction	1–4	5–7	8–10
Goal/Approach Clarity	1–4	5–7	8–10
Leadership	1–4	5–7	8–10
Roles and Responsibilities	1–4	5–7	8–10
Competency to Perform Tasks	1–4	5–7	8–10
Management/Coach Support	1–4	5–7	8–10
Norms/Protocols	1–4	5–7	8–10
Membership	1–4	5–7	8–10
Team Decision Making	1–4	5–7	8–10
Team Maturity	1–4	5–7	8–10
Participation/Influence	1–4	5–7	8–10
Team Meetings	1–4	5–7	8–10
Team Planning	1–4	5–7	8–10
Completion of Team Tasks	1–4	5–7	8–10
Problem Solving	1–4	5–7	8–10
Work Tools/Training	1–4	5–7	8–10
Use of Reward and Recognition	1–4	5–7	8–10
Interpersonal Skills	1–4	5–7	8–10
Team Communication	1–4	5–7	8–10
Team Atmosphere	1–4	5–7	8–10
Handling Conflicts	1–4	5–7	8–10
Inter-Team Management	1–4	5–7	8–10

- Open and active exchange of information

- Methods of recognizing performance that are thoughtful and appropriate

- Respect among peers on the team

The formal team assessment should measure both results and process. Teams may define their own items to be measured and the scale for measuring, or they may use available online instruments that require less work for the team. If a team is constructing its own assessment, it should include the following measures:

Output/Result Measures of Performance

- *Achievement of Team Goals:* how team members have given assistance toward the achievement of team goals; level of activity in establishing the quality, efficiency, and speed of the team

- *Customer Satisfaction:* whether the team meets or exceeds customer expectations; whether the team recognizes the importance of both external and internal customers

- *Quantity of Work:* whether productivity exceeds standards without the team being asked to do so; pride in workmanship, efficiency, and speed

- *Quality of Work:* performance as it relates to process control and continuous improvement; ability to perform tasks accurately

- *Process Knowledge:* extent of job knowledge, technical and professional skill, and ability to meet changing situations; knowledge of multiple jobs

- *Maintenance of Technical Systems:* level of understanding of safety hazards, compliance with safety rules, and work habits; machinery maintenance

Input/Process Measures of Performance

- *Support of Team Process:* level of support for the use of teams to achieve goals; strong positive force in team morale; the level of assistance and support members provide to each other, even under pressure

- *Participation:* whether members lead and participate constructively in team meetings and team tasks, actively encourage the participation of others, and regularly volunteer for various team roles

- *Oral Communication:* use of open, honest, and direct communication; active listening; clarity of speech; willingness to interpret and clarify for other team members; interest in improving communication skills through giving and receiving feedback

- *Written Communication:* willingness to assist in scribing duties; ability to develop and write reports/presentations for the team

- *Collaboration and Collective Effort:* level at which team members respond to others, cooperate readily with all team members, and demonstrate a positive attitude and support for others

- *Conflict Resolution:* ability to see conflict as helpful in promoting different perspectives; ability to freely express views on difficult issues, including nonproductive team behaviors

- *Planning and Goal Setting:* use of proactive planning and goal setting to achieve desired results; ability to be flexible in modifying the plan as needed

- *Participative Decision Making:* level of active exploration of a full range of choices; effort to create mutually supported alternatives or win-win decisions

- *Problem-Solving and Analytical Skills:* contribution to team problem solving; anticipation of potential problems; ability to develop alternatives and suggest best choices

- *Credibility and Trust:* how openly team members express both facts and feelings

- *Work Processes and Procedures:* adherence to standard work processes and procedures

- *Integration of Technical Skills:* ability to learn new skills from other team members (e.g., analyzing financial data, using computer systems)

- *Interdependence:* level of recognition of the importance of others, including the organization as a whole; interest shown in involving others in the identification and solution of problems/issues

- *Managing Skills:* ability to demonstrate management skills, including budgeting, inventory, scheduling, and leadership

- *Commitment:* level of commitment to the idea of work teams

- *Interpersonal Relations:* how team members strive to maintain good relationships with teammates, managers, and other teams and support services

- *Initiation of Ideas:* how frequently team members suggest ideas, alternatives, and solutions

- *Leadership:* how team members share the leadership role; whether they occasionally assume responsibility for leading the team

- *Acceptance of Change and Risk Taking:* how receptive the team is to change; willingness to change its behavior, explore new ideas, stimulate risk taking

Our online tool asks each team member to score the team on a 10-point scale. Since we have developed the tool over time, we are now able to illustrate on the tool a scoring range for phase I, phase II, and phase III teams. For example, the highest a phase I team can score on "team meetings" is a 4, whereas a phase II team can score up to a 7, and a phase III team up to a 10. This scoring range prevents a new team from scoring itself too high.

When the scoring is completed, the team reviews a spider diagram (or radar chart) identifying the composite score of all members for each of the twenty-two items (see Figure 6-7). Using the spider diagram, the team can quickly identify its high- and low-scoring items and can work to develop ways to improve. By using overhead transparencies, a coach with five or six teams can overlay the results of all the teams and see where training needs might apply to more than one team.

The team is responsible for analyzing its results and identifying strategies to drive improvement. Here again, the team will need to set

FIGURE 6-7   Radar Chart of 22 Team Competencies.

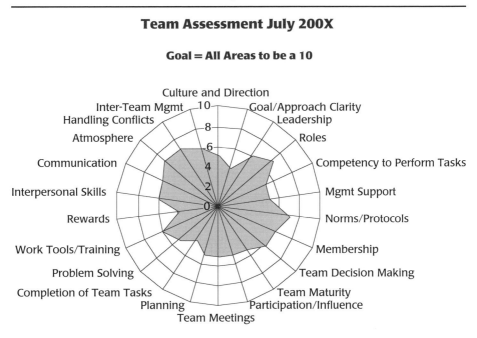

Team Assessment July 200X

Goal = All Areas to be a 10

clear, SMART goals and create the work breakdown plans for how the goals will be achieved by the team.

———— Individual Team Member Assessments ————

When a team is solidly in phase II of teaming, it's appropriate to begin discussing with the team the benefits of providing each member with a personal assessment of his or her contribution to the team. Up to this point, all of the personal assessing has been verbal and very informal, through process observer feedback and discussions with the coach or sponsor. When team members are ready to provide formal feedback to each other, we suggest using an online tool that measures a member's contributions on the same twenty-two competencies that the team used to assess its own performance. For example, under the "roles" competencies, the individual assessment asks the team member and other members to rate the following:

- This team member willingly rotates team roles, including meeting roles and star point roles.

- This team member assumes responsibility for a "fair share" of the duties and tasks on the team.

- This team member rarely has to be reminded to perform the roles assigned.

- This team member actively pursues training to be effective in team roles.

- This team member sees team responsibilities and job responsibilities as his or her "whole job."

— Self-Directed Work Team Evaluation Process —

Here is a sample structure and process that is commonly used by self-directed work teams to evaluate their individual members' performance:

1. The team meets with the coach to set team goals for a specified period of time.

2. Team members receive training on performance planning and evaluating.

3. Team members discuss and establish team and individual performance goals and methods of measuring whether goals have been achieved.

4. The team determines how performance will be reviewed and submits a plan and process steps to the coach for review and approval. Options include the following:

   - All team members evaluate each other, and results are tabulated.

   - Two team members, one chosen by the member being reviewed and one chosen by the rest of the team, conduct and deliver the performance feedback.

- A facilitator selected by the team member being evaluated assembles a group of three or four team members to evaluate performance.

5. Members receive training on coaching skills and assessing performance, as well as on how to receive and process feedback.

6. Throughout the project, the team participates in ongoing coaching and review. The coach and other teams provide regular feedback about the team's progress.

7. As the final review approaches, the team member completes a self-evaluation, and the entire team completes a written (or online) evaluation on the member. In addition, customer surveys and written evaluations from other independent teams may be added. All of the results are tabulated.

8. The two team members or any similar configuration (see step 4) review the information (self-evaluation plus others' evaluation), identify areas of congruence and incongruence, decide how closely objectives were achieved, and pinpoint areas for continued growth.

9. The evaluators meet with the team member and review the information, then complete a final form that combines all the information. The evaluation includes the development of a performance plan including new goals and skill growth for the duration of the project.

Digital Equipment Corporation uses a team of five people as evaluators: a chairperson chosen by the person being evaluated, a manager, two team members selected at random, and the individual being evaluated. Each role is defined and the process steps are identified.[3]

Here are some tips for conducting the team review interview:

- Set a mutually agreeable time for review discussion after all material (self-evaluation, customer surveys, team member reviews) is received and compiled.

- Arrange for private space, and allow no interruptions.

- Warmly greet the team member.

- Explain how the interview process will proceed; ask for suggestions from the team member.

- Offer the team member the opportunity to choose where to begin.

- Ask open-ended questions (how, why) to encourage a two-way discussion.

- Use actual examples of the member's performance to explain reasons for the team's rating.

- In areas needing improvement, discuss behavior that can be changed and the specific improvements desired.

- Stress specific improvement goals, rather than focus on past mistakes.

- Reach agreement on performance improvement goals.

- Summarize discussion points.

- Explain any next steps (such as the completion of the final form).

- Explain the appeal process if the evaluation is negative.

- Schedule follow-up coaching sessions to review the team member's progress.

The following interview behaviors are not acceptable:

- Surprising the team member with an impromptu review

- Not reading through all the evaluations and compiling results into an understandable format

- "Winging it" during the interview

- Generalizing about behavior; providing no specific examples

- Asking the team member to change his or her personality, rather than behavior

- Taking phone calls and allowing other interruptions during the interview

- Dominating the discussion; being unwilling to listen to the team member's explanation

- Being unwilling to admit that the evaluators' assessment of a situation may have been wrong after hearing the team member's explanation

- Suggesting the team member is responsible for the entire success or failure of the team

- Ending the interview without providing a summary and setting new performance goals

- Having no follow-up plan to review ongoing performance

Handling Problem Evaluation Situations

Teams are increasingly finding themselves in the situation of conducting or participating in probationary reviews that may result in discharge. Here are some critical issues for the team to consider:

- Does the team member qualify under a protected class (age, sex, race, national origin, handicap, and so on)?

- Was the team's request for a behavioral change on the part of the new team member reasonable and related to the safe and efficient performance of the job?

- Did the team member receive adequate warning of the consequences of misconduct?

- Did the team investigate the matter before administering discipline?

- Was the team's investigation objective?

- Did the team obtain substantial evidence that the member's behavior was a problem?

- Has the team, and any other team in the organization, applied its rules, orders, and penalties in a manner similar to that of all other teams?

- Did the team identify the desired change in behavior or performance and allow adequate time for the change to occur?

- Do the organization's written policies support the team's activities?

Removing a Member from the Team

During the initial start-up phase of a team, the coach handles all of the team discipline. However, as the team matures and takes on more responsibility, team members begin to provide feedback to people who are not performing at an acceptable level. Removing a member from a team is an act of tremendous significance for both the member and the team. When a person is asked to leave or chooses to leave a team, it is up to the team to handle the situation as effectively as possible.

Once a team has determined that a team member is not working effectively, a procedure for removing the member that basically follows these steps has proven to work with most teams:

1. A team member either volunteers or is selected to speak one-on-one with the problem team member about his or her behavior on the team. The member speaks specifically about the behaviors that are causing a problem for the team. This conversation provides the problem team member with the opportunity to resolve the issue at the simplest level.

2. In the event that the behavior doesn't change, two members of the team either volunteer or are selected to speak with the individual again. They remind the team member of the problem behavior identi-

fied in the first one-on-one discussion and his or her agreement to support the help/hinder list (see Figure 2-1), which defines acceptable and unacceptable behaviors in the team, and they seek commitment from the member to change.

3. If the member refuses to change or no change becomes apparent, the team requests a meeting of the individual with the entire team. This meeting requires a skilled facilitator capable of managing a conflict situation. The team expresses concern about the individual's refusal to address the problem behaviors and spells out in writing what must change immediately and the consequence (recommendation to be removed from the team) if the behavior doesn't change. At this point, the team documents summaries from the one-on-one and two-on-one discussions plus the team's meeting scribe notes. These documents become part of the permanent record and should be reviewed with the coach (and potentially HR) to be certain they have been written correctly.

4. If the member does not respond to the team's written request, the team can decide by consensus of the remaining team members to recommend removal of the problem member.

5. A person designated by the team and the team coach meet with the individual to report the team's decision. It is not helpful at this point to invite the team member back for a final meeting to try to work things through, even if he or she suggests that it would make a difference in his or her behavior.

When a member is removed from the team, it's important to expect a powerful reaction from the rest of the team. The ejection of a team member stirs up deep levels of anxiety associated with the need for approval and belonging. Teams in the forming and storming stages often experience difficulty with the idea of removing a member. Substantial coaching of the team and the problem team member is necessary throughout the process. The coach must demonstrate commitment to the process and impartiality toward all the people involved in the process.

CHAPTER 7

The Teaming Road Map

HOW DO YOU put all the pieces together and transform a workplace into a high-performance, team-based culture? To be successful, there are a number of pieces that have to be strategically placed to bring about the change. This chapter outlines the process of bringing about the transformation. An organizational effectiveness manager in a team-based manufacturing plant once made an important distinction with teaming. She said, "Are we *involving* employees, or *empowering* employees?" Therein lies the difference in the implementation of teams. Some organizations use teams just to involve people (get their opinions and insights) but not engage them in the decision-making process. Others, in vastly reduced numbers, empower employees to run their piece of the organization's real estate—to own it like a home or small business. The teaming roadmap is designed to help the latter type of organizations initiate, plan, execute, and control the teaming process.

—— Building Dissatisfaction with the Status Quo ——

Long before the first team is launched, leadership must begin to introduce to employees why staying where they are will not work for the long term. As leadership shares information about anticipated budget constraints, competitors swallowing up market share, the effect of foreign imports, manufacturing in third-world countries, program consolidations, and the desperate need for change, people develop dissatisfaction with doing things the same way they always have.[1] For example, management might ask: "Can we afford to pay for people watching people watching people watching people and adding all of that overhead to the cost of our product/service?" "Are there synergies that we are not taking advantage of that could make us a market leader?" At this stage, management must allow the problems and plagues to build in order to create the "engine" that will drive the change.

—————— Creating a Compelling Vision ——————

With growing dislike and worry about the current situation, leadership starts to articulate a vision of what the organization might become. Teaming is one of the cornerstones for that vision, a foundation that allows many other pieces (such as Six-Sigma and Lean) to be built upon it. Leadership cannot be wishy-washy about the vision or about teaming at this point. "We will do teams" becomes an important mantra. Often it takes a dynamic, visionary leader to see the value of teams and champion the initiative. In lieu of that type of leader, we have seen unified leadership teams (without the head) drive the same vision successfully. Gaining the support of other stakeholder groups, whether at a corporate level or globally, is critically important at this juncture. Everyone has to agree to the transformation effort at this point or else not proceed. Do not launch pilot teams before building the dissatisfaction with the status quo and gaining leadership support for the compelling vision.

Once dissatisfaction is growing and the vision has been created and accepted by key decision makers, it's time to take the first steps. Too often organizations launch pilot teams as their first steps, even though they are often clueless about what to do and how the teams will interact with the existing structure. There is a better way to proceed that has much greater probability of success. The teaming roadmap provides the transitional structure to lead the organization from where it is to where it needs to go. The roadmap uses an inclusive, dynamic approach that must be customized along the way to the organization's unique requirements; there is no cookie-cutter approach to teaming. However, there are specific strategies that have proven to be successful when supported and encouraged by management.

Creating a Design Team

Managing the organizational upheaval that comes with converting to a team-based organization requires the formation of a design team—a multifunctional representation of the organization charged with *recommending* the new organizational structure to leadership. For example, often there are five salaried and five hourly members on the design team, selected for the first formation of the team by the team sponsor, who is typically the organization's top leader (such as a plant manager or an executive director). The sponsor drafts the team's charter including the team goals and authority level. The job of the design team is to:

- Design a natural, value stream, or virtual work team structure for the organization that supports productivity, safety, and quality goals.

- Determine the launch sequence for all pilot and regular teams, including self-directed, cross-functional, multifunctional, and cross-cultural teams.

- Implement the team structure in a planned, effective fashion.

- Initiate other change support teams including the communication team and the in-house training team.

- Develop and implement systems to monitor and evaluate the progress of the teams.

- Champion the continual improvement of the team structure for the long-term benefit of the organization.

The work of the design team includes numerous components. These are discussed in the following sections.

Articulating the Vision, Values, and Operating Principles in the New Culture

The organization's vision and values are reviewed to determine alignment with a team structure, a graphic representation of the new organization is created, and the key principles of a teaming environment are identified. These principles often include the following:

- Everyone is expected to be a major contributor to the success of the organization and should be encouraged to be engaged and involved.

- Employees are to be provided with the skills, information, tools, and authority necessary to perform in an outstanding manner and deliver customer satisfaction.

- The work environment is expected to foster cooperation and collaboration at all levels to facilitate smarter work structures and quicker problem solving and decision making.

- All employees are to accept responsibility for themselves and their teams under all circumstances.

- Employees are to be valued for their individual and team contributions.

- Everyone is charged with creating an environment of open, four-way communication regarding business and employee concerns. All communication should be open, honest, and direct.

- Leadership is to achieve a constant reputation for reliability, consistency, and credibility.

- Managers, coaches/sponsors, and team members are to be trained and have skills to influence others, communicate, facilitate, and listen effectively.

- The organization is to be operated in a manner that protects the health and well-bring of employees, neighbors, and customers.

- Conflict is seen as healthy and commonplace; people are expected to work to resolve their own conflicts before involving others.

- Consensus decision making achieves the agreement and support needed for effective results; voting is discouraged and silence is treated as disagreement.

- The organization's structure is flat and lean to encourage flexible decision making and quick response at the appropriate levels.

- Authority is increased on a graduated basis as the teams mature.

- The only thing that is constant will be the need to stay flexible and adapt to relentless change.

Understanding and Defining the Organizational Structure

The team drafts an "as is" organizational structure in great detail and brainstorms a "to be" structure based on the idiosyncrasies of the specific organization. The "as is" structure identifies formal and informal reporting relationships, bottlenecks, and constraints. The "to be" structure looks for unexplored synergies between areas that will facilitate improved results. These organizational "maps" are shared with others at all levels of the organization to gain input and reaction prior to any changes. People are continually asked, "What frustrates you with your job?" to uncover the continuous improvement opportunities within the structure. The design team builds a new organizational structure that may include natural work teams, value stream teams, and virtual teams—all integrated to achieve maximum efficiency and effectiveness. The recommended structure is given to management for its review and approval.

Defining New Roles and Responsibilities

The design team defines the roles and responsibilities for leadership, coaches/sponsors, star point leaders (SPLs), subject matter experts (SMEs), teaming facilitators, and any other roles the specific organization wants to include in the team-based design. Definition of the roles includes specific role descriptions and authorities defined in RACI charts for each position. Many times there are difficult role issues to address, such as: "What happens with group leaders, supervisors, and department managers?" Group leaders are usually either reabsorbed into the teams or encouraged to apply for coach, SPL, and SME roles. The organization will want to tap into the talents of people at all levels and move the "best and brightest" into the new leadership roles. Those who have ruled with an iron fist of command and control, however, will find it difficult to secure a role in the new environment unless they commit to changing their behavior.

Not only does the design team define the new roles, but it also makes recommendations about who should fill the roles. The design team typically solicits recommendations from many areas in the organization, defines the criteria for each position, and then scores candidates on a rigorous matrix to select the top choices. Those chosen are provided with extensive training to make the transition. Those with the strongest skills will be used for the first team launches to ensure the greatest probability of success.

Launching the Communication Team

As the design team begins its work on organizational design, it launches a communication team, a cross-functional team composed of salaried and hourly employees responsible for improving the communication dramatically throughout the organization on all issues, including the proposed changes. Communication is abysmal in most organizations and must be addressed if the new structure is going to succeed. The communication team is required to develop a communication plan for the organization that identifies the following:

- What constitutes immediate, high-priority, and moderate-priority communication

- Guidelines for message content for all communication

- Methods of distribution, including the use of communication star point coordinators (SPCs) on the teams

- Relationship authority among the communication team, communication SPL, and organizational leadership as defined by a RACI chart

- Requirements for communication approvals

- Special requirements and strategies for maintaining communication with virtual teams and team members

- A corrective action process if the communication plan is not followed

The communication team assumes responsibility for keeping the organization informed of all the changes taking place, including those located in geographically dispersed locations. The team can accomplish this by publishing a monthly newsletter, maintaining bulletin boards, creating organizational screen-saver messages, and maintaining a website that includes frequently asked questions, communication webinars, personal interest stories, reports on team launches, and success data. One of the goals of the team is to expedite communication faster than the grapevine, a challenge that requires careful coordination between the team and management.

It's important to make a special note here about the unique communication needs of virtual teams. Communication is one of the primary indicators of success for virtual teams; they must learn to overcommunicate to be successful. The communication team can help virtual teams establish communication guidelines and assessment processes to ensure that the necessary communication occurs. The communication team can also work collaboratively with the in-house training team to develop cross-cultural tools and training materials to aid in the understanding of the different communication needs, styles, and approaches of various cultures. For example, an organization in North America may find it difficult for its team members to communicate with French counterparts without misunderstandings. A communication team can provide the necessary tools to guide team members to be more responsive to the needs of each of their cultures.

Launching the In-House Training Team

The design team also launches an in-house training team responsible for providing the training that is pertinent to the development of teams and team members. The training team is composed of ten to twelve members who receive training on adult learning theory and presentation skills in preparation for delivering the team training modules. The design team and the training team work collaboratively to determine the exact training needs of those moving to a team-based structure. Typically, the beginning teaming modules include How Teams Work, which provides an overview of teaming concepts, team development, four core elements of teamwork, and role clarification; Team Meeting Skills, which includes consensus decision making and the team measurement system; and Conflict Resolution Skills, which includes the team conflict protocol. These modules are performed by in-house trainers in pairs after they have been certified to train the module. The second round of training for teams includes the modules Team Problem Solving, Communication Skills, and Managing the Effects of Change.

Selecting Trainers

In-house trainers are selected through recommendation from managers and/or volunteers. There is a rigorous screening process including a short, live presentation by each candidate. In-house trainers spend considerable time away from their regular jobs, especially during the launching of teams; it is therefore paramount that they have the support of their managers prior to participating on the team.

As an example, one recent in-house training team was able to provide twelve hours of training for each of thirteen launching self-directed work teams during a six-week period, more than two thousand hours of training, at no additional cost to the organization. Most in-house trainers show tremendous commitment to their role, because they see the transformation that takes place in the workforce as a result of the training; people move from passive responders to active participants in the organization's future.

Role of the In-House Training Team

The in-house training team, in addition to delivering the training modules, is responsible for assisting with new-hire orientation to teams, maintaining organizational training records, providing ongoing memory tools and training supports to teams as they implement the team process, and sending out training need assessments each year to plan for upcoming trainings. The sponsor of the in-house training team is typically the organization's training manager or coordinator.

The in-house training team works collaboratively with the training SPL and training SPCs to engage the teams in ongoing competency development. Activities may include:

- Developing regular activities and exercises for the training star points to initiate in the team meetings

- Helping training SPCs learn how to assist facilitators and others performing meeting roles during team meetings

- Helping the training SPL design new employee orientation materials for specific teams

- Overseeing the periodic evaluation of training at an organizational level

- Developing cross-training tools and materials to facilitate the learning of new job tasks

- Assisting with the certification process for any skill-based pay systems

- Ensuring that virtual team members are simultaneously trained with others via online webinars, e-room materials, and video conferencing

Training Coaches, Sponsors, and SPLs

Now that the design team has selected the team coaches, sponsors, and SPLs, it's time to train and prepare them to lead their teams. The coaches, sponsors, and SPLs are typically former supervisors, group leaders, and managers who have demonstrated leadership capability and have the attitude and interpersonal skills to work well in a team-based environment. Although all the raw talent is there, the understanding of how to implement effective teams usually is not. Coaches, sponsors, and SPLs must be trained to do an effective job; putting a coach or sponsor in charge of a team without adequate training is a recipe for disaster.

Training of the coach, sponsor, and SPL should include the following components:

- Learning how to draft the team's charter, including SMART goals

- Defining the team's responsibility and authority with a RACI chart

- Developing the responsibility hand-off plan and learning how to delegate effectively

- Understanding the team development process and how to modify coaching approaches and strategies accordingly

- Learning the coach and sponsor's role requirements

- Learning how to "let go" and encourage responsibility building in others

- Understanding the process of team decision making and the transfer of the coach's authority

- Designing team measurement systems and guiding the measurement process

- Rewarding and recognizing team and individual accomplishments

As soon as the coaches are identified, the design team forms the coaches' team to oversee the development of the coaches' platform statements, authority levels, and assessment process. The platform statements are the standards that coaches and sponsors will work to achieve when working with their teams. Without the platform statements, coaches have a tendency to interact according to their personal styles, some being more engaged than others, and the teams will suffer. The standards set the bar of acceptable behavior for all coaches.

Platform Statements

Here are some typical platform statements for coaches; they can also be used for SPLs and team sponsors:

- The coach should interact with the team in some way at least once a day.

- Interaction with individual team members is important, and the coach should do so on a regular basis.

- The coach must demonstrate a belief that teams are the right way to achieve the vision, and that they will be successful.

- The coaching/facilitative/participatory leadership model is the preferred style of managing for the coach; the command and control model of leadership is not acceptable.

- The coach should first try to motivate and encourage a change in team behavior before resorting to negative reinforcement or discipline.

- The coach is to reinforce team member behaviors that support the organization's culture and vision.

- Employees may have a different set of values and beliefs. The coach's response is to listen first to understand before expressing a personal opinion.

- The majority of the coach's time should be spent with those who are or are attempting to perform well rather than with those who are resisting change.

- The coach's action should reflect the developmental level of the team; a one-style-fits-all approach is not effective coaching.

- The coach must promote and demonstrate core organizational values.

- The coach should frequently praise the team for specific accomplishments and offer constructive criticism when invited to do so.

- The coach must demonstrate a belief that most people are trying to do their best.

- When the coach disagrees with a team decision, he or she should initiate dialogue with the team at a point in time when the decision can still be changed.

- When there is a problem with the team or a team member, the coach is expected to take that opportunity to demonstrate his or her excellence as a coach.

- The coach continuously needs to rally support around actions and tangible results.

- The coach's discussion should place priority on the "good of the organization" over the coach's personal goals.

- The coach needs to demonstrate loyalty to the team, including supporting team members whether they perform correctly or not.

- The coach is a teacher, a mentor, an advisor, and a champion for the team, showing faith in the team and pride in its accomplishments.

Coach's Authority Levels

Following are the coach's authority levels for the three phases of team development:

Phase I of Team Development

Level 1: Coach's involvement is a must; team makes minor decisions with input from coach; coach reviews all decisions made by team.

Level 2: Coach's involvement is necessary; coach still makes many decisions; team has increasing input into decision-making process; team makes minor decisions related to team functioning.

Phase II of Team Development

Level 3: Coach's involvement is still needed; team has more participation in decision-making process; coach retains final decision authority.

Level 4: Coach's involvement is minimized; team begins to make its own decisions; team consults with coach prior to implementing decisions.

Phase III of Team Development

Level 5: Team makes decisions on its own, implements decisions, informs coach about decisions.

Level 6: Team makes all decisions within guidelines and procedures; no further action is required.

Coach's Assessment

When a team's authority is being elevated from one level to another, it is time for the team to assess the coach's performance to ensure that the coach is demonstrating the behavior needed to support the team's move to the next level of authority.

The coach's assessment method involves a brief tool completed by the team at each stage of the coach's authority level. Figure 7-1 is a sample coach's assessment at the first and second levels of authority.

After the team completes the coach's assessment, representatives from the team sit with the coach and review the feedback summary, highlighting the coach's strengths and areas needing more work. Ideally, the feedback for the coach is very positive and the team is then ready to move on to the next phase on the teaming roadmap. If the feedback is negative, the coach will need to improve before the team is allowed to progress. This process strengthens the partnership between the coach and the team, because each is dependent on the other for moving forward.

Launching Work Teams

If the organization intends to launch multiple workforce teams within a short period of time, the design team provides the ideal mechanism to organize and orchestrate the rollout. The design team must consider the readiness of the areas where teams will be launched, the rollout schedule for new coaches, the organization's critical areas in terms of workload and schedule, and the feasibility of getting the teams trained. The design team creates the master rollout schedule, notifies the coaches and teams, and oversees the process, troubleshooting as any problems arise.

Realigning Team Rewards and Recognition

The design team also oversees the realigning of rewards and recognition to a team-based environment. No longer can individual recogni-

FIGURE 7-1   Sample Coach's Assessment.

Level I Coaching Assessment

Please rate the following statements using the scale listed below. You will be rating your coach on his/her performance relative to the statements.

  1 = Never 2 = Seldom 3 = Frequently 4 = Most of the time 5 = All of the time

Platform Statement: The Coach should interact with the team in some way at least once a day.

1. The coach performs daily visits to the team's work site or makes daily contact with virtual team sites.

1   2   3   4   5

2. The coach interacts with Star Point coordinators on a regular basis.

1   2   3   4   5

3. The coach attends teams meetings on a regular basis, in person or via teleconferencing.

1   2   3   4   5

Platform Statement: Interaction with every individual is very important and a coach should do so on a regular basis.

1. The coach conducts coaching sessions with individual team members in leadership positions.

1   2   3   4   5

2. The coach links team members to other subject matter experts within the department or area as needed.

1   2   3   4   5

3. The coach links team members to subject matter experts outside the immediate department or organization.

1   2   3   4   5

Platform Statement: The coach must demonstrate belief that teams are the right way to achieve the vision, and that they will be successful.

1. The coach looks for opportunities to communicate organization's vision to be a team culture.

1   2   3   4   5

2. The coach speaks clear statements of support for a team environment.

1   2   3   4   5

3. The coach shares data on the success of teams within and outside the organization.

1   2   3   4   5

FIGURE 7-1   (continued)

Level II Coaching Assessment

Platform Statement: The coaching/facilitative/participatory leadership model is the preferred style of managing for the coach; the command and control model of leadership is not acceptable.

1. The coach uses a participatory style to engage the team in discussion and problem solving.

$$1 \quad 2 \quad 3 \quad 4 \quad 5$$

2. The coach includes members of the team in discussions and decision making.

$$1 \quad 2 \quad 3 \quad 4 \quad 5$$

3. The coach avoids command and control style, especially when pressures build.

$$1 \quad 2 \quad 3 \quad 4 \quad 5$$

Platform Statement: The Coach should first try to motivate and encourage a change in behavior before resorting to negative reinforcement or discipline.

1. The coach organizes sessions to listen to the team's concerns when they arise.

$$1 \quad 2 \quad 3 \quad 4 \quad 5$$

2. The coach uses positive reinforcement (person gets what they want) as a primary form of motivation.

$$1 \quad 2 \quad 3 \quad 4 \quad 5$$

3. The coach avoids the use of threatening statements or behavior.

$$1 \quad 2 \quad 3 \quad 4 \quad 5$$

Platform Statement: The Coach is to reinforce team member behaviors that support our culture and vision.

1. The coach looks for the use of team behaviors and provides positive reinforcement in a timely fashion.

$$1 \quad 2 \quad 3 \quad 4 \quad 5$$

2. The coach reinforces team behaviors by practicing behaviors him/herself (walk the talk).

$$1 \quad 2 \quad 3 \quad 4 \quad 5$$

3. The coach does not reinforce (positively or negatively) behaviors that are not compatible with the vision and culture.

$$1 \quad 2 \quad 3 \quad 4 \quad 5$$

tion be the primary approach. We encourage a combination approach based on team and individual accomplishments, because this better fulfills the needs of the North American culture. Often it is helpful to establish boundaries for the rewards and/or recognition and then allow the team to decide, within the boundaries, what it wishes to do. It is important to track the milestones with teaming, such as completion of each phase of development, and increase the level of recognition correspondingly. Recognition is very important in a team-based culture because the typical external rewards, such as vertical promotions, are no longer occurring on a frequent basis. The design team articulates the principles and the general program that will be applied throughout the organization.

Embedding Other Structural Components

At this point the design team turns to the many different structures within the organization and determines how they will need to be modified to support the team structure. These will include safety, quality, HR, compensation, performance reviews, job descriptions, use of technology, and general policies and procedures. Each will need to be examined with an eye to teaming.

Organizational Development/Effectiveness Manager

The work of the design team moves much more smoothly when the organization has identified an individual to perform the role of organizational development or organizational effectiveness manager. The position is responsible for designing and implementing an empowered and involved employee workforce, including guiding and overseeing the transformation to teams. The job description includes the following duties:

- Operate as an organizational leader and internal consultant to management in the identification, development, and implementation of effective teaming processes.

- Sponsor the design team in all of its responsibilities to implement and monitor a team-based structure.

- Identify and create leadership development programs to ensure that all coaches have the necessary skills to succeed.

- Provide ongoing coaching, guidance, and direction in the development of teams.

- Formulate standards, processes, and solutions to capitalize on continuous improvement efforts.

- Act as a change agent by providing support and structures to implement major changes to the operations of the business/organization.

- Lead the development and implementation of succession planning programs.

- Partner with HR and line management to meet organizational needs.

- Benchmark with other organizations to champion changes that will improve organizational results.

- Conduct regular organizational needs assessments and align resources to address deficient needs.

- Assist in the design and implementation of organizational structures that support the achievement of organizational objectives.

- Develop strategic partnerships with learning institutions offering team-related programs and conducting organizational research.

The organizational development/effectiveness manager is instrumental in spearheading the transformation efforts and unifying management support for the changes. This individual answers the myriad questions that arise with the transformation and demonstrates commitment to the change, even when teams are experiencing what we call "the muck in the middle." The "muck" occurs when teams have launched and begun the changes, but the positive results have not yet occurred. As teams are letting go of the old and familiar and attempting the new and strange, the organizational effectiveness manager champions the vision and direction for managers experiencing the transition as well as for the workforce. This individual must be someone who walks, talks, thinks, and breathes teaming and yet someone who knows and respects the business side of the organization as well.

Virtual Teams

Not only does the design team need to address the local transition, but also the effect on virtual teams in the organization. Virtual teams are defined as teaming networks, or virtual communities, that exist outside geographical boundaries yet are committed to common goals and approaches, similar to colocated teams. To succeed, virtual teams must follow these guidelines:

- Team members must regard communication as part of the work of the team, not as support for work or adjacent to work, but designed as an intentional action with firm rules. Team members must use instant messaging, discussion boards, voice mail, videoconferencing, and e-rooms as seamlessly as co-located members would call out across the hall.

- Logging on is a signal of the team member's arrival in the electronic workplace. Skills in working with electronic tools and virtual operations are required of all team members. Team members must agree on standard technology common to all.

- Team members must believe that virtual members want the same results as they do even though they all work independently. Face-to-face time in the beginning of the team's formation is critical to forming this belief. Mapping the locations of virtual members and placing team member photos on the map help put faces to names and locations.

- Team members must proactively seek out the information needed, rather than wait for the information to come from others. Knowing how to access information within and outside the team is critical to the team's success.

- Coaches must understand that leadership in a virtual team requires the ability to keep the team focused on its overall mission and goals, manage a complex network of dependencies, create and sustain virtual communication and relationships, and present technologies in ways that team members will utilize and embrace.

- Team members must visualize themselves in a teaming community, establishing regular times for team interactions including informal chitchat, socializing, and celebration.

- Team members must learn to test assumptions as a regular part of communicating and give and receive feedback especially with team members who are communicating poorly. Team members must be reminded that the written word can be viewed as much more harsh than the spoken word.

- Although the team's meeting room is a virtual setting via the Internet, e-room, website, or electronic bulletin board, team members must understand that all the roles and meeting protocol requirements are the same as for co-located teams.

Individual Team Road Map

In addition to the organizational team road map, it's possible to create a specific team road map as well. We put together a road map (see

Figure 7-2) for work teams that takes the twenty-two teaming competencies we use for team assessments and identifies three accomplishments for each competency in each phase of the team's development. These competencies are listed for each phase in alphabetical order as a way to guide the team's progress. A coach can review and track the competencies with each team to illustrate the accomplishments being made. Later, when the team is ready for a formal assessment, the roadmap is used as a way to track results. Many organizations find it helpful to make specific tools for each competency available to the teams electronically. A team that has completed each of the three elements in each of the competencies has achieved either a phase I, phase II, or phase III level of teaming. The roadmap provides teams with very specific expectations of behavior that the teams can discuss and measure.

Typically, most teams find themselves between various phases of team development. The teaming roadmap provides a structure for the teams to use that identifies the competencies needed at each phase of teaming and a mechanism for assessing whether they are being demonstrated. As teams accomplish each phase of the roadmap, they can elect various rewards and/or recognition to motivate their advancement. Simultaneously, as the coach increases the level of the team's accountability, the coach is also assessed on his or her skill and development.

FIGURE 7-2   Individual Team Road Map.

Competencies	Phase I	Phase II	Phase III
Atmosphere: Trust and Openness	1. Team training includes trust building exercises 2. Team recognizes the importance of building trust and being open with each other 3. Team members are attempting appropriate trusting behaviors	1. Team members are demonstrating appropriate behaviors conducive to a trusting environment 2. Team is trained on enhancing trust with the team 3. Team displays the behaviors of an open and honest atmosphere both internally and externally	1. The team conducts surveys to ensure trust is still at a high level 2. Team members trust other team members fully 3. Team members continually reinforce each other for the correct behaviors
Competency to Perform Tasks	1. The team knows the tasks it is expected to perform 2. The coach has introduced the Hand Off plan and begun delegation of tasks 3. Competencies required to perform new tasks have been identified	1. Team members are trained in the various competencies to perform tasks 2. Team members are cross-trained on tasks to improve overall team competency 3. A training plan exists for all competencies	1. The team can perform all tasks required in a seamless and uninterrupted fashion 2. The team is accountable for meeting all training requirements per the training plan 3. Certification of tasks is completed by all team members
Completion of Team Tasks	1. The team is in agreement about the tasks to be accomplished 2. Team has a method to hold members accountable for completing tasks 3. Team is assuming ownership of its tasks through the team measurement system	1. Production Star Point schedules and coordinates labor distribution on a daily basis 2. Team members complete tasks when needed 3. All Star Point Roles are being performed at acceptable level	1. Production Star Points review critical processes to improve the team's efficiency 2. All back ups to star point roles are capable of stepping in to complete tasks 3. The team reviews task process efficiency, team alerts coach if task delay will occur

FIGURE 7-2 (continued)

Competencies	Phase I	Phase II	Phase III
Culture and Direction	1. The team's mission and goals are defined 2. The team's charter has been developed and approved 3. The team demonstrates a willingness to understand and participate in team culture	1. Team follows charter and refers to it for clarification of purpose and direction 2. Gradual acceptance of team culture from all team members 3. The team fully participates in building and supporting the teaming culture	1. The team regularly reviews its mission and adjusts for changes in strategic direction 2. The team evaluates and changes negotiable and non-negotiable items in team charter 3. The team reviews various aspects of teaming on own; ensures that reinforcement of behaviors exists
General Communication	1. Team generates a list of ways to communicate effectively (Help/Hinder list) 2. The coach communicates regularly with the team about direction, tasks, and responsibilities 3. Team members actively demonstrate interest in what is being communicated	1. The team creates protocol for effective communication 2. Star Point role coordinators communicate requirements to the team and others regularly and effectively 3. Team members fully understand what is being communicated to them	1. Communication is occurring regularly on both an informal and formal basis 2. The team consistently follows its protocol on communication 3. The communication star point coordinator is effectively delivering communication to the team and maintaining the team's communication systems
Goals and Approach	1. All team members participate in goal development that is prompted by coach and agree to the team's goals 2. The coach and the team work together	1. Team regularly reviews status of its goals 2. Team is able to discuss various approaches to goal attainment and agrees on approach	1. The team initiates goal setting whenever necessary; goals are achievable and relevant to the organization 2. The team is able to recognize when there

FIGURE 7-2   (continued)

Competencies	Phase I	Phase II	Phase III
(Goals and Approach continued)	to develop a commitment to a common approach for achieving each goal which is outlined in the team's work breakdown plan 3. The coach monitors goal attainment with star point coordinators involved and provides regular feedback to the team	3. Star point coordinators track goals accurately and share results with the team	is not agreement to an approach and is able to surface and resolve differences as a team 3. Star point coordinators lead the team in goal setting and tracking
Handling Conflicts	1. The team has been trained in conflict resolution strategies, knows to avoid triangling and stamp collecting 2. The team conflict resolution protocol has been developed 3. The team recognizes and accepts that conflict is normal, requires support from coach during conflict	1. Team members are competent in RISC and PAUSE as methods for giving and receiving feedback from others 2. Team members assume responsibility for resolving team conflicts, offer assistance to other team members who are having work related conflicts 3. The team is trained on group dynamics and understands how to apply learning to improve team functioning	1. The team appreciates the importance of conflict and encourages members to generate different opinions 2. All team members support effective team conflict resolution 3. The team effectively handles conflict, is following and reviewing its conflict protocol
Interpersonal Skills	1. Team members are developing an appreciation for effective interpersonal skills 2. Preliminary training on listening skills	1. The team identifies and creates a list of necessary interpersonal skills each member needs to demonstrate	1. The team fully carries out interpersonal skills including listening, paraphrasing, clarifying, and summarizing

FIGURE 7-2   (continued)

Competencies	Phase I	Phase II	Phase III
	has been completed and team members are able to demonstrate effective listening with each other 3. Team members have completed training on personality styles and know the importance of appreciating different team member styles	2. Team members demonstrate effective listening skills on a consistent basis 3. Team members appreciate style differences of members	2. The team has graduated from an "I" focus to a "We" focus 3. The team members are able to flex personality styles to meet the needs of the team
Inter-Team Management	1. Teams on occasion share ideas and issues with each other as prompted by coach 2. Team is aware of other teams and does not interfere with their functioning 3. Team tries to avoid comparison to other teams that is detrimental to its own growth and development	1. The team is able to identify where inter-team relationships are critical to the team's success 2. The team works effectively with other teams to address critical issues 3. Star point roles interface with others to improve team effectiveness; Star point leaders assist with inter-team relations	1. The team conducts regular review meetings with other teams on critical issues 2. The team has established "service level agreements" that are integral to their success 3. Star point coordinators interface with other star point coordinators on their own
Leadership	1. Leadership is shared most frequently by strong and assertive members of the team 2. Other team members demonstrate willingness to follow leadership 3. Coach often provides leadership direction to team	1. More team members are showing leadership potential and interest 2. Team members support leadership values and understand accountability 3. The coach is providing less direction and encourages others to take leadership role	1. Leadership is shared among all team members 2. Accountability for team actions is supported by all team members 3. The coach has empowered the team to perform own leadership functions within defined boundaries

FIGURE 7-2   (continued)

Competencies	Phase I	Phase II	Phase III
Management Support	1. Management articulates the vision and purpose of the team and functions as "cheerleader" for team results, clarifies boundaries for team in terms of authority, responsibility, and accountability 2. Management often walks around and talks to team on informal basis 3. Management addresses "resistance to teaming" in a manner that reduces resistance	1. Management is "letting go" and actively encourages team growth 2. Management delegates tasks in such a way that the team has a high probability of success 3. Management looks for opportunities to show vocal support for the team	1. Management is available when needed by the team 2. Management provides new challenges for the team to tackle on a regular basis 3. Management openly acknowledges the contribution of the team to the success of the organization
Membership	1. The team works with the coach to identify the skill requirements of the team and assesses member ability; team may need to address any shortfalls 2. New members are provided with descriptions about roles and responsibilities on the team 3. New members are given an orientation about belonging to the team and performance expectations	1. The team takes responsibility for bringing new members "up to speed" and uses "buddy system" effectively 2. The team is involved in providing feedback about potential new members during hiring process 3. The team creates a protocol for team membership	1. The team defines and executes area orientation for all people who work closely with the team 2. The team oversees the selection of members during the hiring process 3. The team effectively follows the protocol for team membership
Norms and Protocols	1. The team Help/Hinder list is created and used during	1. The team updates the Help/Hinder list as needed to	1. The team effectively uses an advanced Help/Hinder list

FIGURE 7-2   (continued)

Competencies	Phase I	Phase II	Phase III
	meetings by the process observer 2. The team has a meeting protocol, decision making protocol, and conflict resolution protocol 3. Members know and practice the protocols and update members regularly; rules and procedures are in writing in the team charter	control team member behaviors 2. Team members update and revise protocols to improve team performance 3. The team utilizes peer pressure and feedback to correct team member behavior; members are being corrected for not following a team protocol	2. The team owns its protocols and generates them whenever clarity and agreement is needed by the team 3. Members seek feedback about their performance to the protocols
Participation and Accountability	1. Team members are attempting to participate; more assertive members have a tendency to dominate 2. The facilitator must actively draw team members into discussion during team meetings 3. Team members let other members know when unable to attend team events or complete agreed upon tasks	1. Most team members are actively participating during discussions 2. Team members respond to facilitator's request for participation 3. Members surface team accountability questions and issues	1. All team members actively participate in discussions without prompting 2. The coach uses an empowering leadership style 3. The team holds members accountable and surfaces issues without prompting from the coach
Planning	1. The planning function is performed by the coach; input from the team is solicited 2. The coach begins to teach the team how to plan and organize effectively	1. The team plans all day-to-day tasks 2. The team is able to look at the "big picture" and identify critical issues for the future	1. The team conducts own planning function, both short-term and long-term 2. The team is involved in long range planning

FIGURE 7-2   (continued)

Competencies	Phase I	Phase II	Phase III
	3. The coach shares financial and organizational information with team to help support the plans	3. The team offers/recommends items for the budget	3. The team prepares and presents a budget for the team to the coach; coach approves
Rewards, Incentives, and Recognition	1. The team is able to give positive reinforcement to members who take on new tasks 2. The team is recognized by the coach for accomplishments 3. The team is trained on reward and recognition principles by the coach	1. The team fully understands the concepts of managing performance and can establish a performance improvement plan 2. Team actively utilizes a program to reward and recognize members who are taking on responsibilities 3. HR/Administrative star point assists in coordinating and planning team celebrations and functions	1. Team members maintain behaviors in a teaming environment without prompting 2. The team has identified extrinsic and intrinsic rewards and recognition that work best for team members and utilizes them to keep the team developing 3. The team creates a performance improvement plan, implements plan, and tracks the plan effectively to ensure positive results
Roles	1. Team members are learning new team roles including meeting roles, star point roles; definition of work includes shared roles 2. Stronger members of the team are assuming responsibility for more difficult roles 3. All star point roles are performed to a "minimum standard" level	1. The team has an established protocol for role rotation; star point roles are rotated according to plan, backup star points are learning their roles 2. Other team members are demonstrating a willingness to assume responsibility for team roles 3. Team members recognize the need for	1. All members willing to assume all appropriate team roles (meeting roles, star point roles) 2. The team achieves effective role transition; back up positions are filled without having to be asked 3. When other responsibilities are added, team assigns to appropriate role or

FIGURE 7-2   (continued)

Competencies	Phase I	Phase II	Phase III
		training to perform roles effectively	creates additional roles as needed; team is able to fine tune the roles; members are assessing the performance of the roles
Team Assessment and Review	1. The team assesses its progress informally with guidance from coach (team thermometers) 2. The team has implemented its measurement system and posts measures on appropriate charts 3. The team conducts its huddle meetings and reviews its results on a daily or regular basis	1. The team sets up routine reviews of the team's progress and reviews with the coach 2. The team tracks measures to ensure achievement of the critical processes 3. Team conducts a more formal assessment of its functioning	1. The team handles own team process improvements and suggestions 2. The team utilizes advanced surveys and reports to provide accurate feedback 3. The team reviews results of assessments on an ongoing basis and recommends change
Team Decision Making	1. The team has learned basic consensus decision making 2. The team is able to use consensus decision making during meetings; members do not need prompting to give consensus signal 3. The team has determined which decisions will require consensus	1. The facilitator is able to lead the team through a simple consensus process 2. Team members are able to disagree and express their disagreement without positioning or attacking each other 3. Some team members are able to generate solution ideas that help bring about consensus	1. All team facilitators are effectively leading the team through consensus decisions 2. Team members readily offer what they can support when disagreeing with consensus 3. The team is able to problem solve to identify "middle ground" solutions that are agreeable to the whole team

FIGURE 7-2   (continued)

Competencies	Phase I	Phase II	Phase III
Team Meetings	1. Team meetings are held regularly without prompting by the coach 2. The team follows its meeting protocol components 3. The team owns development of its meeting agenda; some guidance from the coach is often necessary	1. The team is capable of running its own meeting, including agenda preparation, scribe notes, action items list, process observer report, and timekeeping 2. The team is able to modify its agenda if needed to meet objectives and time requirements 3. Team meetings are productive and result in regular action items being identified and completed	1. Effective team meeting management is the norm 2. The team clearly owns its meeting; the coach is a "guest" at the meetings 3. The team holds itself accountable for updating members if a meeting is missed
Team Problem Solving	1. The team understands what problems it is expected to solve 2. The team is learning to avoid blaming and fault-finding 3. The team receives training on a quality problem solving approach and is able to utilize basic problem solving tools with support from the coach and star point leaders	1. The team assumes responsibility for solving problems without blaming or seeking coach's involvement 2. The team is able to use simple quality problem solving tools with no support from the coach 3. The team is able to use some complex problem solving tools with moderate support from the coach	1. The team is capable of using advanced quality problem solving tools on own 2. The team takes pride in solving its own problems; sees problem solving as part of its job 3. The team proactively works on preventive and corrective actions on its own
Work Tools and Training	1. The team maintains a list of training requirements and completions for each member	1. The team identifies members who need training and makes arrangements for training to occur	1. The team suggests new tools and training needed to perform more effectively

FIGURE 7-2   (continued)

Competencies	Phase I	Phase II	Phase III
	2. Team members are trained on both teaming and job-related skills 3. The team oversees the training for new team members	2. The team records and tracks all team training 3. The team assumes responsibility for conducting new hire on-the-job training and cross-training	2. The team initiates action to coordinate training on own 3. Team trainers certify new team members on job tasks

Notes

Chapter 1

1. Art Kleiner, "Management Bites Dog Food Factory," *Fast Company Magazine*, June–July 1996, 44–46.

2. Charles A. Aubrey II and Patricia K. Felkins, *Teamwork: Involving People in Quality and Productivity Improvement*, White Plains, N.Y.: Quality Resources, 1988, 2.

3. Jack D. Orsburn, Linda Moran, Ed Museelwhite, and John H. Zenger, *Self-Directed Work Teams*, Homewood, Ill.: Business One Irwin, 1990, 15.

4. *Teamwork: Your Role in Developing the Winning Edge. Supervisory Skills Program*, Waterford, CT: Bureau of Business Practice, 1987.

5. Aubrey and Felkins, .

6. Lawrence Miller and Jennifer Howard, *Managing Quality Through Teams: A Workbook for Team Leaders and Members*, Atlanta: Miller Consulting Group, 1991, 109.

7. Lyman D. Ketchum and Eric Trist, *All Teams Are Not Created Equal: How Employee Empowerment Really Works*, Sage, Thousand Oaks, 1992, 85–88.

Chapter 2

1. Irving L. Janis, *Sanctions for Evil*, ed. Nevitt Sanford and Craig Comstock, San Francisco: Jossey-Bass, 1971, 71–89.

2. Cyril R. Mill, *Activities for Trainers, 50 Useful Designs* San Diego: University Associates, 1980; see also John W. Newstrom and Edward E. Scannell, *Games Trainers Play*, New York: McGraw-Hill, 1980, 47–51.

Chapter 3

1. B. Hughes, "25 Stepping Stones for Self-Directed Work Teams," *Training* (December 1991).

2. Adapted from training materials developed by Professional Resources, Inc., Herndon, Virginia.

3. Morton Deutsch, Peter T. Coleman, and Eric C. Marcus, *The Handbook of Conflict Resolution Theory and Practice*, San Francisco: Jossey-Bass, 2006.

4. S. E. Asch, "Studies of Independence and Conformity: A Minority of One Against a Unanimous Majority," *Psychological Monographs*, 70. (No. 9. Whole 416), 1956.

5. D. J. Stang, "Group Size Effects on Conformity," *Journal of Social Psychology*, 98, no. 2 (1976) 175–181.

6. C. Nemeth, J. Brown, and J. Rogers, "Devil's Advocate vs. Authentic Dissent: Stimulating Quantity and Quality," *European Journal of Social Psychology*, 31 (2001), 707–720.

7. S. Moscovici and C. Faucheux, "Social Influence, Conformity Bias and the Study of Active Minorities," in *Advances in Experimental Social Psychology*, vol. 6, ed. by L. Berkowitz, New York: Academic Press, 1972, 149–202.

8. M. C. Flowers, "A Laboratory List of Some Implications of Janis's Groupthink Hypothesis, *Journal of Personality and Social Psychology*, 35 (1977) 888–896. C. R. Leana, "A Partial Test of Janis's Groupthink Model: Effects of Group Cohesiveness and Leadership Behavior on Defective Decisionmaking," *Journal of Management*, 11 (1985) 5–17. G. Moorehead and J. R. Monanari. "An Empirical Investigation of the Groupthink Phenomenon," *Human Relations*, 39 (1986) 399–410.

9. Jerry B. Harvey, *The Abilene Paradox and Other Meditations on Management*, San Francisco: Jossey-Bass, 1988. The original publication of the Abilene Paradox appeared as "The Abilene Paradox: The

Management of Agreement," in *Organizational Dynamics* (Summer 1974).

10. Irving Janis, "Groupthink," *Psychology Today* (November 1971) 43–46, 74–76.

11. G. Strasser, and W. Titus, "Pooling of Unshared Information in Group Decision Making: Bias Information Sampling During Discussion," *Journal of Personality and Social Psychology*, 48, 6, (1985) 1467–1478.

12. R. A. Henry, "Improving group judgment accuracy: Information sharing and determining the best member." *Organizational Behavior and Human Decision Processes*, 62, 2, (1995) 190–197.

13. J. R. Larsen, C. Christensen, T. M. Franz, and A. S. Abbott, "Diagnosing Groups: The Pooling Management and Impact of Shared and Unshared Case Information in Team-Based Medical Decision Making," *Journal of Personality and Social Psychology*, 75, 1 (1998) 93–108.7.

Chapter 4

1. B. W. Tuckman, "Developmental Sequence in Small Groups," *Psychological Bulletin*, 63 (1965): 384–399.

2. D. Garvin and M. Roberto, "What You Don't Know About Making Decisions," *Harvard Business Review*, 79, 8, (September 2001) 4–14.

3. Ibid.

4. Michael A. Roberto, "Lessons from Everest: The Interaction of Cognitive Bias, Psychological Safety and System Complexity," *California Management Review*, v. 45, no. 1 (Fall 2002) 136–137; Michael Klesius, "Life and Death on Everest: The History," *National Geographic*, v. 203, no. 5 (May 2003) 16–40.

Chapter 5

1. Peter Senge et al, *Fifth Discipline Fieldbook*, New York: Doubleday, 1994.

2. Brainwriting is adapted from Bernd Rohrbach, whose form appeared in B. Johannsson, *Kreativität and Marketing*, Switzerland: H. Kern, 1978.

3. Chris Argyris, *Overcoming Organizational Defenses: Facilitating Organizational Learning*, Prentice Hall, 1990. The Ladder of Inference was first put forward by organizational psychologist Chris Argyris and used by Peter Senge in *The Fifth Discipline: The Art and Practice of the Learning Organization*, (1994).

4. W. Edwards Deming, *The New Economics for Industry, Government and Education*, second edition, MIT Press, 2000.

Chapter 6

1. A. M. Mohrman, S. A. Mohrman, and E. E. Lawler, "The Performance Management of Teams," *Performance Measurement, Evaluation and Incentives*, Boston: Harvard Business School Press, 1992.

2. T. Quick, *Successful Team Building*, New York: AMACOM, 1992.

3. C. A. Norman and R. A. Zawacki, "Team Appraisals—Team Approach," *Personnel Journal*, 70, 9 (1991) 101–104.

Chapter 7

1. A change formula was originally created by David Gleicher at Arthur D. Little. See John D. Adams, "Successful Change: Paying Attention to the Intangibles," *OD Practitioner*, 35, 4 (2003) 22–26.

Index